Point of View, Perspective, and Focalization

Narratologia

Contributions to Narrative Theory

Edited by
Fotis Jannidis, Matías Martínez, John Pier
Wolf Schmid (executive editor)

17

Walter de Gruyter · Berlin · New York

Point of View, Perspective, and Focalization

Modeling Mediation in Narrative

Edited by
Peter Hühn, Wolf Schmid
and Jörg Schönert

Walter de Gruyter · Berlin · New York

♾ Printed on acid-free paper which falls within the guidelines
of the ANSI to ensure permanence and durability.

Library of Congress Cataloging-in-Publication Data

Point of view, perspective, and focalization : modeling mediation in narrative / edited by Peter Hühn, Wolf Schmid, Jörg Schönert.
p. cm. – (Narratologia, ISSN 1612-8427 ; 17) (Narratologia ; 17)
"The majority of the papers collected in this volume are based on talks given at the conference ... held at Hamburg University by the Hamburg Research Group "Narratology" (Forschergruppe Narratologie) from October 13 to 15, 2006, titled "Point of View, Perspective, Focalization: Modeling Mediacy."
ISBN 978-3-11-021890-9 (alk. paper)
1. Point of view (Literature) 2. Mediation. 3. Narration (Rhetoric) I. Hühn, Peter, 1939– II. Schmid, Wolf. III. Schönert, Jörg.
PN3383.P64P65 2009
808–dc22
2009012025

ISBN 978-3-11-021890-9
ISSN 1612-8427

Bibliographic information published by the Deutsche Nationalbibliothek

The Deutsche Nationalbibliothek lists this publication in the Deutsche Nationalbibliografie; detailed bibliographic data are available in the Internet at http://dnb.d-nb.de.

Printed in Germany
Cover design: Christopher Schneider, Laufen

Contents

Introduction 1

Part I: Re-Specifications of Perspective

JAN CHRISTOPH MEISTER, JÖRG SCHÖNERT
The DNS of Mediacy 11

URI MARGOLIN
Focalization: Where Do We Go from Here? 41

TATJANA JESCH, MALTE STEIN
Perspectivization and Focalization: Two Concepts—One Meaning? An Attempt at Conceptual Differentiation 59

ALAIN RABATEL
A Brief Introduction to an Enunciative Approach to Point of View 79

GUNTHER MARTENS
Narrative and Stylistic Agency: The Case of Overt Narration 99

DAVID HERMAN
Beyond Voice and Vision: Cognitive Grammar and Focalization Theory 119

BRIAN RICHARDSON
Plural Focalization, Singular Voices: Wandering Perspectives in "We"-Narration 143

Part II: Some Special Aspects of Mediation

VIOLETA SOTIROVA
A Comparative Analysis of Indices of Narrative Point of View in Bulgarian and English 163

TOMÁŠ KUBÍČEK
Focalization, the Subject and the Act of Shaping Perspective........ 183

CHRISTIAN HUCK
Coming to Our Senses: Narratology and the Visual........ 201

Part III: Transliterary Aspects of Mediation

ROLAND WEIDLE
Organizing the Perspectives: Focalization and the Superordinate Narrative System in Drama and Theater........ 221

SABINE SCHLICKERS
Focalization, Ocularization and Auricularization in Film and Literature 243

MARKUS KUHN
Film Narratology: Who Tells? Who Shows? Who Focalizes? Narrative Mediation in Self-Reflexive Fiction Films 259

JAN-NOËL THON
Perspective in Contemporary Computer Games........ 279

Authors 301

PETER HÜHN
(Hamburg)

Introduction

The basic constellation constituting a narrative can be described as a communicative act (narration) through which happenings—including existents such as characters, places, circumstances, etc., within the storyworld (fictional or factual)—are represented and thus mediated through a given verbal, visual or audio-visual sign system. This representation is inevitably shaped—in the selection, combination, perspectivization, interpretation, evaluation of elements—by the agency producing it, ultimately the author who, however, may delegate mediation, particularly in fictional narration, to some intermediary agent or agents, typically a narrator (narrator's voice) and, at a lower level, to one or more characters (character's perspective) located within the happenings (in verbal texts) and, according to some theorists, to the recording apparatus and/or voice-over (in film). This process of transforming and transmitting the story in the discourse, is what is meant by mediation in the broadest sense. One crucial problem concerning mediation in verbal texts as well as in other media is thus the extent and dimensions of its modeling effect, and more particularly the precise relative status and constellation of the mediating agents, i.e. the narrator or presenter and the character(s). The question, then, is how are the structure and the meaning of the story conditioned by these two different positions in relation to the mediated happenings perceived from outside and/or inside the storyworld?

The problem of mediation in narrative was the topic of a conference held at Hamburg University by the Hamburg Research Group "Narratology" (*Forschergruppe Narratologie*) from October 13 to 15, 2006, titled "Point of View, Perspective, Focalization: Modeling Mediacy." The majority of the papers collected in this volume are based on talks given at the conference, supplemented by a few additional articles. In the conference title, "mediacy" was meant as an umbrella term covering all modes, means, and instances of mediation, but since some (presumably above all,

German) readers might associate this word with Stanzel's more limited concept of *Mittelbarkeit*, it was replaced with the comprehensive term "mediation" for the present collection. Like the conference, the book has a twofold aim: to offer a fresh look and a systematic renewal of the notion of mediation in narratology in its traditional focus on literary texts, and in addition to apply this concept to narration in other media, including drama, film, and computer games. Mediation is intended to comprise all possible aspects, forms, and means of constructing and communicating a story in discourse: the selection, ordering, and segmentation of storyworld elements, their transmission through a presenter (e.g. the narrator's voice or equivalent agents in film and drama), their presentation from a particular standpoint or perspective. In its range, this volume does not aim at an exhaustive overview or neat differentiation and definition of the various terms currently in use for this field. Rather, the individual articles address some controversial aspects of the narratological conceptualization and systematization of mediation in their application to both literary and other media.

The first group of articles in this volume—part I—comprises contributions (Meister & Schönert, Margolin, Jesch & Stein, Rabatel, Martens, Herman, and Richardson) whose aim, from various angles, is to re-define, re-specify, or re-model perspective, especially Genette's concept of focalization, typically with regard to its distinction from narrative voice. Jan Christoph Meister and Jörg Schönert's "The DNS of Mediacy" outlines a comprehensive approach to the process of representation inherent in the *histoire/récit* or story/discourse distinction achieved by what they call the Dynamic Narrative System, the instance to which the constitution and communication of the narrative as a whole is attributed. The DNS comprises both voice and perspective (or narration and point of view), modeled as the integrated result of mental activities across the three (interconnected) dimensions of "perception", "reflection" and "mediation". These dimensions differ as to the specific type of mental activity and the constraints exercised by that activity, whether determined, respectively, by epistemological or sensory input: temporal and spatial proximity to the object domain (perception); mental reaction to the input, i.e. the cognitive, emotive and evaluative relation to the object domain (reflection); medial materialization of the output, i.e. the semiotic relation to the object domain (mediation). All three dimensions are organized along the same fundamental opposition of diegetic (narratorial) vs. mimetic (actorial), such that mental activity can shift between the positions of narrator and character(s). The underlying premise is that the rigorous distinction between speaking and perceiving as introduced by Genette, however useful it may be to overcome a confusion between these notions, tends to obscure their inherent interrelations with respect to the modes of mediating stories to readers, since variations in one dimension always entail changes in the other two. By replacing the relatively rigid architecture of structuralist concepts with the variable combination of three scalable parameters, this theoretical model also facilitates a more precise and flexible description and analysis of mediation in practical terms.

Uri Margolin, in "Focalization: Where Do We Go From Here?", rigorously restricts the term focalization to storyworld participants (characters) and their mental (and textual) representation of that world. For him, focalization thus comprises perceptions (through all five senses) as well as acts of simulation or empathy and recollection on the part of characters. It categorically excludes, however, both their acts of planning or projection (because not focused on pre-existing storyworld elements) and the content of an "omniscient", impersonal narrator's voice (because not position-dependent and therefore not restricted). Narrators cannot be focalizers, in Margolin's view, except for certain special cases in which the narrator deliberately limits his perspective to that of a character or situates himself in a concrete situation. Of the two alternative definitions of focalization proposed by Genette—perception and knowledge or information—Margolin thus opts for the former. Basically, for him focalization is restricted to Genette's internal focalization, although he does concede that internal focalization can also occur with homodiegetic or autodiegetic narrators. Margolin's conception of focalization has the merit of clearly marking off mediation in the form of sensory or mental perception, but at the same time it leaves other aspects of mediation unexamined, especially narratorial perspective.

Taking issue with Genette's ambivalent conception of focalization as knowledge (information content) or perception, Tatjana Jesch and Malte Stein, in "Perspectivization and Focalization: Two Concepts—One Meaning? An Attempt at Conceptual Differentiation", propose to redefine the term by separating the two aspects and subdividing the complex of mediation into two different dimensions. Focalization is taken as the selection or withholding of information about the fictional world by the author, whereas perspectivization refers to the subjective perception of the world by a fictive entity, either one or several characters or the narrator (thus partly resembling Margolin's conception of focalization). Since perspectivization is ultimately governed by the author, it can be used by him as a means of focalizing or channeling information.

Based on a different critique of the delimitation and subdivision of Genette's concept of perspective, as also addressed by the two preceding articles, Alain Rabatel's "A Brief Introduction to an Enunciative Approach to Point of View" offers a consistent clarification and simplifycation of the author's model of focalization on linguistic grounds. Rabatel distinguishes between the first speaker or enunciator (who expresses the whole of an utterance, produces the discourse) and the intratextual enunciator (who filters the object of discourse through his evaluations, quailfications, modalizations and judgments). Based on a carefully selected corpus, he then goes on to identify and analyze the linguistic markers which convey point of view as well as variations in perception, thought and speech forming a continuum that passes from narrated through represented to asserted points of view. Speaker and enunciator may or may not coincide, as the enunciator may be located on the same level or on different levels, i.e. that of the narrator or that of the character(s). Analysis of external and internal markers within this framework opens the way to a differentiated description of complex points of view.

Within this broad context of mediating devices, Gunther Martens' "Narrative and Stylistic Agency: The Case of Overt Narration" discusses a specific point: the status and possible functions of overt narration that come into view with the foregrounding of the narrator's act of narration. As a form of mediation, the act of narration must be considered a genuinely narrative device not to be neglected in the face of the widespread privilege granted to presentation through characters' internal focalization since the beginning of the modernist period.

A new comprehensive approach to mediation is presented by David Herman's "Beyond Voice and Vision: Cognitive Grammar and Focalization Theory", drawing largely on the cognitive semiotics and linguistics of Talmy and Langacker. Herman reformulates focalization as a process of conceptualization and construal of a storyworld scene by an embodied mind, specifying a number of parameters which allow for a discriminating description and analysis of mediation as it occurs in a scene: scanning the scene (static vs. dynamic, synoptic vs. sequential); the observer's distance from the scene (distal, medial, proximal); scope (narrow vs. wide); figure/ground alignment (foregrounding vs. backgrounding of characters, elements, etc.); degree of granularity (how detailed the presentation is); spatial and temporal viewpoint (vantage point and orientation within a directional grid); degree of objectivity vs. subjectivity. This system of categories offers a well integrated transmedial approach which covers both narratorial and figural perspectives (voice and vision), cuts across the distinction between information and perception and applies equally well to mono-modal narratives (novels, short stories) and multi-modal texts such as graphic novels.

Discussing "we"-narration and "we"-focalization as a means of presenting collective consciousness, Brian Richardson, in "Plural Focalization, Singular Voices: Wandering Perspectives in 'We'-Narration", analyzes an unusual literary technique which tends to transcend the boundary between homodiegetic and heterodiegetic narration as well as to blur the distinction between narration (voice) and focalization, fluctuating ambivalently between narratorial and figural perspectives. As wandering focalization, this mediating device ultimately undermines the distinctions construed by Genette or, in other ways, by both Jesch and Stein and Rabatel.

The three contributions in part II (Sotirova, Kubíček, and Huck) address relatively unexplored aspects of perspective. A linguistic aspect affecting mediation is the subject of Violeta Sotirova's "A Comparative Analysis of Indices of Narrative Point of View in Bulgarian and English". Emphasizing verbal aspect, Sotirova investigates the influence of the divergent verb systems of Bulgarian and English on the rendering of internal focalization through free indirect discourse, and she identifies areas of differences between the two languages, adding, however, that syntactic analysis of verb forms must be supplemented by that of contextual and semantic features.

A special topic of a different kind is discussed by Tomáš Kubíček in "Focalization, the Subject and the Act of Shaping Perspective", notably Mukařovský's concept of the "subject" of a literary work. The subject, taken as a complex of value-based perspectives on the storyworld, constitutes the overall meaning of a work, comparable to what is termed in other approaches the implied or abstract author. The comprehensive perspective, he argues, is not inherent in the text alone nor determined by it, but ultimately depends on reception by the reader.

Christian Huck, in "Coming to Our Senses: Narratology and the Visual", offers a critique of the sensory foundation of a central dimension of mediation, drawing attention to the pervasive tendency in narratology to literally or figuratively model perspective in analogy to the visual sense (as revealed in the terms "point of view," "focalization," "perspective"), a reflex of the dominant tradition of privileging vision in Western culture. Huck argues that because of the differences among the senses (e.g. in the degree of distance/proximity and detachment/involvement), the visual cannot stand for all senses, even metaphorically, a point he illustrates with reference to two factual 18th-century travelogues. The act of perception and its specific sensory channel ("slant of perception") as the basis of what can be reported by the narrator needs to be studied more thoroughly, with explicit reference to culturally defined default patterns and their privileging of individual senses.

The final group of articles (part III) explores the application of narratological concepts to the analysis of mediation in the non-textual media: drama (as performance), film, and computer games (Weidle, Schlickers, Kuhn and Thon).

While previous narratological studies of drama have concentrated on epic elements contained in the diegetic and hypodiegetic levels (including stage directions), Roland Weidle, in "Organizing the Perspectives: Focalization and the Superordinate Narrative System in Drama and Theater", specifically turns to the extradiegetic level. The agency of extradiegetic narration, which he calls the superordinate narrative system (cf. Meister and Schönert's dynamic narrative system), is predominantly impersonal and covert (close to what others call the implied or abstract author), taking form indirectly by controlling selection, arrangement and focalization, but also through the compositional implication of internal connections (through motifs) or prolepses. Similarly, focalization in drama is usually external, allowing the characters on stage to be apprehended only from the outside (unless they themselves reveal their inner thoughts in direct speech, as in soliloquies). Weidle further highlights these default conditions by referring to rare (and extremely contrived) exceptions, such as the overt appearance of a personal narrative agent (the author in Lauwers' *Isabella's Room*) or the establishment of zero focalization (simultaneous presentation of two chronologically different scenes on stage, as in Marber's *Closer*) or of internal focalization (the enactment of memory on stage, as in Stoppard's *Travesties*).

In "Focalization, Ocularization and Auricularization in Film and Literature", Sabine Schlickers first distinguishes between the implied director (equivalent to the abstract author in literature) and the so-called "camera" as the narrative agent of the film that intermediates between visual and acoustic information. Thus, what is distinguishable as voice and focalization in literary texts appears to be more closely intertwined in film, functioning as perspectivization in general. More precisely, perspectivization operates in the form of focalization (the narrator's knowledge about the characters) in its interplay with ocularization and auricularization (visual and acoustic information about the storyworld). These three terms are then further subdivided into two modes: superior or broad vs. restricted to characters' perspective, resulting in zero vs. internal ocularization, auricularization, focalization (for the latter, an external mode is added in which the spectator's knowledge is more restricted than characters' knowledge). Finally, comparing a few novels with their film adaptations, Schlickers demonstrates the analytic usefulness of these categories in complex examples of filmic mediation, e.g. the combination of zero auricularization and zero ocularization with internal focalization.

Markus Kuhn's article, "Film Narratology: Who Tells? Who Shows? Who Focalizes? Narrative Mediation in Self-Reflexive Fiction Films", is based on a similar system of categories as Schlickers', although the terms employed are somewhat different. Kuhn names the position of the narrator the "filmic narrative agent", dividing it into a "visual narrative instance" and one or more (optional) "verbal narrative instance(s)", roughly equivalent to the traditional distinction of showing and telling. Like Schlickers, he defines focalization on the basis of knowledge (subdivided into zero, external and internal), labeling the visual and auditory aspects of perception ocularization and auricularization. The constellation of the visual and verbal narrative instances is shown to be highly variable in terms of both relative dominance and content, ranging from contradictory through complementary to congruent tendencies. Again, no sharp distinction can be drawn between narration (voice) and perspective (image). Kuhn then goes on to corroborate these findings through the analysis of mediating techniques employed in several self-reflexive multilayered films.

The special setup of the medium of computer games, due primarily to the feature of interactionality, results in substantial differences in how perspective is organized in this medium as compared text-based media. In the concluding article, "Perspective in Contemporary Computer Games", Jan-Noël Thon differentiates three dimensions of perspective for the player, i.e. three positions or "points" from which the game world is presented: the spatial perspective determined by the point of view; the actional perspective determined by the point of action; and the ideological perspective determined by the point of evaluation. Of these, the first and third are similar to the perceptual or spatial and the ideological facets of focalization as they also occur in literary texts, although more restricted in their variability on account of the rigidly agonistic nature of "game-plots". However, the second dimension, actional perspective, is peculiar to computer games, as it also involves the productive position of the author (or the narrator), the interactive player being called on to actively participate in the plot-development.

While a number of the essays collected in this volume seek to clarify and differentiate the terminology of mediation with regard particularly to literary narratives, others represent attempts to apply narratological categories and terms originally designed for the analysis of literary texts to other forms, aspects and modes of narrative communication, and in particular to the media in their various forms. The aim is to explore the great variety of sensory, cognitive, ideological, semiotic and technical modalities of transmitting, representing and structuring happenings in narrative communication. Special emphasis is given to the notion of mediation as a basis for analysis and comparison of these various modalities with respect to the constitution and constellation of mediating instances, but also to the influence of social and cultural contexts and technological conditions on mediation. The ultimate objective is to develop a system of categories to account for mediation within the framework of a general and comparative narratology. Such a system would make it possible to identify features common to all forms of mediation as well as the features characteristic of and peculiar to each specific medium and mode of narration.

***

Note on bibliographical references

In cases where the date of the original publication is important but a later edition or a translation is quoted from the reference will combine the original publication date with the page number(s) of the edition used.

Part I: Re-Specifications of Perspective

JAN CHRISTOPH MEISTER, JÖRG SCHÖNERT
(Hamburg)

The DNS of Mediacy

1 "Who Sees?" and "Who Speaks?": All Questions Answered?

Whatever narrative might be, it is certainly not a simple 1:1 duplication without loss or gain: like any representation it reduces the complexity of its reference domain to the carrying capacity of its medium and to the processing capacity of senders and receivers. By the same token it also adds a specific type of semiotic and performative surplus value: a narrative's content is always narrated content. Narratives do not present us with information per se; they broker information—and mediacy is the signature of this brokering activity which combines quantitative reduction with qualitative (semantic) enrichment.

In literary texts the effect of mediacy is triggered by a complex interaction of epistemological and rhetorical constraints. Some of these can be detected by surface phenomena "hard-wired" into the text, like an explicit narratorial intrusion, while others manifest themselves mainly in the form of readerly inferences. Genette's work on the logic of *discours*, in its double take on "who sees" (with the particular emphasis on "focalization") and "who speaks" ("voice"), pays attention to both types of constraints. However, intuitive as it may be it is exactly the rather reductionist concept of focalization which counts among the most controversial elements in Genette's structuralist heuristics[1]. While some theorists would rather revert to a more holistic and less analytical model like Stanzel's, hard core structuralist narratologists tend to advocate an even more

---

1 In our opinion the methodological status of Genette's taxonomic system is indeed that of a narratological heuristics, not that of a narrative theory—see Genette's own characterization of his approach in *Narrative Discourse* and *Narrative Discourse Revisited* as "a procedure of discovery, and a way of describing" (Genette 1980: 265) or, in short, as "a method of analysis" (23).—The controversy surrounding Genette's concept of focalization is summarized in Jahn (1996) and Jahn (2005); also see van Peer & Chatman (2001).

differentiated analysis. The most advanced approach in this regard is that in Schmid (2005), for here the phenomenon of "perspective" is no longer treated as a distinct medium-level systematic aspect of mediacy. Rather, against the background of his revised ideal-genetic model Schmid conceptualizes perspective as a summary high-level effect of narratives to which the constituent narrative transformations of selection, composition and verbalization equally contribute[2]. In this model perspective integrates aspects of perception and aspects of expression. This integration is an important step towards building a more dynamic model of mediacy.

Our present contribution wants to take the next logical step into this direction. To date neither Genette's critics[3] nor his followers seem to have questioned the methodological premise that forms the shared basis of his and most other approaches towards mediacy. Formalist, structuralist as well as more traditional hermeneutic theories all tend to conceptualize narrative as a given, that is, as an artefact that exists as a complete and stable whole. This is particularly apparent in the ideal-genetic models (cf. Schmid 1982; Genette 1980 and 1988; Rimmon-Kenan 1983) implicitly guided by the question of how a narrative was "made". A narrative, it is implied here, is the outcome of a completed process: it is a product. In a genetic perspective narrative is thus explained as the result of a sequence of creative actions attributed to the empirical author in terms of real-world ontology, or, in terms of systematic logic, to some abstract narrative instance—i.e., to a narrator. Reception theory based models do not really differ in this regard; for they merely address the same question from the opposite angle: how did the reader, on the basis of the narrative, construct a logically (but not necessarily ontologically) preexisting "narrated world"? Of course, such reconstruction is not thought of as a simplistic re-enactment of the genetic process, but as one that is contingent on the particular contexts and world knowledge of readers which no author and narrator can fully anticipate. Cognitive narratology (e.g., Herman 2003),

2 See Schmid (2005: 127–49); the ideal-genetic model presented here is an extended version of the one in Schmid (1982).

3 In the current volume this criticism is represented by Tatjana Jesch and Malte Stein: "Genette's concept of focalization is actually an amalgamation of two wholly independent elements for which—as the author himself might have anticipated—one actually needs two terms. The first element is the perception of the world invented by the author through narrators and other agents also invented by the author; the second element is the regulation of narrative information within the communication between author and reader" (59).

in paying due attention to the cognitive logic of narrative processing, has eventually gone at least half the way: it conceptualizes narrative as a product of cumulative cognitive processes. However, the constituent micro-processes of narrative processing seem to remain below the discriminative threshold, as the cognitivist focus on schematic knowledge representation and synthetic high-level operators for process orientation and control (scripts, frames, types, world knowledge etc.) indicates.

In a sense the quest for a narrative theory that can capture the differential between representation and represented—an ambivalence inherent in the very term "representation", which in the European languages generally denotes the symbolic artefact as well as the performative act of symbolization—is often implicitly guided by two hidden assumptions. The first (and fairly trivial) is the ontological *post hoc, ergo propter hoc* fallacy which manifests itself in our (seemingly "natural") reflex to misinterpret any instance of representation as conclusive proof for the temporal pre-existence of the represented. The second assumption is of a methodological nature and hence more difficult to grasp. We will focus on the latter.

In a given narrative the phenomena so far categorized under the headings of "distance", "focalization" or "perspective" are certainly strong indicators for a differential between representation and represented. Accordingly, it seems to make good sense to analyze them one by one on the basis of distinct systematic typologies. Also, against the background of these typologies, interdependency and interaction between the indicators can then be explored by way of a combinatorial matrix: which type of focalization goes along with which type of mediacy, etc. The method is compelling, for the how of discourse, it seems, can now be concisely defined in terms of its position on the chess-board like tableau of focalization and mediacy.

The main problem with this approach is not one of terminological overlap or inconsistency; rather it lies in the use of permutation logic which combines statements concerning the relation among narrative instance and object domain on the one hand (e.g., attributions of the type "heterodiegetic" vs. "homodiegetic") with statements about the type of information strategy (e.g., types of focalization) on the other. On closer inspection these two types of attributions are in fact categorical apples and pears: the former is ontological, the latter epistemological. Little wonder then that the options for mapping the two typologies onto one another are indeed rather limited[4]. To analyse the phenomenology of discourse in this way—particularly across distinct and logically incompatible categorical dimensions—is possible only if one posits the text "as given and read" in its entirety, and as a stable object that can be dissected from various angles. This, indeed, is the methodological assumption to which we referred above. It has resulted in one of narratological theory's most problematic blind spots: the process character of narrative.

There are many examples of structuralist descriptions which tend to arrest processuality and re-interpret it by way of stratificatory models. One is Genette's: while his taxonomy does of course admit the fact of variable discourse organization in the constituent parts of a given narrative (one can place the narrator piece on the chess-board of discourse differently within every segment, so to speak), it implicitly forces us to model the logic of narrative representation in terms of independent a-temporal systematic layers—a layer of focalization, then a layer of distance, then a layer of order, etc.

The rigid systematic architecture of the analytical approach thus projects a-temporal systematicity onto its object. However, many existing novels and novellas clearly defy this undertaking as our own reading experience shows. Narratives of 19th century realism may have tended to present us with a discourse organization free of contradictory indicators, but modern and particularly post modern literature clearly places more complex demands on readers, and thus on narratological theory. Conscious profiling of the narrator—our attempt to answer the questions of "where / who / how does s/he know / reflect / (dis-)inform"—has become an increasingly difficult task. There is no one narrative instance; rather, "it" is something that is in flux and can change throughout every reading: it is a function, rather than a given.

1.1 Terminology Revisited

One might argue that this simply points us to the need for better definitions and more plausible attributions for the various types of focalization

4 For example, common sense shows that there is a strong affinity between an autodiegetic mediacy and an internal focalization, while an autodiegetic mediacy with (permanent) external focalization makes little *prima facie* sense and can thus be marked as highly unlikely in the matrix of possible combinations.

found in Genette's descriptive apparatus[5]. Some would indeed warrant at least reformulation. For example, Genette's "focalization zero" is certainly counter intuitive in that what it refers to is not a strange nothingness, but rather a universal and "non-restricted" potency: the ability to perceive, gain knowledge and pass on information about a reference domain *ad libitum*. "Autonomous vision" would therefore be a preferable label for this epistemological position from which physical as well as psychological phenomena (via introspection) can be perceived and represented in their absolute totality.

Moreover, the attribution of "autonomy" intuitively signals the ability to change and restrict the representational potential at will: a position of "autonomous vision" allows for the voluntary temporary adoption of a more constrained epistemological vantage point which is either character bound (*Mitsicht* or "co-vision" in Martinez & Scheffel's terminology), or reduced to the mere external aspect (*Außen[an]sicht*) that limits the representation to that of objective physical phenomena (cf. Rimmon-Kenan 1983: "focalized from without").

Genette's "internal focalization" ("restricted focalization") is equally problematic. In addition to a straight forward single character bound epistemology it can also denote the mixed position of "narratorial co-vision" with a defined reflector character which, however, goes along with a reductionist external perspective onto all other characters. Moreover, "internal focalization" can also be used to describe the case of an autobiographic narration where the mode of focalization is completely self-centered. And this does not even exhaust the possibilities for the more vexing constellations in first person narration listed by Stanzel—chronicle, eye witness account, interior monologue, etc.

These examples show that individual definitions could of course be improved on—but the architecture of the analytical model *per se* would still be problematic. So how about a more rigid systematic approach? Perhaps we should set out with a principled distinction, like that between all cases of an objectifying epistemology, of a "looking-from-without", versus all cases of "introspection", i.e. of an empathetic epistemology of "experiencing-from-within"[6]. The scope of the objectifying continuum

---

5 See e.g. Niederhoff (2001); also see the contribution by Tatjana Jesch and Malte Stein in the current volume.

6 It also calls for a clear-cut distinction among epistemology (how can we know what we know?), psychology (how can we feel what we feel?) and ontology (how can we be what we are?). The Genettian distinction of heterodiegetic vs. homodiegetic narrators

could then be marked by concepts such as "autonomous vision—co-vision—self vision—external vision"[7]. All of these refer to cases where the epistemological vantage point remains external to the object domain, even if what one looks at is oneself (though the object remains located in a spatial-temporal position distinct from the point of origin of the enunciative act). By contrast, the second continuum would then integrate the various modes of introspection, of being "focalized from within" (*sensu* Rimmon-Kenan 1983). This continuum could be delineated by the positions of "indexical (subjective) vision—partial introspection—full introspection".

In all of these the empathetic vantage point is centered within an observing and feeling instance. The analysis of a concrete narratorial statement would then amount to a definition of its narratorial position in terms of an intersection of the epistemological and the empathetic. For example, "autonomous vision" can integrate distinct positions of "partial introspection", whereas "co-vision" grants access only to feelings and emotions attributable to the reflector character. "External vision" on the other hand cancels all possibility for "introspection".

The following table is an attempt to systematize the existing terminology. It is based on the binary model of "external vs. internal focalization" as it manifests itself with regard to the object domain of "characters" and their physical and mental states. *n* characters denotes all possible characters existing in a narrated world; *p* stands for a special set of characters in a world that is accessible to one or more actors with perceptive abilities; character *x* (with its different internal states *x1*, *x2*, etc.) stands for a particular actor who perceives.

---

mixes up epistemology and ontology, not to mention the implicit reversal of the Platonian (and Aristotelian) definition of mimesis (domain of the represented content) vs. diegesis (domain of the acts of representation, but also the representation as such—also see footnote 12). With the exception of a first-person real-time report any act of telling is, in a logical sense, a "telling-from-without" and thus "heterodiegetic" in an epistemological sense. The question whether or not a narrator exists within the narrated world is thus an ontological one. However, we already have a term for a narrator who exists within the narrated world—he or she is, quite simply, a narrating character. In the following we will disregard the heterodiegetic/homodiegetic distinction: it is simply not needed.

7 Our definition of this continuum varies slightly from that of Martinez & Scheffel (cf. 1999: 64).

	external focalization	internal focalization
narratorial, unrestricted perception *(autonomous vision / "Übersicht" or "Allsicht" resp.)*	external vision (*"Außen-[an]sicht"*) onto *n* characters	introspection of *n* characters *(full introspection)*
narratorial, partially restricted perception *(co-vision / "Mitsicht" with x)*	external vision onto the *p*-set of characters, excluding character *x*	introspection of *x (partial subjective introspection)*
actorial, partially restricted perception *(self vision of x onto various states of x)*	external vision onto the *p*-set of characters, excluding character *x*	introspection *of x* at different stages *x1, x2* etc. (*complex subjective introspection)*
actorial, restricted perception *(self vision of x in simultaneity to the mediating process: interior monologue)*	external vision onto the *p*-set of characters (excluding character *x*), dominated by subjective introspection	introspection of *x* *(subjective introspection)*, dominating mediation
actorial, restricted perception *(external vision)*	external vision onto the *p*-set of characters, excluding character *x*	marginal to zero introspection (of *x)*

1.2 Before Terminology

This discussion of how narratology's conceptual tool-kit and terminology might be improved with particular regard to the category of focalization will be taken up later in this article. However, in the end all these terminological and pragmatic issues eventually point us back to the more principled problem mentioned above, that of the a-temporal systematicity embedded in structuralist narratology's methodological design. Perhaps the most telling symptom of this orientation is the prevalence of visual metaphors in the narratological terminology dedicated to the analysis of perspective and focalization (*sic!*). These metaphors by their very nature imply that, at least in logical terms, narration is preceded by acts of perception—and even Genette's choice of the more technical concept of focalization, which connotates a camera lens, cannot escape this association either, although it does manage to overcome the anthropomorphism of the "viewing"-metaphor. Generally speaking, the bias on perceptive and sensual input significantly overshadows the mental activities by which we embed the perceived content within the cognitive, emotional and evaluative frame works at our disposal. In fact, as fictional narratives prove we do not even require any sensual or empirical input: perception may be a sufficient trigger for narration, but it is certainly not a necessary prerequisite for it. Rather, the cognitive, emotional and evaluative frame works at our disposal have endowed us with the unique ability to invent the content that will fit them retrospectively and "as if" it had already been perceived. And while such "content-free" fictional narratives might be an extreme case even their factual counter parts are obviously based on the complex procedures of cognitive pre-ordering and pre-processing which characterize all acts of communication.

In the end the terminological predominance of visual, optical and spatial metaphors (perspective, focus, distance etc.) as well as the objectifying systematicity characterizing structuralist narratology both betray its methodological disregard for the processual interdependency and dynamics of acts of perception (real or imagined), acts of cognition / emotion and acts of mediation (of expressing and passing on information). Structuralist approaches have a tendency to "freeze" the narrative into a single snap shot taken right at the end of everything. We are made to believe that one can "see" the logic of discourse in a given scene *ex post* like we "see" the compositional structure of a picture, or a landscape in which everything seems to be present and presented simultaneously.

However, while the (real or hypothetical) objects referred to by a painting or a narrative's constituent symbols might as such indeed be temporal and existential antecedents, their representation as a semiotic construct necessarily develops and unfolds over time—and so does the complementary cognitive and emotive activity of the recipient who transforms the signs into mental images. Before we can have a complete representation in the sense of a complex mental image—the entire tale, the complete picture—we encounter a multitude of representational and interpretive acts that interact with one another. And from time to time, this interplay results in interference rather than coherence.

One way to overcome this restriction is to look at the process of perception in terms of its local and temporal constraints, such as the ideological and linguistic frames of reference within which it takes place. However, relevant analytical approaches such as Rimmon-Kenan (1983) and Schmid (2005) once again focus explicitly on the analysis of an ideal type of how a narrative is narratorially produced. The ongoing mental activity required on the recipient's part and coded into the medium in the sense of processing instructions and controls remains beyond their scope.

2 The Model and its Terminology

In contrast to the terminological discussions which have kept narratology busy over the past two decades we would now like to propose a more fundamental revision of the concept of narration. Our systematic point of departure is not the narrative as an artefact, but rather the processing of a narrative; our goal is to arrive at a model architecture of the communicative process which "drives" narratives. In short, our goal is that of modelling mediacy, which is why our model is called the "Dynamic Narrative System (DNS)"[8]. In order to develop this system architecture we will have to ask questions that go beyond the traditional ones of "who sees" and "who speaks". For the time being the relevance of the DNS model of mediacy is, however, restricted to the sub-set of literary narratives in the narrower sense of the term. The examples given in section 4 (intended to demonstrate the scope of our model and its terminology) will therefore also be restricted to literary texts.

Irrespective of the significant methodological reorientation which we just proposed there is certainly no need to re-invent all the terminological wheels of narratology. The innovation lies in a different type of application of the established narratological concepts: rather than using them to analyze "narrative" in the sense of a stable object and then sort terminologically defined states into the rigid slots of a taxonomy, we will try and work with a scalar description of the variable processes which contribute to narration as a performative phenomenon. However, this approach is also not a licence to a pseudo-Heraclitean stance of "everything flows". In order to identify typical patterns of mediacy we will have to arrest, from time to time, what in reality is an ongoing process. In the continuum of processing time defined points of observation have to be chosen in order to sample prototypical constellations of parameters and

[8] Our concept of "dynamic narrative system" is only loosely related to the concept of "narrative system" referred to by Roland Weidle (see his contribution to the current volume: "Organizing the Perspectives: Focalization and the Superordinate Narrative System in Drama and Theater"). Weidle's approach—which in turn is based on Jahn's concept of the dramatic "superordinate narrative agent" (Jahn 2001: 672)—presents an attempt to define a narrator concept specific to the case of "theatric narration" qua performance.

their values (cf. section 4). In defining these constellations we will try to stick with existing terminology as far as possible, but also complement it by additional concepts and parameters where necessary. Where new concepts are introduced we will try to make sure that they are intuitive, and also translatable across languages without loss. Our aim is not a fully coherent rigid analytical apparatus—rather, we want to try and keep our model sufficiently flexible so that different historical (and perhaps not even yet realized) constellations can be identified with it.

Even so, the model proposed in the following can only cover half of what makes up narrative-in-operation: we will not be able to reflect sufficiently on the readerly aspect of narrative processing. However, it has to be emphasized that our DNS model is not based on the idea of narrative as an abstract and self sufficient semiotic "machine" which runs in and by itself. In the reality of concrete narrative processing each and every component and module of the DNS requires interaction with a human mind in order to be activated. Where and how this mind engages with the architecture and turns it into a live system remains to be explored. For the time being we can only present the architecture as a blue print for the system as such. The model tries to explain how a narrative influences and determines our profiling of its narrative instance, the inferential construct commonly referred to as "narrator". And finally, it is a model—not a theory, and not a taxonomy either: it simply tries to give us an idea of how some of the crucial discourse phenomena are functionally interrelated, taking into account the dimension of time.

3 The DNS (Dynamic Narrative System)

The "discourse/story" distinction is perhaps the most fundamental contribution of narratology to literary theory. As we all know, its conceptual ancestors are Saussure's distinction of *signifiant/signifié* and, perhaps more importantly, the linguistic distinction between expression plane and content. All of these point back to a dichotomy inherent in the basic notion of representation which is preserved in its etymology and ambivalent semantics. Representation has two functional dimensions: the symbolic dimension of "being an image of" as well as the pragmatic dimension of "standing in for"[9]. In both cases representation communicates

[9] As narratologists we generally focus on the semiotic concept of representation, neglecting its wide spread usage in the political and legal sphere. Aestheticians and

something which is not present itself: in the former case a sensory perception which our epistemological conditions do not allow us to make ourselves; in the latter the intention of someone who is not personally present. Narratives often merge these two dimensions of representation, particularly on the level of discourse. Let us try to take them apart again.

3.1 Representation as "Being an Image of"

Narratives have a specific way of informing us about things that happen(ed), the things that they claim to be "an image of". Particular to the narrative representation of "things that happened" is its strong (though not exclusive) focus on events and their temporal ordering. Events need not be restricted to "things that happen in the world" (so-called "object events"), but can also be mental events ("processing events") that take place in the mind of a character, or in that of the narrator, or, if nothing else, in the reader's own mind. Temporality is crucial to the narrative mode of representation. Moreover, temporality is not just the principle that allows for narrative's sequential ordering of snap-shots of the world into connected events, but also the principle by which we position ourselves *vis-à-vis* the flux of events, real or imagined. Narrative representation is, as Ricoeur has argued, therefore perhaps the privileged way for humans to experience temporality. Narratives introduce physical before-after time relations into what they are "an image of"; at the same

---

literary critic's tendency to conceptualize the symbolic representation as an absolute, self-motivating entity might be seen as a consequence of this neglect of the pragmatic dimension of representation. By contrast, the political and legal concept of "representation" features prominently in many contemporary dictionaries, the *Encyclopaedia Britannica* being one. And yet in an etymological perspective the use of the term in the former meaning has clearly preceded the latter significantly, as the *Oxford English Dictionary* (2nd edition) entry on "representation" shows, which differentiates among eight major variants. According to the *OED*, the "fact of standing for, or in place of, some other thing or person, esp. with a right or authority to act on their account; substitution of one thing or person for another" is first documented in 1624, while the "fact of representing or being represented in a legislative or deliberative assembly, spec. in Parliament; the position, principle, or system implied by this" only appears in 1769. As for the semiotic concept of representation, the "action of presenting to the mind or imagination; an image thus presented; a clearly-conceived idea or concept" is first mentioned in 1647; however, the use of the term in the fundamental sense of "an image, likeness, or reproduction in some manner *of* a thing" is already found as early as 1425. This is the first documented occurrence of the term "representation" in the English language and appears in a theological context.

time, they also activate subjective past-present-future positioning via indexical terms ("now", "then" etc.) which transcend the realm of the represented and force us to engage ourselves mentally in the representational game[10]. It is this interplay of time and tense, of the objectively perceived (or imagined) time-line and our subjectively experienced position-in-time which is so highly suggestive and lures us to immerse ourselves into a fictional continuum of events.

3.2 Representation as "Standing in for"

But whose intention does a narrative "stand in for"? Obviously, it can communicate the intentions of (real or fictional) agents that appear on the content plane. More importantly, however, narrative also encourages us to read it as a performative sequence made up partly of observations and reflections, and partly of utterances, all of which we attribute to someone. This "someone" is the product of a typical *post hoc, ergo propter hoc* reasoning: there is a thought, so somebody must have thought it; there is an utterance, so somebody must have uttered it, etc. In everyday terminology this instance is generally called the narrator; referred by structuralists, however, as a "narrative instance" in order to avoid the anthropomorphism. While its ontological status is as problematic as its logical genesis, the narrative instance is nevertheless a useful heuristic device in acts of interpretation. However, if we want to understand how it works then we will need to open the black box. And what we find in there is what we propose to call the "dynamic narrative system".

3.3 Constituents of the Model

In a process oriented perspective narrative representation is the function of intellectual activities that run in parallel and across three dimensions:

---

10 McTaggart refers to these two fundamental principles of temporal ordering and positioning as that of the indexical ("past–present–future") A-line and the physical ("before–after") B-line. Both, however, are logically dependent on the a-temporal C-line of purely numerical or sequential ordering. By the same token one must regard the sequence of words that makes up the narrative's text as a temporally neutral C-line. The narrative text's often claimed "temporality" is in fact entirely induced by acts of interpretation. On the relevance of McTaggart's time philosophy for understanding narrative temporality see Meister (2005); on temporality and narrativity see Currie (2007).

"perception", "reflection", "mediation"[11]. We can describe how these dimensions and the activities taking place in and across them are interrelated by way of what one could call the fundamental representational formula:

$$\text{representation} = \text{function of}\left\{ \frac{\text{perception} * \text{reflection}}{\text{mediation}} \right\}$$

On the basis of this formula, we will start with an abstract overview of the narrative system's components and then go into more detail later. In diagrams 1, 5 and 6 we try to visualize the triangular relationship of mediation with perception and cognition in the form of a three dimensional, dynamic intersection. The internal logic of each dimension is presented in figures 2, 3 and 4. In section 4 the application of our model and taxonomy to concrete literary examples will be demonstrated.

If representation is the "output" of the system, then perception, reflection and mediation are the three functional dimensions in which the system can (and must) perform in order to produce such output. In other words, the system can only come alive and "run" if there is activity in all three systematic dimensions. In order to "make representation happen" we will therefore have to define the system's *modus operandi* in each of the three dimensions: what are the constraints that govern perception, and which goals have been set in this dimension? By the same token, what are the constraints and goals set in the other two dimensions? This overall mix of constraints and goals is what we call "dimensional parameters".

[11] Our term "mediation" refers to the process dimension of narrative representation, whereas "mediacy" is a property of the product, i.e. of narratives. The complexity and variety of narrative mediacy cannot be sufficiently captured in a two or three element order pattern. Visualizations in terms of intersecting and mutually affecting dimensions offer far better possibilities. The three dimensions in our model—perception, reflection and mediation—differ from tabular categorizations (cf. Genette), diagrams (cf. Rimmon-Kenan) or circle sectors (cf. Stanzel) in that they can display overlap to varying degrees. This overlap can change gradually with regard to prototypical constellations (see figure 5). In order to avoid the heterogeneous associations called up by terms such as "point of view", "perspective" and "focalization" our terminology consciously avoids any reference to these. Mediation, on the other hand, was chosen to in order to capture processes of semiosis and representation without reference to specific media, avoiding suggestive categories such as voice or verbalization. The closest resemblance to our model can be found in Rimmon-Kenans parameter called "facet" (cf. Rimmon-Kenan 1983: 78–84) and in Schmid's parameters of spatial-temporal positioning, i.e. *Standort, Zeitpunkt* (for "perception"), *Ideologie* (for "reflection"), *Verbalisierung* (for "mediation") (cf. Schmid 2005: 138–45).

What these dimensional parameters are, which of them are compulsory and which optional, and what values they may take in principle is specific to the type of representational system. In the system architecture of narrative representation all dimensional parameters are organized along one and the same fundamental opposition of "diegetic (narratorial) vs. mimetic (actorial)"[12]. Each of the three DNS dimensions has at least one top level parameter (cf. figures 2 to 4) which defines the dimension and is, as such, not only logically indispensable, but also has the highest level of impact.

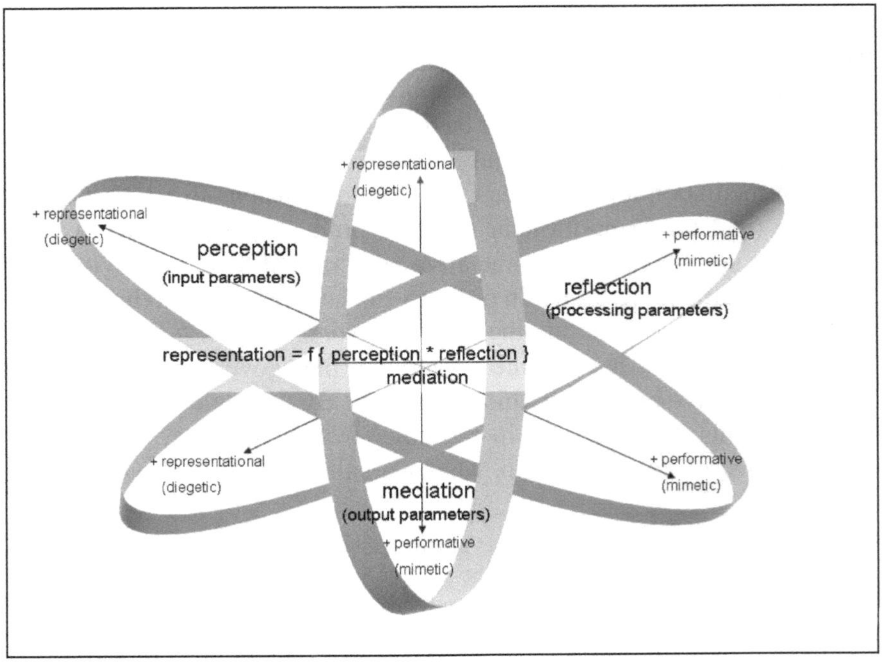

Figure 1: DNS (Dynamic Narrative System) Model of Representation

[12] Our identification of diegetic with "narratorial" and mimetic with "actorial" interprets the Platonian (and Aristotelian) distinction in its narrower sense, i.e. as the two fundamentally opposed representational modes of telling vs. showing, or representational vs. simulative. This is not to be confused with the second meaning of *diegesis* found in Aristotle, where the concept denotes the narrator's utterances *in toto* (i.e. in the modern sense of narrative, *Erzählung* or *rècit*).

In a system's perspective, setting or changing one particular parameter is always of more than just local consequence. Because the representational system is dynamic, any parameterization can potentially affect not only the remaining parameters within the same dimension; it will also result in a systematic predisposition for the other two dimensions. This principle of "change one, change all" is the key to the run-time logic that turns our abstract DNS into a live system.

3.4 The DNS's Constituent Dimensions

Once again: the DNS as such is a model, not a taxonomy, and not even an analytical or descriptive tool. Its intention is not to compete with existing classifications of narrative phenomenology, in particular with those of Genette or Schmid. Rather, its purpose is to provide such classifications with a unifying theoretical frame of reference in order to prepare for the next step (cf. section 4) where we will make a first suggestion towards a typology consistent with our model.

3.4.1 The Dimension of Perception

In order to produce output a system requires some input—the DNS is no exception to this rule. In humans perception is one of three ways to provide us with relevant data, cognition and emotion being the other two. Whether this data is sensory or mentally generated (i.e., thoughts), whether it is real or imagined, true or false is in the end irrelevant: if our aim is to produce representational output, then all of it qualifies as valid input.

In Genette's narrative theory the specific conditions under which perception of narrated content takes place (or rather, is inferred to have taken place) fall mainly under the category of focalization ("zero vs. external vs. internal"). Focalization, it seems, regulates what a narrator or a narrating character can know about the world, his epistemology, whereas the particularities of voice ("hetero- vs. homo- vs. autodiegetic narration") determine the position in the fictional world from which he then utters his communications[13].

However, at least in the case of fictional narrative this distinction between knowing and communicating, between the epistemological and the

[13] This reference to Genette's use of the term focalization is restricted to the aspect of "input". Of course, in Genette's own model "focalization" and "voice" at the same time also account for the narratorial communicative strategy.

ontological constraints under which the representational system operates seems methodologically problematic. Most of our inferences about the narrating instance's perceptive conditions will turn out to be based on the very utterances which we ascribe to it. In other words, the narrating instance's epistemological profile does not exist *a priori*, but is really just a function of performative acts for which we hold it responsible: we "make" the narrator by looking for one. The so-called autodiegetic I-narrator can best illustrate this dilemma: by necessity, its ontological position must be "in" the world "about" which it informs us—ontology and epistemology go hand in hand. Moreover, a narrative instance embodied in the fictional world is in fact just a narrating character, and the quality of information which he can relate to us is not just a matter of abstract epistemological constraints, but also a question of his or her level of cognitive and emotive engagement. It is this mental closeness that matters and profiles the narrating instance, not just temporal-spatial proximity.

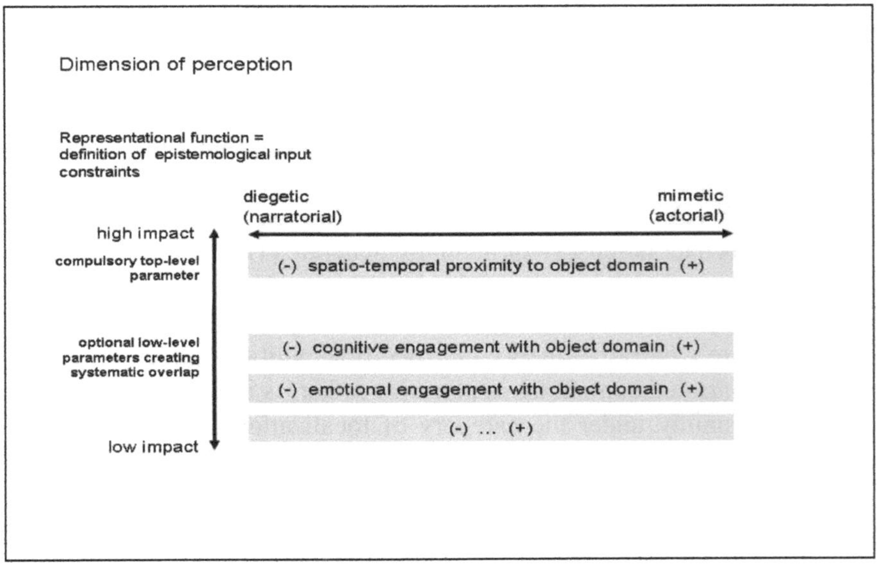

Figure 2: Dimension of Perception

In the DNS model we define the dimension of perception as one which is primarily—but not exclusively!—characterized by epistemological "input constraints" and "parameters"[14]. The compulsory top level parameter defines the constraints of temporal and spatial proximity under which acts of perception take place. When set to a "diegetic" value, such acts are constrained by considerable distance between observer and the domain observed: the typical epistemological position of an omniscient narrator who plays the narrative game with an open deck.

On the other hand, when set to a "mimetic" value the constraints on perception will generate close-ups from the contextually defined point of view of a specific character. As our brief discussion of some of the problems in Genette's system has already indicated, we need to be aware that this first dimensional "take" on the DNS introduces a systematic boundary where, in the reality of system performance, none exists. Perception and processing are closely related, and any change in either dimension will immediately have its effect in its counterpart. While the top-level parameter insists on dimensional specificity, lower-level optional parameters create systematic overlap across dimensions.

3.4.2 The Dimension of Reflection

One of the tenets of structuralist narratology was the formalist conceptualization of narrated characters as mere surface layer representatives for something that drives the narrative's progress on the deep level of action logic: functions. Meanwhile, current narratological theory has begun to rediscover the more traditional notion of character, demonstrating a new interest in characters' phenomenology and anthropomorphic qualities (cf. Jannidis 2004). As a result, actants are extended into "fictional minds" (Palmer 2004), a concept more apt to explain why and how readers engage with narratives across the full spectrum of mental activities.

The narrator, abstract as he or she might be, has never been at a similar risk of being turned into a mere functional variable of representation and

---

14 By mapping identical parameters onto each of the three dimensions, yet in different sequence, we try to demonstrate their difference and interrelation at the same time. For example, sensual perception will always go along with mental processes and rudimentary semiosis. The primacy assigned to the temporal and spatial parameter with regard to "perception" links this dimension to the discussion of "point of view"/"perspective". By contrast, the discussion on focalization is of relevance also to the dimension of "reflection", as it is to the dimension of "mediation" (here with regard to information strategies).

action logic. One reason is that a narrator has a powerful real-life aid: the author as whose *alter ego* he is often misread, if only covertly. One might call this the "narratorial fallacy"—the tendency to react to an inference based construct, which is particular to the narrative type of representation, as if it were "real". This tendency is certainly not just found in cases where readers confuse the categories of author and narrator. It has an even more compelling motivation in what our DNS model integrates as dimension of reflection.

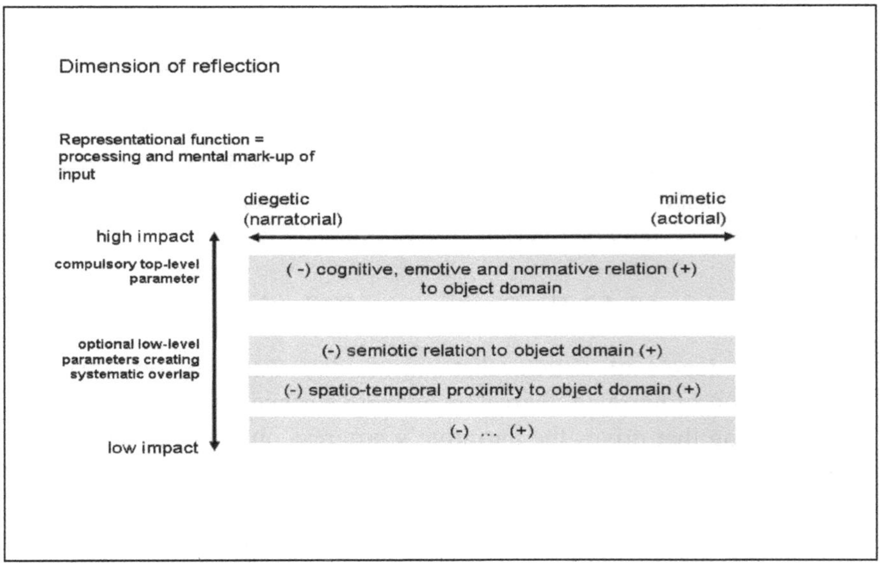

Figure 3: Dimension of Reflection

What is contributed to representation in this dimension is a sort of mental mark-up of the input that was derived in the dimension of perception and then processed by what seems to function like a "mind". The mark-up which it generates defines the narrative system's cognitive, emotive and normative relation to the object domain of the representation. These evaluative stances can be accentuated as diegetic and thus rendered as attributable to the narrator, or mimetic and therefore attributable to characters; they can be contradictory or reinforce each other: in the end they all contribute to what one might call the *Geisteshaltung*, the mentality or, literally translated, the "mind position" of the representation.

A representation lacking this functional component is not narrative—or, to turn the argument around: our success in "narrativizing" a non-narrative representation like for example a photograph hinges to a large degree on our ability to add or identify this dimension in it *post festum*. Its compulsory top level parameter is that of evaluative stance (cognitive, emotive, normative). Optional lower-level parameters include semantic profiling in terms of part-whole-relations, as well as spatial-temporal positioning. Again, these lower-level parameters overlap with the top-level parameters of the other two dimensions.

3.4.3 Dimension of Mediation

In its dimension of mediation the DNS defines the semiotic constraints that regulate the system's output—the materialization of the representation in its double functionality of "being an image of" and "standing in for". This is where the "conditions of possibility" for concrete semiotic realization are negotiated and stipulated, where paradigms, opposites and isotopes are formed and highlighted, and where modes (e.g., tropes, metaphors, register) and media of articulation are selected and posited in relation to the object domain.

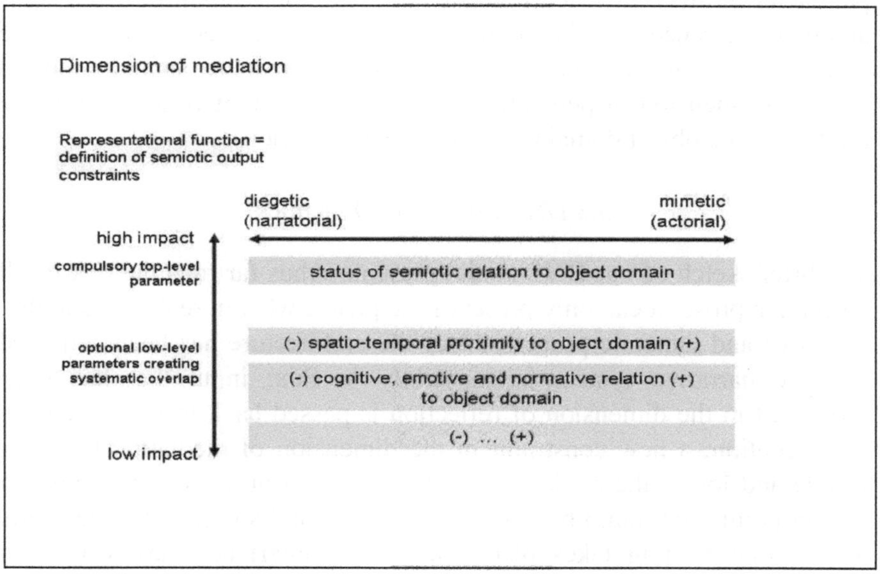

Figure 4: Dimension of Mediation

Must narrative representation meet specific criteria in this regard? Not really, but its outer limits can be defined: a representation devoid of any reference becomes an object in its own right; whereas a representation devoid of any mark of non-identity *vis-à-vis* its referent cancels the referent and usurps its position in totality. Both are no longer representations, but things present. Whether or not such an opaque mimetic representation is indeed possible is hard to decide. One thing is obvious though: in our daily lives the clear distinction between things that "stand for other things" and things that "are" is increasingly hard to make.

We find ourselves directly affected by signs as if they were objects even where these signs explicitly inform us about their semiotic status (take the *Dow Jones Index*). Conversely, we regularly "read" empirical objects and occurrences as "signs for" rather than experiencing them *per se*—we have to do this in order to be able to learn or plan ahead. In short, semiosis in interaction with human practice defies and subverts fixed semiotic categorizations: in our existential practice, things are signs are things are signs etc. Aesthetic semiotic practice, however, need not rely on contextual markers in any event; it indicates its semiotic status inherently, by surplus structuring which indicates its poetic function (*sensu* Roman Jakobson). Against this background the compulsory top-level parameter in this dimension regulates the semiotic relation between signs and their reference domain. Optional lower level parameters include those which were top-level in the other two dimensions, spatial-temporal relation (dimension of perception) and cognitive, emotive and normative relation to the object domain (dimension of reflection).

3.5 DNS Run-Time Dynamics

The brief sketch of our DNS model presented thus far runs the risk of all discursive prose: it can only present in sequence what in reality is a highly recursive and dynamic process. Once the architecture has been activated the live narrative system is constantly in flux: input that has been processed in the dimension of reflection is passed back to the dimension of perception; a new constraint in the dimension of mediation becomes visible and forces the reader to re-run the system in his/her mind up to a certain point, then jump back to the cut point, and so forth. Furthermore, once actual reading takes place the system interfaces massively with human mental processes which are way beyond the scope of our model.

All we can try is to give at least a graphical indication of what the system at work would possible look like: three revolving planes that intersect with one another in different ways on every rotation.

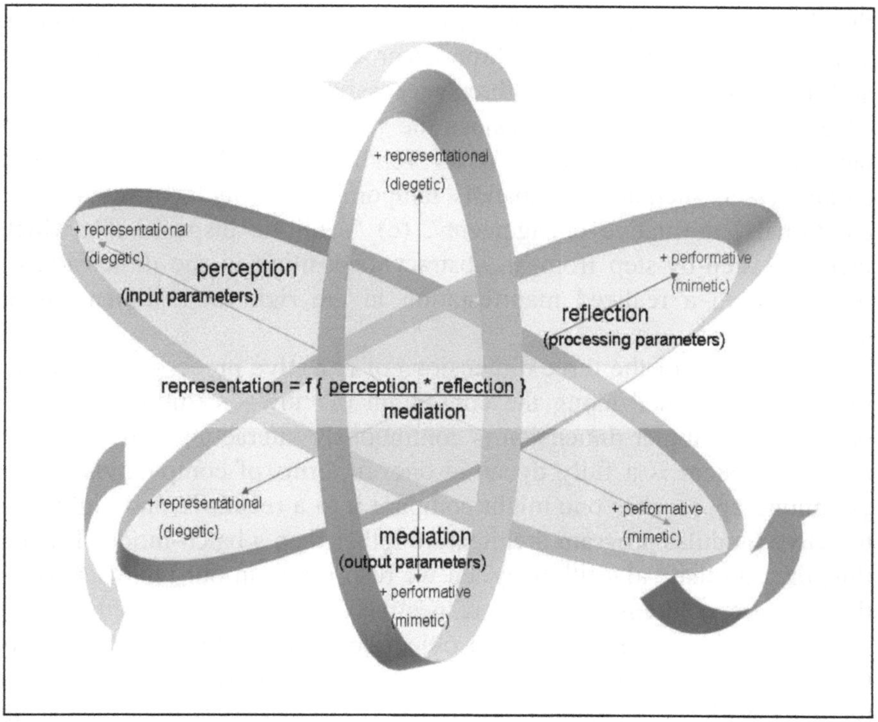

Figure 5: The DNS at "Run-Time", i.e. Performing as a Dynamic Narrative System

4 From the DNS Model to an Analytical Heuristics

In the following we will present a typological table of modes of narrative representation (see page 34). This seems to be in contradiction to our initial criticism of combinatorial attempts to generate typologies. However, our typology is by no means intended to exhaust all valid combinations in parameter settings: it merely tries to project some of the typical constellation that might occur along the three dimensional performative continuum of perception, reflection, and mediation onto a two dimensional table. This is the first step; the second will be an attempt to demonstrate how our abstract model might be applied in the practice of textual analysis[15].

This is how our table should be read: the constituent sub-processes of narration are in the first (systematic, not "real"!) instance determined by the different extensions of the narrative's object domain (1st column). Thereafter, we capture the synchronous processes of perception, reflection and mediation in the form of three successive tabular dimensions (2nd to 4th column). In all three dimensions the standard qualification of a given parameter is measured in terms of its "relation to the object domain". The parameters as such are (a) "spatial / temporal proximity", (b) "cognitive / emotional / normative engagement", (c) "semiotic disposition" (which increases step-by-step from an abstract disposition in the dimension of perception to a realized manifestation in the right-most dimension of mediation).

Within each of the three dimensions of narrative processing these parameters are graded along the continuum of "low—medium—high impact". Every tabular dimension is continuously interacting with the other two: the system is a fully dynamic one; in terms of computational programming approaches one might compare it to a recursive and highly interactive modular program architecture rather than a batch-mode "first do this, then do that" algorithm. When we read a row in our table across its three centre columns and their respective sub-columns we can see the scope of variations in relations to object domain that fall under one particular "representational type". In reality, the number of such types might be huge; we have decided to limit ourselves to just six types which seem to be best documented historically and can thus be cited as exemplary cases. Finally, the two right-most columns compare the traditional Genettian type-term with our suggested terminological replacement.

The measuring of a particular parameter in terms of its relation to object domain value is thus not a question of "yes or no"; it is a question of attributing it a particular position within an array that extends from "high to low". If we want to measure the level of internal influence which the initiating instance of the narrative process (or the textual instances that represent it) can have, then we will differentiate along the axis of low—medium—high interest. If on the other hand our interest lies in measuring the extent to which the process is constrained by text-external (historical and cultural) factors then we will do so along the scale of "fully—medi-

---

15 See Grabienski et al. (2006).

um—low constrained". The values entered in our table are not of an absolute nature; rather they represent an ensemble of tendencies which in their combination allow us to describe the dynamics of narrative processing. From a literary history perspective the few prototypical constellations represented in our table can only capture a glimpse of what has been—or might still be—realized empirically.

The typology of representations is based on the following premises:
(a) The qualification "narratorial" defines a position external to the narrated world. The narrating instance is by default completely autonomous and unconstrained; however, it is marked as narratorial on a gradual scale as soon as a level of limitation affecting its operations in the three dimensions becomes discernable.
(b) The qualification "actorial" defines a position within the narrated world. Again, the narrating instance is marked on a gradual scale in terms of its dimensional limitations: for example, by the spatially and temporally defined position from which the instance observes simultaneously occurring events, as in the case of an eye witness account, or by the simultaneity of experience and narration, e.g. in a protagonist's interior monologue. The latter is in contrast with the so-called autobiographical mode of narration. This mode allows for the narrating instance's choice of different spatial-temporal positions within the dimensions of perception (which is, by definition, experience centered) and mediation (where the focus is primarily on representation). In a typical autobiographical narrative different situations in life are defined by different constellations in the protagonist's cognitive, emotional and normative engagement.
(c) Finally, a third type of mediacy is defined in terms of hybrid positions, which we call "mixed narratorial / actorial". Here the narrator's acts of evaluation and mediation take place from one position, but are combined with acts of perception and reflection bound to a second position that indicates an actorial stance. Actorial mediacy, in these cases, is graded on a scale ranging from "covert" to "overt". An example would be the difference between a completely factual eye witness report, and an affected by-stander's account displaying traces of personal engagement with the ongoings[16].

---

[16] A term we deliberately avoid in our qualification of the six prototypes is "extradiegetic". In our opinion the term is a tautology in that it merely captures the self-evident epistemological prerequisite of all narrative representations: as soon as we talk about "diegesis" in any meaningful way, we have to associate the enunciative act with an enunciator, and dissociate the product of enunciation (the narrative, the text) from it

	NARRATION										
relation to object domain	perception			reflection			mediation			Typology of representations	
	spatial/ temporal proximity	cognitive / emotional / normative engagement	semiotic disposition (virtual)	cognitive / emotional / normative engagement	semiotic disposition (partially actualized)	spatial/ temporal proximity	semiotic disposition (fully actualized)	spatial/ temporal proximity	cognitive / emotional / normative engagement		
	high impact	*medium impact*	*low impact*	*high impact*	*medium impact*	*low impact*	*high impact*	*medium impact*	*low impact*	DNS	Genette et.al.
extension of object domain											
sum total of physical and mental phenomena	medium constrained	low interest	unconstrained	low interest	medium constrained	unconstrained	medium constrained	medium constrained	medium interest	Unconstrained narratorial	Heterodiegetic with omnivision
sum total of physical phenomena + set of agent based mental phenomena	medium constrained	medium interest	medium constrained	medium interest	medium constrained	medium constrained	medium constrained	medium constrained	medium interest	Constrained narratorial	Heterodiegetic, optional phases of co-perception
actorially defined set of physical + agent based mental phenomena	fully constrained	high interest	medium constrained	high interest	medium constrained	medium constrained	medium constrained	fully constrained	high interest	Mixed narratorial / actorial	Heterodiegetic with actorial co-perception
witness defined set of physical phenomena	fully constrained	low interest	medium constrained	low interest	medium constrained	fully constrained	fully constrained	fully constrained	low interest	Covert actorial	Heterodiegetic with external perception
actorially defined set of physical phenomena	fully constrained	medium interest	fully constrained	medium interest	medium constrained	fully constrained	fully constrained	fully constrained	medium interest	Overt actorial	Homodiegetic, external perception
actorially defined set of physical + own mental phenomena	medium constrained	high interest	medium constrained	high interest	medium constrained	medium constrained	fully constrained	fully constrained	high interest	Unconstrained actorial	Autodiegetic with external and self-perception

As we will demonstrate, representational types can be attributed to texts as a whole, but also to passages within texts as we will show below. In some instances the distinction among types is not very clear cut, as in the case of "constrained narratorial representation vs. mixed narratorial / actorial representation": the former type also subsumes phases where the default autonomous vision of the narrating instance is temporarily restricted by constraining its powers of perception and reflection to those attributable to one or more actors; in the latter type the narrative instance is parameterized throughout in accordance with the epistemological and

at the same time. The logical opposite to "extradiegetic" would in fact not be "intradiegetic", but simply "mimetic". The current (Genettian) use of the qualifier "intradiegetic", however, is not intended as a statement concerning the ontological status of the representation as such: it merely tries to point out that the act of narration is, at the same time, its own object; in other words: that diegesis is not organized as a two-level affair of *signifiant vs. signifié*, but rather in the form of nested instances of narration.

reflective position of a particular actor, but the overall semiotic disposition will nevertheless indicate a higher-level narratorial instance.

We will now analyze two textual examples in order to illustrate how the dynamic narrative system's mode of operation might be measured in terms of the continuously changing values which it assigns to the functional parameters in its three interrelated dimensions of perception, reflection, and mediation[17].

Example 1: Charles Perrault *Little Red Riding Hood*

Once upon a time there lived in a certain village a little country girl, the prettiest creature who was ever seen. Her mother was excessively fond of her; and her grandmother doted on her still more. This good woman had a little red riding hood made for her. It suited the girl so extremely well that everybody called her Little Red Riding Hood. One day her mother, having made some cakes, said to her: "Go, my dear, and see how your grandmother is doing, for I hear she has been very ill. Take her a cake, and this little pot of butter." Little Red Riding Hood set out immediately to go to her grandmother, who lived in another village.

As she was going through the wood, she met with a wolf, who had a very great mind to eat her up, but he dared not, because of some woodcutters working nearby in the forest. He asked her where she was going. The poor child, who did not know that it was dangerous to stay and talk to a wolf, said to him: "I am going to see my grandmother and carry her a cake and a little pot of butter from my mother." "Does she live far off?" said the wolf. "Oh I say," answered Little Red Riding Hood, "it is beyond that mill you see there, at the first house in the village." "Well," said the wolf, "and I'll go and see her too. I'll go this way and go you that, and we shall see who will be there first."

The wolf ran as fast as he could, taking the shortest path, and the little girl took a round-about way, entertaining herself by gathering nuts, running after butterflies, and gathering bouquets of little flowers. It was not long before the wolf arrived at the old woman's house. He knocked at the door: tap, tap. [...]

Little Red Riding Hood took off her clothes and got into bed. She was greatly amazed to see how her grandmother looked in her nightclothes, and said to her, "Grandmother, what big arms you have!" "All the better to hug you with, my dear." "Grandmother, what big legs you have!" "All the better to run with, my child." "Grandmother, what big ears you have!" "All the better to hear with, my child." "Grandmother, what big eyes you have!" "All the better to see with, my child." "Grandmother, what big teeth you have got!" "All the better to eat you up with." And, saying these words, this wicked wolf fell upon Little Red Riding Hood, and ate her all up.

Moral: Children, especially attractive, well bred young ladies, should never talk to strangers, for if they should do so, they may well provide dinner for a wolf. I say "wolf", but there are various kinds of wolves. There are also those who are charming, quiet, po-

---

[17] The examples were taken from the web and have not been philologically verified. Yet, for the purpose of a demonstration of our model in application they should suffice.

lite, unassuming, complacent, and sweet, who pursue young women at home and in the streets. And unfortunately, it is these gentle wolves who are the most dangerous ones of all.

These passages taken from a short text present an example for our type 1 ("unconstrained narratorial representation"), including a passage of quasi-mimetic scenic representation marked in italics. In this example the dynamics of the three dimensions could be outlined as follows.

PERCEPTION: the narratorial instance's perceptive abilities are generally not constrained by the spatial or temporal limitations of any single actorial position—the path of the wolf and the path of Little Red Riding Hood are equally followed. Physical objects as well as the mental states of the wolf and Little Red Riding Hood are being presented (viz. the short sequence of introspection at the beginning of paragraph two). However, the perception of narrated events is only marginally intersected by the dimension of reflection. With a view to mediation, these formulations underline the narrator's distanced and ironic position of cognitive superiority *vis-à-vis* the characters, as in this opening: „The poor child, who did not know that it was dangerous to stay and talk to a wolf [...]". This superiority, however, will only be put to full effect in the concluding moral of the story, where the focus of "perception" no longer lies on the fantastic story of Little Red Riding Hood and the wolf, but rather on the real constellations of social life.

REFLECTION: in the beginning, the amount of the narrating instance's cognitive, emotional and normative engagement during the act of perception is minimal, and the semiotic disposition is unmarked. However, long before the final moral is explicated a first sign of reflection-processing is detectable in the narrating instance's normative evaluations of the actors (Little Red Riding Hood is being spoilt by her mother and grandmother; the wolf is hungry and ravenous.) In the final "moral of the story" the normative engagement of the narrative instance increases dramatically from medium to high interest.

MEDIATION: the initially gradual and then suddenly exponential increase in normative engagement is paralleled and supported by the curve which the actualization of semiotic disposition along the mediating process follows. First a number of isolated semiotic determinants manifest themselves (including introspection into the protagonists' state of mind and the representation of character-bound attitudes, even though the latter are not explicitly marked as actorial in their verbalization) before the final moral is presented as an explicit marker of the narratorial activity of "diegesis" (in the Platonian sense).

This first example demonstrated how a description in terms of traditional narratological categories can be formalized in terms of the DNS model. Our second example will now demonstrate the added text analytical capacity which sets the DNS model apart from its precursors.

Example 2: Alfred Döblin *The Murder of a Buttercup*

[a] Yes, he had killed the flower, and it was no business of theirs, and he had the right, which he would defend against all of them. He had the right to kill flowers, and he did not feel obliged to justify it in any more detail. He could kill as many flowers as he pleased for a thousand miles around, north, south, east, west, whether they scoffed at it or not. And if they carried on laughing like that he would leap at their throats. [...] [b1] Again he runs hard against a low fir; it strikes down at him with raised hands. [b2] He breaks his way through violently, the blood running in streams down his face. He spits, lashes out, kicks the trees, yelling, slides down, sitting and rolling, finally runs headlong down the last slope at the verge of the wood toward the lights of the village, his torn frock coat thrown over his head, [c] while behind him the mountain rustles threateningly, shaking its fists, and everywhere trees can be heard cracking and breaking as they run after him, cursing.

This passage (an excerpt from a longer novella) presents a type 3 example ("mixed narratorial / actorial representation"): in [a] free indirect speech is used to represent the thoughts of the protagonist (he has "beheaded" a butter cup with his walking stick). This is followed by the description of a number of actions [b] in which actor centred perception [b1] merges into the externally based perception of a narratorial instance [b2] and then [c] reverts back to actorial perception. The dynamics of the three dimensions could be outlined as follows.

PERCEPTION: as the historical present in paragraph 2 indicates, perception is bound to time and place of the fictional events, yet at the same time it is intermingled to a high degree with actorial emotions and evaluations—and so is the semiotic disposition, which is determined by actor centred patterns. But this is not a fixed constellation: the dimensions of perception, reflection and mediation are being repeatedly and dynamically repositioned against one another. The effect is such that perception, by way of smooth transitions, is also characterized by the evaluations and verbalizations of the narrator. One example is the second sentence in [b2], where „toward the lights of the village“ signals that the predominantly narratorial perception—by way of a merging—is momentarily juxtaposed with a actorial orientation, thus subtly preparing the eventual shift to a fully actorial perception in [c].

REFLECTION: the processing of perceptions mirrors the strong relationship with the actorial dimension: strong in [a], [b1] und [c]; weaker in [b2]. However, semantics and syntax indicate the narrator's intent to demonstrate the intense, pathological state of mind of the actor, without resorting to explicit commentary.

MEDIATION: the predominant commitment to the spatial and temporal position of the actor as well as to his cognitive, emotional and normative position is amplified during mediation processing. However, in its actualization of the semiotic disposition the narratorial instance upholds its claim to perform representational operations which transcend the actorial disposition.

The following presents another example from Döblin's text:

> [a] He was paying, paying for his mysterious guilt. [b] He was performing divine service with the buttercup, [c] and the calm businessman asserted now that each person had his own religion; [d] one had to assume a personal position to an ineffable God. There were things that not everybody could understand. [e] A trace of suffering had appeared in the gravity of his monkey's face; his corpulence had also decreased, his eyes became deep set. [f] The flower, like a conscience, watched over his actions, stringently, from the most important to the smallest everyday deeds.

This is an example for a type 2 constellation ("constrained narratorial representation"). Passages of reflector bound co-vision in [a], [d] and [f] alternate with passages of "unconstrained narratorial representation" [c] and [e], which include the option of introspection and commentary. In between we find passages of gradual transformation from actorial to narratorial profiling of the three dimensions [b].

The summary effect is one of a medium-status which oscillates between "unconstrained narratorial representation" and "mixed narratorial / actorial representation" with gradual transitions. The segments of overlap of the three dimensions change from sentence to sentence. A precise definition of "who sees?" and "who speaks?" is only possible in a few prominently marked positions within this constant flow.

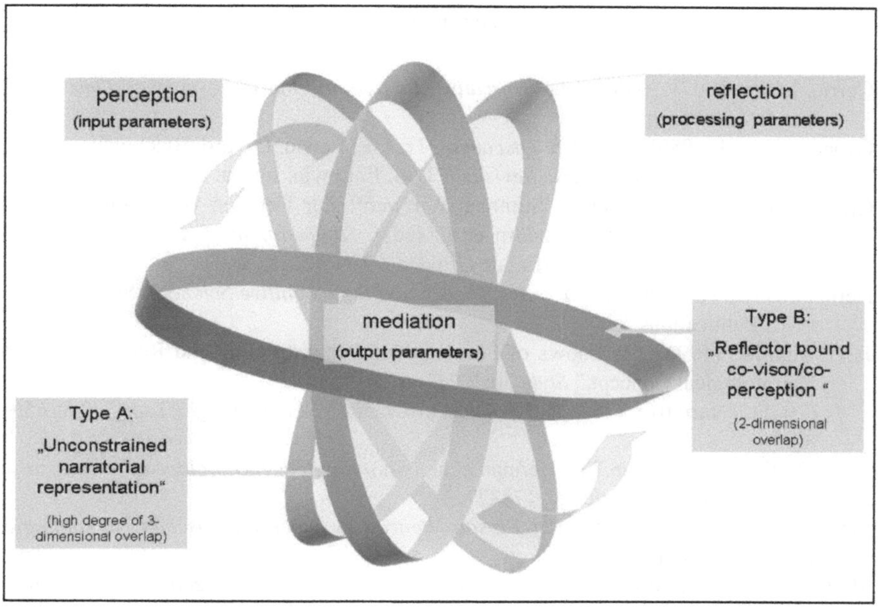

Figure 6: DNS Oscillating Between the Extremes of Type A/B-Mediation

5 Outlook

At this stage our DNS model is a first draft which obviously requires refinement in terms of its design and the analytical categories derived there from. In the current volume the contributions by Markus Kuhn and Sabine Schlickers demonstrate how a literature based Genettian descriptive apparatus can be fruitfully applied to other media: it remains to be seen whether the narratological DNS model and its typology, too, extend in relevance beyond text based representations. However, we believe that two particular characteristics might make our model a strong candidate for such transmedial application: one, its constituent process dimensions and functional parameters "perception—reflection—mediation" do not show the usual bias for a particular medium of representation, nor for visual metaphors. Two, the DNS model is designed to account for the generic as well as the historical dimension of narrative: it conceptualizes the dynamics of narrative processing as one that governs all narrative specimen, yet it always remains susceptible to change and creative "mutation" itself.

References

Currie, Mark (2007). *About Time. Narrative, Fiction and the Philosophy of Time*. Edinburgh: Edinburgh UP.

Genette, Gérard (1980). *Narrative Discourse*. Tr. J. E. Lewin. Oxford: Blackwell.

– (1988). *Narrative Discourse Revisited.* Tr. J. E. Lewin. Ithaca: Cornell UP.

Grabienski, Olaf et al. (2006). "Stimmen-Wirrwarr? Zur Relation von Erzählerin- und Figuren-Stimmen." A. Blöhdorn et al. (eds). *Stimme(n) im Text. Narratologische Positionsbestimmungen*. Berlin: de Gruyter, 195–232.

Herman, David (ed) (2003). *Narrative Theory and the Cognitive Sciences*. Stanford, CA: CSLI Publications.

Jahn, Manfred (1996). "Windows of Focalization: Deconstructing and Reconstructing a Narratological Concept." *Style* 30:2, 241–67.

– (2001). "Narrative Voice and Agency in Drama." *New Literary History* 32:3, 659–80.

– (2005). "Focalization." D. Herman et al. (eds). *Routledge Encyclopedia of Narrative Theory*. London: Routledge, 173–77.

Jannidis, Fotis (2004). *Figur und Person. Beitrag zu einer historischen Narratologie*. Berlin: de Gruyter.

Martinez, Matías & Michael Scheffel (1999). *Einführung in die Erzähltheorie*. Munich: Beck.

Meister, Jan Christoph (2005). "Tagging Time in Prolog. The Temporality Effect Project." *Literary and Linguistic Computing*, Vol. 20. Oxford, UK, 107–24. Electronic publication at <http://llc.oxfordjournals.org/cg>i/reprint/20/Suppl/107> (last seen 01.07.2008).

Niederhoff, Burkhard (2001). "Fokalisation und Perspektive. Ein Plädoyer für eine friedliche Koexistenz." *Poetica* 33:1–2, 1–21.

Palmer, Alan (2004). *Fictional Minds*. Lincoln: U of Nebraska P.

Rimmon-Kenan, Shlomith (1983). *Narrative Fiction. Contemporary Poetics*. London: Routledge.

Schmid, Wolf (1982). "Die narrativen Ebenen 'Geschehen', 'Geschichte', 'Erzählung' und 'Präsentation der Erzählung'. " *Wiener Slawistischer Almanach* 9, 83–110.

– (2005). *Elemente der Narratologie*. Berlin: de Gruyter.

Van Peer, Willie & Chatman, Seymour (eds) (2001). *New Perspectives on Narrative Perspective*. Albany, NY: State U of New York P.

URI MARGOLIN
(Edmonton, Canada)

Focalization: Where Do We Go from Here?

All the papers in this volume show a desire to revise current focalization theory in the hopes of strengthening and improving it, and to try and resolve at least some of the many open issues in this field. The two wishes are closely connected, since it is often the reformulation of assumptions that leads to the resolution of issues. The desire for revision seems to take one of three directions: (1) expansion of the domain of application of focalization theory to other media, with the necessary theoretical modifications (2) reconfiguration (add, delete, replace, rearrange) of the systems of categories and distinctions currently available and (3) a reconceptualization of the whole theory by placing it within a more fundamental theoretical framework, be it fictional world semantics or cognitive linguistics, both of which are ultimately semantic theories. I will try to contribute modestly to both reconfiguration and reconceptualization efforts, but let me start with the most basic question "wozu?" (to what end?) or why do we need a theory of focalization to begin with?

Fortunately, several very good answers to this potentially devastating question have been offered in recent years. In a major article, Mieke Bal (1993) asserts that all cognitive activity is located in the projects and constructions of specifically positioned subjects, and that narrative has the unique capability to map differently positioned subjects in their relation to knowledge and to each other. To this one might add that viewing knowledge as position-dependent enhances one's ability to imagine standpoints different from one's own, with correspondingly different insights regarding the same data, and to accept these other standpoints as alternatives to one's own. In a contribution to a collective volume on narrative perspective Ansgar Nünning (2001) asserts that literature is the only place where the construction of world models is thematized, and that narrative thematizes and structurally reflects the problems attached to the construction of world models. Furthermore, the cognitive processes through which an individual or collectivity actively construct their subjective world models are represented on the story level in the perspectives of the characters. Finally, the Canadian scholar Pierre Ouellet (1996) rightly claims that works of fiction represent the cognitive and perceptual experiences of subjects such as characters and narrators; that the novel in particular is constituted much more by experiences in the phenomenological sense than by objective states of affairs; and that in the modern novel great importance is attached to the representation of perceptual and cognitive processes and activities, to the exploration and dramatization of the mind's movement. But what *is* focalization?

1 Defining Focalization

Focalization is the general term (*Ober-* or *Sammelbegriff*) used to designate at least some of the mental activities just mentioned and their products. One can describe focalization informally as a view of a thing as it presents itself from the personal subjective point of view of a character or narrator. To be more precise (and this is my proposed definition): focalization in narrative involves the textual representation of specific (pre)existing sensory elements of the text's story world as perceived and registered (recorded, represented, encoded, modeled and stored) by some mind or recording device which is a member of this world. In other words, focalization involves at least the internal inscription of external data. Conversely, any state or event mentioned in the text which can possibly be thought of as being perceived in any way can be considered to be the product of an act of focalization, hence indexed to a particular individual, time and place.

1.1 Five Components of Focalization

Occam's razor reminds us that entities should not be multiplied beyond necessity. This lesson is not lost on me, yet I would claim that, as follows from my definition, any adequate description of focalization involves essentially not less than five factors. These are (1) the story-world state or event focalized; (2) the focalizing agent and its make-up; (3) the activity of perceiving and processing this object-focalization as *nomen actionis*; (4) the product of this activity, that is, the resultant take or vision and (5) the textualization of all the above, which is the only thing directly accessible to the reader and not requiring his imaginative reconstruction. It is obviously also the one from which all other components are (re)constructed in the reading process. Moreover, the very basic distinction between who sees and who says, one of the key elements of literary narratology, is ultimately grammar and lexicon based. Let me now expand a little on each.

(1) The object focalized is an element or sector of the story world: states, entities, actions, events and processes, some located in space and time and some internal or mental such as memories of previous acts of focalization. Such an element or sector is the object of the focalizer's attention and subsequent inner processing. Whether everything in the story world can be meaningfully considered as object of potential focalization is a contentious issue to which we shall return (for more on objects of focalization in literary contexts see 3.1 below).

(2) The focalizing agent is a human or human-like story world participant who concentrates or focuses selectively on a portion of the available sensory information. At its core is a mind or recording device with its capabilities, faculties, structures and constraints. These would include embodiment, situatedness or space-time position (=vantage point), architecture (=mechanisms, categories, routines) and, for human minds, also norms, values and epistemic attitudes. A focalizing agent may consequently be termed "perspective" and it is an agent that performs numerous acts of focalization in the course of the story, and is hence a narrative macro element. The inner structure of focalizer–cum–perspective has been the subject of detailed study in recent German narratology, especially by Nünning (2000; 2001) and Carola Surkamp (2003).

(3) Modeling or processing is either a momentary act or an extended activity consisting of perceiving, viewing, selecting, making discriminations, matching information to frames and scripts (=schemas and scenarios), categorizing, gestalt forming, making connections, interpreting, evaluating and so on. These various operations of construal, and their products, are studied in detail in cognitive psychology, especially psychology of perception, and in cognitive linguistics. The narratologist could and probably should employ the distinctions and definitions already available in these disciplines regarding cognitive modeling rather than invent his own. Seen from this perspective, stream of consciousness for example is largely a technique for representing in a non-mediated fashion the process whereby the mind registers incoming instantaneous sensations and tries to identify and relate them to other current or remembered sensory experiences. Similarly, detective novels often highlight the dif-

ficulties involved in perceiving under adverse condition such as in the dark or from a hiding place. Focalization becomes a difficult and drawn out process, almost a struggle, which may end up in failure, partial success or full success (cf. Schubert 2005).

(4) Take or vision of the given, or "mental scene", is the inner representation of information, the product of the perceptual and conceptual processing activity with respect to the focalized, or, in other words, the product of the construal operations brought to bear on the segment of reality serving as the focus of attention. David Herman, in his essay in this volume, discusses in detail the dimensions or parameters involved in an adequate description of such mental products. Informally, one should mention at least the selection, degree of detail and pattern given to the incoming data, and the fore- and backgrounding of information items.

(5) Textual representation includes all the linguistic (tense, modality, deixis) and stylistic devices employed by authors for portraying at least the processing activity and its product, drawing our attention to the fact that what we are facing is a particular character perspective through which entities are being perceived and represented. In an insightful article, Laurel Brinton (1980) has proposed the term "represented perception" to designate some linguistic and stylistic elements that indicate that we are watching the external world being transformed into an internal one (369). Perceptions are thus rendered in an unmediated fashion (i. e., without *verba sentiendi*) as they occur in the characters' minds; through emotionally laden, subjective and evaluative adjectives or verbal forms, such as "darling little spots" or "chuckling, absurd sound", and the flash-like nature of some sensations is rendered through disjointed syntax or nominal phrases (375–81).

(6) Finally, both minds and recording devices may contain an optional self-monitoring component referred to as "consciousness" or self-awareness when humans are concerned. This device may be active during the focalization act, running in parallel to it and providing an internal feedback or commentary. Such a commentary would among others make the perceiver aware that he is engaged in perceiving an object and forming an internal representation of it, and may sometimes also cast doubt on the scope or validity of the take even as it is being formed.

1.2 Terminology: What Are We Talking About?

A large number of terms exist in English language narratology for designating the focalizer, and they can be grouped according to the aspect they highlight:
– mirror, screen, reflector, filter, prism stress the mediating role;
– angle of vision, point of view, origo, focus, vantage point, window and perspective stress the specific situatedness of the agent: spatial, temporal but also conceptual, cultural and epistemic;
– viewer, perceiver, cognizer, and experiencer point to aspects of the mental activity involved;
– (finally) center of subjectivity, awareness or consciousness and mediating consciousness remind us that a human or human-like mind is behind most focalizations in literature.

The resultant take or vision has also had its fair share of terms, but here all of them stress the same point, namely, the difference between the focalized object as such and its particular representation by a given mind or device. Thus we have modeling of an object, perspectival version, projection, prismatic refraction, and mental picture. The most general term is obviously mental representation, and situation model or mental model where sensory perceptions of space-time objects are concerned.

2 Focalization and the Wider Epistemic Context

In classical narratology, the phenomenon of focalization has often been treated as *sui generis* to narrative or even literary narrative, yet it is in fact just one special case of a much larger and far more basic picture of the mind in action, with its representational, semantic and epistemic components. Corresponding wider and more basic frameworks are available in several disciplines, and each of them could actually serve as basis for a reconceptualization of focalization theory. Let me now enumerate several such frameworks in order of increasing abstraction:

– Within narratology, focalization is one component of a general theory of fictional minds, that is, of the literary representation of mental activity in all its varieties.

– In terms of fictional worlds semantics, each take is part of an agent's particular epistemic perspective on the story world. Modally seen, one posits, following Marie-Laure Ryan (1991) a textual actual world consisting precisely of all the facts of this world. Now each agent in it, subject to his information access possibilities and inherent processing capabilities, forms in his mind a take on one or more items of this world, each such take forming an element of his epistemic map of this world or his personal belief world relative to the textual actual one. In text-world semantics, one can speak of each take as component of the textual subworld set up by the focalizer's mental activity.

– For cognitive linguistics, each take on a given situation constitutes one of several possible construals or conceptualizations of this situation, one of several alternative conceptual structures the mind can impose on the same external phenomenon. The specific lexical and grammatical choices made by the author in portraying a given take are viewed as indicators of the perceptual–cum–cognitive operations (process) which gave rise to this (fictional) take, as well as to its specific structure (product). The basic kinds of objects that can be involved in such construal operations are scenes and events, entities and processes, motion and location, and force and causation (cf. Talmy 2006: 542). The basic structures or schemas employed in organizing these objects include the configurational (objects in space and time and their relations), perspectival (location or path of the point at which one places one's "mental eye" to regard a scene), attentional (patterns in which different data are fore-and backgrounded), and force dynamics (relations between entities such as opposition, overcoming, helping and hindering, causing and preventing) (543–44).

Cruse (cf. 2004: 46–73) provides a detailed discussion of the basic construal operations occurring in the mental structuring of data. These include: (1) attention, which encompasses selection, focus, scope and degree of detail and its summary or sequential scanning; (2) comparison, organizing the incoming data into fore- and background elements; (3) perspective or situatedness, defining the vantage point and orientation of the observation, as well as the location and path of attention; (4) the constitution from data of spatio-temporal objects and their interrelations, that is, providing a structure for the experience; and finally, (5) the conceptualization of processes and events as involving different kinds of forces acting in different ways upon the participants of the events.

– For cognitive psychology, focalization as defined in this article could be fully subsumed under perception in the wider sense. Thus, James Pomerantz in his entry on perception (2003) defines perception as the complex sequence of processes by which we take the information received from our senses and then organize and interpret it, which in turn allows us to see and hear the world around us as meaningful, recognizable objects and events, with clear boundaries in space and time. We are also given some basic facts about perception: it is limited, selective, influenced by context and not entirely veridical (=corresponding to facts), and it requires time, memory, and internal representation.

– In terms of Husserl's phenomenology one distinguishes the object of attention or intentional object, the *ego* that has this object in mind, the acts of consciousness applied to it, and the resultant *noema* or intentional content.

– In cognitive science, one speaks of objects of attention, mind, cognitive processing and the resultant mental representation.

– (Finally) in terms of information theory, one speaks of information or data input, an information processor, a series of internal operations based on computation in the wider sense and the resultant information or data output.

The adoption of any such theoretical framework would entail at least the translation of the terms of focalization theory into those of the higher, more powerful theory, and a corresponding reformulation of focalization theory claims in terms of the framework selected. If this operation is successful, focalization theory becomes a sub-theory of the higher one, but quite possibly containing some claims specific to the literary domain, so it cannot be derived from the higher one or reduced to it, and we still get to keep our jobs. Let us further note that if this subsumption under a higher theory succeeds, then many of its insights may also apply to the literary domain, giving us extra knowledge for free, and also suggesting many perspectives and issues that could not occur to us within the narratological context in isolation. The prospects of any such interdisciplinary reconceptualization are daunting indeed, but I am going to evade this task by invoking the scholar's most trite excuse: *ars longa, vita brevis*. Instead, I propose to go back into more specifically narratological issues concerning the revision of current distinctions.

"Focalization" in the narrow sense is an act or activity. One can thus ask about its object (what is the object of this act); agent (who focalizes); and product (or how, that is, kinds of focalization). One can also enquire about combined phenomena, such as the intersection of who and how or agent and manner, which underlies all typologies of focalization. Before we get down to details let us remember that our goal is not to produce some epistemic or psychological general truths or systematics, but rather to provide fruitful heuristic tools for the description of artistic products containing a significant mental component in their content level. And let us further recall that fictional worlds do not necessarily correspond to the actual one that science studies, and need not obey its rules or categories.

3 What, or Contents of Focalization

All focalization is a mental activity, but not all mental activity is focalization. Similarly, not all objects of mental activity are objects of focalization. Focalization concerns only specific kinds of mental activity and limited kinds of content.

– Everybody agrees that incoming data from all five senses as they are being received and processed form an essential component of focalized content. By the same token abstract class concepts, universal truths and so on do not belong here, even though they are part of mental content in general. Analogously, while the registering in the mind of sense impressions is central to focalization, activities of abstract reasoning and inferencing do not belong here.

– Acts of mental simulation or empathy whereby I try to put myself mentally in the place of another and imagine what he is perceiving or perceived from his time space location and how he is or was perceiving it, are objects of second order focalization. Here, both the other's act and its manner, as well as its contents, are objects of focalization.

– Acts of recollection, where an agent activates his own episodic long term memory in order to bring into mind what he experienced through the senses at some earlier time space point and how he did so are parts of focalization.

– Some theorists, like Jahn (1999) and Bal (1997), argue for including under focalization the contents of acts of planning, projection of future scenarios, dreams, delusions and hallucinations, that is, exclusively internally generated perceptions. I find this inclusion problematic. While these contents are indeed specific and inner-sensory in nature (images and sounds) and involve imagined external events and situations, they do not fall under the heading of "pre-existing or existing story world elements as experienced and registered by a mind inside this world" as earlier defined. Moreover, issues of the scope and correctness of any take with respect to the textual actual world, so crucial to our assessment of its focalizer, are by definition inapplicable here. As these phenomena clearly fall outside my initial definition of focalization, I must exclude them for better or worse. On the other hand, when a character recalls the contents and manner of his original past acts of projection or of dreaming, he is concerned with mental episodes that did take place in the actual story world, so these could be considered objects of focalization, and the accuracy of his recollection of them can be meaningfully discussed. To conclude: in my view, it would be fruitful for our theoretical work to include under "contents of focalization" the contents of mental episodes involving sense data stemming from spatio-temporally determinate situations, events and entities, whether these sense data are perceived directly or at a remove of time or person.

3.1 Conventions Regarding Focalization

From contents of focalization we now move to some specific artistic assumptions underlying fictional focalization, since focalization as such is a general discursive category. These assumptions concern access to the contents of characters' focalization acts, as well as to the mental activities involved. In fact, these assumptions are a central part of the constitutive conventions that establish the institution of narrative fiction, and are orthogonal to our default assumptions about embodied human experience in the actual world.

– First and foremost is the convention that mental representations in characters' minds can be accessible to narrator and reader even if not expressed by the characters through words, drawings, or any other public means.

– Secondly, it is assumed that all mental representations are verbal, even though in reality some are propositional and others image based.

– All human focalization is active and transformational, and contains an element of interpretation. Any individual act of focalization is just one particular perspective on the story world, and is always fallible and often skewed, distorted or at least partial. As we know from Kant, human beings can know the world only as a series of mental representations whose shape is determined by the constitutive conditions of the human mind. In narrative fiction, however, there is the assumption that one can know states of affairs *hors de toute focalisation*, fully and with absolute certainty, through the discourse of an impersonal anonymous narrating voice, usually in the third person past tense. Each individual take can thus be assessed relative to this full objective truth. And this in turn enables the reader to evaluate different takes regarding the same data, and also infer back from the nature of a take to the nature of the focalizer behind it (+/-limited, reliable etc.)

4 Who, or the Focalizing Agent

What can be scenically presented or dramatized in focalization are the contents of individual takes and their construction in the mind. The underlying perspective or focalizing mind itself with its architecture can only be reported upon in summary mode, being a set of general features. As we have seen before, it is up to the reader to make further inferences on the nature of a given focalizing mind from what and how it focalizes. Consequently, further questions about the nature of the focalizer as textually represented have to follow the structure of narrative discourse and not psychology. Maximally, the following narrative instances can function as focalizers: a narrative agent or story world participant; some anonymous position in story space (Claude Simon's O in *La bataille de Pharsale*, Banfield's [1987] empty deictic center); a hypothetical agent inside story space (Herman's [1994] hypothetical focalizer); and, in my view, some kinds of narrators all the time and all narrators on some occasions. With so many focalizing instances, is all information in narrative focalized, as Ronen (1994) and Ouelette (1996) claim? Here opinions vary. If focalization is defined as a relation between narrated domain elements and a mind inside this domain (Prince's [2001] internal focalization), then precisely all information coming through minds inside this domain is focalized, and that's it. If, however, focalization is defined as a relation between narrated domain elements and a mind inside the narrated or narrating domain, then information coming through narrators who are or were members of the narrated domain they are reporting about may be considered focalized, at least in the sense that it comes from a personalized instance or center of awareness. On the other hand, no one would consider information coming from an omniscient impersonal voice or speech position focalized, as this kind of narrating function is incompatible with any notion of a restricted experiencing mind or an embodied and situated center of awareness. But even here there is an exception: information coming from such a voice *can* be considered focalized if the voice pretends to look at events through the mind of one or more story world participants, a phenomenon dubbed "reflectorization" by Monika Fludernik (1996).

Two cases that have evoked lots of controversy, but for opposite reasons, are the anonymous focalizer and the personalized narrator. The first, because it is not a textually inscribed speech position, and the other because, according to scholars like Chatman (1986) it is nothing but a speech position. Let us begin with the anonymous focalizer.

4.1 The Anonymous Focalizer

In many cases we encounter in fiction a passage that looks like a take on a given spatio-temporal situation from some inside subject position, as indicated by scenic immediacy, deictics and so on. But no story world participant is textually indicated as the observer-experiencer or origin of this take. So who sees then? In such cases we sometimes postulate a nameless observer as the focalizer. Monika Fludernik (1996) suggests we call this operation "figuralization," as we are attributing to some anonymous observer figure the information in question. Let us not forget, however, that this observer is a mere interpretive *Hilfskonstruktion,* the product of an operation of naturalization. But what does this anonymous observer or witness position, which Herman (1994) has dubbed "unspecified virtual witness," mean? We are in fact claiming that the specific nature of the given information can be realistically motivated by positing as its origin a standard observer position on the scene whose location can sometimes be pinpointed. Following Herman's notion of hypothetical focalization we could also say: this is what would be seen by whoever, any human observer, including the reader, if they were located at this space time position. All the same, whether or not a given passage represents a take to begin with, and, if so, whose exactly, are often interpretive and context-dependent decisions, and we may arrive at no clear answer or at several alternate equally plausible ones. Also, the transition from one take to another, or from a take by one person to that by another, are often textually unmarked and subject to interpretive debates. Such indeterminacy is the constructive principle of Vargas Llosa's novel *Conversación en la Catedral*, for example.

4.2 Narrators as Focalizers?

Quite probably, no issue in focalization theory has generated more controversy than whether or not narrators can be focalizers. I believe the question is wrongly put. After all we are dealing with artificial artistic constructs, not with facts of nature. I think the question should accordingly be reformulated as follows: in what cases is it meaningful or fruitful to consider a narrator as a focalizer as well, in view of our initial definition of focalization. I believe it makes perfect sense in some cases, and the categorical refusal to do so stems from a failure to distinguish between role or function and individual and to realize that a focalizer or a narrator are not flesh and blood monolithic entities which remain constant throughout, but artistic constructs which can repeatedly change roles in the course of a text according to the author's informational needs at each juncture. The one thing everybody agrees on is that only a personalized or individuated narrating instance with a clear I-here-now *Ich-origo*, self reference, subjective semantics etc. can function as a potential focalizer. Beyond this I think it is better to distinguish situational varieties rather than jump to universal claims whether or not narrators can function as focalizers. There are three varieties I can think of right now:

– The first and most obvious case, ignored by most narratologists, is a narrator, who is also observer or agent in the narrated sphere, reporting on events and situations taking place in the narrated sphere simultaneously with his act of narration. In this case, person, time and place of narrator and narrative agent are clearly the same, and the individual cannot but report events and entities, including himself, as he observes and experiences them at the moment of narration. Such a narrator fulfils two distinct functions, saying and seeing, and must function as focalizer, focusing on the setting, other agents, or himself *qua* agent, since focalization is his only way to acquire any knowledge of the world around him as it unfolds.

– An individuated narrator who is currently reporting on earlier events or situations in the narrated domain in which he acted as observer or agent is the standard case. Obviously, such narration involves current acts of recall whose content are earlier acts of witnessing or experiencing. As agent or observer of the events as they occurred, this narrator *qua* story world participant was clearly able to focalize. So our problem concerns not this, but rather the status of his current acts of recollecting and reporting on his own past acts of focalization. Are they too acts of focalization? I think the answer depends on the kind of current mental activity. Recall can be a distanced analytic retrospective summary "I saw X, I experienced Y", which is not focalization since it lacks the immediacy and experientiality essential to focalization. But recall may also be more like an attempt to relive or re-experience the original act of focalization or sensory experience and its resultant take, effecting a mental shift of deictic center. A clear indicator of this kind of recall is the switch from past to present tense. In Proust's famous madelaine scene, the narrator starts by "one day in winter, on my return home." He then describes dipping the cake in the tea and sipping the tea: "I raised to my lips a spoonful of the tea...I drink a second mouthful" (Proust 1981: 48). Following Edminston (cf. 1989: 739–42) one could say that the narrator now adopts the intradiegetic vision of himself then, presenting his own mental activity and view of others (and himself) at the moment of the event. The narrator restricts himself accordingly to the experiencing self then with its deictic center, in a word, not doing any further retrospective information processing. (On this point see also Shen [2003].) I feel very strongly that it would be quite sensible and useful to include this kind of recollection under focalization. It goes without saying, though, that all acts of recollection of any kind are fallible, since memory is an active faculty, not a passive slate.

– Chatman, the great enemy of narrator as focalizer, remarks that a narrator could look at events and existents in the discourse world or space of narration he occupies, to the extent that this world is fleshed out (cf. 1990: 143–44). The same observation has been made by James Phelan (2001), a friend of narrator as focalizer. This rare agreement opens up a third area of narrator as focalizer. Any individuated narrator, whether or not he is a participant in the narrated domain, can always be considered a focalizer when his object of attention is his current situation as narrator, his activity of telling and so on. The specification and emphasis on the narratorial sphere at the expense of the narrated, on the narrator's immediate context and his writerly activities, has a long history going back at least to Cervantes (cf. Alter 1975), and is a hallmark of postmodernism. As Brian Richardson points out in his paper in the present volume, even the anonymous teller at the beginning of Conrad's *Heart of Darkness* perceives immediate sights and sounds, including the voice of Marlow, on the boat on the Thames, and can therefore be considered a limit case of focalizer.

5 What, or Typologies of Focalization

The traditional external vs. internal focalization is valuable, but the terms are polysemous, designating three different binary oppositions: the identity of the focalizer and his location in the narrated and/or narrating system; the nature of the focalized, that is, public sense data or internal mental ones; and the possibility of access to the minds of others. Another well-known typology deals with levels of focalization and its possible hierarchical and embedded nature (cf. Bal 1997). More recent is Jahn's (1999) interesting scale of focalization, starting from "strict" individual perception of an object, followed by "ambient" one, where two focalizers observe simultaneously the same object from different points. The next stage is "weak" focalization where there is still an object but no determinate point or center of awareness, and finally no object and no point of observation.

Broader Horizons: Beyond the Limits of Space and Time

I would like to conclude by discussing briefly several additional cases going beyond the singular focalizer and act of focalization, involving second order focalizations, and including embedded, transferred, and joint ones. I think they can be systematized in terms of original and transferred systems of personal coordinates, consisting of person, time and space. The truth table method indicates eight possible combinations of these three factors, ranging from I-here-now to not-I, not-here, and not-now. The I-here-now is of course the prototypical or standard kind of focalization. Proceeding to I not-now and optionally also not-here we get the case of recollection of past acts of focalization we spoke of before. The "I" can also juxtapose here several past acts of focalization concerning the same object, as Proust's narrator does towards the end of *A la recherche*, where he juxtaposes in an extended act of recollection several mental snapshots of the princess de Guermante dating from different times in his life. This is by definition embedded or second order focalization. How about "I+now but not here"? The focalizer in this case tries to place himself imaginatively in a situation currently occurring elsewhere and project what he would see, hear etc. if he were there himself now. This is not far-fetched at all. Every Canadian who, in the dead of winter, spoke on the phone to a friend basking in the Caribbean sun has experienced this kind of vicarious hypothetical focalization.

The "not-I cases" are even more interesting. In all of them, the focalizer tries to bracket out his own mental makeup, and possibly time space location as well, put himself in the spatial, temporal and perceptual position of another mind, and simulate how this other mind would process situational information and what the resultant take would be like. We usually refer to this mental exercise as "taking the point of view of another" or "putting oneself in someone else's position or shoes" or "seeing things from someone else's perspective", sometimes quite literally. Characters can do it to one another, and of course a personalized narrator can do it with respect to one or more characters. The act of simulation is most poignant when one tries to simulate the other's take on the simulator himself (what do I look like to her?). In this case the simulator literally looks at himself as if he were another. I suggest we call all the foregoing varieties "transferred" focalization.

Brian Richardson in this volume and myself some years ago have drawn attention to the possibility of trans-individual focalization. This too could be viewed as a chain whose first link is provided by Jahn's notion of ambient focalization. Jahn describes ambient focalization as a case where spatial deictics are relaxed and the vision is mobile, hence beyond that of a single individual. One variety would be where the narrator's words convey the simultaneous takes of several individuals on the same object. He cites an incident from Virginia Woolf's *To the Lighthouse* where two focalizers, James and Cam, sitting at two opposite ends of a boat are simultaneously observing the people seated in the center of the boat. The singular textual representation of these people consequently involves two points of view from which they are observed concurrently. Note that the individual ingredients of any simultaneous composite vision or take may be overlapping or complementary, but they may also fail to coincide, creating a discordant focalization, like a Cubist painting.

In Jahn's example the individual acts of focalization were concurrent but not coordinated. But cases also exist which tend towards a coordinated vision. One is that of focalizers negotiating a joint consensual take, a clear example of the social mind in action. Two or more people can seek to formulate a jointly held vision of a person, situation, object or event either by comparing and adjusting their individual ones to yield one unified homogeneous picture, or by each contributing a piece of the puzzle, a partial vision needing to be complemented by all others in a resultant composite picture. Either process can be seen when witnesses to the same car accident for example discuss their visual and auditory impressions of it. In the case of the unified picture one starts with a plurality of individual visions in dialogue, interacting and intersecting and, if a joint one is attained, one ends with a plural "we" discourse conveying it, such as "we saw" or "we felt" etc. This is the last variety, that of the uniform communal vision where the individual experiencers feel themselves as one and speak in the collective "we" (or even "I" in some choruses of

Greek tragedy) about their collective vision, a subject developed in detail in Brian Richardson's paper.

References

Alter, Robert (1975). *Partial Magic*. Berkeley: U of California P.

Bal, Mieke (1993). "First Person, Second Person, Same Person: Narrative as Epistemology." *New Literary History* 24, 293–320.

Bal, Mieke (^{2}1997). *Narratology*. Toronto: U of Toronto P.

Banfield, Ann (1987). "Describing the Unobserved: Events Grouped around an Empty Centre." N. Fabb et al. (eds). *The Linguistics of Writing*. New York: Methuen, 265–85.

Brinton, Laurel (1980). "Represented Perception: A Study in Narrative Style." *Poetics* 9, 363–81.

Chatman, Seymour (1986). "Characters and Narrators: Filter, Center, Slant and Interest-Focus." *Poetics Today* 9, 189–204.

– (1990). *Coming to Terms*. Ithaca: Cornell UP.

Cruse, Alan D. (2004). *Cognitive Linguistics*. West Nyack, NY: Cambridge UP.

Edminston, William (1989). "Focalization and the First Person Narrator: A Revision of the Theory." *Poetics Today* 10, 729–44.

Fludernik, Monika (1996). *Towards a "Natural" Narratology*. London: Routledge.

Herman, David (1994). "Hypothetical Focalization." *Narrative* 2, 230–53.

Jahn, Manfred (1999). "More Aspects of Focalisation: Refinements and Applications." *GRAAT* 21, 85–110.

Nünning, Ansgar (2001). "On the Perspective Structure of Narrative Texts." W. van Peer & S. Chatman (eds). *New Perspectives on Narrative Perspective*. Albany: SUNY Press, 207–23.

Nünning, Vera & Nünning, Ansgar (eds) (2000). *Multiperspektivisches Erzählen*. Trier: VWT.

Ouellet, Pierre (1996). "The Perception of Fictional Worlds." C. A. Mihailescu & W. Hamarneh (eds). *Fiction Updated*. Toronto: U of Toronto P, 76–90.

Phelan, James (2001). "Why Narrators can be Focalizers—And why it Matters." W. van Peer & S. Chatman (eds). *New Perspectives on Narrative Perspective*. Albany: SUNY Press, 51–64.

Pomerantz, James R. (2003). "Perception." L. Nadel (ed). *Encyclopedia of Cognitive Science*, Vol. 3. London: Nature Publishing Group, 527–37.

Prince, Gerald (2001). "Point of View on Points of View or Refocusing Focalization." W. van Peer & S. Chatman (eds). *New Perspectives on Narrative Perspective*. Albany: SUNY Press, 43–50.

Proust, Marcel (1981). *Remembrance of Things Past*, Vol. 1. Tr. C. K. Scott Moncrieff & T. Kilmartin. New York: Random House.

Ronen, Ruth (1994). *Possible Worlds in Literary Theory*. Cambridge: Cambridge UP.

Ryan, Marie-Laure (1991). *Possible Worlds, Artificial Intelligence, and Narrative Theory*. Bloomington: Indiana UP.

Shen, Dan (2003). “Difference behind Similarity: Focalization in Third Person Center-Of-Consciousness and First Person Retrospective Narration.” C. Jacobs & H. Sussman (eds). *Acts of Narrative*. Stanford: Stanford UP, 81–92.
Schubert, Christoph (2005). “Fallible Focalization.” *GRM* 55, 205–26.
Surkamp, Carola (2003). *Die Perspektivenstruktur narrativer Texte*. Trier: VWT.
Talmy, Leonard (^{2}2006). “Cognitive Linguistics.” *Encyclopedia of Language and Linguistics*, Vol. 2. Amsterdam: Elsevier, 542–46.

TATJANA JESCH, MALTE STEIN
(Hamburg)

Perspectivization and Focalization: Two Concepts—One Meaning? An Attempt at Conceptual Differentiation

The study of focalizations "has caused much ink to flow" in the estimation of the scholar who coined this narratological term "a little too much" (Genette 1988: 65). To begin with, we would like to justify our desire to invest a bit more ink in the discussion of focalization by stating our initial question about the topic: on what grounds, we asked ourselves, did the author of *Narrative Discourse* title one chapter of his *Narrative Discourse Revisited* "perspective" and the other "focalizations," especially given the fact that he had originally introduced the term "focalization" in order to avoid terminology like "vision or point of view"—all terms with "too specifically visual connotations" (Genette 1980: 189). As Genette explains again in *Narrative Discourse Revisited*, his remarks on focalization should not be seen as anything more than a "reformulation" (Genette 1988: 65) of the classic descriptions of perspective. But—as an avowed follower of Occam—why had he not abandoned the term "perspective" altogether?!

In the following, we will demonstrate (section 1) that Genette's concept of focalization is actually an amalgamation of two wholly independent elements for which—as the author himself might have anticipated—one actually needs two terms. The first element is the perception of the world invented by the author through narrators and other agents also invented by the author; the second element is the regulation of narrative information within the communication between author and reader. In the latter, in our assessment, lies the innovative potential of the discourse about focalization. This potential, however, is overlooked by narratologists, who have wholeheartedly adopted the new term as a mere substitute for the older one (section 2). We would like to suggest that the terms focalization and perspective—in clear differentiation from one another—be retained (section 3) and, using the example of Kafka's *The Metamorphosis*, we will attempt to demonstrate the relevance of this terminological differentiation to textual analysis (section 4).

1 Focalization in Genette: One Concept—Two Meanings

Genette first introduced the term focalization in his *Narrative Discourse* as a replacement for the term "point of view": "To avoid the too specifically visual connotations of the terms *vision*, *field*, and *point of view*, I will take up here the slightly more abstract term *focalization*" (Genette 1980: 189). As explained here, the goal of replacing these terms was to make clear, on a terminological level, that an analysis of perspectival structures should not be limited to the visual:

> There would have been no point in taking great pains to replace point of view with focalization if I was only going to fall right back into the same old rut [the narrowing of meaning to visual perception, T. J. & M. S.]; so obviously we must replace *who sees?* with the broader question of *who perceives?* (Genette 1988: 64)

Genette criticizes the terms "vision", "field" and "point of view" for implying the visual too strongly. Thus, he suggests the question "who perceives?" clearly as a means to include not only optical perception, but also the constructive, meaningful awareness that a character or a narrator gains as a result of his or her "capacities of knowledge" (Genette 1980: 162).

Later, however, in his *Narrative Discourse Revisited*, Genette gave another definition of the term focalization, this time based on wholly different criteria. In place of the question "who perceives?" one finds the implicit question "what can the reader know?":

> So by focalization I certainly mean a restriction of "field"—actually, that is, a selection of narrative information with respect to what was traditionally called *omniscience*. In pure fiction that term is, literally, absurd (the author has nothing to "know", since he invents everything), and we would be better off replacing it with *completeness of information*—which, when supplied to a reader, makes him "omniscient". The instrument of this possible selection is a *situated focus*, a sort of information-conveying pipe that allows passage only of information that is authorized by the situation. (Genette 1988: 74)

With this definition, Genette no longer stresses the mode of perception of a fictive entity, but rather the transfer of information between author and reader. At the same time, he presupposes that the choice of a limited narratorial or figural perspective—a "restriction of 'field'"—will always bring about an equivalent limitation or "selection of narrative information" available to the reader.

Although Genette continues to claim in the same volume that "narratology has no need to go beyond the narrative situation" (137), his (new) conception of focalization requires him to return to the author's communication with the reader. He had already done this in his *Narrative Discourse*, when he mentioned in the passage on "alterations":

> [...] the case of a novel [...], where the narrator, a trusting husband, is present at scenes between his wife and a male friend that he recounts without thinking anything amiss but whose meaning cannot escape the least subtle reader. This excess of implicit information over explicit information is the basis of the whole play of what Barthes calls *indices*. (Genette 1980: 197–98)

As we see here, Genette's narratological practice leads him to presuppose an author (as a communicative entity) whose messages to the reader are to be drawn out of the text (as an "excess of implicit information") even when they contradict the point of view of the fictional perceiving subject: "here it is as if the narrator [...] did not understand what he relates; this in no way prevents the reader from interpreting it in conformity with the author's intentions" (198)[1]. In examples such as this one, it becomes evident that one must clearly differentiate between perspective (understood as "focus of perception" [Genette 1988: 64]) and focalization (understood as "selection of narrative information" [74] available to the reader). For it is always possible (and in literature no rarity) that the fictional perceiving subject does not see (realize, comprehend, understand, etc.) something of which the reader is made fully aware. Contrary to what even Genette at times presumes—see the definition of focalization in *Narrative Discourse Revisited*—a limited narratorial or figural perspective in no way rules out the possibility for the author to communicate the "completeness of information" (74) with the help of interspersed indices. The reader can know more about the "actual world" (cf. Ryan 1991) than the fictional perceiving subject, which leads to the conclusion that perspective and focalization are independent of one another.

In a footnote to his *Narrative Discourse Revisited*, Genette refers to François Jost's works "on the difference between focalization and 'ocularization' (information and perception)," which he judges to be "the most relevant contribution to the debate on focalization and to the necessary

---

1 See also Genette (1988: passim).

refining of that notion" (Genette 1988: 73–74). Regardless of this, it has become commonplace in narratological discussions simply to substitute the term perspective for focalization and, "despite the shift in terminology, to continue thinking within the categories of perspective and point of view" (Niederhoff 2001: 16)[2].

2 The Prevailing Reception of the Term "Focalization"

Instead of giving an overview here of the numerous positions within the discussion of focalization, we choose two works out of the abundance of publications on the topic. Of these two, Rimmon-Kenan (1983) has already achieved the status of a seminal work in the field and can thus serve as representative of the prevailing use of the term. The second work, on the other hand, is a more contemporary plea for a terminological differentiation between focalization and perspective.

Rimmon-Kenan begins her explanation of focalization with the demarcation, established by Genette, of the acts of perceiving and speaking. The perspectival position underlying a narrative speech act (and influenced by the perceiver's knowledge and values) need not necessarily represent the position of the narrator: "speaking and seeing, narration and focalization, may, but need not, be attributed to the same agent" (72). However, in the simple two-part breakdown of types of focalization that she subsequently proposes, she departs from Genette's formulations. The (implied) underlying criterion of Genette's typology of focalizations, at least in *Narrative Discourse Revisited,* is the differentiation between a non-restricted and a restricted regulation of information vis-à-vis the reader:

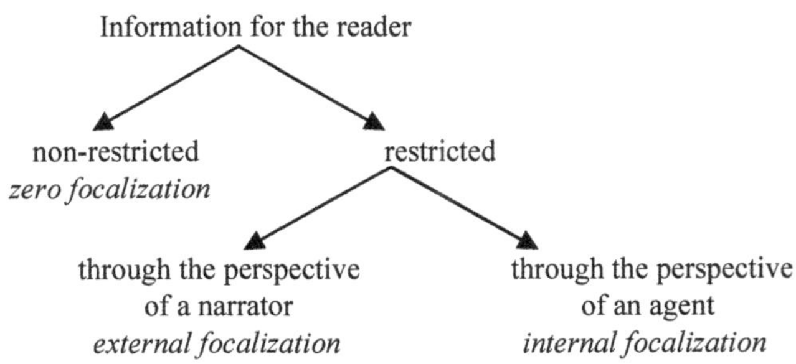

Figure 1: Types of Focalization According to Genette (1988)

[2] Tr. of quotations from Niederhoff (2001): Tracy N. Graves & Katherine McNeill.

Rimmon-Kenan, on the other hand, consistently uses the term focalization as a synonym for perception (i.e. perspective) and divides the types of focalization according to the "position relative to the story" (74) that the perceiving subject ("center of consciousness") holds. Her opposition of external versus internal is based upon this criterion, which she then—in the course of differentiating perspective into "perceptual", "psychological" and "ideological" facets—connects with further oppositional features:

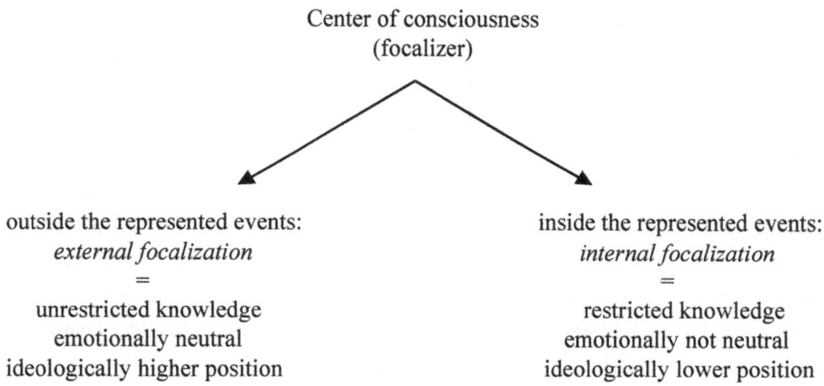

Figure 2: Types of Focalization According to Rimmon-Kenan (1983)

It becomes clear that the limitation of information plays no role in her typology when Rimmon-Kenan writes about the "external focalizer (or narrator-focalizer)" that he knows in principle "everything about the represented world" (79)[3]. He can, however, limit "his knowledge"—she

[3] The postulate that an "external focalizer (or narrator-focalizer)" is in principle omniscient (emotionally neutral and ideologically superior) in relation to the represented world may be applicable to many narrative texts, but cannot be maintained in theoretical terms. "Omniscience" in respect to the represented world can only be assumed in fictional narrative for those who invented or composed this world. This term (as Genette [1988] makes clear) thus applies only to the author, who determines with what "perceptual", "psychological," and "ideological" characteristics he provides the (also invented) narrating entity. Just like any character in the story, a narrator can also serve the author as a *goulot d'information*, an "information-conveying pipe" (Genette 1988: 74). Rimmon-Kenan probably does not consider this possibility because she virtually equates the narrator with the author and as such analyzes "narrative fiction" on the basis of a communicative model that only encompasses the (fictional) communication between character and narrator, but ignores that of the author with the reader.

probably means the communication of his knowledge—"out of rhetorical considerations" (79). In Genette's model, this would be the transition from zero focalization to external focalization. When Rimmon-Kenan speaks of external focalization, she refers to both the restricted and non-restricted communication of knowledge as long as the narrator remains the center of consciousness (the focalizer) and his omniscience can be assumed. Instead of emphasizing, as Genette (1983) does, that the possible knowledge of the reader is restricted through focalization, she merely returns to the (hypothetical) state of knowledge of the fictional perceiving subject. Therefore, her understanding of focalization remains within the framework of the conventional description of perspective.

Burkhard Niederhoff recently expressed a legitimate criticism of such a use of the term focalization, in which he objects "that the advocates of focalization often think in the categories of perspective" (Niederhoff 2001: 1) and that they can only justify the change in terms with "unconvincing arguments" (5)[4]. He holds the view, similar to ours, that Genette's "neologism" "includes aspects of narratorial communication, which are not covered by the related terms of perspective or point of view" (5). Thus, Niederhoff also sees a "conclusive decision in favor of one of the two terms" as "neither necessary nor desirable" (1–2).

Based on definitions from the *Oxford English Dictionary*, what Niederhoff then seeks to establish are similarities between the two terms. According to him, "both terms imply a limitation of the power of the narrator to communicate information" (7). In addition, their "most important similarity" consists in "that they describe a subjectification and restriction of perspective" (9). As has become apparent in the above statements, Niederhoff, too, has a tendency to infer from the boundaries of perception and knowledge of the fictive entities (narrator or character) an equivalent restriction of the information communicated to the reader. From the outset, he does not factor in the possibility that an author uses clues to reveal

---

4 There are above all two reasons that critics, with an appeal to Genette, have repeatedly introduced and occasionally played against each other, although neither of the arguments has any substance. The first argument reads that the term focalization is more appropriate than perspective to differentiate between voice and perception in narratological analysis—an argument that Genette did not formulate even once in his *Narrative Discourse*. The other argument claims that the use of the term focalization makes it clearer that the question "who perceives?" does not refer solely to the visual component of perception. As the term chosen by Genette comes from the field of optics, this argument is equally unjustifiable.

more to the reader than the narrator or agents (can) perceive and know—in other words, the possibility of an "excess of implicit information over explicit information" (Genette 1980: 198). Just like those whom he reproaches for having an understanding of focalization that is too perspectival he links Genette's term above all back to (figural and narratorial) perception. The only difference between the two terms consists for him "in the element that creates the restriction of perception" (Niederhoff 2001: 9). While with perspective this is the spatial "position", the restriction of perception with focalization is a result of the "choice of a particular kind of reality" (9). He writes: "If one places a camera at a particular point, the perspective becomes fixed, but not the focus. One can focus on the flowers in the foreground or the rock face in the background" (9). We will not consider here the feasibility of applying such a differentiation taken from photo-optics to the field of narratology, nor the question as to how much insight one actually gains from such a comparison. In any case, it remains to be said that behind both of the aspects of analysis named by Niederhoff lies, once again, only the question of the perceptual horizon and scope of knowledge of the narrator and/or agent. However, the question of the author's management of information is wholly disregarded.

3 Recommendations for a Conceptual Clarification

Taking up Genette's definition from *Narrative Discourse Revisited*, we recommend that focalization be defined as the author's temporary or definitive withholding of information from the reader. Under the term "perspectivization"[5], on the other hand, we understand the representation of something from the subjective view of a fictive entity (narrator or character). At the same time, this mode of viewing is always a part of that which the author depicts for the reader. A connection between focalization and perspectivization can exist to the extent that perspectivization often serves to account for a restriction of information within the fictional world. As such, perspectivization can become a way to achieve focalization. Once again, however, perspectivization is not focalization, for a

[5] We are consciously not using the term perspective here, but rather perspectivization, in order to indicate that the structure found in this case—just as with focalization—can be traced back to a constructive activity on the part of the author.

text can contain (implicit) information that transcends the figural and/or narratorial capacities of knowledge.

In order to determine whether the communicated information in a particular passage of the text is complete (as regards the events that have been narrated up to this point), one must have a standard for measuring the completeness of information. One must specify under what conditions one can say that the author enables the reader's "omniscience". This is the case, according to our assessment, when the reader is placed in a position in which (up to a certain point of the narrative discourse) he can:
(a) order the depicted incidents chronologically and spatially (coherence level I),
(b) recognize the said incidents as to be expected within the represented world (i.e., according to a stereotype or schema)[6] or as eventful (i.e., diverging from the stereotype)[7] (coherence level II),
(c) comprehend the incidents in their causal, final and consecutive relations (coherence level III).

Coherence Level	Type of relation	Activities of the reader
I	Temporal and spatial *first x, then y, then z;* *x here, y there, z there*	Ordering of the presented incidents according to their chronological sequence in the represented world. Mapping of the presented incidents onto spaces.
II	Correlative *If x, then also y*	Ordering and expansion of the presented incidents according to intra-, inter- and extratextually established schemata.
III	Causal/ultimate/consecutive *y because of x* *y in order to x* *x so that y*	Comprehension of the presented incidents with regard to causes, motivations and consequences.

Table 1: Levels of Coherence in the Reconstruction of Narrated Stories

6 Compare to the procedure of sequence formation as Barthes has described it in several works (collected in Barthes [1985]).

7 Such breaks in schema on the level of the "histoire" are repeatedly described as a structural characteristic essential for the narratability of events. Barthes speaks in this context of "narrative transgression" (1985), Quasthoff of "plot disruption" (1980), Lotman (1977), Renner (1983) and Schmid (1992) of an "event" and Herman (2002) of "non-stereotypic actions and events".

We assume in traditional narratological fashion that a narrative is the representation of a story comprising at least one action. As Bremond has already demonstrated, every plot is sequentially structured insofar as it is made up of multiple phases. The reconstruction of a plot can thus take place on the basis of a universal sequencing schema, such as Bremond's elementary sequence, which is composed of a "possibility" (*éventualité*), a "process of actualization" (*passage à l'acte*), and an "outcome" (*achievement*) (Bremond 1973: 131). We offer another schema here in its place, out of which one more clearly sees:

(a) that the so-called "possibility" is based upon a subjective perception of situation and a subsequent (conscious or unconscious) formation of intention,

(b) that the "process of actualization" can have effects that the agent could not foresee.

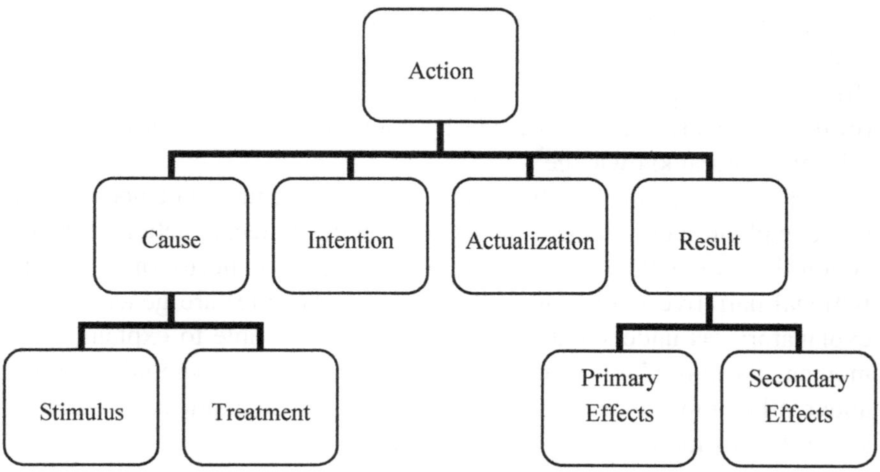

Figure 3: Sequencing Schema "Action"

Complete knowledge with reference to an action is achieved as soon as the reader comes to know its cause, its underlying intention(s), its actualization and its results. If the corresponding information (in relation to the events presented up to this point) is not communicated to the reader, he is dealing with focalization.

It is also necessary to further specify the mode of the communication of knowledge: when can a piece of information be seen as communicated or withheld by the author? The explicitness of a piece of information cannot be the criterion of differentiation in this regard, for even a text whose semantics remain closely attached to a conventionally and invariably fixed literality contains implicit information. In the domain of the "Implicit I", which is connected to the wording and in which the recipient moves without any lack of information, focalization can therefore not exist (cf. Linke & Nussbaumer 2001: 437). The "Implicit II", on the other hand, is understood as "non-literal" and "variable" because it does not belong to the semantics of the wording and demands pragmatic inferences on the part of the reader. Even so, it also conveys deducible propositions to an adequately competent reader. Focalization does not occur in this case either.

One can only speak of withheld information, then, in the case of a proposition:

(a) that the reader needs in order to reconstruct the occurrence in the "actual world" (cf. Ryan 1991) according to coherence level III (see table 1),

(b) that is not explicitly given where the reader would need it,

(c) that the reader cannot discover by combining given propositions with relevant cultural knowledge[8].

In the practice of narrative analysis, it is of course not necessary to make explicit every element of the sequencing schema "action" for each action that is mentioned in the text. However, the majority of actions (in fictional narrative worlds as well as in everyday life) are generally self-explanatory, as understanding a plot means being able to explain at any moment its individual elements. Thus, one's attention should be drawn above all to those elements of the sequence whose explication—as a result of focalization—seems difficult or disputable.

8 Whether cultural knowledge that is activated in the reception process holds factual relevance can be determined through its power of integration or its functionality. We can apply here, for example, the rules formulated by Titzmann, which determine when a potentially relevant piece of knowledge can be considered functionalized, and thus factually relevant in the text (cf. Titzmann 1977: 360). This is the case when a conclusion which can be reached through a textual proposition with the help of this piece of knowledge (a) is "itself a textual proposition," or (b) is "in its turn functionalized" as the implicit condition of another proposition.

4 Perspectivization and Focalization in Kafka's *The Metamorphosis*

If one conceives of perspectivization and focalization as we have suggested, then theoretically, there are four possible alternatives in fictional narration:

– focalization through perspectivization,
– perspectivization without focalization,
– focalization without perspectivization,
– neither focalization nor perspectivization.

To give an especially concise example of each of these possibilities would have required referring to several texts in what follows. However, we have decided to reference only one text in order to make it clear that conclusions about focalization—conclusions about what the reader (oneself) can know about a depicted world—necessitate a larger hermeneutic intensity than the mere description of which fictive entity perceives whom or what, from which position and by what means.

4.1 Focalization through Perspectivization

In Kafka's story *The Metamorphosis* (1915), the events are told primarily from the perspective of the protagonist Gregor Samsa. This is apparent from the outset in the strong limitations of the field of vision presented to the reader (when Gregor is confined to his room, the accounts and descriptions of the other family members are restricted to acoustic impressions or to the speculations of the protagonist about their actions). Gregor's perspective is also apparent in the absence of direct insight into the mental processes of other characters: assertions about the unspoken thoughts, feelings or intentions of the characters other than Gregor are rendered only in his subjective interpretation of them. For the most part, these interpretations turn out to be unfounded, a fact that the recipient will sometimes only recognize retrospectively. In such cases, the perspectivization becomes associated with a temporary focalization.

After Gregor Samsa's transformation, his parents and sister complain above all "that since they could hit on no way of moving Gregor, they could not give up this apartment, which was much too large for their present circumstances" (172). The family members express an intention—they want to change apartments—and complain at the same time about a circumstance that would make the realization of that intention impossible.

However, the obstacle is invalidated by the depiction of incidents from Gregor's perspective:

> Gregor, however, realized it was not just their consideration for him that held them back, for they could have easily transported him in a suitable crate with a couple of air holes in it. The main obstacle to the family's relocation was their utter despair and their sense of being struck by a misfortune like no one else among their friends and relatives. (172)

The protagonist recognizes that a problem with his transportation cannot be what is hindering the Samsas in their move. The real reason that the family stays in their old apartment, as he sees it, is the "utter despair" into which they have fallen because they have had to take care of themselves since he ceased to be the breadwinner. For this reason, he infers, they have reached the limits of their "strength" (172). Towards the end of the story, when Gregor dies, there is a change in the perspectivization to the narrator's perspective[9], which allows for selective insight into the thoughts of the figures (187–92). With this shift, a completely contrary picture emerges: as it turns out, Gregor's surviving family members look into their future full of confidence, as "their jobs were all exceedingly advantageous and also promising" (192). After their former provider has passed away, they make hopeful plans including the rapid realization of the move, which they had put off until then:

> Naturally, the greatest immediate improvement in their situation could easily be brought about by their moving; they hoped to rent a smaller and cheaper apartment, but with a better location and altogether more practical than their current place, which had been found by Gregor. (192)

Only retrospectively can the reader discern that it is not perhaps "utter despair" that hindered Gregor's parents and Grete in their move. It seems, rather, that it was out of consideration for their physically changed son and brother, who they did not want to take with them to their new dwelling. Hence Gregor's death appears as the liberation of his family members: "Then all three of them left the apartment together, which they had not done in months, and took the trolley out to the countryside beyond the town" (191–92). At this moment, specifically the daughter of the family

---

9 A distinct indicator for this change in perspective is the change in the way characters are referred to. The characters belonging to the family are no longer called "father," "mother" or "sister," but rather simply "Mr. and Mrs. Samsa," "daughter" and "Grete" (cf. Kafka 1915: passim).

feels better than ever. Since her brother's transformation Grete has changed gradually as well—she "had blossomed into a lovely, shapely girl" (192).

4.2 Perspectivization without Focalization

During his life Gregor shows a tendency to be possessive of his sister. Although it is not apparent to him, it is made recognizable to the reader through the inclusion of certain details in the story:

> He was determined to creep all the way over to the sister, tug at her skirt to suggest that she take her violin and come into his room, for no one here would reward her playing as he intended to reward it. He wanted to keep her there and never let her out, at least not in his lifetime. For once, his terrifying shape would be useful to him; he would be at all the doors of his room simultaneously, hissing at the attackers. His sister, however, *should* remain with him not by force, but of her own free will. (180; emphasis added)

In the passage above, the figural perspectivization does not lead to focalization but, on the contrary, serves to inform the reader about the protagonist's tendency toward denial. One notices instantly the discrepancy between Gregor's desire to have his sister stay with him of her own free will and the prescriptive nuance resonant in the modal verb "should", which becomes even stronger through his own deterrent behavior. Such protective behavior seems unwarranted especially given the fact that the text gives no indication of any outside aggression directed towards Grete. Instead the reader receives clear information that Gregor, who "wanted to keep her there [in his room] and never let her out," longs for intimate togetherness:

> She should sit next to him on the settee, leaning down to him and listening to him confide that he had been intent on sending her to the conservatory [...]. Gregor would lift himself all the way up to her shoulder and kiss her throat, which she had been keeping free of any ribbon or collar since she had first started working. (180–81)

4.3 Focalization without Perspectivization

As is generally known, Kafka's story begins with a discovery that is surprising to both the reader and the protagonist alike: "One morning, upon awakening from agitated dreams, Gregor Samsa found himself, in his bed, transformed into a monstrous vermin" (119). The fact that a human being, identified as such by virtue of his name and by mention of his

sleeping habits, has had his body transformed overnight into that of an animal cannot simply be put down to the (extratextually anchored) world view of Genette's "potential reader" (Genette 1988: 138).
Given the change in condition of the protagonist, it is a matter, rather, of a break with expectations or, as Jurij Lotman would suggest, a matter of an "event" in the emphatic sense (see also Renner [1983]). Every event of this kind raises the question of its cause, for which, in this instance, the reader does not find any information in the introductory passage cited above. Readers of modern narratives are confronted again and again with similar deficiencies of information at the beginning of texts. Often, as with detective stories, readers are not introduced to the depicted world of such stories step-by-step, but rather they are pushed abruptly into them. They must negotiate their own way in these worlds, even if the necessary information to do so is not provided.

If, as in the beginning of the story, such a case of focalization exists, it is not necessarily motivated by the limited viewpoint of the protagonist. It is not due to Gregor's limited state of consciousness that the circumstances of his transformation at the beginning of the story are completely unknown. In fact, only later in the text does the protagonist express his perplexity about his changed condition: "What's happened to me?" Gregor wonders (119), much like the other characters subsequently do. On the level of the author's communication, this general wonderment is an indication of the fact that the hero's metamorphosis is a matter of an exceptional incident in the depicted world, one that, as such, demands an explanation. And this explanation remains unrevealed to and unexpressed by the fictive entities at the text's culmination—a fact that says nothing about the conclusions the reader might be able to draw in the end. To assume (as the debate over focalization does to a large extent) that the reader's state of awareness is limited by the awareness of the characters and of the heterodiegetic narrator would mean to insinuate that the author has transgressed the "conversational maxim" of adequate information (cf. Grice 1975). Because this presumption can only be justified—if at all—after reading the story in its entirety, readers will initially assume that the missing information will be given gradually.

4.4 Neither Focalization nor Perspectivization

Immediately after Gregor has examined his changed body, his gaze turns to an object above:

> He lay on his hard, armorlike back, and when lifting his head slightly, he could view his brown, vaulted belly, partitioned by arching ridges, while on top of it, the blanket, about to slide off altogether, could barely hold. His many legs, wretchedly thin compared with his overall girth, danced helplessly before his eyes [...]. Above the table, [...] hung the picture that he had recently clipped from an illustrated magazine and inserted in a pretty gilt frame. The picture showed a lady sitting there upright, bedizened in a fur hat and fur boa, with her entire forearm vanishing inside a heavy fur muff that she held out toward the viewer. (119)

This change in the figural line of vision—from his own covered body to the body of the woman in the picture—is communicated by the narrator only belatedly and, even then, only incidentally. Nevertheless, the turn of the gaze is a (figural) action and the attentive reader will ask why Gregor—under these exceptional circumstances—looks at the portrait of the woman. On the level of literality[10] and denotation[11], the author does not impart any information at all about the cause and intention of Gregor's eye movement. However, the omission of this information is neither perspectivally motivated—in other cases the narrator renders Gregor's thoughts—nor is it a sign of focalization. For, at the moment that the reader becomes aware of the progression of Gregor's gaze, there are also indications of its motivation: through interpretative inference it is already possible to explain the movement of Gregor's gaze at the moment of its narration.

If one compares the woman dressed in fur with Gregor's insect body, both figures turn out to be creatures belonging to the isotopy "animal". The "vaulted belly" ("gewölbter Bauch") of the metamorphosed Gregor, in turn, can be considered compatible with the isotopy "feminine", which is also to be attributed to the woman. Whereas the "arching ridges" ("bogenförmige Versteifungen") that he notices in his abdomen after waking up conform to the opposite isotopy "masculine".

---

[10] See Linke & Nussbaumer (2001: 436–37).

[11] See Barthes (1964).

Taking into account cultural knowledge contemporary to the text[12] allows for the hypothesis that, underneath the woman's fur, which reminds one of a growth of pubic hair covering the whole body, a kind of phallus is hidden in the form of "her entire forearm." This allows the isotopy "masculine" to be attributed to the woman in the picture as well. Like Gregor, the woman, therefore, also combines both of the classemes "masculine" and "feminine". In this lies a noticeable commonality between the two figures—in addition to their shared animal traits.

Moreover, the illustration of the beauty in fur hanging on the wall of Gregor's bedroom also brings to mind Sacher-Masoch's novel *Venus in Furs* (1869), in which the Gregor (!) of that text, alias Severin, also has two pictures of Venus-figures in fur hanging on his walls: an original of a dominatrix armed with a whip and a copy of Titian's Venus, whose fur, as the reader will learn, has become a "symbol" of feminine "tyranny and cruelty" (Sacher-Masoch 1869: 9–10). Sacher-Masoch's hero Gregor[13] is seduced by the Venus in furs, who with her erotic, over-encoded fur-fetish and the dominance she exercises over her lover, seems to be a phallic female figure. She is symbolic of feminine dominance in a relationship based on subordination and satisfies the desires of the man in her abuse of him.

As far as the motivation of the eye movement of Kafka's Gregor is concerned, two hypotheses can, consequently, be formulated. First, it is Gregor's intention, in looking at the female form in the picture, to compare his strange new body to an ideal figure framed in gold (at which point it is confirmed that there are certain similarities between himself and the lady). Second, in depicting this comparative gaze (and intertextually alluding to Sacher-Masoch's *Venus in Furs*[14]), the author insinuates that

---

[12] See Freud's thesis that the sexual fetish is an imaginary phallus (1905; 1910). Next to feet and undergarments, fur, according to Freud, belongs to the most often chosen of fetish-objects, which "no doubt [...] owes its origins to an association with the hair of the *mons Veneris*" (Freud 1905: 155).

[13] Kafka's Gregor owes his first name to this figure; the last name "Samsa" could be close to an anagram of the first two letters and first three letters, respectively, of the author's name, Sacher-Masoch.

[14] This reference will be continued throughout the text, e.g. when one of the moralizing critiques issued by Sacher-Masoch's *Venus*—"And if any of you ever has had the courage to kiss my red lips, he then goes on a pilgrimage to Rome, barefoot and in a penitent's shirt [...]" (5)—is transferred to Kafka's text. In order to alleviate the "burning pains in his abdomen" (Kafka 1915: 132), Kafka's Gregor crawls "quickly" up to the picture of the "woman clad in nothing but furs" and presses his body "against the

Gregor's transformation is connected to a crisis in his psychosexual development. The protagonist's gender identity is (has become) problematic—as shortly thereafter it is pointed out that he is jealous of those colleagues of his who "live like harem women" (Kafka 1915: 121).

These hypotheses also help to demonstrate the increasing neutralization of the introductory focalization, through which the author seeks to ensure that the reader remains, at least initially, in the dark about the cause of Gregor's metamorphosis. Once one has perceived Gregor's psychosexual problems, it appears obvious to look for an explanation about the mysterious metamorphosis of the hero in his identity-forming family relationships.

5 Conclusion

Through the textual examples given from Kafka's *Metamorphosis*, it should have become clear that the question of "Who (of the fictive entities) perceives (how much)?" can be clearly separated from the question of "What can the reader know about portrayed world(s)?". The fictional perspectivization, on the one hand, and the regulation of information within the communication between the author and reader, on the other hand, are two wholly independent phenomena and, therefore, must be conceptually differentiated from one another. Whether temporary and definitive withholding of information can be readily denoted by the term focalization—or whether one ought not to refer to them with the term "filtration"—is, as a quarrel over terminology, not what we would like to discuss here[15].

---

glass, which held him fast, soothing his hot belly" (161). After his mother catches a glimpse of him in this position and faints, crying out "Oh God, oh God!" (162), he tears himself away from the lady and feels "tortured by self-rebukes" (163)—in the sense of the script previously sketched out by Sacher-Masoch's *Venus in furs*.

15 As Chatman has already determined (cf. Chatman 1990: 143–53) "filtration" (and also "filter") is "a good term for capturing something of the mediating function of a character's consciousness—perception, cognition, emotion, reverie—as events are experienced from a space within the story world" (144, 149). Chatman sees the advantage of the term "filter" in the fact "that it catches the nuance of the choice made by the implied author about […] which areas of the story world [he] wants to illuminate and which to keep obscure" (144). We could also agree with this argument. However, we believe that the definition of the concept as provided is too broad. In suggesting, namely, that the term "filter" applies to every "point of view" of a figure—"the […] range of mental activity experienced by characters in the story-world" (143)—Chatman

What deserves further discussion, however, is how much cognitive inference is required on the part of the reader before a piece of information can no longer be considered textually communicated. We have taken an extreme position with our claim that there is no focalization whenever all needed information can at least be inferred (even if it requires a great effort to do so). Should it (on the basis of cognitive psychology) be possible in the future, to distinguish between different degrees of implicitness within the "Implicit II" (cf. Linke & Nussbaumer 2001), one could also speak of levels of focalization—depending on how narrowly defined the "information-conveying pipe" (Genette 1988: 74) is in each case.

Translated from German by Tracy N. Graves and Katherine McNeill.

References

Barthes, Roland (1964). "Éléments de sémiologie." *Communications* 4, 91–141.
– (1985). *L'aventure sémiologique.* Paris: Seuil.
Bremond, Claude (1973). *Logique du récit.* Paris: Seuil.
– (1964). "Le Message narratif." *Logique du récit.* Paris: Seuil, 1973, 11–47.
Chatman, Seymour (1986). "Characters and Narrators: Filter, Center, Slant and Interest-Focus." *Poetics Today* 9, 189–204.
– (1990). *Coming to Terms: The Rhetoric of Narrative in Fiction and Film.* Ithaca: Cornell UP.
Freud, Sigmund (1905). *Three Essays on the Theory of Sexuality* [*Drei Abhandlungen zur Sexualtheorie*]. J. Strachey et al. (eds). *The Standard Edition of the Complete Psychological Works of Sigmund Freud,* Vol. VII. London: Hogarth Press and the Institute of Psychoanalysis, 1953, 123–245.
– (1910). *Leonardo da Vinci and a Memory of his Childhood* [*Eine Kindheitserinnerung des Leonardo da Vinci*]. J. Strachey et al. (eds). *The Standard Edition of the Complete Psychological Works of Sigmund Freud,* Vol. XI. London: Hogarth Press and the Institute of Psychoanalysis, 1953, 57–137.
Genette, Gérard (1972). "Discours du récit." *Figures III.* Paris: Seuil, 65–278.
– (1980). *Narrative Discourse.* Tr. J. E. Lewin. Oxford: Blackwell.
– (1983). *Nouveau discours du récit.* Paris: Seuil.
– (1988). *Narrative Discourse Revisited.* Tr. J. E. Lewin. Ithaca: Cornell UP.
Grice, H. Paul (1975). "Logic and Conversation." *Syntax and Semantics* 3, 41–58.
Herman, David (2002). *Story Logic: Problems and Possibilities of Narrative.* Lincoln: U of Nebraska P.

---

assumes that figural perspectivization categorically accompanies a curtailing of the information available (149: "distortion of story information"). With this move, he also allows for a jumbling of two terms, for whose clear and strict separation we have argued here.

Kafka, Franz (1915). "The Metamorphosis" ["Die Verwandlung"]. *The Metamorphosis and Other Stories.* Tr. J. Neugroschel. New York: Charles Scribner's Sons, 1993, 119–92.

Linke, Angelika & Nussbaumer, Markus (2001). "Konzepte des Impliziten. Präsuppositionen und Implikaturen." K. Brinker et al. (eds). *Text- und Gesprächslinguistik. Ein internationales Handbuch zeitgenössischer Forschung.* Berlin: de Gruyter, 435–48.

Lotman, Jurij (1972). *The Structure of the Artistic Text.* Tr. R. Vroon. Ann Arbor: U of Michigan P, 1977.

Niederhoff, Burkhard (2001). "Fokalisation und Perspektive. Ein Plädoyer für eine friedliche Koexistenz." *Poetica* 33:1–2, 1–21.

Quasthoff, Uta M. (1980). *Erzählen in Gesprächen. Linguistische Untersuchungen zu Strukturen und Funktionen am Beispiel einer Kommunikationsform des Alltags.* Tübingen: Narr.

Renner, Karl Nikolaus (1983). *Der Findling. Eine Erzählung von Heinrich von Kleist und ein Film von George Moorse. Prinzipien einer adäquaten Wiedergabe narrativer Strukturen.* Munich: Fink.

Rimmon-Kenan, Shlomith (1983). *Narrative Fiction. Contemporary Poetics.* London: Routledge, 2002.

Ryan, Marie-Laure (1991). *Possible Worlds, Artificial Intelligence, and Narrative Theory.* Bloomington: Indiana UP.

Sacher-Masoch, Leopold (1869). *Venus in Furs* [*Venus im Pelz*]. Tr. J. Neugroschel. New York: Penguin, 2000.

Schmid, Wolf (1992). "Cechovs problematische Ereignisse." *Ornamentales Erzählen in der russischen Moderne. Cechov, Babel, Zamjatin.* Frankfurt a. M.: Peter Lang, 104–34.

Titzmann, Michael (1977). *Strukturale Textanalyse. Theorie und Praxis der Interpretation.* Munich: Fink, 1993.

ALAIN RABATEL
(Lyon)

A Brief Introduction to an Enunciative Approach to Point of View

Even when narrowed down to the field of language, the concept of point of view borrows from a variety of other fields ranging from vision ("a spectacular point of view") to the expression of an opinion which is more or less justified, but which is distinct from a scientific truth ("this is a point of view which I share"), and including the adoption of a central narrative perspective (referred to differently by Genette as "focalization"), not to mention the linguistic operation of foregrounding important information, in particular through an emphatic operation (as in: "The text by Genette that I particularly have in mind is *Narrative Discourse*").

Point of view (POV) is defined, in an enunciative approach, in terms of the linguistic means with which a subject[1] envisages an object[2], and encompasses all the meanings of the term "envisage"[3], whether the subject be singular or collective and the object concrete or linguistic. The subject, who is responsible for the referential values of the object, expresses his POV either directly, in explicit commentaries, or indirectly, through the construction of referential values, in other words through choices concerning the selection, combination, and realization of the linguistic material, and does so in all circumstances, ranging from the most subjective choices to those which appear to be the most objectivizing, and from the most explicit markers to the most implicit clues.

---

1 Or focalizer (Genette [1972; 1983]), enunciator (Ducrot [1984]), subject of consciousness (Banfield [1982]), modal subject (Bally [1965]), locus of empathization (Forest [2003]), centre of perspective (Lintvelt [1981]; Rabatel [1997]), etc.

2 Or "object of focalization" (*focalisé*) (cf. Bal 1977).

3 Going from perception to mental representation, as expressed in, and through, discourse.

An examination of POV based on linguistic markers makes it possible to advance the discussion of opposable arguments, but at the same time has the disadvantage, at least in a first analysis, of appearing to be valid only for a particular language, such as French (the language in which I have conducted practically all my research), because of the specificities of each linguistic system. In point of fact, this is not at all the case, given the similitude between cognitive phenomena[4] and markers which play an identical role in numerous languages. It can therefore reasonably be claimed that the POV theory presented in the present study is to a certain extent generalizable, as long as the greatest care is taken not to transpose unchanged those analyses and markers which might not have an equivalent in another system—for all languages, beyond their distinctive differences, are the vehicles of enunciative heterogeneity, in other words the interweaving of the voices of others in one's own discourse, and this is a phenomenon which is fundamental to POV theory.

Given the still dominant nature of Genettian theories, with which I am in strong disagreement,—hence the abandonment of the term "focalization"—I might have begun by giving a brief presentation of the specificity of my own position compared to that of Genette, but I prefer to commence by presenting my own framework for enunciative analysis[5], examining the instances of point of view (1) and the various modalities of POV (2), before presenting the external or internal markers of POV which contribute to the more or less subjectivizing or objectifying expression of these instances (3). In the final part of this study, I bring together the points on which Genette and I differ, while clearly underlining the nature of my enormous debt to him (4). In short, I would ask readers to bear with me before I lay out my reasons, so they can better appreciate, on the basis of the evidence presented, why I distance myself from the Genettian model.

---

4 See Uri Margolin's contribution in the current volume.

5 Especially as: (i) Genette does not claim that his is an enunciative approach, (ii) his essentially structuralist conception of focalization is grounded, it is worth noting, on a very limited number of linguistic clues, and (iii) the users of his model often disagree over the analysis of focalizations – see Rabatel (1997, ch. 12).

1 The Instances of Point of View

Enunciative linguistics, of which Beneveniste (1966) was the pioneering proponent, seeks to analyse the way in which the enunciator's choices of exophoric linguistic reference influence the addressee. It is in this context that the links between, or disconnection of, discourse and situation of utterance have been studied through the examination of person and space-time markers. Rather than speak of "the subjectivity of the enunciator" (cf. Kerbrat-Orecchioni 1980), however, it is preferable to favor the notion of point of view, since a point of view is not necessarily subjective (cf. Latour 2006[6]). Furthermore, traces of a point of view are not exclusively restricted to markers relating to "I–here–now"; rather, they are to be found widely distributed in the way the enunciator constructs discourse objects. In my approach to POV (freely inspired by Ducrot [1984]), the speaker is the instance that expresses an utterance which is localized either deictically or anaphorically, while the enunciator[7], who is similar to Bally's modal subject, takes charge of the utterance, insofar as the evaluations, qualifications, modalizations, and judgements on the objects of discourse are filtered through his subjectivity[8]. It is, however, important to distinguish the prime enunciator, the one who takes responsibility for the utterance made by a speaker, from secondary enunciators who are the sources of a POV, where these POVs are not expressed in words. Ducrot insists on the fact that the expression of POV is not necessarily embodied in "precise words":

---

6 "What makes you think that 'adopting a point of view' means 'being restricted'? or being particularly 'subjective'? [...] If it is possible for you to see a statue from different points of view, it is because the statue itself is three-dimensional and allows you, yes, *allows you* to walk round it. If something makes such a multiplicity of points of view possible, it is because it is complex, intricate, well-organized and beautiful, yes, objectively beautiful. [...] Do not believe all the nonsense that is written about the fact of being 'restricted' to your own perspective. Each science has invented ways of shifting from one point of view to another, from one frame of reference to another. [...] This is what relativity is all about. [...] If I want to be a scientist and attain objectivity, I need to be able to move from one frame of reference to another, from one point of view to another. Without such shifts I really would be restricted to my own narrow point of view." (Latour 2006: 210–13)

7 See Charaudeau & Maingueneau (2002: 220–24, 226).

8 It is useful for the theory to make a distinction between these two actualizations, even if they often go together, see Rabatel (2005a) and Rabatel (2008b: ch.15).

> I call "enunciators" those entities which are considered as expressing themselves through the act of enunciation, though precise words may not necessarily be attributed to them; if they can be said to "speak," it is only in the sense that enunciation can be seen as expressing their point of view, their position or their attitude, but not, in the concrete sense of the term, their actual words. (Ducrot 1984: 204)

This is why it is necessary to make a distinction between cases where the speaker is superimposed over a single enunciator (himself) and those where this superimposition is complicated by the co-presence of several different enunciators. The former case corresponds to situations in which utterances are built on a syncretism between speaker and enunciator, as on each occasion the speaker thinks what he says and says what he thinks—or pretends to say what he thinks: this can be observed in pleas, threats, oaths, or again in declarations of love, or orders (see the following quotations in [1] and [2]):

> (1) Behold, thou art fair, my love; behold, thou art fair; thou hast doves' eyes. (KJV:[9] Song of Solomon 1:15)
> (2) And the LORD said unto Moses, stretch out thine hand over the sea, that the waters may come again upon the Egyptians, upon their chariots, and upon their horsemen. (KJV: Exodus 14:26)

However, the prime speaker/enunciator may also develop in his discourse certain POVs[10] which he does not necessarily share, as in the case of irony, hypotheses, free indirect discourse, or again in delocutive utterances expressing a point of view[11], in reported heterodiegetic narratives in the past, as in:

> (3) Le Philistin regarda et, quand il aperçut David, il le méprisa : *c'était un gamin, au teint clair et à la jolie figure*. (TOB:[12] Premier Livre de Samuel 17:41)
> (And when the Philistine looked about, and saw David, he disdained him: *for he was but a youth, and ruddy, and of a fair countenance.* [KJV: 1 Samuel 17:42])

Genette's model of focalization would be hard put to account for the above example in so far as it contains few linguistic markers of internal focalization, essentially free indirect discourse or internal monologue. However (3) is not a case in point of such forms. While, admittedly, one might be tempted to analyze (3) as an instance of free indirect discourse, this can only be achieved by stretching the example somewhat since, in

9 *The Holy Bible (Authorized King James Version).*
10 Having as a reference point an intratextual enunciator.
11 Marked in italics in (3) and in subsequent examples.
12 *Traduction Œcuménique de la Bible.*

accordance with the generally admitted norm, free indirect discourse depends on the presence of a reporting verb or, more rarely, of a verb of thought (cf. De Mattia 2001), neither of which is present here[13]. The text positions Goliath as the perceptual subject, he "looked about," and describes the precise nature of the intentional perception: "he disdained him". Here, in the French translation, *quand* ("when") is equivalent to "as soon as", indicating that Goliath deliberately looked at David to see whether the latter might be a formidable adversary. The text does not just predicate the act of perception, in the plane of historical enunciation (whose prototypic tense, in French, is the simple past), by giving an overall view of this event. With the use of the imperfect tense copula, *était* ("was")[14], by virtue of the secant view which it expresses, the reader finds

13 See the studies of free indirect discourse in English (De Mattia [2001]; Poncharal [2003]) and on the value of demonstratives in the marking of point of view in Swedish (Jonasson [2002]), et al. While, I agree with Authier-Revuz (1992 and 1993) on the need to stress the close relationship between free indirect discourse and POV in cases of free indirect discourse without a reporting verb or verb of thought, and while I also share, with Rosier (1999) and Fludernik (1993), the idea of a continuum of forms, I would not go so far as to place POV on the same level with free indirect discourse, or to consider POV as one of the various forms of reported speech, contrary to the position wrongly attributed to me by Marnette (cf. 2005: 61, 277). Admittedly, when seen in the context of dialogism, perceptual reports are close neighbours to the reports of speech and thought found in reported speech, since a prime speaker/ enunciator (the narrator) envisages things from the point of view of a secondary enunciator (a character), even when there is no explicit discourse, as will be seen infra with example (3), but Baxtinian dialogism is much a broader phenomenon than the notion of reported speech. See Rabatel (2008b, ch. 15 to 17).

14 The markers of POV are broadly the same in French and English apart from the tense systems. The French imperfect is the prototypic tense of the second plane (cf. Combettes 1992). The use of the word "prototypic" here is to be understood as meaning that it is the tense which is most often encountered, but it should be noted that this role can also be played by other verb forms, such as the present participle, as in the Hebrew text. The above analyses are valid for French, and cannot be applied unchanged to the English verb system. It is clear that in example (3) the French imperfect has to be translated by a simple preterite; however, it should in no way be concluded that the English simple preterite is equivalent to the French imperfect, but simply that it shares certain aspectual characteristics with the latter. Poncharal (personal communication) observes, moreover, that the imperfect rarely corresponds to a form in "be+-ing", and that there is often more affinity between the simple preterite and the imperfect than between the simple preterite and the French simple past. As for the rest, the English translation of example (3) denotes a POV, by virtue in particular of the aspectual values of "was", but also by virtue of the presence of "for" (cf. Danon-Boileau 1995: 26), not to mention other choices involved in exophoric reference.

himself at the heart of the perception: at this point the text reveals details or parts of this perception (general appearance, complexion, face). The reader thus realizes, without the Philistine having to say a word, that the term "youth" and the allusion to his "fair countenance," in short his quasi feminine grace, are more characteristic of women than of men, and connote the disdain of the virile male of mature years for an upstart who is not part of the world of virile men, and hence not a worthy adversary for a man of his strength.

This explanation will, it is hoped, enable the reader to obtain a better grasp of Ducrot's definition, quoted above, of the (intratextual) enunciator. Thus, the utterance in (3), written by the narrator, who corresponds to the prime speaker/enunciator, involves an intratextual enunciator, Goliath, who is the enunciative origin of a POV, even though this POV in no way corresponds to discourse uttered by Goliath, since the latter has said, literally, nothing. To put it another way, the POV represented is a descriptive fragment which could, perhaps, be paraphrased by a sort of implicit internal monologue along the lines of: "I'll soon make short work of this pretty young man!" The prime speaker/enunciator conveys this POV without endorsing its disdainful connotation[15], even though he confirms the denotation of the propositional content, the youth and beauty of David, in the absence of any epistemic distancing[16].

What, then, are the narratological conclusions that we can draw from this enunciative analysis? If the origins of POV are enunciators, then cat-

---

15 Axiological distancing, though of a discreet nature, is nevertheless present in the contrast between the verb "disdained" and the description of David: the positively orientated attributives would not normally indicate disdain, unless they are seen through the sadistic prism of a man who has full confidence in his strength, and reduces human relationships to a man-to-man fight to the death. This distancing indicates a dissonance between the narrator and the character/perceiver. In the contrary case, we speak of consonance, see Cohn (1978); Rabatel (1998: ch. 4; 2001 and 2008b: ch. 19).

16 This is why I distance myself from Fludernik (1993) when she treats speech and thought as a whole, even going so far as finding similarities between perceptions and thoughts in the case of narrated perceptions. While I share the idea of scalarity in the subjective expression of speech, thought and perceptions, I do not go so far as to consider the latter three as equivalent to each other. Furthermore, her conception of free indirect speech (FIS) is based on the idea that the distinction between mode and voice is unfounded. My analysis of (3) shows that the distinction remains pertinent as long as the enunciator's POV is expressed through exophoric linguistic reference, even if he does not pronounce any words, since it is the voice of the narrator who envisages things from the character's point of view.

egories of POV, linked to these enunciative sources, can only exist by virtue of their relationship with a linguistic substrate. This enunciative reality explains why an authentic narrational POV is undoubtedly present when the objects of discourse are referenced without being seen through the perspective prism of one of the main characters. This would be the case in (4) if David was described with the same terms, without reference to Goliath:

(4) David appeared. *He was but a youth, and ruddy, and of a fair countenance, an adversary unworthy of respect.*

The concept of zero focalization (which Genette glosses as an absence of focalization, the point of view of the narrator or variable focalization resulting from all the other focalizations—which are, for a scientific definition, incompatible, contradictory glosses) does not stand up to scrutiny. Nor does external focalization, despite Rivara's claims[17]. Bal (1977), some time ago, stressed the confusion between focalization "by" (a focalizing subject/an instance) and focalization "on" (a focalized object) and reassigned external focalization to objective description of the focalized entity. My proposals are paralleled by the Anglo-American approach, which only makes a distinction between external point of view (that of the narrator) and internal point of view (that of the character), even if the linguistic justification for the qualification as "external" is questionable. This enunciative consideration is the nub of my difference of opinion with Genette. It would take too much space to reiterate my 1997 demonstration (one which has never been refuted since): the supposed examples of external focalization are actually attributable either to a character's POV or the narrator's POV "with an external view", in other words limited to the description of some "external" aspect of an object[18], such as the description of someone's clothing or of an object and expressed in objectifying utterances whose enunciation is historical, and above all to a description from which manifest traces of subjectivity are absent[19].

[17] See Rabatel (2009) for a detailed discussion of this point.

[18] The physical ("external") description of David, therefore, shows traces of the ("internal") subjectivity of Goliath; this is why I felt it necessary to abandon this dichotomy (cf. Rabatel 1997), which is unfounded from the linguistic point of view.

[19] See Rabatel (1997: ch. 3, 4 and 12, and 2003c).

2 Different Modalities of Point of View: Dialogism of Represented, Narrated and Asserted Points of View

POV, then, corresponds to those elements which, in the exophoric linguistic reference to the objects (of discourse), reveal, from a cognitive and an axiological point of view, a particular enunciative origin and indicate, explicitly or implicitly, the latter's representations and, where relevant, his judgements on the referents. This definition makes it possible to give an explanation for the close relationships between POV and reported discourse, on the one hand, and POV and assertion, on the other, without limiting POV to perceptions or to the narrative genre alone: a POV exists when reference to the object also entails the representation of an enunciator, even in the absence of explicit judgements, whether the object of discourse be an opinion or a perception, and whether the latter appear in a description, a narrative, a news item, an explanation or an argumentation.

This means that POV is not limited to the expression of represented perceptions, as analyzed by myself in Rabatel (1998), even though I do not disown my analyses; quite simply, these analyses are not, and never claimed to be, the final word on POV. In this sense, reported discourse (cf. Rosier 1999) and POV are subsets of the general problematic of dialogism. Speech, thought and perceptions may be reported/represented using identical syntactic and enunciative patterns by means of direct, indirect, free indirect and free direct reporting. The fragment in italics in (5) is a direct account of perception, which is largely analogous, at the syntactic level, to its paraphrases containing direct discourse, as proposed in (6), or containing indirect discourse in (7), free direct discourse in (8), free indirect discourse in (9), and psycho-narration in (10):

(5) And the angel of the LORD appeared unto him in a flame of fire out of the midst of a bush: and he looked, *and, behold, the bush burned with fire, and the bush was not consumed.* (KJV: Exodus 3:2)

(6) And the angel of the LORD appeared unto him in a flame of fire out of the midst of a bush: Moses looked <u>and said to himself</u>, "*the bush is burning with fire, and the bush is not consumed.*"

(7) So Joshua sent messengers, and they ran unto the tent. <u>They cried out</u> *that it was there, hid in his tent, and the silver underneath.* And they took them out of the midst

of the tent, and brought them unto Joshua, and unto all the children of Israel; and laid them out before the LORD[20].

(8) So Joshua sent messengers, and they ran unto the tent; *and there, indeed, it is, hid in his tent, and the silver underneath.* And they took them out of the midst of the tent, and brought them unto Joshua, and unto all the children of Israel; and laid them out before the LORD.

(9) And when Pharaoh drew nigh, the children of Israel lifted up their eyes, and, behold, the Egyptians marched after them; and they were sore afraid: and the children of Israel cried out unto the LORD. (KJV: Exodus 14:10)

(10) So Joshua sent messengers, and they ran unto the tent and saw that *what Achan had said was true*. And they took [it and the silver] out of the midst of the tent, and brought them unto Joshua, and unto all the children of Israel; and laid them out before the LORD.

These variations objectify the cognitive and linguistic continuums between perception, thought and speech, and explain, at the semiotic level, the similarities of their textual values in the construction of reality effects (*mimesis*), in the provision of information (*mathesis*) and the handling of textual structuring (*semiosis*), according to Adam and Petitjean (1989). All these various accounts of perception can be grouped together in a continuum, labelled as follows, according to their greater or lesser degree of visibility and their greater or lesser aptitude to express the enunciator's interiority, subjectivity and reflexivity:

– "Embryonic" or narrated POV (cf. Rabatel 2001; 2004), corresponding to perceptual points of view limited to traces on the first plane, as in (10);

– Represented POV (cf. Rabatel 1998: 54), expressing the accounts of perception (possibly associated with speech or thought) developed in the second plane, as in the passages in italics in (3), (5);

– Asserted POV (cf. Rabatel 2003b; c; Rabatel 2008b: ch. 15 to 17), corresponding to POVs expressed in word or thought, as exemplified by conventional forms of reported discourse (cf. [6] to [9]) or in assertions, outside of the context of reported discourse, as in the examples below.

Beyond the question of labelling, one should not lose sight of the underlying affinity between these forms which are capable of expressing the POV of a character or that of the narrator: thus, the embryonic POV is not an absence of POV, but is rather a minimal, minor POV, one which, while less reflexive and subjectifying than an asserted POV, is nevertheless already a POV. One should never lose sight of their affinity or their

---

[20] Examples (7), (8) and (10) are based on the Biblical text: "So Joshua sent messengers, and they ran unto the tent; and, behold, it was hid in his tent, and the silver under it" (KJV: Joshua 7:22).

complementarity in the expression of mimetism and reflexivity (cf. Rabatel 2003e), without forgetting that the dialogism of POVs goes beyond the framework of reported discourse, since every assertion, or even a word, expresses, in one way or another, a POV, as can be seen in the enumerations of the names of countries in which the pleasure of the Jews in naming the different parts of their promised land is clearly perceptible or, again, can be found in the genealogies which, through the enumeration of filiations which have ensured the survival of Israel (Joshua 15–21, or 1 Chronicles 2), give a glimpse of the hard-earned pleasure of enduring.

But, besides these forms of dialogism (cf. Bakhtin 1929; Rabatel 2008b: ch. 13), all propositional content, even that which is not concerned with perception, thought or speech, expresses by default the POV of the prime speaker/enunciator, or that of an intratextual enunciator. Thus, the selection of information in the construction of propositional content is highly significant. This is the case in the First Book of Chronicles 11:1: the narrative, which states that "Then all Israel gathered themselves to David unto Hebron," elides seven and a half years of the reign of David over Hebron (while Ishbosheth, one of the sons of Saul, ruled over the rest of Israel), so as to give it to be understood that the reign of David concerned "all Israel," and that nothing having to do with Saul was of any importance. This is confirmed by the ensuing direct discourse, in which "all Israel" declares to David: "Behold, we are thy bone and thy flesh. And moreover in time past, even when Saul was king, thou wast he that leddest out and broughtest in Israel:" (KJV: 1 Chronicles 11:1–2).

3 Markers of Point of View

Parallels are often drawn between the linguistic nature of POV and the idea contained in a proposition. All propositions, being centered on propositional content (=PC) express a POV. Does this, then, mean that there can be no POV above the level of the proposition, for instance at the text level, or below the level of the proposition, for instance at the word level?

It is relevant to consider that the PC is the heart of any POV, for it relates to a predication which, in an assertion, always already expresses the point of view of the speaker by virtue of the choice of words. But that does not imply that the lower threshold of POV is predication, as a single word can at times suffice to express a worldview, relating back to a POV, as long as the word links back to an enunciator and a POV which can both be clearly identified for a given linguistic community. Above the propositional level, it is desirable[21] to group PCs together according to referential content (all the PCs concerning the same referent), enunciative origin (all the PCs having the same enunciative origin) and argumentative orientation (all the PCs sharing the same orientation to which, if necessary, could be added PCs with a contrary orientation integrated into the argumentative drift of the principal enunciator)—in short, according to the similarity of the effects of the POV upon the reader.

The external markers are the opening or closing markers indicating the beginning and the end of a POV. Such markers are fragile, once one moves outside the clearly marked-out framework of written direct discourse. With an asserted POV, the external markers are those of reported (or represented) discourse, and only direct discourse has clear external markers (and even then, this is only true of written discourse), for with indirect discourse, while there is unquestionably an opening marker, the closing marker is often far from being present in every case. The difficulties with external delimitation increase with free indirect discourse and narrativized discourse. For the represented POV, the opening limit is indicated by a perceptual predicator—most often a verb, but also conceivably a noun—and a related perceiving subject; in the absence of such markers, the perceptual process may be inferred from a verb of motion; the opposition between global tense forms (such as the preterite or the historical present) and secant forms (such as the French imperfect or pluperfect) which play an opening role (passage from the first to the second plane) or closing role (passage from the second to the first plane) comparable to what happens with free indirect discourse (cf. Vuillaume 2000)[22]. With an embryonic POV, we move on from external markers to internal markers.

Generally speaking, the more tenuous the external markers, the more internal markers of modal actualization act as signals of enunciative alterity and have the merit of embodying the instances behind the POVs. Numerous lexical elements are capable of playing this role such as, at the level of the cohesion between nominals, lexical designations containing

---

21 In order to optimize the cognitive processing of information, the multiplication of myriads of enunciators should be avoided.

22 Tense alternation such as, in French, preterite—>perfect—>preterite, does not necessarily signify the end of a particular point of view and a return to narrative text. As was shown in Rabatel (2003a), it also indicates the transition from a represented to an embryonic point of view (or vice versa), in other words different degrees in the reflexive apprehension of percepts by an intratextual enunciator.

positive or negative value judgements (11) or phenomena of actualization of nouns (12). As examples (11) to (23) cover, with some variations, the same ground as example (3), it will not be necessary to restate the original analysis. Suffice it to say that the POV remains both the same and, in terms of expressivity, not quite the same. We would remind the reader that the part in italics corresponds to the expression of the POV as analyzed in example (3), and that the term(s) underlined correspond(s) to the internal markers which intensify the original POV and generally give it a specific semantic colouring, which can be more or less expressive, depending on their particular value. It is particularly important, therefore, to stress that each of these markers contributes to the location of the POV, and more particularly, to its expressivity (underlined); hence the more numerous these markers are, the more strongly marked is the POV:

(11) And when the Philistine looked about, and saw David, he disdained him: *for he was but a youth, an ephebe, and ruddy, and of a fair countenance.*
(12) And when the Philistine looked about, and saw David, he disdained him: *this youth, ruddy, and of a fair countenance.*

At the level of logical cohesion, this function is also fulfilled by presentatives (cf. Rabatel 2008a, ch. 3), connectors, spatio-temporal markers and intensifiers, by virtue of their enunciative-argumentative value (cf. Rabatel 2008a: ch. 4) (13):

(13) And when the Philistine looked about, and saw David, he disdained him: *for he was barely a youth, but his ruddy complexion and fair countenance could not hide his shifty look.*

At the verbal level, temporal-aspectual distinctions, the semantic content of verbs (cf. Rabatel 2003a), etc., also contribute to modal actualization in the representation of events.

At the syntactic[23] level, most of the markers indicating dialogism act as internal markers, skewing the account of perception towards one of speech or thought, and confirm that the POV is that of Goliath: thus, the dialogue markers which go to make up the *dictum* (propositional content) reinforce the reflexive content of the perceptions, whether the case be one of an interrogative (14), a rhetorical question (15), presupposition or negation (16), a cleft sentence (focus, foregrounding) (17), a concessive (18), opposition (19), confirmation (20), rectification (21) or intensification (22):

[23] Their syntactic basis is, of course, inseparable from their semantic dimension.

(14) And when the Philistine looked about, and saw David, he disdained him: *who was to be the enemy's champion? For he was but a youth, and ruddy, and of a fair countenance.*
(15) And when the Philistine looked about, and saw David, he disdained him: *had anyone ever seen such a ridiculous enemy? He was but a youth, and ruddy, and of a fair countenance.*
(16) And when the Philistine looked about, and saw David, he disdained him: *the enemy really was not to be feared, for he was but a youth, and ruddy, and of a fair countenance.*
(17) And when the Philistine looked about, and saw David, he disdained him: *the enemy's champion, he was but a youth, and ruddy, and of a fair countenance.*
(18) And when the Philistine looked about, and saw David, he disdained him: *for even if the enemy looked bold, he was but a youth, and ruddy, and of a fair countenance.*
(19) And when the Philistine looked about, and saw David, he disdained him: *for he was not a battle-hardened fighter, he was but a youth, and ruddy, and of a fair countenance.*
(20) And when the Philistine looked about, and saw David, he disdained him: *yes, he really was but a youth, and ruddy, and of a fair countenance.*
(21) And when the Philistine looked about, and saw David, he disdained him: *he was a young man, in fact, but a youth, and ruddy, and of a fair countenance.*
(22) And when the Philistine looked about, and saw David, he disdained him: *for he was but a youth, an effeminate weakling in fact, and ruddy, and of a fair countenance.*

These dialogue markers make the potential underlying responsive dimension in (3) explicit: for instance, the dialogic perceptual account of (15) is a response to a presupposed implicit objection; (16) and (18) are answers to a prior objection (or at any rate anticipate such an objection), and so on. All these markers (the list of which is not exhaustive; cf. echoic repetition, travesty, irony, the hypothetic, etc.) participate in the construction of intratextual modal subjects.

Inversely, the POV can delete these markers, or even erase verbs of perception (in some contexts, it is the perceiving subject who is implicit), as long as there are enough clues in the exophoric reference to the object for it to be understood as the source of the perception:

(23) The Philistine advanced towards his enemy: *he was but a youth, and ruddy, and of a fair countenance.*

Thus, in function of the dialogism of the linguistic markers[24] involved in the exophoric reference of perceptions, the latter denote perceptual processes which may be more or less intentional and more or less associated

[24] By dialogism, we mean the fact that an utterance allows several voices, which answer each other, to be heard. This concept is often confused with that of polyphony, but it is desirable to make a distinction between the two, see Rabatel (2008b: ch. 13).

with epistemic and axiological dimensions, to the point that the saturation of dialogue markers blurs the distinction between, on the one hand, perception and, on the other, thought and speech[25].

4 Marked Differences With the Genettian Model of Focalization

Besides the fundamental disagreement with Genette over the number and nature of instances of POV, there are differences as to the status of first- or third-person narrative utterances, a question which intersects with that of the status of utterances with a heterodiegetic narrator and those mediated by a character, on the plane of the expression of subjectivity and knowledge.

As the previous markers may be present with an “I- or he-POV”, it follows that a POV expressed in the first person is not necessarily subjectifying by virtue of its expression, no more than a third-person point of view necessarily implies an objectifying utterance. This scale of subjectivity in the expression of POV is due to the fact that what is perceived is expressed, be it with an “I” or a “he”, through lexical or syntactic markers—much in the same way as were those mentioned in connection with examples (11) to (23); and these markers, by virtue of their presence, indicate the reactions of a subject toward an object. Thus, the “I-POV” in (24) is totally subjectifying, through the comparison of the loved one with a gazelle or a young stag. The “I-POV” in (25), describing Ezekiel’s vision of the construction of the new temple, is objectifying, whereas the same prophet’s vision of glory in (26) is a combination of various objectifying data from which there emerge, despite his desire to describe faithfully what he had seen in a dream, a certain number of subjective reactions:

(24) The voice of my beloved! behold, he cometh leaping upon the mountains, skipping upon the hills. My beloved is like a roe or a young hart: behold, he standeth behind our wall, he looketh forth at the windows, shewing himself through the lattice. (KJV: Song of Solomon 2:8–9)

(25) So he measured the court, an hundred cubits long, and an hundred cubits broad, foursquare; and the altar that was before the house. And he brought me to the porch of the house, and measured each post of the porch, five cubits on this side, and five cubits on that side: and the breadth of the gate was three cubits on this side, and three cubits on that side. (KJV: Ezekiel 40:47–48)

[25] See also Fludernik (1993) and supra, note 16.

(26) And I looked, and, behold, a whirlwind came out of the north, a great cloud, and a fire infolding itself, and a brightness was about it, and out of the midst thereof as the colour of amber, out of the midst of the fire. Also out of the midst thereof came the likeness of four living creatures. And this was their appearance; they had the likeness of a man. And every one had four faces, and every one had four wings. And their feet were straight feet; and the sole of their feet was like the sole of a calf's foot: and they sparkled like the colour of burnished brass. And they had the hands of a man under their wings on their four sides; and they four had their faces and their wings. (KJV: Ezekiel 1:4–8)

The presence and the combination of lexical and syntactic markers produce the same effects of subjectifying or objectifying expression with a "he-POV": the heterodiegetic POV of Solomon, describing the temple, is objectifying in (28), the POV taking the form of a description of actions:

(27) And in the most holy house he [Solomon] made two cherubims of image work, and overlaid them with gold. And the wings of the cherubims were twenty cubits long: one wing of the one cherub was five cubits, reaching to the wall of the house: and the other wing was likewise five cubits, reaching to the wing of the other cherub. And one wing of the other cherub was five cubits, reaching to the wall of the house: and the other wing was five cubits also, joining to the wing of the other cherub. The wings of these cherubims spread themselves forth twenty cubits: and they stood on their feet, and their faces were inward. And he made the vail of blue, and purple, and crimson, and fine linen, and wrought cherubims thereon. (KJV: 2 Chronicles 3:10–14)

The heterodiegetic POV in (3), on the other hand, includes numerous subjectivemes, as was seen above. For its part, the following extract from Genesis occupies an intermediary position:

(28) In the beginning God created the heaven and the earth. And the earth was without form, and void; and darkness was upon the face of the deep. And the Spirit of God moved upon the face of the waters. And God said, Let there be light: and there was light. And God saw the light, that it was good: and God divided the light from the darkness. And God called the light Day, and the darkness he called Night. And the evening and the morning were the first day. (KJV: Genesis 1:1–5)

The same reasoning denies the pertinence of the erroneous simplifications which portray the POV of a heterodiegetic narrator as, by definition, objective, and a character's POV as, by definition, subjective[26]. This type of confusion between the origin of and the linguistic expression of subjectivity relies in an overly naive fashion on the mistaken idea that narration is so "objectifying" that "no one is speaking here, the events seem to narrate themselves," as Benveniste (cf. 1966: 241) claims in an as-

---

[26] See supra the quotation from Latour, note 6.

sertion which is contradicted by the presence of all sorts of subjective markers (cf. Kerbrat-Orecchioni 1981), even in written texts whose enunciation is historical, because anaphoric localization still does not prevent traces of the modal subject from coming to the surface (cf. Rabatel 2005c: 117–20), as can be verified if one reflects on the presence or absence of such-and-such a linguistic marker, as in examples (11) to (23), opening the way to the possibility for a narrator's or a character's POV to be more or less objectifying or subjectifying.

The last point of disagreement concerns the attribution of a volume of untouchable knowledge contiguous with each perspective, ranging from narratorial omniscience to the maximum retention of information in external focalization, whereas this is only a theoretical possibility. This eventuality is accepted as far as the narrator is concerned, even if, in practice, he is confined to omniscience[27], while on the other hand characters are denied variability in the volume of their knowledge. Now, omniscience is a datum which is not always verified in texts, depending on the genre, the type of narrator, expositional strategy, etc.; nor, moreover, is it reserved exclusively to narrators, insofar as it is manifest, since there exist knowledgeable characters and since, generally speaking, the thesis according to which the point of view of characters is a limited one (restricted to external vision, according to Vitoux [1982]), because they are supposedly unable to have access to the thoughts of other characters, quite simply does not stand up to close linguistic inspection, as is shown by the examples analyzed in chapter 12 of my 1997 book. The fact that a character can indeed evoke the thoughts of others, particularly in reported discourse, is the surest indicator that characters, as the centers of narrative perspective, can have access to other characters' interiority or, at least, represent this interiority, as the narrator does, with the same margins of certainty and error. What is certain is that the existence of this actorial knowledge about other characters is not guaranteed: in this sense, there is a clear difference between the authorial and the actorial instance[28], but it

[27] See Rabatel (2009) for a more detailed analysis of straightforward examples of omniscience or of an equally obvious absence of omniscience, and for the development of a bridge between the enunciative approach to point of view and an interactional conception of narration which gives all due importance to the reader/co-enunciator. See also Pier (2004) and Coste (2006).

[28] It could be objected that the characters' knowledge depends on their status as "narrator"-characters, who are the authors of embedded narratives. This objection, however, backfires on those who voice it: the fact that a character can act as a second-level

is one that has to do with the fiduciary relationship. In short, it is possible for a character to have access to the introspection of someone else, contrary to what J. Lintvelt writes: "adopting the perspective of an actor, the narrator is limited to the extrospection of this actor-perceiver, with the result that he will only be able to give an external presentation of the other actors" (Lintvelt 1981: 44).

But beyond the differences, what remains—and this is one of Genette's unsurpassed (and unsurpassable) achievements—is the distinction between mode and voice, in other words the possibility for the narrator to tell a story with his own voice while allowing other enunciative sources to be heard, even when they do not take the form of discourse. In my own work, up to now, I have constantly endeavoured to identify the linguistic markers which allow one to hear these POVs, with their profoundly dialogic nature, within the framework of a continuum, by paying particular attention to the least obvious forms of subjectivity, in contexts of enunciative effacement, in which traces of a modal subject are nevertheless perceptible[29].

These different forms function conjointly (cf. Rabatel 2001; 2005b), allowing the prime speaker/enunciator to—more or less explicitly—express his own point of view or adopt that of the characters, or even to superimpose or oppose various narrative perspectives, inviting the reader, on the basis of the effects produced by the POV, to get ever closer, through empathy, to the characters' reasons, as to those of the narrator, since the former are expressed through the voice of the latter. This is why the necessarily schematic presentation of forms and markers must be confronted with texts and their interpretations, which it has not been possible for me to do here, having chosen to demonstrate and substantiate the deep underlying enunciative unity which brings together such a diversity of linguistic forms. But the reader may wish to refer to the numerous publications[30] in which critics have been good enough to point out the thor-

---

narrator exposes the vacuousness of the arguments that relegate characters to a role which only allows them limited knowledge. This in no way reduces differences in function and status: the cognitive superiority of the character-narrator, which is higher than that of all other characters, remains lower than that of the first narrator.

29 For a more complete approach, see my re-reading of Genette, in Rabatel (1997 and 2008b: ch. 2).

30 See, in particular, my analyses of the Bible (cf. Rabatel 2008a, ch. 6 to 8), Maupassant (cf. Rabatel 2008a: ch. 9 and 10), Pinget (in Bouchard et al. [2002]), Ernaux, Renaud Camus or Semprun (cf. Rabatel 2008b: ch. 8 to 10).

oughness of the linguistic descriptions and the resulting interpretative advances.

Translated from French by Rodney Coward (University of Tours), including the quotations from Ducrot (1984), Latour (2006) and Lintvelt (1981).

References

Adam, Jean-Michel & Petitjean, André (1989). *Le texte descriptif.* Paris: Nathan.

Authier-Revuz, Jacqueline (1992). "Repères dans le champ du discours rapporté" (1). *L'information grammaticale* 55, 38–42.

– (1993). "Repères dans le champ du discours rapporté" (2). *L'information grammaticale* 56, 10–15.

Baxtin, Mixail (Bakhtin, Mikhaïl) [Vološinov (Volochinov), V. N.] (1929). *Marxisme et philosophie du langage.* Paris: Editions de Minuit, 1977.

Bal, Mieke (1977). *Narratologie*. Paris: Klincksieck.

Bally, Charles (1932). *Linguistique générale et linguistique française*. Berne: Francke, 1965.

Banfield, Ann (1982). *Unspeakable sentences: Narrative and representation in the language of fiction.* London: Routledge & Kegan Paul.

Benveniste, Emile (1966) *Problèmes de linguistique générale* 1. Paris: Gallimard.

Bouchard, Robert et al. (2002). "'Déclencher le mécanisme'... de la construction / déconstruction du texte romanesque." E. Roulet & M. Burger (eds). *Les modèles du discours au défi d'un "dialogue romanesque": l'incipit du roman de R. Pinget, Le Libera.* Nancy: PU de Nancy, 153–211.

Charaudeau, Patrick & Maingueneau, Dominique (2002). *Dictionnaire d'analyse du discours*. Paris: Seuil.

Cohn, Dorrit (1978). *Transparent Minds. Narrative Modes for Presenting Consciousness in Fiction.* Princeton: Princeton UP.

Combettes, Bernard (1992). *L'organisation du texte*. Metz: Centre d'Analyse Syntaxique.

Coste, Didier (2006). "Le récit comme forme-mouvement." *Acta Fabula* 7:5, <http://fabula.org/revue/document1641.php>.

Danon-Boileau, Laurent (1995). *Du texte littéraire à l'acte de fiction : lectures linguistiques et réflexions psychanalytiques*. Paris: Ophrys.

De Mattia, Monique (2001). "Mrs Dalloway de Virginia Woolf ou l'instabilité du discours rapporté." M. De Mattia & A. Joly (eds). *De la syntaxe à la narratologie énonciative*. Paris: Ophrys, 227–64.

Ducrot, Oswald (1984). *Le dire et le dit*. Paris: Minuit

Fludernik, Monika (1993). *The Fiction of Language and Languages of Fiction*. London: Routledge.

Forest, Robert (2003). "Empathie linguistique et point de vue." *Cahiers de praxématique* 41, 85–104.

Genette, Gérard (1972). "Discours du récit." *Figures III.* Paris: Seuil, 65–278.

– (1980). *Narrative Discourse*. Tr. J. E. Lewin. Oxford: Blackwell.
– (1983). *Nouveau discours du récit*. Paris: Seuil.
– (1988). *Narrative Discourse Revisited*. Tr. J. E. Lewin. Ithaca: Cornell UP.
Jonasson, Kerstin (2002). "Références déictiques dans un texte narratif. Comparaison entre le français et le suédois." M. Kęsik (ed). *Références discursives sur les langues romanes et slaves*. Lublin: Wydawnictwo Uniwersytetu Marii-Curie-Sklodowskiej, 107–21.
Kerbrat-Orecchioni, Catherine (1981). *L'énonciation. La subjectivité dans le langage*. Paris: Colin.
Kleiber, Georges (2003). "Adjectifs démonstratifs et point de vue." *Cahiers de praxématique* 41, 33–54.
Latour, Bruno (2006). *Changer de société–Refaire de la sociologie*. Paris: Éditions de la Découverte.
Lintvelt, Jaap (1981). *Essai de typologie narrative*. Paris: Corti.
The Holy Bible (Authorized King James Version) [KJV] (1992). Oxford: Oxford UP.
Marnette, Sophie (2005). *Speech and Thought Presentation in French*. Amsterdam: John Benjamins Publishing Company.
Pier, John (ed) (2004). *The Dynamics of Narrative Form: Studies in Anglo-American Narratology*. Berlin: de Gruyter.
Poncharal, Bruno (2003). "Divergences énonciatives et stylistiques au DIL en anglais et en français." G. Mathis et al. (eds). *Stylistique et énonciation: le cas du discours indirect libre*. Nanterre: Publications de l'université de Paris 10, 249–66.
Rabatel, Alain (1997). *Une histoire du point de vue*. Paris: Klincksieck/CELTED.
– (1998). *La Construction textuelle du point de vue*. Paris: Delachaux et Niestlé.
– (2001). "Fondus enchaînés énonciatifs. Scénographie énonciative et points de vue." *Poétique* 126, 151–73.
– (2003a). "Une lecture énonciative des hypothèses aspectuo-temporelles et commentatives dans les suites PS + IMP : point de vue du locuteur ou de l'énonciateur ?" *Journal of French Language Studies* 13:3, 363–79.
– (2003b). "Le point de vue, entre langue et discours, description et interprétation : état de l'art et perspectives." *Le point de vue. Cahiers de Praxématique* 41, 7–24.
– (2003c). "Entre usage et mention : la notion de re-présentation dans les discours représentés." R. Amossy & D. Maingueneau (eds). *L'analyse du discours dans les études littéraires*. Toulouse: Presses universitaires du Mirail, 111–21.
– (2004). *Argumenter en racontant*. Brussels: De Boeck.
– (2005a). "La part de l'énonciateur dans la construction interactionnelle des points de vue." *Marges linguistiques* 9, 115–36, <http://www.marges-linguistiques.com>.
– (2005b). "Une catégorie transversale, le point de vue." *Le français aujourd'hui* 151, 57–68.
– (2008a). *Homo narrans. Pour une analyse énonciative et interactionnelle du récit. Tome 1. Les points de vue et la logique de la narration*. Limoges: Éditions Lambert-Lucas.
– (2008b). *Homo narrans. Pour une analyse énonciative et interactionnelle du récit. Tome 2. Dialogisme et polyphonie dans le récit*. Limoges: Éditions Lambert-Lucas.

– (2009). "Pour une narratologie énonciative ou pour une approche énonciative des phénomènes narratifs ?" J.-M. Schaeffer et al. (eds). *Narratologies contemporaines*. Paris: CNRS Éditions (forthcoming).

Rivara, René (2000). *La langue du récit. Introduction à la narratologie énonciative*. Paris: L'Harmattan.

Rosier, Laurence (1999). *Le discours rapporté*. Brussels: Duculot.

Traduction Œcuménique de la Bible [TOB] (1975). Paris: Cerf.

Vitoux, Pierre (1982). "Le jeu de la focalisation." *Poétique* 51, 359–68.

Vuillaume, Marcel (2000). "Le style indirect libre et ses contextes." *Cahiers Chronos* 5, 107–30.

GUNTHER MARTENS
(Ghent; Brussels; Antwerp)

Narrative and Stylistic Agency: The Case of Overt Narration

1 Introduction

This article mainly discusses aspects of style (rhetorical figures, imagery) in relation to the question of agency. Narrative theories distinguish various textual agents such as “narrators”, “focalizers”, “focal characters” or “reflector-characters” and invest them with differing degrees of autonomy, power and causation. This article first reviews some recent cognitive attempts to turn formerly central stylistic elements of narratorial agency into triggers and even objects of internal focalization. On the basis of this inquiry, I argue that any account which treats narratorial discourse as a kind of default “stylistic norm” is reductive in terms of stylistics. Its reductiveness becomes evident when marked stylistic and rhetorical features of the narratorial discourse are seen as intrusive interventions and authoritative points of view of the narrator and thus infractions on the carefully perspectivized text. This conception of narratorial agency, which I call institutionalist, can be remedied by approaching overt aspects of narration from a rhetorical and stylistic point of view. In order to illustrate this approach, I address a number of cases in which stylistic features complicate the establishment of perspective, features that can then be described as part of a lesser-known, more encompassing register of overtness.

2 On Triggers of Internal Focalization

Existing narratological approaches to the establishment of (internal) perspective encounter problems when attempting to link narratorial agency with stylistic elements. This can be illustrated by referring to the remarkable discussion surrounding the initial sentence of Joyce’s *Eveline* in *Dubliners*: “She sat at the window watching the evening invade the avenue” (Joyce 1961: 34). According to Chatman, the metaphor “invade” cannot belong to the diction of the protagonist. Because the metaphor is said to reflect an inventive, literary mind, it is considered to be the narrator's or even the author's infraction on the character's perspective. In other instances, the text conveys how the character would phrase or verbalize that perception in Eveline's "true idiom", which is characterized by colloquialisms ("the man out of the last house") and strong deictic anchoring (such as exclamations) (cf. Chatman 1978: 204–06). Attridge, however, claims that the rhythms of the patterned sounds (evening invade, avenue) are in fact "graceless, the metaphors dead and the diction commonplace." (Attridge 1990: 5) Echoing Genette's typically structuralist argument for internal focalization (the substitution test, cf. Genette 1972: 210; 1988: 194), Attridge argues that "the passage can be translated into first-person present tense with no difficulty," thus ruling that "the narrator's style has given way to one that mimics the speech and thought patterns of the character" (Attridge 1990: 5). Other theorists (cf. e.g. Füger 1993: 51; Jahn 1997: 461–64; Rimmon-Kenan 2002: 51) have continued to refine the account of why this passage is internally focalized from the very beginning, linking the discussion about what one can assume the character to know or command with detailed attention to shifts in the anchoring of the deictic center. Increasingly, however, aspects of free indirect discourse that indicate the lingering indirectness of the framing narration are interpreted as a key to the internality of a focalization, taking familiarizing articles and perception indicators (such as "watching", "she heard") to be marking "transitions to figurally focalized passages" (Jahn 1997: 463), while imagery is delegated to narratorial intervention[1]. From a cognitive point of view, Jahn even makes a case for the view that the frame of internal focalization, once cognitively established, easily overrules the remnants of the narrator's perceptibility. In this register, Jahn's most adventurous claim is that even conspicuous elements of the narratorial discourse pointing to indirect speech, such as the *inquit* and *percepit* formulae, will not only act as triggers (and hence, as an identification of objects) of internal focalization, but can also be integrated within that internal focalization. I aim to question Jahn's sugges-

1 "Narratorial localization typically uses descriptive imagery while reflector-mode focalization is usually cast in a "mind style" comprising referentless pronouns, the familiarizing article, minimized narratorial perceptibility, in actu presentation." (Jahn 1996: 257)

tion that these incipits are standardized and have lost their framing trigger function. I will do so by illustrating that this level of indirectness can expand into a stylistic register with relevance to the agency of narration. By arguing that even direct discourse and *inquit formulae* are amenable to internal perspective, Jahn tries to evacuate the site of the narrator's agency by giving a receptive twist to it: thus "Mrs. Dalloway's mind is [...] only minimally involved in the conversation, passively registering her own automatic questions" (Jahn 1997: 456). In a later article, Jahn (1999: 104) specifies the "much-needed excuse for treating third-person, past-tense passages such as [a similar, typical Hemingway-passage of covert figuralized narration] as fully 'internally focalized' segments": it is provided by backgrounding "deictic residue". Specific (modernist) texts featuring stream of consciousness (such as *Mrs. Dalloway*) may strive towards that evacuation, but this does not prevent other (not only older, even modernist and postmodernist) texts and genres from experimenting with types of narration with a former particular historical sedimentation[2].

From a rhetorical point of view, it is striking to note that the metaphoric element "invade" continues to be discussed in terms of diegetic appurtenance (cf. Genette 1972: 48) or "rooting" (cf. Stanzel 1979: 297). As such, its discussion remains restricted to the circumscription of idioms as guidelines for attributing individual voices and visions: Jahn proposes to consider "invade" as a "piece of the puzzle of one's mind" (Jahn 1997: 462) in tune with the character's feeling of being "beleaguered" (462) by impressions. By extending the isotopy as the character's frame of reference, Jahn gives a receptive twist to metaphor as an experiential repertoire in line with Lakoff and Johnson's conceptual metaphor. Nevertheless, Jahn's suggestion testifies to a rather resultative approach that tends to disregard the narrative function of indirect, stylistic aspects such as figurative patterns.

To conclude this section, a number of ideal-typical positions can be distilled from this debate. On the one hand, the substitution test for internal focalization (cf. Genette 1972: 210, with reference to Barthes 1966: 40), which points to the structuralist legacy of narratology, remains inconclusive with regard to stylistic agency, precisely because structuralism saw the radical formalization and construction of the object as one of its

---

[2] In fact, Jahn (1999: 105) allows for such "more active interferences between narratorial and reflectorial conceptualizations" to be grouped under Stanzel's label "colouring".

strengths. Aczel rightly criticized that in classical narratology "the central criterion for overtness remains the speaker's relationship to the discourse spoken (i.e. the position, level and time from which the story is told), and not the quality of the discourse itself. Distinctive idiomatic traits are not seen as indicators of voice" (Aczel 2005: 635)[3]. According to Fludernik, most approaches to perspective or focalization "unfortunately" (Fludernik 1993: 75) continue to stress the transformational nature of free indirect discourse as a kind of linguistic clue from which to infer a clear-cut substitution of agency or an effacement of narrative command. On the other hand, the cognitive models which continue to advance refinements and nuances in the register of internal focalization tend to diminish the agency of the narrator as such in favour of a discussion of narrative in terms of "embedded narratives": "Real readers conceive of canonical fictional language (that is, narrative without a narrator) as self-constituting rather than emanating from a fictional teller" (Galbraith 1995: 32). Jahn's argument is somewhat akin to Galbraith's position, which he quotes approvingly (cf. Jahn 1999: 103–04). Jahn is of course right to criticize what he considers to be the "attributive fallacy" and what shall be termed here an institutionalist-logical understanding of the attributive frame. However, the fact that Jahn resorts to the term "conative solicitude" (borrowed from Bonheim; cf. Jahn 1997: 456) is particularly telling. This terms at least suggest that texts that are highly aware and expressive of their attributing activity and of their orientation towards the addressee (in Jakobson's term) are "solicitous", i.e. overly and redundantly meticulous in a register which in fictional texts "goes without saying" on institutional and conventional grounds[4].

In the following, I aim to group the extended range of stylistic expressivity under a less evaluative version of the term "overtness". In doing so, I assume that the conditions for "covert narration" have sufficiently been detailed in the many models which add refinements to internal focalization. What is left out of Jahn's cognitive account is precisely that some types of narration do in fact foreground and expand the narratorial frame

3 In his rhetorical approach to fictionality, Walsh discusses the concept of voice in three senses, as "instance," as "idiom," and as "interpellation" (cf. Walsh 2006: 89-101).

4 Although Bonheim needs to be credited for his awareness that authors like Henry James are "real acrobats of the inquit" (Bonheim 1982: 78), Collier comments that in fact Bonheim "displays a covert endorsement of unobtrusive or minimal tagging" (Collier 1991/1992: 48).

and the concomitant indirectness, and that this expansion fulfils the added narrative function of reflecting the act of delegation itself. Both Chatman's and Jahn's interpretive moves are variations of the similar assumption that the metaphor "invade" must presuppose either a narrator or a character as agent or deictic centre. Jahn's conception of "ambient focalisation" (Jahn 1999: 98), which may be that of an overt communal narrator who adopts or substitutes the perception of one or more characters, comes close to the descriptive-summary textual phenomena that will be studied in section 5 of this article. Yet, despite the sophistication of Jahn's account, he continues to define in negative terms as vagueness and lack of spatio-temporal situatedness what is in fact—in terms of style—a highly profiled, interpellative dimension of narrativity. In what follows, I aim to consider how reading in terms of overtness may thwart the very effort of ascribing such stylistic traits to either narrator or character, inviting us to consider the concept of narrative agency in relation to that of stylistic agency.

3 Concepts of Overtness: A Critical Round-Up

Before I go on to theorize perspective in relation to agency, some further terminological clarifications are in place. First, I need to clarify what exactly is meant by overt narration. Overt narration (from the French *ouvert*, in turn derived from Latin *aperire*) "can comment both on the content of the narration (story world) and on the narrating function itself; the address to a narratee is a part of this meta-narrative performance" (Fludernik 1993: 443). Especially heterodiegetic overt narration continues to be associated with older texts[5]. Within the scope of this article, it is not possible to discuss the conceptual history of overt narration. It needs to be noted that in Stanzel's version of overt narratorial mediacy, the speaker is

[5] Prince defines overtness as "a narrator presenting situations and events with more than a minimum of narratorial mediation, an intrusive narrator." He only refers to classical texts as evidence: "*Eugénie Grandet, Barchester Towers, Tom Jones, Tristram Shandy*" (Prince 1988: 69). In a passionate attack on the "neo-modernist" leanings of Genette's system, Sternberg argues that "assumptions that omniscience's time has passed" are "counterfactual" and stated "in blissful disregard for the evidence" (Sternberg 2008: 716). According to Sternberg, Genette and even more his followers fashion "zero-focalisation" as "marginal and uninteresting, if at all discussible" (715), whereas this "licensed excess of knowledge" (715) is rather common and not limited to mythological or biblical, law-making narrative with its typical epithetic overtness.

necessarily personified. In Stanzel's opinion, the authorial narrator leads us to infer the role of a companiable, talkative, intrusive speaker very similar to Wayne Booth's "dramatized narrator". Stanzel exempted from what I would call the overt type of narrative mediacy summaries, gnomic comments and synoptic titles (as typical of satirical literature), which he regarded as a kind of degree zero of narrativity or even non-narrative "direct information". Stanzel's theory features a second, covert type of mediacy as the dominant trend of modern(ist) literature, in which the reflector-character functions as a kind of autonomous "medium", escaping the narrator's control as mediating agent. It is not so much the way in which Stanzel juxtaposed these two types of mediacy, but rather the organicist overtones of his terminology and its visualization that met with critique[6]. Genette is less outspoken about overtness. While Genette maintains that the structuralist-linguistic inspiration of his model as well the specific case of Proust (with special reference to metaphor) cut across and foreclose in principle any (backwards-)compatibility with the telling-showing distinction (cf. Genette 1972: 188), a kind of ironic dialogue with the standard definition of overt narration is carried out in the footnotes. Although Genette playfully denegates a penchant for "Flaubert, James, and Hemingway" at the expense of "Fielding, Sterne, and Thomas Mann" (Genette 1988: 54), he distances himself ironically from the authorial style of Fielding in a footnote (cf. Genette 1988: 95) and finally leaves the business of stylistics (which is still relevant to Stanzel's definition of colouring) to linguistic predecessors (52). Both Stanzel and—to a lesser extent—Genette take into consideration overtness, accompanied either by aperspectivism or zero-focalization. But in both cases, the aforementioned "telling-style" utterances are mainly held to affect and thematize the status of fictionality, they are judged to display a typified, standardized capacity whose actual textual surface is only relevant in quantitative terms of presence and visibility (see also Martens [2008]). Apart from being embedded in a different interpretation of the rhetorical tradition, the apotropaic gestures towards extreme summary mentioned above may have a common ground: In non-fictional narrative, telling-style phenomena like summary, abstract and metanarrativity are very much linked to their institutional speech act functions: they are

6 In this respect, see also the thoughtful contribution to this volume by Tatjana Jesch and Malte Stein, pages 59–77.

meant to signal that instead of turn-based interaction, a longer stretch of narrative report is coming up next (cf. Zipfel 2001: 130). There is no explicit need to signal this in fiction, although several authors (from Sterne to Robert Walser) see stylistic opportunities in questioning this institutional self-evidence.

Although it could be argued that neutral functional descriptions of narrators as instances of mediation do exist (cf. e.g. Nünning 1997), especially theories that conceptualize the "role" of the narrator in terms of a more neutral logical necessity (cf. Ryan 1981), a set of narratorial functions (cf. Ryan 2001) or a deictic field of orientation, tend to assume that the narratorial level of transmission or attributive quotationality functions as a kind of "stylistic default". Basically, they tend to discuss narratorial discourse as "a neutral and merely functional ground on which the peculiarities of characters' diction in passages of free indirect discourse are set into relief" (Fludernik 2001b: 627). This conception entails the institutionalist-logical account of narratorial agency as exemplified in the discussion of *Eveline*. It may explain the basically substitutional quest for either "plain production sentences" as expressive of the narrator's idiom or "plain action sentences" as embedded focalization. This conception of agency inevitably pitches the local and particularized agent of focalization against the logical but (ideally) reduced agency of the overall narration. This conception ultimately rests on the assumption that vision is a more flexible, individualized and diverse (multi-facetted) quality (cf. Warhol 1996; Horstkotte 2005), whereas the prominence and indirectness of the overt narratorial framing discourse is deemed potentially detrimental to the readers' immersive activity: On account of its proximity to a "voice of a collective subject, [...] offered in a mode of persuasion" (Culler 2004: 31), Culler assumes it to be more prone to become the mouthpiece of generalization, typification and standardization[7]. In fact, Chatman's own usage of the term "overtness", as illustrated in the *Eveline* example above, and his explanatory distinction between the narrator's "slant" and the characters' "filter" promptly testify to the institutionalist conception of agency illustrated above: "slant" casts "the narrator's attitudes and other mental nuances" as a kind of ontological "attitude" and bias which the poor narrator cannot really help. "Slant captures the psychological, sociological, and ideological ramifications of the narrator's attitudes,

[7] See, however, Nünning's concept of "secondary mimesis" (cf. Nünning 2001: 21).

which may range from neutral to highly charged" (Chatman 1990: 143). "Filter", on the other hand, is intended to give a more positive and active twist to "the much wider range of mental activity experienced by characters in the story world—perceptions, cognitions, attitudes, emotions, memories, fantasies, and the like" (Chatman 1990: 143). Shifting away from the polemical overtones used to treat overtness in terms of "(omni)-presence,"[8] Fludernik rightly stressed the local nature and functional flexibility of the signals responsible for the "establishment of internal perspective through the deictic centre" (Fludernik 2001a: 107). The same focus on "small-scale linguistic features that trigger readers' establishment of narrators, reflectors, and observers" (102–03) needs to be applied to the markers of overtness. Unlike first-person overt narration, which is currently widely discussed in the instantiation of unreliable homodiegetic narration, anonymous overt narration often refuses or fails to pay off in terms of extracting or divinating both the real "persona" of the narrator or in extracting the real past course of events and causalities obfuscated in the overly phatic communication itself. The overt comment on the performance may take the form of an "axiological overdetermination" (Schmid 2005: 79) without growing into a personified presence. It is strictly this type of non-personified overtness I will be concerned with in this article.

While personified, psychologically motivated overtness has been widely discussed with regard to homodiegetic or unreliable narration, its anonymous counterpart, which is prominent but nevertheless lacking in clear-cut spatio-temporal situatedness and "individuating features" (Nünning 2001: 212) cannot adequately be discussed in terms of experience or individual perception. What threatens to get obfuscated by this stress on the mental and the receptive is precisely a neutral assessment of the interactive nature and function of overt narration, which can be said to occur no less frequently[9]. In conversational story-telling, a narrator, instead of

---

8 In Chatman's view, an overt narrator is necessarily a distinct, personified agent. The overt narrator "writes of the burdens of authorship, modestly disavows artistic competence, speaks freely of the need to push this narrative button, tip that lever, and apply a brake now and then [...]. This squeaky machinery may annoy us if we are overly committed to the smoothly purring Jamesian style, and it hardly inspires a profound contemplation of the nature of narrative artifice" (Chatman 1978: 248).

9 In this respect, see also Nünning's foregrounding of the narrator function (cf. Nünning 2001: 39).

setting out to embody or quote the actual words and intonation of a speaker (letting other people in on the actual experience), frequently makes short shrift of this speech or thought representation by abstracting the conversation, using epithets, metaphors and proverbs to characterize the general speech habitus of the represented person rather than the actual event or content. Such narrative performances are characterized by dissociation, distancing, disengagement rather than by immersion. In this respect, we enter the domain of distancing and irony, not devoid of conative (but by no means imperative) and phatic aspects of bonding (confiding) with the addressee at the expense of the reported experience. In this type of narration, one can foreground the experiental clues it offers in relation to an inferred speaker, but one can also highlight the extent to which the level of ongoing communication (with its addressee-oriented rhetoric) outweighs the past experience reduced to summary. By exempting from default narrativity the more resultative or evaluative summary and thought report typical of overt and authorial narration, one risks to ignore a dimension of style that is bound to fail the deictic substitution test because it is established in a more dynamic, interpellative way. Both Herman (cf. 2002: 365) and Palmer (cf. 2004: 57, 59) already warned that this stress on internality may run the risk of implying a certain degree of egocentricity in narratological terminology. Herman argues in favour of resituating deixis in a wider, more sociocentric "network of (more or less) virtualized speech positions" (366).

Ultimately, Herman's aim to discuss focalization in terms of "experiential repertoires" and competences differs from the present article's concern to discern types of stylistic agency that may run counter to storyworld agency. In what follows, I will contrast the standard approach to overtness (as intrusive, opinionated comment, hinging on an a priori personified speech position) with a possible alternative: according to this alternative conception, readers may infer, on the basis of figurative constellations and other stylistic phenomena, marked shifts in agency which supplement or even rival the more common (grammatical, deictic) indexes of narratorial agency. To that purpose, I shall discern a free-floating dimension of stylistic overtness, which is more likely to obtain in the case of (but not limited to) an overt profiling of the narratorial discourse. Such a more flexible and dynamic understanding of narrative agency has already been reached by focusing on areas in which the agency of narration is less dependent on prototypical historical instantiations, as in the thorough theorization of hybrid "you"-narration by Monika Fludernik and

David Herman. In contrast to first or third-person narration, "you"-narration, by virtue of its double appeal to both the virtual-imaginable and the particular, turns out to be rather indeterminate in terms of attributing internality or externality. One of its striking features is that it challenges readers to negotiate and compare the suggested "experiential repertoires" (Herman 2002: 344) wavering between actual and virtual experience. Below, I will not focus on "you"-narration nor on metaphor, which would require a more sustained text-related approach. Instead, I will focus on what I think poses a similar challenge to the narratological enterprise, namely on less straightforwardly deictic elements of anchoring, as evidenced in rhetorical and stylistic aspects of narrative texts such as summary characterization and *praeteritio*.

4 A Rhetorical Approach to Stylistic Agency

As one of the most straightforward and palpable elements of the establishment of internal perspective, one tends to rely on familiarizing elements such as "etic" (Stanzel 1979: 216) descriptions and the familiarizing article. That such familiarizing strategies may cease to function as seemingly automatic cataleptic references and intuitive "figural triggers" when set within texts of overt narration can be illustrated with reference to the Swiss author Robert Walser. In many cases, Walser's narrators feel the need to explicate straightforward deictic references by means of parentheses.

> the hot-headed lout of a Pole, that is, none other than our Master Steward happened to surprise me at my quiet, attentive reading. (Walser 1990: 88)
> Concerning a keg of the finest rye whiskey that, to the delight of the steward and that of a certain additional person—namely to my very own, grinning, hand-rubbing delight—showed up only to be closely inspected and quite thoroughly investigated and examined by the two abovementioned important or insignificant personages, I shall take care not to waste another word. (Walser 1990: 88)

While going in many, even contradictive evaluative directions, these utterances do not really allow for the inference of a troubled, yet consistent individual mind. In fact, they point to an interface for which the interaction with the reader ("our") is a constant task, sublimated in a quasi-automated display of codes of politeness, confession and self-referentiality. A variation of this technique is particularly exploited in Walser's highly overtly narrated *Der Räuber* (1925, published posthumously 1972), in which the inescapably thetic and artificial quality of the figural trigger is foregrounded:

> The Robber now came to a house that was no longer present, or, to say it better, to an old house that had been demolished on account of its age and now no longer stood there, inasmuch as it had ceased to make itself noticed. He came, then, in short, to a place where, in former days, a house had stood. These detours I'm making serve the end of filling time, for I really must pull off a book of considerable length, otherwise I'll be even more deeply despised than I am now. (Walser 2000: 74–75)

Walser's narrator stumbles over the fact that one assumes focalization to be silently maintained: the accumulative utterances concerning "an old house that is no longer there" markedly refuse to lend experiential credibility to this perception, which normally would familiarize the reader with a real or virtual observer within the textual world[10]. The narrator goes to great lengths to clarify that probably the "house that was no longer there" had been demolished due to old age. The statement that the house "had ceased to make itself noticed" is of course, by the time it occurs, a performative self-contradiction from the readers' point of view. The digressive legitimations lead up to the mock (metacompositional) motivation that the accumulation of verbal material is there for the book to be long enough. Here the narrator slips into the present tense, with clear-cut metaleptic overtones. The stylistic "detours" of the narratorial discourse, motivated by the need to produce "a book of considerable length," continue to resonate with an agent covering a lot of distance in the storyworld. Throughout this novel, the narrator keeps on linking his (or, given Walser's unsettling narration, one could also say her) own spatio-temporal position and motion as intradiegetic observer with the quantitative aspects of the operation of both narrating and writing—and ultimately the reader's "progression" through the novel. This is a classic and playful case of overt narration: the reference to material writing acts as a comment on the performance of the narration. In addition, the quote illustrates in a striking—though ambiguous—way that overt heterodiegetic-extradiegetic narration can no longer simply be equated with "performative authoritativeness" (Culler 2004: 26). Although seemingly redun-

10 In order to make the stylistic contrast clear: Joyce's *Eveline* unequivocally integrates a similar reference to a disappeared object within the (however distal) deictic spatio-temporal frame of the character: "One time there used to be a field there in which they used to play every evening with other people's children" (Joyce 1961: 34).

dant, the contrived stylistic variation points to an underlying logic of *amplificatio* which at times suggests that the quantity of the verbal and its materiality playfully reflects and iconically mimics its content[11]. In referring to the first Walser-passage, one may be reminded of Booth's attempts to demonstrate the impossibility of a narrative that remains fully within the compass of a single character (cf. Booth 1989). However, the latter's hypothetical formulations were somewhat contrived and precisely geared towards displacing the modernist canon. Instead, I argue that this passage points towards lesser-known conative and otherwise rhetorical aspects of narrative communication, which may obtain both in homo- and in heterodiegetic narration.

The purpose of the analysis of the next example in this section is to illustrate that stylistic overtness does not necessarily signal a narration fully in control of things. In fact, stylistic overtness may attach to narrators whose stated ambition it is to remain covert. This can briefly be illustrated by means of Günter Grass' novella *Im Krebsgang*. Grass' novella installs a homodiegetic narrator who aims to remain at a distance from the events to be related: the narrator, a journalist by profession, survived the sinking of the *Wilhelm Gustloff* in his mother's womb. In its multi-tiered frame narrative, the novella displays an awareness of its attributive indirectness, which is meant to caution against self-victimization and the retrospective attribution of causality. Grass' narrator does so by means of the master trope of the crab's movement (*seitlich ausscherend*, scuttling sideways) as well as with numerous caveats against the self-propelling and self-serving nature of non-reflexive narrativization, summed up by the mechanical activity of "abspulen" (cf. Grass 2002: 8, 54; "unreeling"). Nevertheless, his attempt at distance is thwarted on the thematic level by the fact that the narrator's son Konrad turns out to have committed a crime inspired by the historical events. Based on his apologetic stance towards anti-Semitism and Nazi ideology, Konny killed an internet friend whom he thought to be Jewish and who had defended the sinking of the ship as a legitimate act of retribution. In this context, it is all the more striking to see that the narrator momentarily lapses from his self-awareness and his

---

[11] "Snow does not fall lickety-split, but slowly, i.e. bit by bit, which means flake by flake, down to the earth." (Walser 2002: 135) Originally in German: "Schnee fällt nicht Knall auf Knall, sondern langsam, d.h. nach und nach, will sagen flockenweise zur Erde" (Walser 1978: 369).

stylistic control of the narration. At a crucial point in the novel, the narrator summarizes his son's speech of defence in court: "After that Konrad offered a fairly vivid account of the state funeral rites in Schwerin."[12] Konrad refers to the historical event in Schwerin commemorating the Nazi Wilhelm Gustloff, who had been murdered by a Jew. Although the narrator says that Konny's evocation of this event was both ample as well as "bildhaft" (colorful, vivid), the narrator carefully aims to bracket and evacuate its ideological bias by means of the passing summary. In addition, the meta-narrative utterance "ablaufen" continues to stress the mechanical and foreseeable aspects of Konrad's act of narrating[13], and the causative use of "lassen" strategically mixes quasi-metaleptic implications of causation with connotations of "allowing for, indulging". All the while the narrator's summary aims to convey that Konrad's evocation of the event is biased. The narration's conundrum at this point can be summarized as follows: the narrator's summary is there in order to avoid giving the floor to an ideological type of discourse which it frames as highly infectious and conative. Yet, in order not to do so, it has to make use of the same linguistic strategies of partiality. While this might be considered to be a momentary lapse, still setting off the narrator's self-consciousness from the "tabloid-style sensationalism" (Dye 2004: 481) employed by Konny, it is hard to ignore the fact that, by similar means, the novel frames not only the ideology but also the youth's preferred medium (internet communication) in its entirety as suspect, conatively solicitous and liable to abuse.

Despite the narrator's declared intention to remain unobtrusive, the stylistic option discussed constitutes a kind of stylistic overtness which leads the reader to reflect on the very mechanism of delegation and attribution. The strategic decision to reduce reflectorial delegation is rooted in either frequent situational constraints (in conversational story-telling) or in deliberate decisions of narrators not to spell out the dialogue or the "in actu presentation" of thought and perception designated by Jahn as "mind-style" (Jahn 1996: 257). One could interpret the ensuing texture as another sign of the I, as a sign of the narrator's judgmental or mental dis-

---

12 "Danach ließ Konrad den in Schwerin abgefeierten Staatstrauerakt ziemlich bildhaft ablaufen" (Grass 2002: 190). Here, as in the following, English translations of German texts are mine, if not indicated otherwise.

13 Cf. "[D]och setzte sich die Rede meines Sohnes wie selbsttätig fort" (Grass 2002: 191); "But my son's speech sped on, as if under its own steam" (Grass 2004: 206).

tance, but that would ignore its dynamic nature as an interferential, compound phenomenon.

In literary studies, such strategic bracketing of access to a character's mindset continues be associated with ironic and satirical purposes, although in fact recent research has shown that the narrative function of stylistic agency extends well beyond this particular usage (cf. Biebuyck 2007). In the case of the "acrobats of the inquit" (cf. Bonheim) I will briefly deal with in the following, it is quite obvious that the information is not presented as a result of action or as we "may have speculatively come to learn" (Culler 2004: 31), but by way of parentheses and appositions, highlighting iterative and typical features of characters that often anticipate further developments. Nevertheless, such drastic parentheses are even to be found in modernist novels normally considered to be devoted to the expansion of figural viewpoint(s):

> Mamsell Jungmann, who was now already 35 years old and who could pride herself on having withered away at the service of affluent circles [...]. (Mann, *Buddenbrooks*, 1901: 159)

> Clarisse's governess—a family heir-loom, pensioned off in the honourable guise of serving as an assistant mother [...]. (Musil, *The Man Without Qualities,* 1930: 902)

In its more moderate form, the iterative and incriminating description may match the common, socially codified disregard of servants of that period. In its extreme form of thematized narratorial command either enhancing or disrupting fictionality, it climaxes in the topos of the narrator losing sight of characters or forcefully "throwing" characters out of the novel.

> And what about his brother Fritz? We make no secret of it that he does not interest us. Not a single word from his mouth has been handed down to us. Even if it had been handed down, it would not interest us. (Schneider, *Schlafes Bruder*, 1992: 51) [14]

This kind of abbreviation mainly affects *personae minores*. Whereas the appositions could be explained as a placeholder while a crucial phase in the biography of a more important character is recounted, iterative characterization can also occur during center-stage events. This is the case in

---

[14] For more violent ways of eliminating potential perspective-bearers with metaleptic overtones, see Deupmann (2001) on Doderer. In most cases mentioned so far, the iterative description of flat characters is accompanied by hypothetical focalizations: see also the exit of the midwife in Schneider (1992: 19–20).

Musil's *The Man without Qualities*, when the attempt to find a single unifying "idea" for the modern age is abandoned:

> a Frau Weghuber, a manufacturer's wife with an impressive record of charitable works and *quite impervious to any idea that there might be something more pressing than the objects of her concern*, rose promptly to her feet. She advanced a proposal for a Greater Austrian Franz Josef Soup Kitchen to the meeting, which listened politely. [...] Had they [="those present"] been asked on their way to this meeting whether they knew what historical events or great events of that sort were, they would certainly have replied in the affirmative; but confronted with the weighty imperative of making up such an event on the spot, they slowly began to feel faint, and something like rumblings of a very natural nature stirred inside them. (Musil 1930: 183–84; italics added)

In this case, the apposition is underscored by the ensuing hypothetical focalization which, through its stylistic dissonance, highlights the impossibility for the characters to articulate or even allow for the recognition of this mundane feeling (i.e. of hunger) themselves. This summary characterization may seem outrageously biased against the character(s) and may strike many readers as parody. However, such appositional shortcuts possess a jarring, satirizing effect of paralepsis only in texts that adhere to presenting events in a more or less realistic way and that abide by the unity and primacy of the storyworld as the focus of narrativity. In the case of Musil's meta-novel, however, this narrative short-circuiting even affects the protagonist. Although his mindset is rendered more consonantly, the protagonist is not exempted from similar abbreviations, such as the lopsided and quasi-tautological reference that "two weeks later" he had had a lover "for fourteen days" (Musil 1930: 26). While expressive of the modernist suspicion of the retrospective establishment of narrative causality, the overtness goes to signal that there is in fact no unpredicated version of a reality that one could get to know otherwise[15].

One could of course argue that "diegetic summary, focusing exclusively on the commonality of the topic and ignoring individual variations of manner and inner verbalization," with its inherent tendency towards "typification, schematization of recognizable shared stances, perspectives, views or common opinions" (Margolin 2000: 605) is straining the nature of narrativity as such. In fact, it has been argued, that its occurrence is in fact more widespread in (hybrid) essayistic writing, "sociological and

---

[15] Since I deal with this at length elsewhere, the reader is referred to the examples and markers of overtness I quote and discuss in Martens (2006).

historical discourses" (Margolin 2000: 606) or even more appropriate to journalism or lyrical writing (cf. Margolin 2001: 253). Ultimately, this touches upon culturally determined preferences, i.e. the question whether we see the narrative representation of reality as emanating from individual mental activity rather than vested in a collective interaction, ridden with argumentative and imaginative moves as a kind of contest of perspectives.

Stylistic overt agency comprises more than the conventionalized illusion-shattering display of personified narratorial agency. There is a wide variety of less spectacular forms of authorial mediation that obtain more than just a metafictional or metacompositional valency: the use of parenthesis and apposition (cf. Martens 2006), "distancing appellations" (Cohn 2000: 137), "alienating comments" (143) and various degrees of nominalization and appropriation (cf. Fludernik 1993) need to be taken into account in order to systematize the effects of narratorial overtness. "Diegetic summary, content paraphrase" (Rimmon-Kenan 2002: 109), and we could add: gnomic we-utterances can be a narratively productive undertaking too[16]. More than often in those cases "representation is schematic in content and projected rather than quoted in its verbalization" (Margolin 2000: 606), yet, as illustrated in the passage by Günter Grass, such rhetorical and stylistic features may encode an alternative version of agency, thus acting as a kind of prosody of narrative performance or a diacritical surplus adding focus to the information distribution. This allows for the conclusion that the scope of overtness "is finally realized to be greater than the occasional slippage into the first person" (Aczel 1998: 472). Elements of stylistic agency may reinforce the profile of an individual narrator, but they may also refuse to reinforce deictic localization; in such case, they rather supplement or even contradict the construction of well-defined focalizers or narrators (e.g. when imagery fails to be classified as either diegetic or non-diegetic). If one accepts the idea that stylistic agency may reshape the profile of narrative agents (cf. Martens & Biebuyck 2007: 355-356), this phenomenon can be treated as the paranarrative dimension of narrative communication, which in itself does not

[16] Whilst only gnomic utterances have made it into Stanzel's theory of narrative, De Temmerman (2007) sets out to reinsert the broader rhetorical techniques of characterization (such as *chreia*) as outlined in the *progymnasmata* into narrative studies.

result in the construction of a distinctive agent next to focalizers or narrators: figurativeness as "second order agency"

> does not give rise to the construction of a second order agent, a paranarrator or a paracomposer. For it is clearly the recipient who performs or carries out the actions, even though he or she is nothing more than the executor. [...] there is not one single narrating "voice" to be detected in the paranarrative; the figurative forms always entail a multiplicity of voices. (Biebuyck 2007)

The paranarrative is similar, but not entirely assimilable to related concepts such as hypothetical focalization (cf. Herman) and the disnarrated (cf. Prince). The paranarrative differs from the widely known aspects of metanarrativity in that the former does not give rise to the inference of a personified textual agent. It should have become sufficiently clear by now that considering narratorial discourse as either an intrusive blockage or a neutral stylistic default from which to distinguish character perspectives poses problems when dealing with the stylistic aspects of overt narration. When analyzing the agency of narration as a kind of interactional relay of information, even stylistic elements acting precisely as an impediment to the attribution of individualized perspective can be considered as functional parts of that interaction.

Conclusion

The outline presented here proposes a redefinition of the scope of overt narration. This redefinition has taken as its point of departure the observation that the techniques and strategies of narrators going covert are well-documented and currently even being expanded, whereas the conception of narratorial agency as either a "stylistic default" or an opinionated intrusion is itself difficult to reconcile with the objectives of stylistics and rhetorical narratology. Instead, the criteria for stylistic overtness, often unilaterally considered to be non-narrative schematic descriptions or illusion-shattering disruptions of fictionality, contribute to alternative versions of stylistic agency. Hence, this article has documented a number of stylistic, rhetorical and narrative elements (especially in the domain of summary and epithet-like descriptions) that are not straightforwardly deictic and yet relevant to narrative agency. These elements can be said to primarily invite a reflexive reconsideration of the agency involved in the act of narration. Further studies will need to systematize in what ways the agency of narration relates to rhetorical and argumentative patterns present in texts. As such, the hypothesis of stylistic agency is a topic in need of further investigation with relation to a broader corpus[17].

References

Aczel, Richard (1998). "Hearing Voices in Narrative Texts." *New Literary History* 29: 3, 467–500.

– (2005). "Voice." D. Herman et al. (eds). *The Routledge Encyclopedia of Narrative Theory*. London: Routledge, 633–36.

Attridge, David (1990): "Reading Joyce." D. Attridge (ed). *The Cambridge Companion to James Joyce*. Cambridge: Cambridge UP, 1–30.

Barthes, Roland (1966). "Introduction à l'analyse structurale des récits." R. Barthes et al.: *Poétique du récit*. Paris: Seuil, 1977, 1–57.

Biebuyck, Benjamin (2007). "Figurativeness figuring as a Condenser between Event and Action. How Tropes Generate Additional Dimensions of Narrativity." *Amsterdam International Electronic Journal for Cultural Narratology* 4. Electronic publication at <http://cf.hum.uva.nl/narratology/a07_biebuyck.htm>.

Bonheim, Helmut (1982). *The Narrative Modes: Techniques of the Short-Story*. Cambridge: Brewer.

Booth, Wayne (1989). "Are Narrative Choices Subject to Ethical Criticism?" J. Phelan (ed). *Reading Narrative: Form, Ethics, Ideology*. Columbus: Ohio State UP, 57–78.

Chatman, Seymour (1978). *Story and Discourse: Narrative Structure in Fiction and Film*. Ithaca: Cornell UP.

– (1990). *Coming to Terms. The Rhetoric of Narrative in Fiction and Film*. Ithaca: Cornell UP.

Cohn, Dorrit (2000). *The Distinction of Fiction*. Baltimore: The Johns Hopkins UP.

Collier, Gordon (1991/1992). "Style at the interface: Speech-tags." *REAL* 8, 33–107.

Culler, Jonathan (2004). "Omniscience." *Narrative* 12:1, 22–34.

De Temmerman, Koen (2007). "A Narrator of Wisdom. Characterization through gnomai in Achilles Tatius." <http://www.princeton.edu/~pswpc/pdfs/detemmerman/030701.pdf> (17.07.2008).

Deupmann, Christoph (2001). "Ein fragwürdiges Kapitel. Erzählte Gewalt und gewalthaftes Erzählen bei Heimito von Doderer." *Text+Kritik. Zeitschrift für Literatur*, Vol. 150: Heimito von Doderer, 48–56.

Dye, Elizabeth (2004). "'Weil die Geschichte nicht aufhört': Günter Grass's *Im Krebsgang*." *German Life and Letters* 57:4, 472–87.

Fludernik, Monika (1993). *The Fictions of Language and the Languages of Fiction: the Linguistic Representation of Speech and Consciousness*. London: Routledge.

– (1996). *Towards a "Natural" Narratology*. London: Routledge.

[17] The author is Postdoctoral Research Fellow of the Fund for Scientific Research—Flanders. I wish to thank the anonymous reviewers and the editors for their suggestions.

– (2001a). "The Establishment of Internal Focalization in Odd Pronominal Contexts." W. van Peer & S. Chatman (eds). *New Perspectives on Narrative Perspective.* Albany: SUNY Press, 101–13.
– (2001b). "New Wine in Old Bottles? Voice, Focalization, and New Writing." *New Literary History* 32:3, 619–38.
Füger, Wilhelm (1993). "Stimmbrüche: Varianten und Spielräume narrativer Fokalisation." H. Foltinek et al. (eds). *Tales and "their telling difference": Zur Theorie und Geschichte der Narrativik. Festschrift für Franz K. Stanzel.* Heidelberg: Winter, 43–60.
Galbraith, Mary (1995). "Deictic shift theory and the poetics of involvement in narrative." J. F. Duchan et al. (eds). *Deixis in Narrative: a cognitive science perspective.* Hissdale, NJ: Lawrence Erlbaum, 19–60.
Genette, Gérard (1972) : "Discours du récit." *Figures III.* Paris: Seuil, 65–282.
– (1980). *Narrative Discourse.* Tr. J. E. Lewin. Oxford: Blackwell.
– (1983). *Nouveau discours du récit.* Paris: Seuil.
– (1988). *Narrative Discourse Revisited.* Tr. J. E. Lewin. Ithaca: Cornell UP
Grass, Günter (2002). *Im Krebsgang. Eine Novelle.* Munich: DTV.
– (2004). *Crabwalk.* Tr. K. Winston. New York: Harvest Books.
Herman, David (2001). "Towards a Socionarratology. New Ways of Analyzing Natural-Language Narratives." W. van Peer & S. Chatman (eds). *New Perspectives on Narrative Perspective.* Albany: SUNY Press, 218–46.
– (2002). *Story Logic: Problems and Possibilities of Narrative.* Lincoln: U of Nebraska P.
Horstkotte, Silke (2005). "The Double Dynamics of Focalization in W. G. Sebald's *The Rings of Saturn.*" J. C. Meister (ed). *Narratology beyond Literary Criticism. Mediality, Disciplinarity.* Berlin: de Gruyter, 25–44.
Jahn, Manfred (1996). "Windows of focalization: deconstructing and reconstructing a narratological concept." *Style* 30, 241–67.
– (1997). "Frames, Preferences, and the Reading of Third-Person Narratives: Towards a Cognitive Narratology." *Poetics Today* 18:4, 441–68.
– (1999). "More Aspects of Focalization: Refinements and Applications." *GRAAT* 21, 85–110.
Joyce, James (1961). *Dubliners.* Harmondsworth: Penguin.
Mann, Thomas (1901). *Buddenbrooks. Verfall einer Familie.* Frankfurt a. M.: Fischer, 1975.
Margolin, Uri (2000). "Telling in the Plural: From Grammar to Ideology." *Poetics Today* 21:3, 591–618.
– (2001). "Collective Perspective, Individual Perspective, and the Speaker in Between: On 'We' Literary Narratives." W. van Peer & S. Chatman (eds). *New Perspectives on Narrative Perspective.* Albany: SUNY Press, 241–55.
Martens, Gunther (2006). *Beobachtungen der Moderne in Hermann Brochs "Die Schlafwandler" und Robert Musils "Der Mann ohne Eigenschaften". Rhetorische und narratologische Aspekte von Interdiskursivität.* Munich: Fink.
– (2008). "Revising and extending the scope of the rhetorical approach to unreliable narration." E. D'hoker & G. Martens (eds). *Narrative Unreliability in the Twentieth-Century First-Person Novel.* Berlin: de Gruyter, 77–105.

Martens, Gunther & Biebuyck, Benjamin (2007). "On the Narrative Function of Metonymy in Chapter XIV of Heine's *Ideen. Das Buch Le Grand.*" *Style* 41:3, 342–65.

Musil, Robert (1930). *The Man without Qualities*. Tr. S. Wilkins. New York: Picador, 1997.

Nünning, Ansgar (1997). "Die Funktionen von Erzählinstanzen: Analysekategorien und Modelle zur Beschreibung des Erzählerverhaltens." *Literatur in Wissenschaft und Unterricht* 30:4, 323–49.

– (2001). "On the Perspective Structure of Narrative Texts: Steps toward a Constructivist Narratology." W. van Peer & S. Chatman (eds). *New Perspectives on Narrative Perspective*. Albany: SUNY Press, 209–23.

Prince, Gerald (1988). *A Dictionary of Narratology*. Aldershot: Scolar P.

Rimmon-Kenan, Shlomith (2002). *Narrative Fiction: Contemporary Poetics*. London: Routledge.

Ryan, Marie-Laure (1981). "The Pragmatics of Personal and Impersonal Fiction." *Poetics* 10:6, 517–39.

– (2001). "The Narratorial Functions: Breaking Down a Theoretical Primitive." *Narrative* 9:2, 146–52.

Schmid, Wolf (2005). *Elemente der Narratologie*. Berlin: de Gruyter.

Schneider, Robert (1992). *Schlafes Bruder. Roman*. Leipzig: Reclam.

Stanzel, Franz K. (1979). *Theorie des Erzählens*. Göttingen: Vandenhoeck & Ruprecht.

Sternberg, Meir (2007). "Omniscience in Narrative Construction: Challenges Old and New." *Poetics Today* 28:4, 683–794.

Walsh, Richard (2007): *The Rhetoric of Fictionality. Narrative Theory and the Idea of Fiction*. Columbus: The Ohio State UP.

Warhol, Robyn R. (1996). "The Look, the Body, and the Heroine of Persuasion: A Feminist-Narratological View of Jane Austen." K. Mazei (ed). *Ambiguous Discourse: Feminist Narratology and British Women Writers*. Chapel Hill: U of North Carolina P, 21–39.

Walser, Robert (1972). *Der Räuber. Roman*. Frankfurt a. M.: Suhrkamp, 1986.

– (1978). "Winter." *Das Gesamtwerk VIII. Verstreute Prosa I. (1907–1919)*. Frankfurt a. M.: Suhrkamp.

– (1990). "Tobold II." *Masquerade and Other Stories*. Tr. S. Bernofsky. Baltimore: The Johns Hopkins UP, 80–100.

– (2000). *The Robber*. Tr. S. Bernofsky. Lincoln: U of Nebraska P.

– (2002). *Selected Stories*. Tr. C. Middleton. New York: NYRB Classics.

Zipfel, Frank (2001). *Fiktion, Fiktivität, Fiktionalität. Analysen zur Fiktion in der Literatur und zum Fiktionsbegriff in der Literaturwissenschaft*. Berlin: Schmidt.

DAVID HERMAN
(Columbus, OH)

Beyond Voice and Vision: Cognitive Grammar and Focalization Theory

1 Introduction

1.1 Perspective, Construal, and Cognitive Narratology

This essay draws on ideas from cognitive linguistics to explore the structure and dynamics of narrative perspective[1]. More specifically, I suggest the advantages of supplementing narratological accounts of focalization with cognitive-grammatical research on construal or conceptualization—factoring in related ideas developed by Leonard Talmy (2000) under the rubric of cognitive semantics. In the approach outlined here, perspective takes its place among a wider array of construal operations—ways of organizing and making sense of domains of experience—that are anchored in humans' embodied existence and that may be more or less fully exploited by a given narrative. Besides attempting to recontextualize previous frameworks for research on narrative perspective, my essay also has a broader goal: namely, to suggest that by incorporating into the domain of narrative analysis research exploring the nexus of language, mind, and world, theorists can help promote the development of cognitive narratology as one of a number of "postclassical" approaches to narrative inquiry. At issue are frameworks for narrative study that build on the work of classical, structuralist narratologists but enrich that work with concepts and methods that were unavailable to story analysts such as Roland Barthes, Gérard Genette, Algirdas J. Greimas, and Tzvetan Todorov du-

---

1 Herman (forthcoming a) sketches a less developed version of part of the analysis presented more fully in section 2 of this essay. I am grateful to Jeroen Vandaele for insightful comments and criticisms that led to revisions of the earlier version of the analysis and that also inform the expanded treatment given here.

ring the heyday of the structuralist revolution[2]. Cognitive narratology constitutes one such framework, or rather cluster of frameworks, and in the present essay I outline a cognitively grounded approach to the problem of perspective to suggest directions for research in this wider, emergent area of narrative inquiry[3].

Further, my essay tests the descriptive and explanatory power of a cognitive approach to perspective by using as case studies both monomodal print narratives (namely, stories from Joyce's 1914 collection *Dubliners*) and a multimodal text, namely, Daniel Clowes's 1997 graphic novel *Ghost World*[4]. By focusing on cognitive dimensions of focalization in different kinds of narrative texts, I suggest, story analysts can overcome limitations arising from the restricted corpora on which scholars working in separate traditions of research have based their concepts and methods. In particular, by cross-comparing how perspectives are represented and interpreted in different narrative media, theorists can explore the scope and relevance of ideas developed by cognitive linguists for stories not solely dependent on verbal language. My research hypothesis is that ideas from cognitive grammar and cognitive semantics help illuminate perspective-taking processes in narratives that exploit multiple kinds of semiotic resources—e.g., graphic novels that involve a coordinated interplay of verbal and visual information tracks. Hence, in the model proposed here, cognitive narratology should be viewed as a subdomain of the broader enterprise of cognitive semiotics (cf. Brandt 2004; Fastrez 2003)—to which cognitive linguistics also belongs. Cognitive semiotics is the super-category containing frameworks for studying how the use and interpretation of sign-systems of all sorts are grounded in the structure, capacities, and dispositions of embodied minds. Cognitive narratology, for its part, studies the design principles for narratively organized sign-systems, drawing on

---

2 For a fuller account of classical versus postclassical approaches to narrative theory, see Herman (1999). For accounts of the structuralist revolution and of the way it shaped structuralist theories of narrative in particular, see, respectively, Dosse (1997) and Herman (2005).

3 See Jahn (2005) for a synoptic account of developments in cognitive narratology; see also Herman (2003 and forthcoming b).

4 Multimodal narratives can be defined as narratives that exploit more than one semiotic channel to evoke a storyworld (for a fuller account, see Herman [forthcoming c]). On methods for studying multimodality in textual artifacts and in face-to-face communication interaction, see Kress & van Leeuwen (2001) and Norris (2004), respectively.

tools from (cognitive) linguistics, ethnography, the philosophy of mind, social and cognitive psychology, and other disciplines to explore the interfaces among narrative structure, semiotic media, and humans' fundamental cognitive abilities[5]. I return to these distinctions and relationships in my concluding section, using the analysis outlined in sections 1–3 as the basis for a reassessment of the place of cognitive narratology within the architecture of inquiry.

1.2 The Illustrative Narratives

To illustrate the advantages of moving from talk of focalization to talk of conceptualization, and to suggest the productiveness of this approach for the analysis of various kinds of narratively organized sign-systems, multimodal as well as monomodal, I focus here on two case studies. My first case study, discussed in detail in section 2, involves a literary (i.e., monomodal print) narrative—more precisely, three stories from Joyce's *Dubliners* (1914): "Araby", "Ivy Day in the Committee Room", and "The Dead". All of them completed between 1904 and 1906, the three stories form something of a comparison set; I use them to redescribe contrasting modes of focalization as, instead, alternative patterns of construal or conceptualization. The three stories respectively exemplify the first-person, authorial, and figural narrative situations described by Stanzel (1979); the stories thus enable me to test out the implications of the model presented in this paper for print texts using a range of strategies for encoding perspectives on narrated situations and events. "Araby" is told retrospectively by a homodiegetic narrator revisiting his thwarted attempt to buy at a local bazaar a gift for a girl with whom he had become infatuated. "Ivy Day", which takes place on election day as well as the anniversary of the death of the Irish political leader Charles Stuart Parnell, is told almost exclusively through dialogue and set in a meeting room where a group of men canvassing for the local candidates discuss the issues of the day. Finally, "The Dead" is told in the third person but refracted through the vantage-point of Gabriel Conroy, who undergoes an adventure of consciousness and a rethinking of his own attitudes and values when he learns about a former

---

5 See Herman (2007) for a fuller discussion of the challenges and opportunities of integrating cognitive narratology into the domain of interdisciplinary research on the mind-brain—and vice versa. See also section 4 below.

lover of his wife who (at least in Gretta Conroy's interpretation of events) died for her sake.

Section 3 of my essay then turns to a second case study—specifically, a single page from Daniel Clowes's graphic novel *Ghost World*. In Clowes's text, the coordinated interplay of two semiotic channels or information tracks, words and images, marks shifts in the vantage-point on—more broadly, the construal of—represented situations and events. The narrative focuses on two teenage girls trying to navigate the transition from high school to post-high-school life, standing out contrastively against the backdrop afforded by the tradition of superhero comics. Far from possessing superhuman powers, Enid Coleslaw[6] and Rebecca Doppelmeyer struggle with familial and romantic relationships, resist the stereotypes their peers try to impose on them, and are bought face to face, on more than one occasion, with the fragility and tenuousness of their own friendship. In this way, closer in spirit to the female Bildungsroman than action-adventure narratives, *Ghost World*, which was originally published as installments in the underground comics tradition and subsequently assembled into a novel, overlays a graphic format on content matter that helped extend the scope and range of comics storytelling generally. My discussion of the illustrative page from Clowes's graphic novel focuses on how constellations of verbal and visual signs encode processes of construal that are fundamentally isomorphic with those structuring monomodal print texts. Analysis of word-image combinations in *Ghost World* thus reinforces the central claim of this essay: namely, that narrative perspective is best understood as a reflex of the mind or minds conceptualizing scenes within storyworlds. Accordingly, construal constitutes the common root of voice and vision—the common denominator shared by types of narrative mediation, no matter how many semiotic channels (or what specific channels) may be involved in the mediational process.

2 Beyond Voice and Vision: Rethinking Focalization Theory

In essence, the study of narrative perspective concerns how vantage-points on situations and events in the storyworld are encoded in narrative discourse and interpreted as such during narrative processing. In this section, after discussing foundational research on narrative perspective (2.1) and

6 As reported by Taylor (2001), "Enid Coleslaw" is an anagram for "Daniel Clowes".

reviewing Jahn's (1996 and 1999) own proposals about how to reconceptualize that earlier work (2.2.1), I explore how ideas from cognitive grammar might enable narrative scholars to circumvent impasses created by classical narratological theories of focalization (2.2.2 and 2.3). Narrative perspective, as I have suggested, can be interpreted as a reflex of the mind or minds conceptualizing scenes represented in narrative texts, such that construal becomes the common root of voice and vision. This approach has wide-ranging consequences for previous accounts of perspective in stories[7]. For one thing, the focus of analysis shifts from taxonomy building, or the classification of types of focalization, to a functionalist account of perspective as sense-making strategy.

Joyce's three stories constitute my main test cases in this section. Although I refer to the stories in their entirety, my discussion will use the following three passages as "touchstones" or specific illustrative examples:

(a) Mr Hynes sat down again on the table. When he had finished his recitation [of "The Death of Parnell"] there was a silence and then a burst of clapping: even Mr Lyons clapped. The applause continued for a little time. When it had ceased all the auditors drank from their bottles in silence. ("Ivy Day", Joyce 1914: 135)
(b) I watched my master's face pass from amiability to sternness; he hoped I was not beginning to idle. ("Araby", Joyce 1914: 32)
(c) The piano was playing a waltz tune and he [Gabriel Conroy] could hear the skirts sweeping against the drawing-room door. People, perhaps, were standing in the snow on the quay outside, gazing up at the lighted windows and listening to the waltz music. The air was pure there. In the distance lay the park where the trees were weighted with snow. ("The Dead", Joyce 1914: 202)

Then, in section 2.3, I draw on another passage from "The Dead", represented as (d), to draw together the strands of my discussion and underscore the advantages of moving from classical narratological theories of

[7] Likewise, Grishakova (2002 and 2006) richly synthesizes semiotic, narratological, and cognitive-linguistic research to argue that "Genette's 'voice' and 'vision' ('perception') are the two sides of the same process of sense-generation" (Grishakova 2002: 529)—that "perception is the common root of different modes of sense-production (verbal, visual and others)" (529). As I do in the present study, Grishakova draws on Langacker's ideas to underscore the parallelism of perception and conception and to challenge "Genette's understanding of 'focalization' as pure perception, on the one hand, and the existence of [...] 'non-focalized' narration, on the other" (Grishakova 2006: 153). See Broman (2004) for a comparable critique of Genette's attempt to drive a wedge between narration and focalization.

focalization to a postclassical account informed by Langacker's cognitive grammar and Talmy's cognitive semantics:

> (d) When he saw Freddy Malins coming across the room to visit his mother Gabriel left the chair free for him and retired into the embrasure of the window. The room had already cleared and from the back room came the clatter of plates and knives. Those who still remained in the drawing-room seemed tired of dancing and were conversing quietly in little groups. Gabriel's warm trembling fingers tapped the cold pane of the window. How cool it must be outside! How pleasant it would be to walk out alone, first along by the river and then through the park! The snow would be lying on the branches of the trees and forming a bright cap on the top of the Wellington Monument. How much more pleasant it would be there than at the supper-table! ("The Dead", Joyce 1914: 192)

2.1 Narrative Perspective: Classical Accounts

In the narratological literature, the concept of focalization, originally proposed by Genette as a way to distinguish between who sees and who speaks in a narrative, has generated considerable debate. In the Genettean tradition, focalization is a way of talking about perceptual and conceptual frames, more or less inclusive or restricted, through which participants, situations, and events are presented in a narrative (cf. Prince 2003: 31–32; Herman 2002: 301–30). Thus, in what Genette (1980) calls "internal focalization," the viewpoint is restricted to a particular observer or "reflector" whereas in what he calls "zero focalization" (which Bal [1997] and Rimmon-Kenan [1983] term "external focalization") the viewpoint is not anchored in a localized position. Also, internal focalization can be fixed, variable, or multiple. Hence the focalization in "Araby" and "The Dead" is, in Genette's terms, internal: as suggested by passages (b) on the one hand and (c) and (d) on the other hand, the younger, Experiencing-I is the focalizer in "Araby" whereas in "The Dead" Gabriel Conroy provides the vantage-point on situations and events in the storyworld. Meanwhile, "Ivy Day" (a) relies mainly on externalized views of the group of election workers commemorating the anniversary of Parnell's death. Hence, whereas the focalization is fixed and internal in "Araby" and "The Dead", "Ivy Day" uses what Genette (as opposed to Bal and Rimmon-Kenan) would term external focalization, in which "what is presented [is] limited to the characters' external behavior [words and actions but not thoughts or feelings], their appearance, and the setting against which they come to the fore" (Prince 2003: 32). There is, however, a departure from (what Genette might call a paraleptic "infraction against") this dominant code of focalization when the narration dips briefly into the contents of Mr Crofton's mind and reveals that he refrains from speaking because "he considered his companions beneath him" (Joyce 1914: 142).

So far, so good: the structuralist approach to focalization yields important insights into the contrasts and commonalities among texts like Joyce's—and, in principle, among all texts categorizable as narratives. Yet the classical picture of narrative perspective is complicated both by (1) tensions between different approaches within the Genettean framework and by (2) a separate tradition of research stemming from the work of Franz K. Stanzel (1979) on "narrative situations", which is inconsistent with or at the very least orthogonal to Genette's approach. In the first place, Shlomith Rimmon-Kenan (1983) and Mieke Bal (1997) are among the narratologists who argue that processes of focalization involve both a focalizer, or agent doing the focalizing, and focalized objects (which can in turn be focalized both from without and from within). Yet Genette (1983) himself disputes these elaborations of his original account. Invoking Occam's razor, Genette maintains that only the *gestalt* concept of focalization is needed to capture the modalities of narrative perspective[8].

Stanzel for his part assimilates narrative perspective to the more general process of narratorial mediation, which he characterizes in terms of three clines or continua: internal vs. external perspective on events, identity vs. non-identity between narrator and narrated world, and narrating agent (or teller) vs. perceptual agent (or reflector). For example, the figural narrative situation, exemplified by "The Dead" globally and also locally in passages (c) and (d) above, obtains when a given stretch of narrative discourse is marked by an internal perspective on events, a position toward the reflector end of the teller-reflector continuum, and non-identity between narrator and storyworld. Authorial (=distanced third-person) narration, exemplified by passage (a), obtains when the discourse is marked by an external perspective, a position toward the teller end of the teller-reflector continuum, and, again, non-identity between narrator and storyworld. More generally, whereas Genette and those influenced by him

8 Broman (2004) notes a further division among researchers working within the Genettean tradition: namely, between those who follow Genette himself in developing a global, typological-classificatory approach, whereby differences among modes of focalizations provide a basis for categorizing novels and short stories, and those who follow Bal in developing "the minute analysis of shifts in points of view between text passages and sentences, and in certain cases even within the same sentence" (71).

strictly demarcate who speaks and who sees, voice and vision, narration and focalization, the Stanzelian model suggests that the voice and vision aspects of narratorial mediation cluster together in different ways to comprise the different narrative situations. Furthermore, for Stanzel, these aspects are matters of degree rather than binarized features. As the gradable contrast between the authorial and figural narrative situations suggests, the agent responsible for the narration can in some instances, and to a greater or lesser degree, fuse with the agent responsible for perception—yielding not an absolute gap but a variable, manipulable distance between the roles of teller and reflector, vocalizer and visualizer (cf. Shaw 1995; Nieragden 2002; Phelan 2001). Contrast Kate Chopin's *The Awakening*, which shuttles back and forth between the authorial and figural modes in order to extrapolate general truths from internal views of Edna Pontellier's situation, with Franz Kafka's *The Trial*, which suggests the impossibility of any such extrapolation by remaining scrupulously close to Josef K.'s position as reflector.

As even this cursory overview suggests, the lack of consensus or even convergence among researchers after several decades of research in this area, as well as the problematic incommensurability of the Genettean and Stanzelian paradigms, points up the need to rethink foundational terms and concepts of focalization theory itself. After providing in section 2.2.1 a brief overview of Manfred Jahn's (1996 and 1999) innovative proposals along these lines, in sections 2.2.2 and 2.3 I use ideas from cognitive linguistics to outline another strategy for reconceptualizing the study of narrative perspective.

2.2 Reframing the Classical Accounts

2.2.1 Jahn's Model

Jahn (1999) has developed a powerful model of focalization based on folk understandings of the structure of vision as well as the cognitive science of seeing. Figure 1 reproduces what Jahn characterizes as a mental model of vision (Jahn 1999: 87; cf. Jahn 1996: 242)—a model grounded in how we think we see things, as opposed to a precise mapping of the physiology of vision. In this model, focus-1 corresponds to the "burning point of an eye's lens" (Jahn 1999: 87) and also suggests an origo or vantage-point on perceived scenes within a larger storyworld, i.e., "a point at which all perceptual stimuli come together, a zero point from which all spatio-temporal and experiential coordinates start" (Jahn 1996: 243). Focus-2, meanwhile, corresponds to the focused-upon object or scene within a field of vision that is in turn nested within the surrounding environment or world.

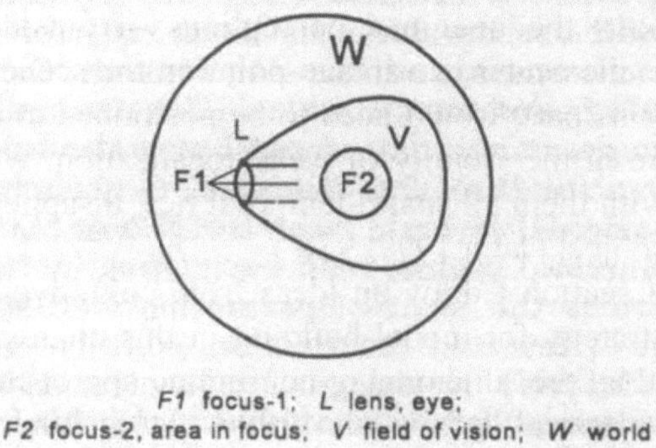

Figure 1: Jahn's Mental Model of Vision (Jahn 1999: 87)

Jahn (1999) builds on this basic model to suggest a scale of focalization possibilities, ranging from zero focalization (where no particularized center of consciousness filters the focused-upon events) to strict focalization of the sort found in first-person narration or figural narration such as that used by Kafka. Figure 2 reproduces the scale at issue.

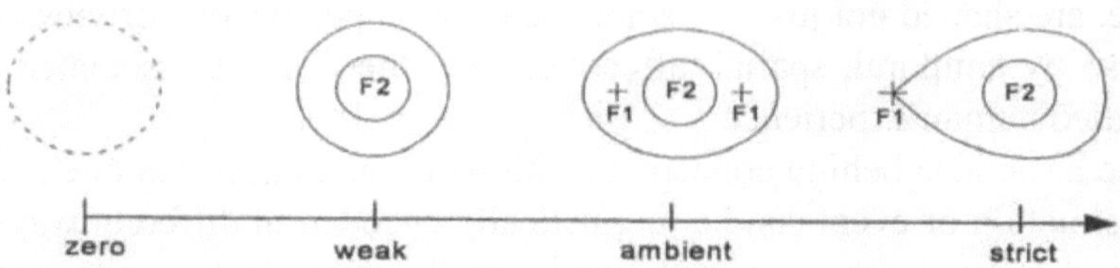

Figure 2: A Scale of Focalization Possibilities (Jahn 1999: 96)

The passages from Joyce quoted above would occupy different positions along this scale. For example, passage (b) would be located at the rightmost position along the scale, it being strictly focalized through the vantage point of the Experiencing-I of "Araby". Here focus-2, the schoolmaster's face, "is perceived from (or by [focus-1, i.e., the Experiencing-I]) under conditions of precise and restricted spatio-temporal coordinates" (Jahn 1999: 97). By contrast, passage (c) from "The Dead" can be located at a position to the left of passage (b), since in addition to Gabriel Conroy's perceptions the imagined perceptions of outside observers serve briefly as a deictic center or vantage-point on the scene. Passage (a) from "Ivy Day", for its part, would need to be positioned to the left of passage (c), somewhere in the vicinity of weak focalization, where all focalizing agents, "and with them all spatio-temporal ties, disappear," leaving only a focused-upon object (Jahn 1999: 97).

In my next section I draw on ideas from cognitive linguistics to suggest another strategy for model-building in this context—a strategy likewise motivated by the "dilemma of conflicting approaches" to focalization theory in its classical form (Jahn 1996: 241). Whereas Jahn rethinks earlier accounts via mental models of vision, the heuristic framework outlined next emphasizes the inextricable interconnection between narrating and perspective-taking. In other words, all storytelling acts are grounded in the perceptual-conceptual abilities of embodied human minds.

2.2.2 From Focalization to Conceptualization

Building on studies by Langacker (1987) and Talmy (2000), among others, the present section suggests how narrative analysts can move from classical theories of narrative perspective toward a unified account of construal or conceptualization processes and their reflexes in narrative. Such construal operations, which underlie the organization of narrative discourse, are shaped not just by factors bearing on perspective or viewpoint, but also by temporal, spatial, affective, and other factors associated with embodied human experience.

The basic idea behind conceptualization or construal is that one and the same situation or event can be linguistically encoded in different ways, by means of locutions that are truth-conditionally equivalent despite more or less noticeably different formats (for a detailed overview, see Croft & Cruse [2004: 40–73]). Langacker (1987) suggests that a range of cognitive abilities, including comparison, the deployment of imagery, the transformation of one construal into another or others, and focal adjustment, support the processes of conceptualization that surface as dimensions of semantic structure. In other words, these cognitive abilities are also design parameters for language. A subset of the parameters at issue—namely, those associated specifically with focal adjustment—derives from the enabling and constraining condition of having an embodied, spatio-temporally situated perspective on events.

A brief thought-experiment can illustrate the general processes at issue. Assuming that (i)—(vi) all truly apply to the same spatiotemporal configuration of participants and circumstances, differences among them reflect humans' ability to mentally "construe" one and the same situation in alternative ways:

(i) The family of raccoons stared at the goldfish in the pond.
(ii) The goldfish in the pond were stared at by the family of raccoons.
(iii) A family of raccoons stared at some goldfish in a pond.
(iv) The family of raccoons stared at the goldfish in the pond over there.
(v) That damned family of raccoons stared at the goldfish in the pond.
(vi) The family of raccoons stared at those damned goldfish in the pond.

(i) and (ii) show how alternate figure-ground relationships afford contrasting conceptualizations; (i) and (iii) how different locutionary formats can represent different construals of hearer knowledge; (i) and (iv) how conceptualizations can be more or less subjective in Langacker's sense of that term, i.e., include the situation of utterance more or less prominently in the scene being construed; and (i), (v), and (vi) how different affective registers can surface in alternative construals. Although cognitive grammarians tend to study such construal operations at the clause and sentence level, my claim is that the operations themselves are scalable and can be mapped onto discourse-level structures in narrative.

To return to the parameter of focal adjustment in particular, Langacker (1987) identifies a number of sub-parameters relevant for the study of how perspective shapes the construal of events. Combined with Talmy's (2000) account of perspective as a "conceptual structuring system", Langacker's account yields a rich framework for studying perspective-taking processes in narrative contexts. Langacker decomposes focal adjustment into the following sub-parameters (and sub-sub-parameters):

(1) selection, which concerns the scope of a predication, i.e. how much of the scene that one is construing is included in the conceptualization;
(2) perspective, which includes
(2.1) figure-ground alignment, i.e., foreground-background relations (see also Talmy [2000, 1: 311–44]),
(2.2) viewpoint (=vantage point + orientation within a directional grid consisting of vertical and horizontal axes);

(2.3) deixis (deictic expressions include some reference to the "ground" or situation of utterance in their immediate scope of predication),
(2.4) subjectivity/objectivity (for Langacker, the degree of subjectivity of a construal varies inversely with the degree to which the ground is included in the immediate scope of a predication: the more the ground is included, the more objectivized the construal); and
(3) abstraction, which pertains to the level of specificity of a construal, i.e., its degree of granularity (how much detail is included).

Meanwhile, in Talmy's (2000) cognitive semantics, perspective constitutes a schematic system. On the basis of this system, languages establish "a conceptual perspective point from which [a referent entity can be] cognitively regarded" (1: 68). In parallel with Langacker's model, Talmy's account of the perspective system encompasses several categories or parameters that find reflexes in the semantic system of a given language (1: 68-76), including
(α) the location of a perspective point within a "referent scene";
(β) the distance of a perspective point from the regarded scene (distal, medial, proximal);
(γ) perspectival mode, including motility, i.e. whether the perspective point is stationary or moving, and mode proper, i.e., synoptic versus sequential viewing;
(δ) direction of viewing, i.e., "sighting" in a particular direction (spatially or temporally) from an established perspective point.
My larger point here is that classical theories of focalization, deriving from the work of Genette and Stanzel, capture only part of this system of perspective-related parameters for construal.

By shifting from theories of focalization to an account of the processes and sub-processes involved in conceptualization, story analysts can explore how narratives may represent relatively statically (synoptically) or dynamically (sequentially) scanned scenes (or event-structures). Scenes will have a relatively wide or narrow scope, focal participants and backgrounded elements, an orientation within a horizontal/vertical dimensional grid, and a more or less objective profile (i.e., encompass the ground of predication to a greater or lesser extent). Scenes are also "sighted" from particular temporal and spatial directions, and viewpoints on scenes can be distal, medial, or proximal, that is, range from being far away to being up close. Each such distance increment, further, may carry a default expectation about the degree of granularity (or level of detail) of the construal. Closer perspectives on scenes generally yield finer-grained (=more granular, more detailed) representations; more distant perspectives generally yield coarser-grained (=less granular, less detailed) representations.

Analysts can investigate how these parameters for construal are realized textually (or, more broadly, semiotically)—and in turn how particular kinds of textual or semiotic cues guide readers' efforts to parse narrative representations into scenes that are variably structured, paced, and distributed over the course of a given story. Passage (a), for example, can be redescribed as an instance of narrative discourse in which the conceptual perspective point is static rather than dynamic and situated at a medial distance from the regarded scene, yielding a medium-scope construal of the characters and their environment. Yet, despite the constant distance between the vantage-point on the scene and the scene itself, there is a shift in the level of granularity of the representation: over the course of the passage, the focal participants move from particularized individuals (Mr Hynes, Mr Lyons) to the characters viewed as a group ("all the auditors"). Conversely, passage (c) (and also passage d, discussed in my next subsection) is remarkable for the way fluctuations in perspectival distance do not affect the degree of granularity of the construal. Gabriel is at a proximal distance from the drawing room, but as the sentential adverb "perhaps"[9] indicates, his vantage-point is distally located vis-à-vis the scenes he imagines to be outside: namely, the quay and, still farther away, the park. Yet there is no appreciable difference in the granularity of the construals afforded by shifts along this chain of vantage-points. Working against default expectations about how much granularity is available from what perspectival distance, Joyce's text evokes the power of the imagination to transcend the constraints of space and time—both here and again at the end of story, when Gabriel imagines how the snow is general all over Ireland. The conceptualization processes portrayed in the story thus emulate the spatio-temporal transpositions accomplished by Joyce's own fictional discourse; the concern in both contexts is the process by which one set of space-time parameters can be "laminated" within another, to use Goffman's (1974) term. In other words, the scene outside the party becomes proximate to Gabriel's mind's eye through the same process of transposi-

---

[9] In Fauconnier's (1994) terms, "perhaps" functions here as a space-builder, opening within the storyworld an embedded mental space constructed by Gabriel's imagination. This space could also be characterized, in Paul Werth's (1999) terms, as a subworld within the text world evoked by Joyce's story as a whole.

tion that allows readers to relocate, or deictically shift (cf. Zubin & Hewitt 1995), to the spatial and temporal coordinates occupied by Gabriel as the reflector through whom perceptions of the fictional party are filtered.

In passage (b), meanwhile, what is noteworthy are the cross-cutting directions of temporal sighting: the older, Narrating-I looks back on the younger, Experiencing-I, whose observation of the increasingly dissatisfied expression on his schoolmaster's face is in turn forward-oriented. This bidirectional temporal sighting, the signature of first-person retrospective narratives (whether fictional or nonfictional), is complemented by a combination of synoptic and sequential scanning. The passage reveals a construal of the master's face as undergoing change over time, but the construal itself is summative, compressing into a single clause an alteration that one can assume unfolded over a more or less extended temporal duration.

2.3 Underscoring the Advantages of a Cognitively Grounded Approach

Drawing on the enriched analytic framework outlined in my previous subsection, theorists can ask questions about narrative perspective that could not even be formulated within the classical models, while still preserving the (important) insights afforded by Genettean and Stanzelian focalization theory. The approach thus affords a more unified, systematic treatment of perspective-related aspects of narrative structure that previous narratological research treats in a more piecemeal or atomistic way. These gains can be underscored by a somewhat more extended analysis of one textual segment, namely, the portion of "The Dead" excerpted as passage (d) above.

In this passage, the Genettean analyst would speak of internally focalized narration; the Stanzelian, of narration in the figural mode. As he does throughout the story, Gabriel functions in the quoted passage as the reflector. Accordingly, although the narrator remains distinct from Gabriel (hence the use of the third person pronoun "he"), the narration is filtered through Gabriel's vantage-point on the scenes he encounters over the course of the story. Further, drawing on the "speech-category" approach to consciousness representation (cf. Cohn 1978; Palmer 2004: 53–86), the classical narratologist interested in tracing moment-by-moment shifts in the perspective structure of the passage would be able to note the movement from actual to imaginary perceptions in the second half of the passage. In particular, the last four sentences of the passage feature imaginative projections by Gabriel—hypothetical forays into the way it is or would be like outside the house where the party is taking place. For one thing, the exclamation marks suggest sentiments or thoughts that have forcibly struck Gabriel, and that are therefore linked to his subjectivity rather than the neutral, non-exclamatory discourse of the narrator. In addition, the sequence of clauses containing verbs with modal auxiliaries ("How cool it *must be*...," "The snow *would be* lying...," "How pleasant it *would be*...," etc.) exemplifies a process that linguists have termed the *irrealis* modality. This modality encompasses all the semantic resources that enable language users to signal that they that are not fully committed to the truth of a proposition about the world (cf. Frawley 1992: 387–90). In this case the main resource is the subjunctive mood signaled by the auxiliary verbs. Coupled with the exclamation marks that express Gabriel's subjectivity, the subjunctive indicates that Gabriel is again framing inferences about the storyworld, but in this case inferences based on probabilistic reasoning rather than on evidence to which he has direct, perceptual access.

Beyond the study of such expressivity markers, however, recruiting from Langacker's and Talmy's frameworks allows the analyst to capture how the factor of perspective bears on a wider range of textual details, and to uncover systematic interconnections among those details that remain hidden when classical narratological approaches are used. In Talmy's terms, passage (d) reveals how Gabriel's perspective constitutes a conceptual structuring system, in which Freddy Malins and his mother are, initially, the focal participants in a sequentially scanned scene. The past-tense indicative verbs indicate that the scene is sighted from a temporal viewpoint located later on the time-line than the point occupied by the represented events. Spatially, the scene is sighted from a viewpoint situated on the same plane as the represented action: Gabriel is not observing the scene from below, for example, as is the case when he construes Gretta as "a symbol of something" at the top of the stairs (Joyce 1914: 210)[10]. Further, Gabriel's initial medium-distance viewpoint on the scene (from

[10] Likewise the factors of orientation and (spatial) sighting come into play in passage (c). Gabriel first imagines others looking up at the lighted windows and listening to the music in the house; then, mentally shifting to the deictic coordinates occupied by those hypothetical outside observers, he imaginatively takes up their vantage-point and sights the imagined scene in the park along a horizontal rather than vertical axis.

the chair next to Mrs Malins) affords a medium-scope representation with a corresponding, mid-level degree of granularity or detail. Then, when Gabriel takes up his new position in the embrasure of the window, his distance from the scene increases, producing a wider-scope conceptualization of the scene that has a correspondingly lower degree of granularity: Gabriel construes the scene in terms of groups rather than individuals. As they did in passage (c), then, the factors of distance, scope, and granularity of construal co-vary systematically: as you get farther away from something, you see more of the context that surrounds it but with less overall detail, and these perspectival constraints on people's mental lives also shape how they use language—for example, how they produce and interpret narratives. Meanwhile, Gabriel has now moved much closer to the window, his position affording a proximal, narrow-scope, and highly granular, detailed representation of his own fingers tapping the cold pane. The shift to free indirect thought in "How cool it must be outside!" marks the onset of a new conceptualization—this time of an imagined scene outside. As the new construal gets underway, distance, scope, and granularity again co-vary: the hypothetical scene is farther away than the window, encompasses the whole area by the river and through the park, and is not envisioned in any detailed way. But then Gabriel imagines specific features of the scene, the degree of granularity increasing dramatically to the point where the snow on the branches of trees and on the top of the Wellington monument comes into focus. Working against default expectations about how much granularity is available from what perspectival distance, Joyce's text once again evokes, structurally as well as thematically, the power of the imagination to transcend the constraints of space and time.

In short, in contrast with earlier focalization theory, a cognitive-grammatical approach points the way toward a more unified, integrative account of perspective and its bearing on other aspects of narrative production and processing, including stylistic texture (e.g., verb tenses and moods), the spatio-temporal configuration of storyworlds, the representation of consciousness, and narrative thematics. A task for future research is to consider other ways in which the idea of construal might afford new foundations for narrative inquiry—for the study of how strategies for telling are inextricably interlinked with strategies for conceptualizing the world told about. In my next section, rather than venturing to explore these further domains, I sketch the relevance of the approach outlined here for transmedial narratology. Though cognitive grammar and cognitive semantics were of course designed for linguistic analysis, my argument is that these frameworks are extensible for the purposes of cognitive-semiotic and also cognitive-narratological research, insofar as they point to general capacities and constraints associated with embodied human cognition. These capacities and constraints can be assumed to shape the use and interpretation of all sign-systems, nonverbal as well as verbal, whether narratively organized or not. I now turn to the perspective-indexing functions of word-image combinations in graphic narratives to test this research hypothesis.

3 Perspective and Construal in Multimodal Narratives

My case study in this section is the page from *Ghost World* represented as figure 3 (see next page). The visual-verbal organization of this page or sequence of panels encodes information about how the scene is being construed, and by whom, across the corresponding sequence of time-slices in the storyworld. At issue is a temporally structured representation consisting of shifting figure-ground alignments, changes in the vantage-point or location of the perspective point within the referent scene, and alterations in perspectival mode and direction of viewing. Again, classical theories of focalization capture only part of this system of perspective-related parameters for construal, and furthermore tend to be geared toward perspective-marking features of print texts. The model proposed here, by contrast, allows story analysts to study how the logic of narrative perspective intersects with the constraining and enabling properties of particular modes (=semiotic channels viewed as a means for the construction or design of a representation) and media (=semiotic channels viewed as a means for the dissemination or production of a given representation)[11]. In this way, study of perspective-marking resources of different storytelling environments constitutes a key aspect of transmedial narratology (cf. Herman 2004 and forthcoming c). Theorists can hold constant the underlying, cognitively grounded system of capacities that supports narrative perspective-taking, while comparing and contrasting how different storytelling environments (print texts, films, graphic narratives, plays, etc.) promote or inhibit the reliance on various elements of that system to encode perspective-based information in a given instance.

---

[11] The distinction between mode and medium articulated here is drawn from Kress & van Leeuwen (2001) and Jewitt (2006).

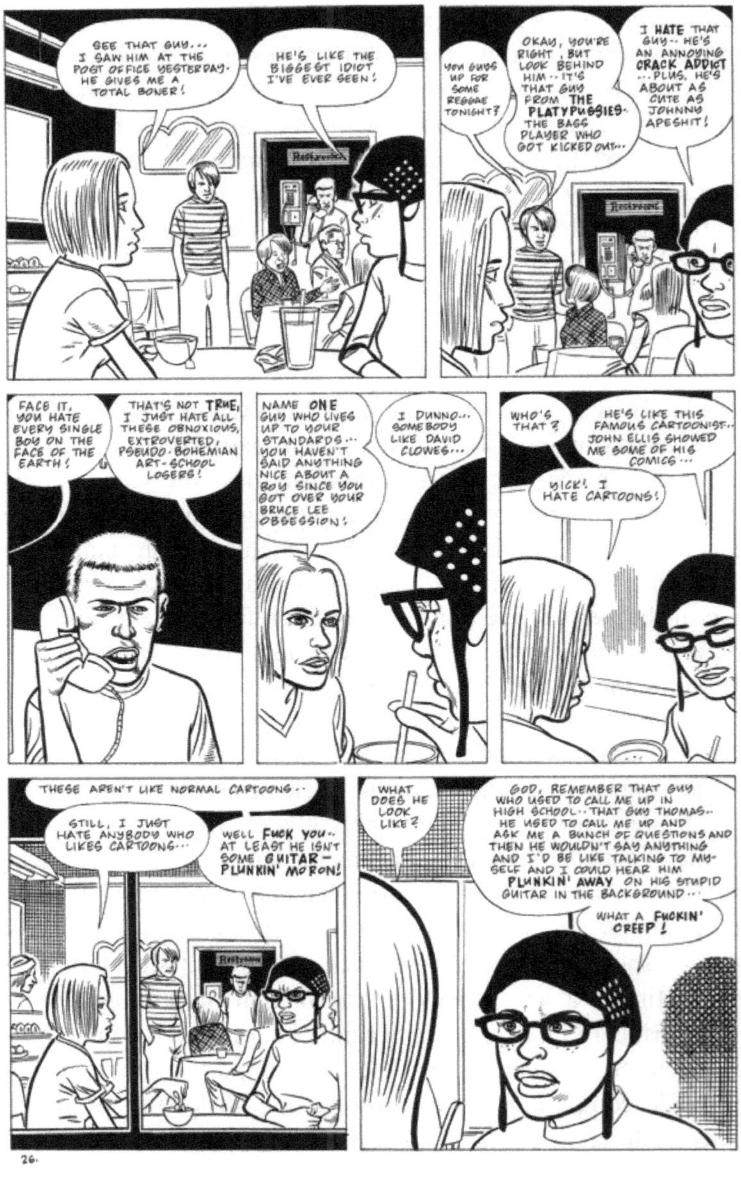

Figure 3: Page from Daniel Clowe's Graphic Novel *Ghost World* (1997: 26). Copyright © 2008 Daniel Clowes; courtesy of Fantagraphics Books (Fantagraphics.com).

In the opening panels of the page reproduced as figure 3, the text's word-image combinations encode variable vantage-points on the scene, indexing construal processes operative at multiple levels. In the first panel, the perspective point is encoded via the inclusion of Rebecca's and Enid's bodies within the first panel, putting the reader in a position of looking over the characters' shoulders in order to construe their own construal processes; these processes form the common root of the verbal and visual mediations of narrated content and find reflexes in the direction of the two main characters' gazes, the orientation of their torsos, and the structure as well as the topical content of their utterances[12]. To reiterate: the perspective structure of both the first and the second panel situates the reader at a point from which he or she can construe Rebecca's and Enid's own joint or at least coordinated acts of construal, which in turn center on the non-focal characters' second-order acts of mutual observation. Here processes of construal involve a telescopic chain of observational acts.

Note, however, that the two information tracks of the text feature different focal participants: the verbal track foregounds the visually backgrounded male characters, whose smaller size suggests their distal position vis-à-vis the orienting perspective point; by contrast, the visual track represents Rebecca and Enid as the focal participants, thanks to their larger size and implied proximity to the orienting viewpoint. In this instance readers are not likely to have any difficulty reconciling these information tracks within the larger perspective structure of the text. Other multimodal narratives, however, might create more jarring discordances as interpreters attempt to integrate reflexes of construal manifest in different information tracks. For example, the affective dimension of construal might be thematized (and thus de-automatized) by disjunctive information presented simultaneously through different semiotic channels, as when a film soundtrack overlays on distressing, horrific images ebullient extradiegetic music, or vice versa.

To return to Clowes' graphic narrative, as readers move to the third panel on the page, they can use the context established by the visual design of first two panels, together with the patterning of speech attributions in the form of word balloons, to draw an inference concerning the

[12] To adapt Langacker's terms: the ground of the characters' discourse is placed within the immediate scope of their predications, thanks to demonstrative pronouns and deictics in expressions such as "see that guy" and "look behind him."

status of the image represented in this third panel. Specifically, interpreters are likely to infer that this image of the former bass player is mediated through the perceptions of one of the two main characters—most probably Rebecca's, given her physical location and the orientation of her torso and gaze in the preceding panel[13]. That inference is reinforced by the absence of a speech balloon in the third panel, even though the bass player is shown talking on the phone—and even though the narrow-scope or proximal representation makes the male character the focal participant in the visual track. Here readers can assume that, because of the representation of the male character's location at the far side of the restaurant in the first two panels, Rebecca cannot hear what he is saying on the phone—although he has acquired focal status in the domain of visual perception. By contrast, in the second panel on the page, in the case of the utterance represented by means of the leftmost speech balloon, readers can assume that this remark was made within Rebecca's and Enid's perceptual range and is therefore included in the visual report of their perceptions at this point in the unfolding action.

In panels 4 and following, the interplay of words and images prompts readers to pull back from the internalized view of the ex-bass player in panel 3 and adopt shifting perspectives during Rebecca's and Enid's debate concerning what Rebecca characterizes as Enid's impossibly high standards for men. In a manner reminiscent of the shot/reverse-shot technique in cinematic narratives, the text first provides, in panel 4, an over-the-shoulder view of Rebecca from Enid's perspective, followed in panel 5 by an over-the-shoulder view of Enid from Rebecca's perspective. Then in panel 6 the perspective shifts again, to a more externalized view that captures Enid's angry expression as she defends her preference for the cartoonist over the "guitar plunkin' moron" (=ex-bass player) whom Rebecca had alluded to favorably. Such shifts between perspective points more or less proximally positioned vis-à-vis elements of the storyworld are structurally homologous with (and arguably derive from the same cognitive capacities as) third-person or heterodiegetic narration that moves

[13] Although it is arguable that this panel shifts away from the characters' acts of construal to a straightforward narratorial report of a moment of storyworld time, Rebecca's use of the demonstrative pronoun in "I just hate all these obnoxious, extroverted, pseudo-bohemian art-school losers" might also be interpreted as a reference to a feature of the storyworld that falls within the domain of the characters' current perceptions.

along a spectrum from relatively more external to relatively more internal views—that is, from external focalization (in Stanzel's terms: the authorial narrative situation), where the vantage-point on events is not associated with a character in the storyworld, to internal focalization (in Stanzel's terms: figural narration), where the vantage-point is in fact a character's.

Thus, in graphic narratives like Clowes's both the design of individual panels and sequential links between panels align readers with particular vantage-points on the storyworld. More precisely, constellations of verbal and visual cues encode shifts in the foreground-background relations—and fluctuating distances from focused-upon elements of scenes—that structure the processes of construal represented within the text. Integral to the interface between mind and world, and thus shaping the design and use of all semiotic systems, these processes underlie narrative across media. However, as Clowes's text also suggests, in multimodal narratives exploiting more than one information track, cognitive capacities and constraints associated with what Langacker terms the parameter of focal adjustment (and what Talmy calls a perspective-based conceptual structuring system) can be distributed across more than one semiotic channel, requiring interpreters to integrate these reflexes of perspective-taking processes into a more or less coherent mental representation of a given time-slice of the storyworld. A task for future research on narrative perspective is to explore the processing mechanisms supporting integration of this sort—and the relation of those processing mechanisms to the ones brought to bear on manifestations of construal in monomodal print texts such as Joyce's.

4 Conclusion: Narrative Perspective, Cognitive Narratology, and the Architecture of Inquiry

In the model sketched in this paper, cognitive semiotics is the broadest domain in which study of cognitive bases for perspective-taking—that is, processes of construal—can be situated. In this domain, the question is how the perspectival structure of embodied human experience finds reflexes in sign systems of all kinds, and how perspective-based information is parsed out in monomodal versus multimodal texts (or communicative practices). To restate the question: how do relevant cognitive capacities and constraints affect the organization and sequencing of constellations of signs—in sign systems that may exploit either a single semiotic channel or else multiple channels to encode perspectivally enabled and constrained construals of a storyworld? Treatments of perspective in cognitive linguistics are narrower in scope, focusing on how underlying cognitive abilities related to perspective are reflected in the organization of verbal language in particular. Meanwhile, cognitive-narratological research on perspective—that is, research on the cognitive bases for perspective-taking processes in narratively organized sign systems of all sorts, verbal as well as nonverbal, monomodal as well as multimodal—is situated at an intermediate level of generality. Compared with cognitive semiotics, cognitive narratology takes a more targeted approach: it explores the perspectival grounding not of sign systems as such but rather of sign systems that exhibit a narrative profile. Compared with cognitive-linguistic research on perspective, the cognitive-narratological approach is at once more general and more specific: it is not restricted to the study of construal processes in narratives conveyed through verbal language, but by the same token it limits itself to how construal operates in narratively organized discourse as opposed to language use more broadly.

Although the present paper explores ideas pertinent for each of these domains of inquiry, its chief concern has been to begin characterizing what a specifically cognitive-narratological approach to perspective might involve—to start detailing the distinctive scope, methods, and aims of such an approach. As I hope to have demonstrated, further work in this area will require closer scrutiny of the areas of intersection among processes of construal, dimensions of narrative structure, and the representational properties and capacities of the particular semiotic environments through which stories are told. In turn, integrative research of this kind will have the added benefit of helping to establish the place of cognitive narratology within the architecture of inquiry. For the purposes of further theory building, including but not limited to future work on cognitive aspects of narrative perspective, the following working definition may suffice: cognitive narratology is the domain of study whose essential concern is the nexus of narrative and mind, that is, the mind-relevant aspects of storytelling practices, wherever—and by whatever means—those practices occur.

References

Bal, Mieke ([2]1997). *Narratology: Introduction to the Theory of Narrative*. Toronto: U of Toronto P.

Brandt, Per Aage (2004). *Spaces, Domains, and Meaning: Essays in Cognitive Semiotics*. Frankfurt a. M.: Peter Lang.

Broman, Eva (2004). "Narratological Focalization Models: A Critical Survey." G. Rosshold (ed). *Essays on Fiction and Perspective*. Frankfurt a. M.: Peter Lang, 57–89.

Clowes, Daniel (1997). *Ghost World*. Seattle, WA: Fantagraphics Books.

Cohn, Dorrit (1978). *Transparent Minds: Narrative Modes for Presenting Consciousness in Fiction*. Princeton: Princeton UP.

Croft, William & Cruse, D. A. (2004). *Cognitive Linguistics*. Cambridge: Cambridge UP.

Dosse, François (1997). *History of Structuralism*, Vol. 1. Tr. D. Glassman. Minneapolis: The U of Minnesota P.

Fastrez, Pierre (ed) (2003). *Sémiotique Cognitive—Cognitive Semiotics*. Special issue of *Recherches en communication/Research in Communication* 19.

Fauconnier, Gilles (1994). *Mental Spaces: Aspects of Meaning Construction in Natural Language*. Cambridge: Cambridge UP.

Frawley, William (1992). *Linguistic Semantics*. Hillsdale, NJ: Lawrence Erlbaum.

Genette, Gérard (1972). "Discours du récit." *Figures III*. Paris: Seuil, 65–278.

– (1980). *Narrative Discourse*. Tr. J. E. Lewin. Ithaca: Cornell UP.

– (1983). *Nouveau discours du récit*. Paris: Seuil.

– (1988). *Narrative Discourse Revisited*. Tr. J. E. Lewin. Ithaca: Cornell UP.

Goffman, Erving (1974). *Frame Analysis: An Essay on the Organization of Experience*. New York: Harper.

Grishakova, Marina (2002). "The Acts of Presence Negotiated: Towards the Semiotics of the Observer." *Sign Systems Studies* 30:2, 529–53.

– (2006). *The Models of Space, Time and Vision in V. Nabokov's Fiction: Narrative Strategies and Cultural Frames*. Tartu: Tartu UP.

Herman, David (1999). "Introduction." D. Herman (ed). *Narratologies: New Perspectives on Narrative Analysis*. Columbus: Ohio State UP, 1–30.

– (2002). *Story Logic: Problems and Possibilities of Narrative*. Lincoln: U of Nebraska P.

– (2004). "Toward a Transmedial Narratology." M.-L. Ryan (ed). *Narrative across Media: The Languages of Storytelling*. Lincoln: U of Nebraska P, 47–75.

– (2005). "Histories of Narrative Theory (I): A Genealogy of Early Developments." J. Phelan et al. (eds). *The Blackwell Companion to Narrative Theory*. Malden: Blackwell, 19–35.

– (2007). "Storytelling and the Sciences of Mind: Cognitive Narratology, Discursive Psychology, and Narratives in Face-to-Face Interaction." *Narrative* 15:3, 306–34.

– (forthcoming a). "Cognitive Approaches to Narrative Analysis." G. Brône et al. (eds). *Foundations for Cognitive Poetics*. Berlin: de Gruyter.

– (forthcoming b). "Cognitive Narratology." J. Pier et al. (eds). *The Living Handbook of Narratology*. Berlin: de Gruyter.

– (forthcoming c). “Word-Image/Utterance-Gesture: Case Studies in Multimodal Storytelling.” R. Page (ed). *New Perspectives on Narrative and Multimodality*. London: Routledge.

– (ed) (2003). *Narrative Theory and the Cognitive Sciences*. Stanford, CA: Publications of the Center for the Study of Language and Information.

Jahn, Manfred (1996). “Windows of Focalization: Deconstructing and Reconstructing a Narratological Concept.” *Style* 30:3, 241–67.

– (1999). “More Aspects of Focalization: Refinements and Applications.” *GRAAT* 21 (Issue Topic: “Recent Trends in Narratological Research”), 85–110.

– (2005). “Cognitive Narratology.” D. Herman et al. (eds). *Routledge Encyclopedia of Narrative Theory*. London: Routledge, 67–71.

Jewitt, Carey (2006). *Technology, Literacy, and Learning: A Multimodal Approach*. London: Routledge.

Joyce, James (1914). *Dubliners*. New York: Penguin, 1967.

Kress, Gunther & van Leeuwen, Theo (2001). *Multimodal Discourse: The Modes and Media of Contemporary Communication*. London: Hodder Arnold.

Langacker, Ronald W. (1987). *Foundations of Cognitive Grammar*, Vol. 1. Stanford: Stanford UP.

Nieragden, Göran (2002). “Focalization and Narration: Theoretical and Terminological Refinements.” *Poetics Today* 23:4, 685–97.

Norris, Sigrid (2004). *Analyzing Multimodal Interaction: A Methodological Framework*. London: Routledge.

Palmer, Alan (2004). *Fictional Minds*. Lincoln: U of Nebraska P.

Phelan, James (2001). “Why Narrators Can Be Focalizers—and Why It Matters.” W. van Peer & S. Chatman (eds). *New Perspectives on Narrative Perspective*. Albany: SUNY Press, 51–64.

Prince, Gerald (^{2}2003). *A Dictionary of Narratology*. Lincoln: U of Nebraska P.

Rimmon-Kenan, Shlomith (1983). *Narrative Fiction: Contemporary Poetics*. London: Methuen.

Shaw, Harry (1995). “Loose Narrators.” *Narrative* 3, 95–116.

Stanzel, Franz K. (1979). *A Theory of Narrative*. Tr. C. Goedsche. Cambridge: Cambridge UP, 1984.

Talmy, Leonard (2000). *Toward a Cognitive Semantics*, Vols. 1 and 2. Cambridge, MA: MIT Press.

Taylor, Craig (2001). “Girls’ World.” *The Guardian*, November 3, 2001. <http://www.guardian.co.uk/Archive/Article/0,4273,4290067,00.html>.

Van Peer, Willie & Chatman, Seymour (eds) (2001). *New Perspectives on Narrative Perspective*. Albany: SUNY Press.

Werth, Paul (1999). *Text Worlds: Representing Conceptual Space in Discourse*. London: Longman.

Zubin, David A. & Hewitt, Lynne E. (1995). “The Deictic Center: A Theory of Deixis in Narrative.” J. F. Duchan et al. (eds). *Deixis in Narrative: A Cognitive Science Perspective*. Hillsdale, NJ: Lawrence Erlbaum, 129–55.

BRIAN RICHARDSON
(College Park, MD)

Plural Focalization, Singular Voices: Wandering Perspectives in "We"-Narration

"We"-narration and focalization is little studied and poorly known; apart from the recent studies of Adelaide Morris, Uri Margolin, Celia Britton, Joel Woller, and Amit Marcus, it has been largely unexplored in the history and theory of narration. Nevertheless, I believe it is a compelling type of perspective that has a substantial (if largely unknown) history, and poses very powerful questions concerning basic assumptions of narrative theory as currently understood. Though this is a somewhat new and fairly uncommon practice in the West, in other cultures it is widespread, even standard. Hertha D. Sweet Wong has analyzed collective speaking subjects in traditional and recent Native American women's autobiography. She notes that "a Native autobiographer, whether a speaking or a writing subject, often implies, if not announces, the first person plural—we—even when speaking in the first person singular. 'We' often invokes *a* (sometimes *the*) Native community" (Wong 1998: 171)[1]. She also notes that contemporary Native American writers use the technique in a less literal manner, gesturing toward a larger community that is invoked rather than depicted by the pronoun. As we will see, some indigenous South African speakers also employ first person plural narration.

It goes without saying that a first person narrator who frequently uses the plural pronoun to denote the action of a group is not unknown in fiction. In a recent story by Eilis Ni Dhuibhne, for example, the narrator, referring to herself and her sister's perspective, states, "The only tolerable part of the expedition occurred immediately after this, when we bought

1 Thus, one Yukon Native begins the story of her life with a history of her nation, the histories of her mother and other close relatives, and the origin myth of her people. "She does not even get to her own birth until page 52 (and then it is buried in a long list of her brother and sisters arranged in birth order)." (174)

souvenirs at a stall [...]. There we stood and scrutinized the wares on display: beads, statuettes, medals, snowstorms. Reverting to our consumerist role, we [...] do I mean I? I assume my sister felt the same about it all [...]" (Wong 1988: 117). This is an unproblematic case of first person perspective, with the appropriate epistemic boundaries of conventional fiction firmly in place. Not even a sister always knows what is passing through the mind of her sibling. The purpose of this essay is not to examine the many kinds of usages of "we" in ordinary discourse, an analysis that has been admirably performed by Margolin. Instead, the narratives I am concerned with differ from natural narratives insofar as they produce a tension concerning the identity, speech situation, or knowledge claimed by the "we" voice. This occurs when, for example, an "I" pronoun is never used in the text, despite its appropriateness at many points, when the focalization is unrealistically broad, or when the "we"-speaker possesses knowledge that they cannot normally have acquired. These are distinctively literary uses and are not normally found in natural narratives.

The first sustained example of first-person plural narration seems to be Joseph Conrad's *The Nigger of the "Narcissus"* (1899). The work opens in the conventional manner of standard, omniscient third person narrative. Soon, a collective focalization is established through third person plural reports of the crew's perceptions. "We"-focalization does not appear until a common bond develops among the seamen and "we" becomes the primary perspective: "We hesitated between pity and mistrust" (36). Conrad uses different types of narration in counterpoint to the consciousness of the men he is depicting: the greater their cohesion, the more insistent the use of "we". At a few points later in the voyage, as sailors retreat back into their own individual selves, the classic third person form returns. It might be noted that collective focalization seems more transgressive when it appears in "we"-narration as opposed to "they"-narration, no doubt because a character narrator cannot know the thoughts of other, under the conventions of mimetic narration.

"We" in this text refers to most of the crew, not the officers, the resentful Donkin, the West Indian James Wait, or old Singleton, the boatswain. The seamen's perceptions of Donkin are represented in terms that express difference: "He stood on the bad eminence of a general dislike. [...] Our sea-boots, our oilskin coats, our well-filled sea-chests, were to him so many causes for bitter meditation: he had none of these things, and he felt instinctively that no man, when the need arose, would offer to share them with him" (40). Intriguingly, in this passage the "we"-narration is focalized through the mind of Donkin, something of course a first person narrator, singular or plural, is not supposed to be able to do.

As the narration continues, similar or shared thoughts are depicted as if they were part of a single mind. This practice, however, grows more odd (and less susceptible to a realistic recuperation) the longer it continues, as can be seen in the progression in the following passages: "We were appalled. We perceived that after all Singleton's answer meant nothing. We began to hate him for making fun of us. [...] We suspected Jimmy, one another, and even our very selves" (43). Especially curious is the claim that "we suspected each other," since each individual is said to be entirely united in distrusting the others. For the most part, "we"-narration and its peculiar kind of collective focalization appear to be entirely reliable, a modest approximation of the third person narration elsewhere in the narrative. At times, however, what might be called "group unreliability" strikes: the crew is convinced that Wait's desire aided by Wamibo's presumed magic spells delayed the ship in the open seas (142). At other times, the unreliability becomes self-conscious and openly acknowledged: "we [...] sympathised with all [Wait's] repulsions, shrinkings, evasions, delusions" (139). That is to say, the "we"-perspective affirms what it wishes to believe even when it knows it is mistaken.

The "we"-perspective appears for the final time as the "Narcissus" comes into its port (166). Once on land, the collective perspective in a different manner as "they"-narration is used to depict the men in their last moments together in the shipping office where they are paid off. And in the last paragraphs of the novel, Conrad introduces his final, concluding transformation, as an "I"-narrator suddenly intrudes into the text and continues the story seamlessly: "Charley and Belfast wandered off alone. As I came up I saw a [...] woman [...] fall on Charley's neck" (170). Collective narration and focalization are over; the narrator goes off by himself, with nothing but his money, his memories, and an isolated consciousness.

Conrad's use of "we"-narration transcends the strictures of realism in the alternation of the "we" and "they" segments, since within a mimetic framework, the "we"-voice cannot know the private thoughts of many of the seamen. More audaciously, the two collective perspectives are not clearly separated and often glide into each other. This juxtaposition of mutually exclusive narrative stances can be seen prominently in passages where a sentence of "we"-narration is followed in the next line by a third person plural account: "Our little world went on its curved and unswerving path carrying a discontented and aspiring population. They found comfort of a gloomy kind in an interminable and conscientious analysis of their unappreciated worth" (103). From the perspective of a mimetic theory of narration, the speaker either is or is not part of the group and therefore one of the pronouns is entirely misleading. Other examples are even more resistant to a realistic recuperation. As many Conrad critics have pointed out, the entry into the consciousness of Singleton, Wait, and others is incompatible with the narrator's claims of having performed physical action onboard: "Groaning, we dug our fingers in, and very much hurt, shook our hands, scattering nails and drops of blood" (68). If the narrator is a character on the ship, he cannot enter the minds of others or report conversations he has not observed; if he is omniscient, he can't break fingernails onboard. The narrator, that is, is simultaneously homodiegetic and heterodiegetic.

In the history of this narrative technique after Conrad, we find a number of repeated issues and concerns. The precise nature and identity of the "we" is often varied and modulated as groups change or themes alter. The "we"-form raises interesting issues concerning reliability: insofar as it is a subjective form, it is enmeshed in issues of reliability and discordance, but these are issues that are potentially different from those in first person singular narratives since they may involve more accurate intersubjective beliefs as well as communal misprisions or even mass delusion. In addition, the "we"-perspective is used to present the collective consciousness of a tightly joined group who can be expected to share closely aligned ideas and emotions, and the novels focus on groups like merchant seamen, soldiers, revolutionaries, peasants, and even mice in the case of Kafka's "Die Sängerin Josephine". Henri Barbuse's *Feu,* a 1916 novel about World War I, is mostly narrated in the "we"-form. It explicitly discusses the unusual nature of the individuals that have come to form its collective subject: "Despite all the variations in age, origin, education and status, and everything that used to be, despite the gulfs that used to divide us, broadly speaking we're the same. Behind the same crude shape we conceal and exhibit the same manners, the same habits, the same simplified character of men who have reverted to their primal state" (18). And, we might add, the same set of perceptions. We find other early examples in the work of Victor Serge, Ignazio Silone, William Faulkner, and Raja Rao.

A striking and sustained use of "we"-narration and focalization appears in a nonfictional text, Richard Wright's *12 Million Black Voices* (1941). As Joel Woller (1999) has remarked, the first chapter "is narrated in a cross-generational voice. [...] It functions as a kind of prologue, articulating a collective memory of the middle passage and slavery" (348). In a paragraph describing the horrors of the middle passage, the iterative narration includes the experiences of both the living and the dead: "In the summer, down in the suffocating depths of those ships, on an eight- or ten-week voyage, we would go crazed for lack of air and water, and in the morning the crew of the ship would discover many of us dead" (14). At the time of its appearance, the work was castigated by some reviewers for its author's temerity in presuming to speak for many other subjectivities from within the "we"-perspective. This strategy would be greatly extended by Ayi Kwei Armah in his novel, *Two Thousand Seasons* (1973). His "we" are black Africans, and the term is a tool of resistance; it is routinely opposed to the discourse of a colonizing "they", Arab or European. The "we" here is especially inclusive, stretching for a thousand years. This leads to some particularly daring effects of voice, focalization, and temporality, as when "we remember" a prophet speak to a "we" that existed ten centuries ago to inform it of events that will soon ensue, even though "we" have also seen its tragic results centuries later (12–13). As such, this practice is a most interesting embedding of chronological relations within a largely iterative framework. This voice produces other compelling features, including a collective memory which is set forth as authoritative and a denunciation of the notion of an individual consciousness:

> Of unconnected consciousness is there more to say beyond the clear recognition this is destruction's keenest tool against the soul? [...] That the passion and the thinking and the action of any one of us should be cut off from our communal consciousness by mere physical things, walls of wood or walls of stone—that would indeed be the manic celebration of death's white empire. (128–29)

Uri Margolin has correctly noted that the "we" may "shift in identity, scope, size, and temporal location in the course of the narration" (Margolin 2001: 245), and observes that, in Faulkner's "A Rose for Emily", "most 'we' references are to the townspeople, a community that encompasses three different generations, not all of whom could be alive together at any given moment" (245). Wright and Armah show just how extensive this "we" can be[2].

---

[2] As Margolin points out, in Armah's novel "no less than half a dozen reference groups with complex relations of inclusion or partial overlap can be distinguished, including all Africans of the past one thousand years" (Margolin 2001: 245).

We may now identify the main kinds of "we"-narration and -focalization. An inventory of the most salient varieties of "we"-narration, differentiated according to the degree to which they diverge from the poetics of realism, could be aligned as follows:

(1) Standard: Largely realistic narration that nevertheless stretches verisimilitude at key points, especially when the narrator discloses the inner thoughts, perceptions, or feelings of a group. For instance, in Joan Chase's novel, the "we"-voice of shared experience and the third person accounts of each girl's individual actions cannot be realistically squared. *During the Reign of the Queen of Persia* (1983) is a narrative centered on a group of cousins: "There were four of us—Celia and Jenny, who were sisters, Anne and Kate, sisters too, like our mothers, who were sisters" (48). In the course of the narrative, each girl is described in the third person with zero focalization. This means that the writer of the narrative must at some points be (misleadingly) referring to herself and her actions in the third person, something not normally done in realistic representation. In the few cases where this occurs, such as Henry Adams referring to himself in the third person in *The Education of Henry Adams*, we all know very well that it is a first person narration that is told in the third person form. In Chase's novel, however, we don't know and cannot determine who the narrator is. The "we"-sections, however, are internally focalized and present a single perception or emotion shared by three or four individuals.

Another example can be adduced to show how standard "we" narration regularly examines its own practices self-reflexively within the work itself. In Jeffrey Eugenides's *The Virgin Suicides* (1993), the "we"-narrator is a partially indeterminate collection of neighborhood boys who, despite years of investigation and speculation, never begin to understand the motives of the girls who commit suicide. This novel includes a number of subtle, self-reflexive allusions to the idea of a multiple, protean subject, including the depiction of a shared consciousness with a single focalization: while reading one of the girl's diary together, "we learned about their lives, came to hold collective experiences of times we hadn't experienced, harbored private images of Lux leaning over the side of a ship to stroke her first whale" (42–43). Here Eugenides describes a realistic experience that is an analogue of his narrative practice that strays beyond the boundaries of realistic representation.

(2) Nonrealistic: In the texts by Conrad and Wright noted above we have more flagrant violations of the parameters of realistic representa-

tion. Conrad's are done solemnly without remark; Wright's narrator (like that of Armah) discloses sentiments that stretch over centuries and range across continents. Even more interesting in this context is a recent novel by Zakes Mda, *Ways of Dying* (1995). Mda provides the most playful and sustained interrogation of the curious epistemology of the "we"-narrator; an early passage in *Ways of Dying* reads as if it were intended to answer critics of the practice of Conrad, Wright, and many of their successors concerning what should be mimetically impossible kinds of knowledge and acts of focalization:

> We know everything about everybody. We even know things that happen when we are not there; things that happen behind people's closed doors deep in the middle of the night. We are the all-seeing eye of the village gossip. When in our orature the story-teller begins the story, "They say it once happened ...", we are the "they". (12)

In an attempt to ground the impossible knowledge of the contents of other minds in a first person form, the speaker playfully locates the source of such knowledge in a more unreliable (yet widely believed) source, village gossip, and then goes on to associate this narration with the well-spring of traditional oral literature. The speaker continues with some salient reflections on the control and selection of narratives in this kind of speech community and a direct address to a potentially skeptical audience: "No individual owns any story. The community is the owner of the story, and can tell it the way it deems fit. We would not be needing to justify the communal voice that tells this story if you had not wondered how we became so omniscient" (12). Here we have a slyly ironic and politically charged explanation (or pseudo-explanation) for information not available under a rigorously mimetic framework as well as a defense of traditional practices of narration and focalization from the vantage point of a first person plural voice.

As in Native American "we"-narration, there is also a socio-historical component to this choice of pronoun. As Mda states:

> The communal voice "we" is quite common in both the Nguni and the Sotho groups of languages—especially in the day-to-day speech. In Sepedi, for instance, it is respectful to address a person in the plural form. In the storytelling traditions of folk tales the communal voice is not that common since most stories are told in the third person. But in the narration of legends, myths and history (and often the boundaries are blurred here) we do find the communal voice sometimes, depending on the storyteller and his/her distance to the events.[3]

[3] Private communication to the author, 18 December 2006.

(3) Our final category is the Antimimetic: Sarraute's *Tu ne t'aime pas* (1989) eschews realism altogether, and functions instead as experimental constructions of multiple discourses that can inhabit a "we". This novel is a representation of a collection of contiguous voices, some of them contradictory, that seem to form a single, polymorphous decentered consciousness. Here, the instabilities that flavor nearly all "we"-narration are blended into the voices of a deconstructed self. As one of the voices complains at the out-set of the book: "We all do that all the time. What else can we do? Every time one of us shows himself to the outside world he designates himself as 'I,' as 'me,' [...] as if he were the only one, as if you didn't exist" (Sarraute 1990: 2). This continues: "Of course, we were a little restless, a little ill at ease, embarrassed ... Not all of us, though ... We never turn out in full force ... there are always some of us who are dozing, lazing, relaxing, wandering ... this 'we' can only refer to the ones who were there when you came out with that remark" (2, Sarraute's ellipses). The work is not so much a psychological study as a philosophical allegory of the multiple subjectivities and voices bound together in a self; its unstable, shifting, and always incomplete "we"-voices provide an apposite image of this polydirectional entity. Intriguingly, this practice yields a multiple subject with multiple focalizers. I refer to this as an anti-mimetic type of "we"-narration since it traduces the conventions of nineteenth century realism—even though the author (and many others) might well claim it is a more accurate representation of mental events than that found in realist works; Sarraute views the "self" as composed of many selves, not unlike a flock of birds in flight. Hazard Adams' novel *Many Pretty Toys* (1999) also contains extended anti-mimetic narration of a fragmented collectivity (e.g., "All of us—or rather most, for there are always believed to be dissenters—insist finally that how we reach agreement is the major part of the story, in fact is the story, of its form, or frame, or the sanction, in short, for our existence—if we exist—everything else being a filter, as it were" [16]).

In his 1996 article, Uri Margolin suggested that "we"-narratives are rare for three related reasons: because the exact scope of the "we" may remain ambiguous and may contain different members at different points in the narrative, because the question of the narrators' mental access of others' minds remains inherently unresolved, and because the sense of a collective subject is more easily conveyed in lyric or meditative texts. The examples above, I would argue, suggest a different conclusion on all three points. As recent critical studies are making apparent, "we"-narration is increasingly shown to be a supple technique with a continuous history of over a century that continues to be deployed in a considerable number of stories and novels, particularly those that emphasize the construction and maintenance of a powerful collective identity. It has been utilized by a considerable number of major twentieth century authors as well as significant figures prominent in oppositional literatures. Substantial examples of its sustained use appear in every decade of the twentieth and twenty-first centuries and its practitioners include Conrad, Kafka, Faulkner, Ignazio Silone, Raja Rao, Richard Wright, Robbe-Grillet, Butor, Sarraute, Vargas Llosa, Cortázar, Patrick Chamoiseau, Zakes Mda, Jeffrey Eugenides and Joyce Carol Oates[4].

It is certainly the case that it is an excellent vehicle for expressing a collective consciousness; the relative rarity of its use enhances its ability to highlight traditional formulas and foreground its difference from the autonomous individual consciousness associated with the rise of the novel in England and the development of modernist techniques of representing minds. For socialists, feminists, and Third World intellectuals who denounce the extremes of bourgeois egoism and the poverty of an isolated subjectivity, "we"-narration must seem a prefiguration of the new, more communal, and more egalitarian society they are working to promote. The form is also singularly adept in expressing the shared perspectives of a number of different groups, including Conrad's seamen; the isolated rural communities of Silone, Rao, and Faulkner and the preindustrial *Gemeinschaft* they share; the revolutionaries of Armah; the segregated urban poor of Mda; the soldiers of Barbusse; the children's sensibility depicted by Faulkner and Vargas Llosa; the crass cliques portrayed by Joyce Carol Oates; and even the society of mice depicted by Kafka.

Margolin's second objection has been partially answered by Margolin himself in a later study of narration in the plural (2000). In this article he clarifies that collective representations of mental activity

> are best interpreted as typification, schematization, or contraction of recognizable shared stances, perspectives, views, or common opinions held by numerous members of the group. The specific words employed are supposed to echo what most or all group members may have thought on a given occasion, but rather than being a verbatim quotation, they are in fact a condensation of numerous expressions, an image of collective inner speech, projected or invented by the narrator. (605–06)

---

4 I discuss many of these examples at greater length in my book, *Unnatural Voices*.

These comments indicate something of what is at stake in the use of such narration and focalization. I feel, however, that it is most useful to see the "we"-narrator as a different kind of figure from the realistic type of first person narrator and more like a postmodern first person narrator who refuses to be bound by the epistemological rules of realism; the same is true of "we"-focalization[5]. I argue that "we" is an essentially dialectical perspective that typically (and most successfully) plays with its own boundaries. As Celia Britton observes,

> its extreme elasticity provides a point of view that is not limited to any one character or period of time but moves around from one to another. [...] As such it creates a different representation of intersubjective relations between the individual characters, suggesting that people's most intimate feelings are known to the community. (Britton 1999: 142)

Rather than an inherently flawed, problematic, or scandalous technique, "we"-focalization is instead an extremely flexible strategy that works precisely because of its variable referents. The drama created for the reader is thus to determine how literally and how figuratively to take each such expression of shared mental events. The "we" glides between the individual subjectivity and collective omniscience, between a strict and a more lax denotation, and between mental experiences that are entirely, partially, or minimally shared. Its focalization remains fixed even as those whose perspective it describes shift positions, change, and grow larger or smaller. Much of the drama of reading such a work comes from observing the fluctuations in the group that constitutes the "we", assessing its explicit epistemological statements concerning the origin and veracity of its beliefs, attending to moves away from realism and toward a more paradoxical discourse, and noting fundamental changes in the general reliability of the "we"-narrator.

Indeed, one of the great challenges of reading this kind of fiction is to establish the relative objectivity or subjectivity of the "we". One may even discern a general, if intermittent, historical trajectory that moves from more reliably intersubjective narrators earlier in the century to ever more unreliable ones and then back again to a playful, postmodern "communal omniscience". The "we"-narrators of Silone, Rao, Wright, and (most of the time) Conrad, when confined within their own spheres of ex-

---

[5] Indeed, the most recent criticism and theory of "we"-narrations often explicitly rejects the parameters of realism: see Britton (1999: 136); Woller (1999: 346–48); Fulton (2003: 1113, note 3).

perience, are utterly reliable. Those of Eugenides are fallible, while Mda self-consciously provides his narrator with the authoritative knowledge he should not normally be able to possess. The "we" of Wright can even include the perspectives and voices of the dead.

Margolin's latest treatment of the subject still attempts to provide a mimetic framework that can explain these phenomena. But there is no need to insist on such a framework: if an author ignores these parameters, as Conrad does, or gives them a postmodern wink, as Mda prefers, then the "problem" dissolves. If Conrad's depictions of his crew's sensibilities are inherently unresolvable given the existing models based on realist conventions, then we should not limit ourselves to realist conventions when grounding our theories.

The larger theoretical problem foregrounded by more extreme forms of "we"-narration is starkly present in Mario Vargas Llosa's *The Cubs* (*Los cachorros* [1967]). In this text, "we" and "they" forms alternate, not merely in successive sections or passages, but within the same sentence: "They were still wearing short pants that year, we weren't smoking yet, of all the sports they liked football best, we were learning to ride the waves [...]" (Vargas Llosa 1989: 1). As Jean O'Bryan-Knight (1997: 340) comments, "in a single sentence [...] we observe the group [of four boys] subjectively and objectively". Vargas Llosa has thus compressed the epistemological antinomy devised by Conrad into a starkly unnatural form, thereby foregrounding the transgression that "we"-narration always threatens to enact: the collapsing of the boundary between the first and the third persons and thereby minimizing the foundational difference between the implicit fallibility of all first person narration and the inherent infallibility of third person fiction.

Such epistemic slippage has appeared before in the history of the novel: many classic examples of first person narration and focalization are by no means innocent of the transgressions apparent in "we"-narratives. As Peter Rabinowitz points out,

> Anton Lavrent'evich, the narrator of Dostoyevsky's *Possessed*, offers a limited perspective on events at the beginning of the novel. But while he remains the nominal narrator throughout the text, his persona and limitations fade away for long passages in the middle, where we receive a great deal of information to which he could have no possible access. (Rabinowitz 1987: 126–27)

Genette discusses a number of such examples, which he terms "paralepses," in Proust (cf. Genette 1980: 207–11), including

> the last thoughts of Bergotte on his deathbed, which, as has often been noted, cannot have been reported to Marcel since no one—for very good reason—could have knowledge of them. That is one paralepsis to end all paralepses; it is irreducible by any hypothesis to the narrator's information, and one we must indeed attribute to the "omniscient" novelist—and one that would be enough to prove Proust capable of transgressing the limits of his own narrative "system". (208)

We have, Genette explains, a "paradoxical—and to some people shameful—situation of a 'first-person' narrating that is nevertheless occasionally omniscient" (252). Genette offers a way out of this impasse by concluding that the "decisive criterion is not so much material possibility or even psychological plausibility as it is textual coherence and narrative tonality" (208)—typical features, it will be noted, of "we"-narration. Through this analysis, Genette provides us with the tools by which we can best comprehend "we"-focalization (though he himself unfortunately dismisses "the collective witness as narrator" as an unremarkable variant of homodiegetic narration [245]).

Later work by Dan Shen and by Henrik Skov Nielsen has further explored and foregrounded this elusive kind of oscillating narrative perspective. Shen writes that paralepses "draw attention not only to the limitations of the violated modes of focalization, but also to the fact that the barriers between modes of focalization are very much conventional" (Shen 2001: 172). Nielsen takes his analysis further, arguing for two separate theoretical entities in the case of such paraleptic texts: the narrating-I and what he calls the "impersonal voice of the narrative." The latter

> can say what a narrating-I cannot say, produce details that no person could remember, render the thoughts of other characters, speak when the character remains silent, etc. It speaks, however, in the first person, both when the possibilities of the person referred to by the first person are abandoned and when it says what this person cannot say. (Nielsen 2004: 139–40)

We can now further pinpoint the distinctive theoretical differences of "we"-narration. Genette has stated that the novelist must choose between two narrative postures, either "to have the story told by one of its 'characters', or to have it told by a narrator outside the story" (Genette 1980: 244). Whenever a text uses a first person plural narrator to depict the thoughts of others, it tends to straddle the line between first and third person fiction, as a homodiegetic character narrator discloses that which can only be known by an external heterodiegetic intelligence. These narrations are thus simultaneously first and third person discourses, and thus transcend either subtly or flagrantly the foundational oppositions set forth in different ways by Stanzel and Genette (though, as we have noted, Genette is able to see these fused in Proust). Whereas most second person narration oscillates between these two poles, "we"-narration curiously occupies both at once. Genette mentions two instances of sudden shifts in narration where the hero moves from "I" to "he" or "he" to "I" (cf. Genette 1980: 246); he calls these cases "narrative pathology" but goes on to admit that "the contemporary novel has passed that limit [...] and does not hesitate to establish between narrator and character(s) a variable or floating relationship, a pronominal vertigo in tune with a freer logic and more complex conception of 'personality'" (246). It is, I suggest, this pathology that needs to be investigated fully, and this floating relationship that needs to be theorized by narratologists.

"We"-narration, as I describe it above, is an artificial perspective that shares the characteristic features of the two other, more common, perspectives. But they too, of course, are themselves artificial conventions. The distinguishing feature of third person narration, as Käte Hamburger and others have insisted, is the disclosure of the thoughts and mental events of persons other that the narrator. This of course is not possible in life by human beings, and is an ability granted by convention to such a narrator. The first person is equally, if differently, a construct. In addition to the slippages just noted in the work of Proust and Dostoevskij, violations which could be added to indefinitely, there is the curious situation that a governess, writing in the first person, may not know what she has not perceived, but she may write in a highly (and unlikely) compelling narrative style, and one that reads just as if it were written by Henry James. Further, as Alan Palmer has recently stressed, interior monologue is not an entirely accurate representation of the jumble of thoughts, impressions, and subvocalized speech that goes on inside our heads, but rather a stylized and often misleading technique of representing consciousness. Finally, in fiction the borders between first and third person narration are often more porous than many theorists would allow. Nikolai Gogol in his 1842 story, "The Overcoat", draws attention to both of these conventions. As his protagonist is strolling in the streets of St. Petersburg at night in his new overcoat, he sees a salacious figurine in a shop window and smiles. The narrator asks a few rhetorical questions concerning the cause of this smile, before going on to aver that there is no creeping into a man's soul and finding out what he thinks. Throughout the text, however, he has been doing just that, revealing private thoughts, disclosing scenes that were unobserved, and generally assuming the prerogatives of an omniscient third person narrator—even as he complains that his memory is growing dim and he cannot recall all the details of the events he narrates. Gogol is obviously mocking these conventions and refusing to be bound by them; he is clearly telling his reader that when it comes to narration, he can do whatever he pleases—a sentiment many other novelists have obviously shared.

Concerning a theory of narration, we need both the traditional opposition of first and third person or homo- and heterodiegetic forms, as well an additional category that generally exists only in fiction which deliberately conflates the other two perspectives. Concerning focalization, I suggest that in addition to the standard conception of "who sees", in Genette's shorthand, which is limited to the narrator in first person texts and to character focalizers in third person texts, we should add an additional term, "wandering focalization", which partakes of both of the others to describe the peculiar features of "we"-narratives. We might add this to the growing list of concepts to depict unusual or deviant forms, including Genette's paraleptic focalization, David Herman's "hypothetical focalization" (cf. Herman 2002: 309–23), and what I have elsewhere called "pseudo-focalization" (Richardson 2006: 89) to designate apparent heterodiegetic depictions of a character's consciousness that turn out to be projections by a homodiegetic narrator, as found in most of the depictions of thoughts and emotions in Ian McEwan's *Atonement*, a novel that seems to be an omniscient, third-person work until it is revealed at the end to have been written by one of its characters.

References

Adams, Hazard (1999). *Many Pretty Toys*. Buffalo: SUNY Press.

Adams, Henry (1907). *Democracy, Esther, Mont saint Michel and Chartres, The Education of Henry Adams*. New York: Library of America, 1983, 715–1192.

Armah, Ayi Kwei (1973). *Two Thousand Seasons*. London: Heinemann.

Barbusse, Henri (2003). *Under Fire*. Tr. R. Buss. New York: Penguin.

Britton, Celia (1999). "Collective Narrative Voice in Three Novels by Edouard Glissant." S. Haigh (ed). *An Introduction to Caribbean and Francophone Writing*. Oxford: Berg, 135–47.

Chase, Joan (1983). *During the Reign of the Queen of Persia*. New York: Harper and Row.

Conrad, Joseph (1899). *The Nigger of the "Narcissus". Complete Works*. London: Doubleday, 1921.

Eugenides, Geoffrey (1993). *The Virgin Suicides*. New York: Farrar, Straus, and Giroux.

Fulton, Dawn (2003). "*Romans des Nous*: The First Person Plural and Collective Identity in Martinique." *The French Review* 76:6, 1104–114.

Genette, Gérard (1972). "Discours du récit." *Figures III.* Paris: Seuil, 65–278.

– (1980). *Narrative Discourse*. Tr. J. E. Lewin. Ithaca: Cornell UP.

Herman, David (2002). *Story Logic: Problems and Possibilities of Narrative.* Lincoln: U of Nebraska P.

Marcus, Amit (2001). "A Contextual View of Narrative Fiction in the First Person Plural." *Narrative* 16:1, 46–64.

Margolin, Uri (1996). "Telling Our Story: On 'We' Literary Narratives." *Language and Literature* 5:2, 115–33.

– (2000). "Telling in the Plural: From Grammar to Ideology." *Poetics Today* 21, 591–618.

Mda, Zakes (1995). *Ways of Dying.* New York: Farrar, Straus, and Giroux.

Morris, Adalaide (1992). "First Persons Plural in Contemporary Feminist Fiction." *Tulsa Studies in Women's Literature* 11, 11–29.

Ní Dhuibhne, Éilís (1988). *Blood and Water.* Dublin: Attic Press.

Nielsen, Henrik Skov (2004). "The Impersonal Voice in First-Person Narrative Fiction." *Narrative* 12, 133–50.

O'Bryan-Knight, Jean (1997). "From Spinster to Eunuch: William Faulkner's 'A Rose for Emily' and Mario Vargas Llosa's *Los cachorros*." *Comparative Literature Studies* 34, 328–47.

Palmer, Alan (2004). *Fictional Minds.* Lincoln: U of Nebraska P.

Rabinowitz, Peter (1987). *Before Reading: Narrative Conventions and the Politics of Interpretation.* Ithaca: Cornell UP.

Richardson, Brian (2006). *Unnatural Voices: Extreme Narration in Modern and Contemporary Fiction.* Columbus: Ohio State UP.

Sarraute, Nathalie (1989). *Tu ne t'aimes pas.* Paris: Gallimard.

– (1990). *You Don't Love Yourself.* Tr. B. Wright. New York: Brazilier.

Shen, Dan (2001). "Breaking Conventional Barriers: Transgressions of Modes of Focalization." W. van Peer & S. Chatman (eds). *New Perspectives on Narrative Perspective*. Albany: SUNY Press, 159–72.

Silone, Ignazio (2000). *The Abruzzo Trilogy: Fontamara, Bread and Wine, The Seed Beneath the Snow.* Tr. E. Mosbacher. South Royalton, VT: Steerforth Italia.

Vargas Llosa, Mario (1989). *The Cubs and Other Stories*. Tr. G. Kolovakos & R. Christ. New York: Noonday.

Vargas Llosa, Mario (1967). *Los jefes; Los cachorros*. Barcelona: Seia Barral, 1982.

Woller, Joel (1999). "First-person Plural: The Voice of the Masses in Farm Security Administration Documentary." *Journal of Narrative Theory* 29:3, 340–66.

Wong, Hertha D. Sweet (1998). "First Person Plural: Subjectivity and Community in Native American Women's Autobiography." S. Smith & J. Watson (eds). *Women, Autobiography, Theory: A Reader.* Madison: U of Wisconsin P, 168–78.

Wright, Richard (1941). *12 Million Black Voices.* New York: Thunder's Mouth, 1988.

Appendix: Bibliography of "We"-Narratives

Narratives Entirely or Substantially Composed in the "We"-Form

Joseph Conrad (1899). *The Nigger of the "Narcissus"*.
Henri Barbusse (1916). *Feu.*
Franz Kafka (1924). "Die Sängerin Josephine, oder das Volk der Mäuse".
Thomas Mann (1929). "Mario und der Zauberer".
Ignazio Silone (1930). *Fontemara.*
William Faulkner (1930). "A Rose for Emily".
– (1931). "That Evening Sun".
– (1931). "A Justice".
– (1931). "Divorce in Naples".
– (1932). "Death Drag".
– (1935). "That Will Be Fine".
– (1943). "Shingles for the Lord".
– (1948). "A Courtship" .
Raja Rao (1938). *Kanthapura.*
Richard Wright (1941). *12 Million Black Voices.*
Alain Robbe-Grillet (1954). "The Way Back".
Hans Erich Nossack (1963). "Das Mal".
Mauro Senesi (1963). "The Giraffe".
Michel Butor (1964). "La Gare Sainte-Lazare".
Amos Oz (1966). *Elsewhere, Perhaps.*
Mario Vargas Llosa (1967). *Los Cachorros.*
Gabriele Wohmann (1971). Stories in *Gegenangriff.*
– (1975). Stories in *Ländliches Fest.*
Pierre Silvain (1971). *Les Eoliennes.*
Ayi Kwei Armah (1973). *Two Thousand Seasons.*
Arlette and Robert Brechon (1974). *Les noces d'or.*
Edouard Glissant (1975). *Malemort.*
– (1981). *La Case du commandeur.*
Donald Barthelme (1978). "We dropped in at the Stanhope ...".
Julio Cortázar (1981). "Queremos Tanto a Glenda".
Mark Helprin (1981). "North Lights" .
John Barth (1982). *Sabbatical.*
Joan Chase (1983). *During the Reign of the Queen of Persia.*
T. C. Boyle (1985). "Greasy Lake".
Jim Crace (1988). *The Gift of Stones.*
Louise Erdrich (1988). *Tracks.*
Elfriede Jelinek (1989). *Lust.*
Nathalie Sarraute (1989). *Tu ne t'aimes pas.*
Jeffrey Eugenides (1993). *The Virgin Suicides.*
Zakes Mda (1995). *Ways of Dying.*

Patrick Chamoiseau (1997). *L'Esclave vieil homme et le molosse.*
Joyce Carol Oates (1999). *Broke Heart Blues.*
Hazard Adams (1999). *Many Pretty Toys.*
Alice Elliott Dark (2001). "Watch the Animals".
Jill McCorkle (2002). "Billy Goats".
Nadine Gordimer (2003). "Visiting George", "Look-Alikes", "Karma". *Loot and Other Stories.*
Yiyun Li (2005). "Immortality," "Persimmons." *A Thousand Years of Good Prayers.*

Narratives with Significant Sections in the "We"-Form

Gustave Flaubert (1857). Beginning of *Madame Bovary.*
Yevgeny Zamyatin (1924). *We.*
Victor Serge (1931). *Naissance de notre force.*
Gertrude Stein (1937). *Everybody's Autobiography*, chapter 4, "America."
Albert Camus (1947). *La Peste.*
Samuel Beckett (1950). *L'Innommable.*
Vladimir Nabokov (1951). *Speak Memory*, chapter 15.
Carlos Fuentes (1964). "Alma Pura".
Maurice Roche (1966). *Compact.*
Ngugi wa Thiong'o (1967). *A Grain of Wheat.*
Toni Morrison (1970). *The Bluest Eye.*
Julia Alvarez (1991). *How the Garcia Girls Lost Their Accents.*
Jean Echenois (1992). *Nous trois.*
Patrick Chamoiseau (1992). *Texaco.*

Part II: Some Special Aspects of Mediation

VIOLETA SOTIROVA
(Nottingham)

A Comparative Analysis of Indices of Narrative Point of View in Bulgarian and English

1 Aspectual Differences Between Bulgarian and English

In her 1993 book, *The Fictions of Language and the Languages of Fiction*, Monika Fludernik notes with regret that we know little as yet about how narrative viewpoint is expressed in free indirect discourse in languages such as Russian and Japanese, or other non-indo-European languages. She calls for new studies of free indirect discourse in underinvestigated languages, suspecting that knowledge of their linguistic features would have an impact on the theories narratologists construct to account for the presentation of viewpoint and consciousness. Fludernik herself outlines some of the features of free indirect discourse in Russian and she compares these with the linguistic cues she identifies for free indirect discourse in English, German and French (cf. 100–02). Although Fludernik's comments cannot be accepted as entirely justified because work on Russian and Japanese has been carried out (cf. Kuroda 1973, 1987; Pascal 1977; Schmid 2003), her monumental study of the linguistic technique of free indirect discourse hints at the possibility of using cross-linguistic evidence when attempting to theorize the form and function of free indirect discourse.

My aim in this paper will be to examine features of free indirect discourse across two languages, Bulgarian and English, and to analyze these features in relation to some unresolved issues in narrative theory. I shall focus in particular on the use of tense and aspect—two verbal categories where the differences between the two languages are most prominent and which also bear significantly on the narratological issues of voice and perspective.

Although similar to Russian in many respects, Bulgarian offers a richer system of aspectual, tense and mood categories which present complex possibilities for rendering past events and states. Similarly to verbs in other Slavonic languages, Bulgarian verbs are marked on the stem for aspect. So, pairs of verbs with the same meaning exist in the language, the only difference between them being their "finished"/perfective or "unfinished"/imperfective aspect. This aspectual distinction would roughly correspond to the English simple and progressive aspect, although one has to bear in mind that aspect in English is grammaticalized, while in Slavonic languages it is considered to be lexical. Unlike English, Bulgarian only allows the imperfective verb to be used in the indicative mood in present tense. The perfective stem is reserved for certain modal constructions and can also be used with the future marker. Where the differences between the aspectual systems of the two languages are most apparent is with the so called class of stative verbs (cf. Quirk & Greenbaum 1977: 47). Bulgarian, unlike English, maintains the aspectual distinction even on stative verbs which in English cannot take the progressive aspect. Stative verbs which according to Leech fall into four main semantic types, can in most cases be expressed in Bulgarian with either of a pair of verbs[1]:

– verbs of inert perception (feel, hear, see, smell, taste)
– verbs of inert cognition (believe, forget, hope, imagine, know, suppose, understand)
– state verbs of having and being (be, belong to, contain, consist of, cost, depend on, deserve, have, matter, own, resemble)
– verbs of bodily sensation (ache, feel, hurt, itch, tingle) (cf. Leech 1971)

Verbs of inert perception	*Perfective stem*	*Imperfective stem*
I feel:	почувствам	чувствам
I hear:	чуя	чувам
I see:	видя	виждам
I smell:	помириша	мириша
I taste:	опитам	опитвам

Verbs of inert cognition	*Perfective stem*	*Imperfective stem*
I believe:	повярвам	вярвам
I forget:	забравя	забравям
I hope:		надявам се

[1] I base my analyses of Bulgarian verbs on Andreichin et al. (1998).

I imagine:	представя си	представям си
I know:	узная	зная
I suppose:	предположа	предполагам
I understand:	разбера	разбирам

State verbs of having and being	*Perfective stem*	*Imperfective stem*
I am:	бъда	съм
I belong to:		принадлежа
I contain:		съдържам
I consist of:		състоя се
I cost:		струвам
I depend on:		завися
I deserve:	заслужа	заслужавам
I have:		имам
I matter:		знача
I own:		притежавам
I resemble:		приличам

Verbs of bodily sensation	*Perfective stem*	*Imperfective stem*
it aches/hurts me:	заболи ме	боли ме
it itches me:	засърби ме	сърби ме
it tingles me:	защипе ми	щипе ми

The semantic difference between the two aspectual types in Bulgarian—"finished" and "unfinished"—lies in the way in which they present the event or situation. Similarly to other languages, the finished aspect is synthetic, it views the event as a whole in its completion. The unfinished aspect is analytical and views the event in progress, in the process of unfolding. All verb stems in Bulgarian belong to one of the aspectual classes: perfective/finished or imperfective/unfinished, with most of them having an aspectual counterpart. Some verb stems only exist in one of the classes and their corresponding aspectual partner is formed through affixation. The use of a prefix (по-; за-) in the case of "feel" and "ache" is thus normal in the transformation of an imperfective stem into a perfective verb. But while in some cases the difference between such pairs of verbs is purely aspectual, in others there is also a more perceptible change in lexical meaning (e.g. the verb becoming inchoative or semelfactive). However, the aspectual distinction is present, even if the lexical meaning also undergoes a change when transforming these imperfective verbs into perfective. Bulgarian morphologists explain the existence of these so called "defective" verbs with the fact that their lexical meaning does not readily allow them to take the perfective. Such would be the case with most of the verbs in Leech's class of "state verbs of having and being". However, the other semantic classes of stative verbs can take either of a pair of verbs in Bulgarian. Stative verbs, then, are of special interest because in one of my languages for the purposes of this comparison we have two possibilities, while in the other, in English, only the simple aspect is allowed by the grammar. The Bulgarian pairs of verbs I have given in the tables are both in the present tense. Further, more complex distinctions would be present in the rendering of past states.

What emerges so far from the brief sketch of aspectual differences between Bulgarian and English is that dynamic verbs in most cases would be translatable with equivalent forms across the two languages, but the rendering of stative verbs would be more intricate because of the two aspectual possibilities in Bulgarian. This difference between the two languages would be interesting to pursue, not only for a purely linguistic comparison, but also because it bears on some important issues in narrative theory.

2 Implications for Narrative Theory

It has already been noted by narratologists that stative verbs in the past tense make sentences of free indirect discourse indistinguishable from narration because they cannot take the progressive aspect. This class of stative verbs also poses problems for another reason. They usually denote some kind of mental state of the character and as such hover on the brink between narration and character point of view. There is disagreement as to whether such sentences should be classed as free indirect discourse or whether they stem from the narrator's point of view. All such sentences, containing mental verbs, such as "believe, know, feel, suppose, suspect, expect", etc. fall under Short et al.'s (1996) category of "internal narration" which the authors add to Leech & Short's (1981) cline of modes of speech and thought presentation after extensive work on a large corpus of narrative texts. The need for new categories is suggested by the numerous examples drawn from these texts, or as the authors assert: “In fictional texts, narrators may provide reports of characters’ cognitive activities and emotional states which do not fall under any of Leech and Short’s categories for thought presentation” (Short et al. 1996: 124).

Short et al.’s examples of Internal Narration include sentences, such as: “Her approval filled the military young man with happiness” (Aldous Huxley, *Point Counter Point*); “For a moment he was rendered motionless by surprise, a kind of respect” (Rupert Thomson, *The Five Gates to Hell*). The reason why the presentation of these states does not fit into the Leech & Short (1981) model is that all of the categories associated closely with the character’s point of view in this initial taxonomy are verbal categories. Most importantly, free indirect thought has to be translatable into direct thought in order to qualify as such. What we have in these examples, on the other hand, are states that are not necessarily verbalized or articulated in inner speech. When Short et al. (1996) introduce this new category of Internal Narration, they position it at the leftmost end of their cline, next to pure narration. This means that the narration of internal states is viewed by them as almost fully in the narrator’s control and not tinged with the character’s voice or perspective, or as they say: “we are given insights into a character’s internal states or changes, but no representation of specific thoughts of the character.” (125) The reason for their interpretation of sentences of internal narration as akin to narratorial discourse, I think, lies not least in the fact that these states are not readily verbalized into inner speech. But no more elaboration on these decisions is given at this stage than simply to state: “clearly, NI lies at the interface between narration and thought presentation” (125). The speech and thought presentation clines then look like this:

						Norm		
Narrator in control	*N*	*NV*	*NRSA*	*IS*	*FIS*	*DS*	*FDS*	*Character in control*
	N	*NI*	*NRTA*	*IT*	*FIT*	*DT*	*FDT*	
				Norm				

N—Narration
NV—Narrator’s report of voice
NRSA—Narrator’s representation of speech act
IS—Indirect speech
FIS—Free indirect speech
DS—Direct speech
FDS—Free direct speech

N—Narration
NI—Narration of internal states
NRTA—Narrator’s representation of thought act
IT—Indirect thought
FIT—Free indirect thought
DT—Direct thought
FDT—Free direct thought

Sentences of internal narration are thus less closely associated with the character's internal point of view than sentences of indirect thought or even narrative reports of thought acts, examples of which would be: "Jed thought he understood" (Rupert Thomson, *The Five Gates to Hell*); "As she walked down the Charing Cross Road, she put to herself a series of questions" (Virginia Woolf, *Night and Day*). More surprisingly, Short et al. draw a further distinction between "cognitive or emotional experiences" which fall under internal narration and "reports of characters' perceptions, whether the stimuli are internal ('She felt a pain in her stomach') or external ('She felt the softness of his hair')" which they say "would be coded as narration" (Short et al. 1996: 125).

This type of sentence, rendering the mental states of characters, is classed as psychonarration by Dorrit Cohn (1978). Cohn explains that such sentences can give us a glimpse into the character's almost unconscious states and as such allow for non-articulated thoughts and feelings to be presented to the reader. Fludernik later identifies psychonarration with "the narrative's external description of figural consciousness" (Fludernik 1993: 136). Although Cohn considers the mode of psychonarration important, she like Short et al. privileges what Palmer calls "the speech category account" of the presentation of fictional minds (Palmer 2002: 28). Palmer takes issue with this account because he thinks that all of the modes for the presentation of thoughts and states of the mind, identified by narratologists and stylisticians, tend towards viewing the content of consciousness as internalized speech and because "these concepts do not add up to a complete and coherent study of all aspects of the minds of characters in novels" (Palmer 2002: 28). What he identifies as missing from existing accounts of thought presentation is "the role of thought report in describing emotions and the role of behavior descriptions in conveying motivation and intention" (28), or all of these sentences that Short et al. would class under their category of Narration of Internal States.

Palmer is right in arguing that analyzing consciousness as consisting of articulated, verbalized speech would result in viewing it as highly self-reflective. This tendency is apparent in a number of stylistic accounts of free indirect discourse where features of direct discourse, such as direct questions, exclamations, imperatives, are seen as some of its central indices. Only perception among the non-verbal processes of consciousness has been recognized as part of free indirect discourse and only by some theoreticians (Brinton [1980]; Banfield [1982]). But perception as a valid component of free indirect discourse only encompasses characters' perceptions of the external narrative world that surrounds them. It is usually identified by the use of deixis: progressive aspect or proximal deictic adverbs and its content refers to the character's outside world. The kind of states of the mind that Palmer is arguing have been excluded from studies of narrative or simply relegated to a less important position in the presentation of fictional minds include, in his words, "mental phenomena as mood, desires, emotions, sensations, visual images, attention, and memory" (Palmer 2002: 31). These can be exemplified by one of the extracts that he quotes from Austen's *Emma* (1816):

> Not that Emma was gay and thoughtless from any real felicity; it was rather because she felt less happy than she had expected. She laughed because she was disappointed; and though she liked him for his attentions, and thought them all, whether in friendship, admiration, or playfulness, extremely judicious, they were not winning back her heart. She still intended him for her friend. (362; cited in Palmer 2002: 35)

Here Emma is reflecting on Frank Churchill's behavior towards her. Her emotional response to his "attentions", which we as readers know were misjudged, is captured in a series of sentences that contain either a verb, or an adjective, or an adverb, or a noun that corresponds to a mental state of the character: "gay, thoughtless, felicity, felt, happy, expected, laughed, disappointed, liked, thought, heart, intended". Palmer captures all such narrative sentences under a category which he argues is equally, if not more, important than what has traditionally been defined as free indirect discourse: what he calls "thought report" (Palmer 2002: 30). One of the reasons behind the neglect of this category by narratologists and stylisticians he sees in the fact that the presentation of consciousness here is done by the narrator, whereas narratologists have tended to privilege modes of presentation that stem more directly from the character or are perceived as more mimetic (cf. 31).

Palmer's argument then clashes with the other stylistic and narratological accounts reviewed here in respect of the importance of the different categories used for the presentation of minds in fiction. He argues for a more inclusive and more comprehensive analysis of the different ways in which readers can have a glimpse of characters' fictional minds. But he concurs with them on one important point: that the report of internal states which corresponds to Short et al.'s category of internal narration is under the narrator's control. I would agree with Palmer that bracketing out the internal states of characters from our analysis would mean to miss out a very important dimension of characterization in narrative. But I would question the understanding of internal states as closely related to narration and as stemming entirely from the narrator.

3 Case-studies

If Bulgarian offers two alternatives for most stative verbs denoting mental states of characters, then this should complicate the position adopted by Short et al. that such sentences are entirely in the narrator's control. I will begin my comparison of the use of aspect as a cue of narrative view-point across two passages from Lawrence's *Sons and Lovers* (1913) and their Bulgarian translations:

> (A) One day in March he *lay* on the bank of Nethermere, with Miriam sitting beside him. It *was* a glistening, white-and-blue day. Big clouds, so brilliant, *went by* overhead, while shadows *stole along* on the water. The clear spaces in the sky *were* of clean, cold blue. Paul *lay* on his back in the old grass, looking up. He *could not bear* to look at Miriam. She *seemed* to want him, and he *resisted*. He *resisted* all the time. He *wanted* now to give her passion and tenderness, and he *could not*. He *felt* that she *wanted* the soul out of his body, and not him. All his strength and energy she *drew* into herself through some channel which *united* them. She *did not want* to meet him, so that there *were* two of them, man and woman together. She *wanted* to draw all of him into her. It *urged* him to intensity like madness, which *fascinated* him as drug-taking *might*. (239; italics added)

Most of the sentences in this passage would probably be classed not as free indirect discourse, but as internal narration or even narration on Short et al.'s model. They contain verbs of cognition and emotion which on their analysis presuppose an external reporter of the state of the character, i.e. the narrator. Because Bulgarian offers at least two alternatives for most of these verbs, it would be interesting to follow through their Bulgarian translations.

One of the complications arising at this point would be that apart from the aspectual distinction on the stem of the verb, in the past tense Bulgarian also offers two alternative endings. These are regarded as tenses by Bulgarian linguists: the Past Complete Tense, or the Aorist, and the Past Incomplete Tense, or the Imperfect[2]. Most commonly, verbs with perfective or finished stems would take Aorist endings and verbs with imperfective or unfinished stems would take Past Incomplete endings. But crossovers are also possible and new shades of meaning are created. Thus, imperfective stems can take Aorist endings in which case most typically

[2] Strictly speaking, this distinction in the past tense is also aspectual.

they usually mean that the action is completed in the past but it has had a certain duration while being carried out. For example, in a sentence like: "For nine years he *wandered about*, homeless, sleepless, restless"[3], the imperfective verb would be combined with the Aorist to express this meaning of duration and completion at the same time. Or, it is also possible to combine imperfective verbs with the Aorist in order to express iterative events within a limited period of time: e.g. "Several times during the night I was *awoken* by the loud barking of the dog".

The Past Incomplete Tense, or the Imperfect, denotes events in progress, concurrent with another past orientational moment, which may not have finished before the moment of speaking. Most typically, the Past Incomplete Tense combines with imperfective or unfinished verb stems. But perfective stems can also take the Past Incomplete Tense in some special circumstances. Usually, this combination of perfective verb stem with Past Unfinished Tense, or Imperfect, results in modal meanings—conditional, optative etc.: e.g. "If this *happened*, then the trip would be most delightful; If only the damned telegram would *arrive*". And finally, perfective stems in the Past Incomplete could express habitual events: "He *would get up* in the morning, *lay* the table and *begin to wait* for the others". Thus, a four-way distinction of past meanings is possible in Bulgarian, a feature unique to Bulgarian and Macedonian, which does not occur in other Slavonic languages. Most typically, however, perfective verbs would take the Aorist and imperfective verbs the Imperfect past tense endings. This is the case in the first Lawrence passage that I quote above. All of the verbs I have underlined are rendered by the Bulgarian translator as imperfective verbs in the Past Incomplete Tense. In the table below I have given both the imperfective form in the Past Incomplete and the perfective counterpart in the Aorist in order to highlight the possibility of an alternative choice.

he lay:	легна (perfective Aorist) – лежеше (imperfective Imperfect)
was:	беше (imperfective Imperfect)
they went by:	се понесоха (perfective Aorist) – се носеха (imperfective Imperfect)
they stole along:	се прокраднаха (perfective Aorist) – се прокрадваха (imperfective Imperfect)

3 Examples are directly translated from Bulgarian examples in Andreichin et al. (1998).

they were:	се синяха (perfective Aorist) – се синееха (imperfective Imperfect) [verb derived from "blue"]
he could not bear:	нямаше сили (imperfective Imperfect) [had no strength]
she seemed to want:	пожела (perfective Aorist) – желаеше (imperfective Imperfect) [desired]
he resisted:	съпротиви (perfective Aorist) – съпротивяваше (imperfective Imperfect)
he wanted:	поиска (perfective Aorist) – искаше (imperfective Imperfect)
he could not:	не можа (perfective Aorist) – не можеше (imperfective Imperfect)
he felt:	почувства (perfective Aorist) – чувстваше (imperfective Imperfect)
she drew:	изсмука (perfective Aorist) – изсмукваше (imperfective Imperfect) [suck out]
she did not want:	не поиска (perfective Aorist) – не искаше (imperfective Imperfect)
it urged:	изпълни (perfective Aorist) – изпълваше (imperfective Imperfect) [filled throughout]
it fascinated:	омая (perfective Aorist) – омайваше (imperfective Imperfect) [fascinated, intoxicated]

In all of the sentences that focus on Paul's internal states the translator has chosen the imperfective verb with Past Incomplete endings. This renders the experience as being in the process of unfolding. Bulgarian linguists point out that the Past Incomplete corresponds in all of its meanings to the present tense and as such, when used in quasi-direct discourse, it denotes experience which is current and immediate for the character. These semantic properties of the Past Incomplete and of imperfective verbs give a different shade of meaning as opposed to perfective verbs in the Past Complete. Each and every sentence of this passage could have been translated using perfective verbs in the Past Complete. However, their typical value of denoting punctual events, completed in the past, and arranged chronologically might not have been entirely adequate stylistically. I think that given the semantic properties of all the verbs in the passage, and given the meaning of the whole episode, the translator's decision to choose imperfective verbs in the Past Incomplete has been sensitive and justified.

But apart from rendering the episode successfully in a foreign language, the translator's choices also signal the strong semantic connotations of these sentences: they are closely associated with the character's experiences and as such stem from his point of view. Translating all of these events and states in a tense and aspect that foreground the progress of the experience makes this experience more immediate.

An immediate conclusion that can be reached at this point is that mental verbs which denote states of the character are always translated as imperfective verbs in the Past Incomplete. But it is not the case, as the following passage from the same novel demonstrates:

> (B) Morel *watched* her shyly. He *saw* again the passion she *had had* for him. It *blazed* upon her for a moment. He *was* shy, rather scared, and humble. Yet again he *felt* his old glow. And then immediately he *felt* the ruin he *had made* during these years. He *wanted* to bustle about, to run away from it. (243; italics added)

Interestingly, the verbs in this passage are mostly rendered as perfective Aorists. The list of pairs of verbs, where available, is included below:

he watched:	погледна (perfective Aorist)—гледаше (imperfective Imperfect)
he saw:	усети (perfective Aorist)—усещаше (imperfective Imperfect) [=felt]
it blazed:	припламна (perfective Aorist)—припламваше/пламтеше (imperfective Imperfect)
he was shy:	се притесни (perfective Aorist)—се притесняваше (imperfective Imperfect) [=got anxious]
he felt:	усети (perfective Aorist)—усещаше (imperfective Imperfect)
he felt:	почувства (perfective Aorist)—чувстваше (imperfective Imperfect)
he had made:	се е превърнал (Past indefinite) [=had transformed himself into]
he wanted:	прииска му се (perfective Aorist)—искаше му се (imperfective Imperfect)

There is only one imperfective form in the Imperfect in the whole passage and that is the form of the first verb "watched". In all other instances where the English verb is in the Past Simple the Bulgarian translator has chosen to render it with a perfective verb in the Aorist. Although some verbs in the passage could have been rendered in the Imperfect with imperfective verb stems, the choice has in this case fallen on the perfective

Aorist. I use this passage to demonstrate that both alternatives are available in the language. If we are only guided by the type of verb, stative verbs can be translated as imperfective Imperfects as we saw in passage (A) and they can also be translated as perfective Aorists as we see here in passage (B). The question now would be: is this a random decision on the part of the translator?

This passage, as opposed to the one quoted in (A), displays certain signals of temporal ordering that might perhaps account for the translator's choice of perfective Aorists. In sentence two where the translator switches to perfective Aorists, we have the adverb "again" which suggests a new occurrence of an event and as such punctuates the series of events. The adverb features in the Bulgarian translation and might be taken as a signal of a particular moment in the chronological development of the narrative. Sentence three also displays an adverbial phrase which denotes instantaneousness: "for a moment". The verb that the translator uses here begins with a prefix "при-" that is a common perfective prefix on verb stems. There is a possibility to derive an imperfective verb from this perfective stem, but its meaning in this case would be of an intermit-tent event, e.g. it can be used with the verb "to light" as in "присвятква" (=there are lightnings). Without the prefix the imperfective form of the verb could readily take the Imperfect and mean simply "it was blazing". Since here English also offers a choice between simple and progressive, the translator has adhered closely to the writer's choice of verb, but also has observed the semantic restrictions imposed by the adverbial phrase. The verb in the next sentence "he felt" is a stative verb, so its form in English is limited to the Past Simple, but the Bulgarian form chosen is again of a perfective Aorist. It seems to me that the presence of the adverbs "yet again" is once more taken as a contextual clue for the punctuality and chronological ordering of the events described.

A similar reasoning might have resulted in the choice of a perfective Aorist for the verb "he felt" in the next sentence. Here, the explicit chronological adverb "then" and the punctuality denoted by the other adverb "immediately" have probably triggered the choice of verb form made by the translator. Bulgarian would not permit the combination of either of these adverbs with an imperfective verb in the Imperfect. Although here the translator omits "then", "immediately" on its own imposes the same restriction. The final sentence would permit the use of an imperfective Imperfect verb, but what seems to have happened here is that the constraints on some of the verbs in the passage influence the rest of the verb choices. Perhaps switches from one aspectual class to another within the boundaries of a short paragraph like this would have resulted in incoherence, or as Jacob Mey describes this phenomenon, here we have the principle of "interpretative obstination" or "syntactic inertia" (Mey 1999: 33). In other words, unless strongly prompted to reshape an interpretation, a reader will keep an established interpretation within sentence boundaries, and even across sentences and within paragraphs. Once the pattern of using perfective Aorists is established in sentence two, the translator adheres to it throughout the paragraph, thus suggesting an interpretation of these sentences as stemming from the narrator's point of view. A shift to the other aspectual class would have resulted in a shift to the character's point of view which if chosen in the final sentence alone would have required too big an interpretative leap.

The translator's choices of verb forms in (A) would strongly suggest that character states are not entirely in the narrator's control. Even though they cannot, and probably are not, consciously articulated by the character, it is semantically implausible to position them under the narrator's control on Short et al.'s cline of modes of thought presentation if a narrative internal viewpoint is suggested through the use of imperfective verbs in the Imperfect past tense. On the other hand, the verb forms used in the translation of (B) would seem to support the position adopted by Short et al. since perfective Aorists would imply that these states are viewed holistically as punctual, discrete and completed events in the past. Perhaps this would support the hypothesis that these states, precisely because they cannot be verbalized by the character are more likely to stem from the narrator's viewpoint. Another passage from *Sons and Lovers*, quoted in (C), would address this issue further:

> (C) Miriam *was astonished* and *hurt* for him. It *had cost* him an effort. She *left* him, wanting to spare him any further humiliation. A fine rain *blew* in her face as she *walked* along the road. She *was hurt* deep down; and she *despised* him for being blown about by any wind of authority. And in her heart of hearts, unconsciously, she *felt* that he *was trying* to get away from her. This she *would never have acknowledged.* She *pitied* him. (241; italics added)

Only in the first sentence the translator has chosen to render the English past tense with two perfective verbs in the Aorist. All of the other English verbs in the past simple appear in the Bulgarian translation as imperfective Imperfects:

she was astonished:	се учуди (perfective Aorist)—се чудеше (imperfective Imperfect)
she was hurt:	й домъчня (perfective Aorist)—беше й мъчно (imperfective Imperfect)
had cost him:	му бе струвало
she left him:	си тръгна (perfective Aorist)—си тръгваше (imperfective Imperfect)
she walked:	(из)вървя (perfective Aorist)—вървеше (imperfective Imperfect)
it blew:	запръска (perfective Aorist)—пръскаше (imperfective Imperfect)
she was hurt:	прониза (perfective Aorist)—пронизваше (imperfective Imperfect)
she despised him:	презря го (perfective Aorist)—презираше го (imperfective Imperfect)
she felt:	почувства (perfective Aorist)—чувстваше (imperfective Imperfect)
she would never have acknowledged:	никога не би признала

What is of particular interest in this passage is the sentence: "And in her heart of hearts, unconsciously, she felt that he was trying to get away from her." The explicit lexical signals that the feelings of the character are buried deep beneath the level of consciousness and that they are indeed unconscious would perhaps prompt some analysts to attribute this sentence to the narrator. After all, Miriam is not consciously aware of these feelings and what is more she would never have acknowledged them. But interestingly, this transcription of what is supposedly hidden from the character herself is rendered once again in Bulgarian with verbs that very much implicate her own experience of these states in the text. Do we, therefore, need to posit an external observer for the presentation of these states; is the voice of the narrator necessary in sentences of character internal states for the reasons that Short et al. list?

On the evidence of the examples so far I would argue that the element of unconscious half-sensing of certain states on the part of the character is not a valid reason to attribute sentences of this kind to the narrator. A language like Bulgarian that allows aspectual distinctions for these kinds of verbs can be used as a nice test-case of the two possibilities of attributing such sentences to the narrator or to the character. My passage (A) offers evidence that the internal states of the character are more strongly linked with that character's viewpoint than with the narrator's voice. Passage (B), on the other hand, shows that imperfective Imperfects are not the only available option for rendering past tense stative verbs into Bulgarian and that contextual signals impose semantic restrictions on the interpretation of viewpoint in the paragraph as a whole. The most instructive example, perhaps, is the passage quoted in (C). It shows that Bulgarian allows the use of imperfective verbs in the Imperfect, even where we are explicitly told that a character is unconscious of a certain state. In this case it seems that the semantic properties of the verbs which denote mental states are so strongly linked with character subjectivity that their imperfective forms coupled with the Imperfect are considered to be the stylistically appropriate option. The interpretation of the passage, thus, is once again as arising from Miriam's point of view, rather than as a report delivered by a controlling narrator.

Further confirmation of the strong semantic links between stative and mental verbs and character point of view is also witnessed in the comparison of a passage from Woolf's *To the Lighthouse* (1927) with its Bulgarian counterpart:

(D) But his son *hated* him. He *hated* him for coming up to them, for stopping and looking down on them; he *hated* him for interrupting them; he *hated* him for the exaltation and sublimity of his gestures; for the magnificence of his head; for his exactingness and egotism (for there he *stood,* commanding them to attend to him); but most of all, he *hated* the twang and twitter of his father's emotion which, vibrating round them, *disturbed* the perfect simplicity and good sense of his relations with his mother. By looking fixedly at the page, he *hoped* to make him move on; by pointing his finger at a word, he *hoped* to recall his mother's attention, which, he *knew* angrily, *wavered* instantly his father *stopped.* But no. Nothing *would make* Mr Ramsey move on. There he *stood,* demanding sympathy. (44; italics added)

he hated:	намрази (perfective Aorist)—мразеше (imperfective Imperfect)
he stood:	застана (perfective Aorist)—стои (present)
vibrating:	не спряха (perfective Aorist)—не спираха [did not stop (to flutter)]
he hoped:	се надяваше (imperfective Imperfect)
he knew:	узна (perfective Aorist)—знаеше (imperfective Imperfect) разсърди (perfective Aorist)—сърдеше (imperfective Imperfect)
wavered:	се разсея (perfective Aorist)—се разсейваше (imperfective Imperfect) [got distracted]

would make:	не беше в състояние (imperfective Imperfect) [nothing was in the ability to]
he stood:	застана (perfective Aorist)—стоеше (imperfective Imperfect)

The pattern of choosing imperfective Imperfect verbs is repeated here as well. In some cases, as with the verb "hope", the translator has had no alternative; in others, as with the non-stative verb "stood", the alternative perfective Aorist could have been chosen. But all of the mental verbs that denote states of the character are once again rendered with imperfective verbs in the Imperfect. What is perhaps most revealing about this extract is that in one place the translator spontaneously chooses the present tense verb: appropriately, this occurs in the clause inserted in parentheses that interrupts the coherence of the series of parallel clauses beginning with "he hated him." There are no strict rules about the sequence of tenses in Bulgarian which allows the use of the present in subordinate clauses for example, so these transitions from past to present are perceived as far less ungrammatical than in English. In this case, the digression in the character's mind which is inserted in parentheses, is felt by the translator to be an experience so immediate that she renders the verb in an aspect and tense that foreground the duration of the event and its presentness, thus placing us amidst its unfolding.

On the evidence of the Bulgarian translations of (A), (C) and (D), then, I would like to suggest that the narrative internal observation point from which the events and states described in these passages are viewed is the character's. The imperfective aspect, coupled with the Past Incomplete, creates this sense of experientiality. In the three passages from Lawrence and Woolf—(A), (C) and (D)—we have witnessed a consistent pattern of choosing imperfective verbs in the past Imperfect which strongly suggests that the semantic cues of the three passages foreground the character's own experience of the situation. Even when these experiences are not verbalized and even when they are explicitly stated to be unconscious states of the character, the aspectual rendering of the verbs in Bulgarian provides evidence that we are still within the character's consciousness. Example (B), on the other hand, which makes consistent use of perfective verbs in the Aorist, brings to the fore the role played by other contextual signals, such as adverbial expressions. In both cases, where imperfective Imperfect verbs are chosen and where perfective Aorist verbs are chosen by the translator, the semantics of the whole passage has obviously played the strongest part in these decisions.

This analysis does not mean that for English speakers such sentences sound more removed from the character's viewpoint than for Bulgarian speakers. The semantic properties of these verbs suggest strongly enough the character's internal experience of events and states, regardless of whether the language system grammaticalizes or lexicalizes these semantic meanings in aspectual distinctions. In English, grammar and meaning part in that the grammar does not allow stative verbs to take the progress-sive aspect of experientiality. In Bulgarian, these distinctions are available and it is the context that determines whether one chooses the imperfective or the perfective. Once this choice is made, the interpretation of viewpoint is very strongly suggested by the verbal aspect and past tense ending, with the imperfective Imperfect placing us inside the character's consciousness and the perfective Aorist denoting an external report of the states of consciousness experienced by the character.

4 Conclusions

From a narratological and stylistic standpoint, then, sentences denoting the internal states of characters merit a semantic analysis. Simply assigning them to narration, or placing them on the borderline between narration and the other modes of thought presentation does not capture adequately their effects on readers. The fact that such sentences cannot readily be transformed into direct speech should not be taken as proof that they are not expressive of the character's point of view, but rather should prompt us to question the transformational account of free indirect discourse. If we revisit some of our examples so far, we will find that there are enough many other markers of subjectivity in these sentences to warrant an interpretation of character internal point of view: in the *Emma* passage, all of the words denoting emotion from different classes ("gay," "thoughtless," "felicity," "happy," "disappointed," etc.), the intensifier "extremely"; in passage (A) from *Sons and Lovers*, the modal verb "could," the proximal deictic "now," and again a series of nouns subjectively referring to the inner life of the protagonist ("soul," "strength," "energy," "intensity," "madness"); in passage (C) from *Sons and Lovers*, the past perfect of character's past experience ("it had cost him"), the progressive of "he was trying," the proximal deictic "this"; and finally, in passage (D) from *To the Lighthouse*, the evaluative "exaltation," "sublimity," "egotism," "twang and twitter of his father's emotion," "perfect simplicity," "angrily". These contextual signals, along with the verbs which denote mental and emotional states of the character are the semantic guarantors for reading these passages as stemming from the character's point of view and perhaps should be included in a broader definition of the free indirect mode, not as discourse, but as a particular style of writing consciousness. On the other hand, passage (B), with its contextual signals of punctuality of the states and events and of their chronological ordering would perhaps invite also from English readers a more narrator-orientated interpretation. Ultimately, what cross-linguistic comparisons of this kind bring to light is the importance of semantic and contextual analyses rather than purely syntactic transformational accounts of the different modes of consciousness presentation.

As McHale (1978: 263) points out, already Vološinov (1973) had shown that free indirect discourse, or his quasi-direct discourse, cannot be theorized in purely syntactic terms as a fusion of two possible modes of report, direct and indirect. Rather, he, and later Baxtin (1975), see it as the collision or sounding in harmony of two voices, of two angles of vision, of two points of view. This argument in favor of a semantic analysis of free indirect discourse does not mean that the syntactic properties of this mode should be ignored, but syntax should not be allowed to determine an interpretation; it should only be an explanatory tool in the process of unpacking interpretations. The semantic argument that Vološinov and Baxtin advance is fully justified linguistically by Adamson (1994) who finds the semantic roots of the free indirect mode in the everyday practices of empathetic deixis and echoic, or quotative, modalized utterances. On this analysis, the style of writing character point of view emerges as an independent form which is not derived from a transformation of a pre-existing construction (direct or indirect) or as a blend of two constructions, but is based on linguistic practices that also have their psychological counterpart: empathy and echolalia. This semantic account of the free indirect style opens up the possibility of broadening out its parameters. It does not have to be the product of a syntactic transformation, but is governed by the semantics of experience. If we set it apart from its alleged base forms: direct and indirect discourse, then the connection that many have seen between sentences of free indirect discourse and inner speech also becomes more tenuous and the name "discourse" itself becomes questionable.

References

Adamson, Sylvia (1994). "Subjectivity in Narration: Empathy and Echo." M. Yaguello (ed). *Subjecthood and Subjectivity*. Paris: Ophrys, 183–98.

Andrejčin, Ljubomir et al. (1998). *Bulgarska gramatika na suvremennija literaturen ezik. Tom 2: Morfologija* [*Bulgarian Grammar of the Contemporary Literary Language, Vol. 2: Morphology*]. Sofia: Abagar.

Austen, Jane (1816). *Emma*. London: Penguin, 1966.

Baxtin (Bakhtin), Mixail (1975). "Slovo v romane" ["Discourse in the novel"]. *Voprosy literatury I ėstetiki* [*Questions of literature and aesthetics*]. Moscow: Xudožestvennaja literatura, 72–233.

Banfield, Ann (1982). *Unspeakable Sentences: Narration and Representation in the Language of Fiction*. Boston: Routledge & Kegan Paul.

Brinton, Laurel (1980). "Represented Perception: A Study in Narrative Style." *Poetics* 9, 363–81.

Cohn, Dorrit (1978). *Transparent Minds: Narrative Modes for Presenting Consciousness in Fiction*. Princeton, NJ: Princeton UP.

Fludernik, Monika (1993). *The Fictions of Language and the Languages of Fiction*. London: Routledge.

Kuroda, Shigeyuki (1973). "Where Epistemology, Style and Grammar Meet: A Case Study from the Japanese." P. Kiparsky & S. Anderson (eds). *A Festschrift for Morris Halle*. New York: Winston, 377–91.

– (1987). "A Study of the So-Called Topic *wa* in Passages from Tolstoi, Lawrence, and Faulkner (of course, in Japanese translation)." J. Hinds et al. (eds). *Perspectives on Topicalisation. The Case of Japanese "wa"*. Amsterdam: Benjamins, 143– 61.

Lawrence, David Herbert (1913). *Sons and Lovers*. London: Penguin, 1973.

– (1990). *Sinove i ljubovnitsi* [*Sons and Lovers*]. Tr. L. Aleksandrova. Sofia: Profizdat.

Leech, Geoffrey (1971). *Meaning and the English Verb*. London: Longman.

Leech, Geoffrey & Short, Mick (1981). *Style in Fiction: Linguistic Introduction to English Fictional Prose*. London: Longman.

McHale, Brian (1978). "Free Indirect Discourse: A Survey of Recent Accounts." *Poetics and Theory of Literature* 3, 249–87.

Mey, Jacob (1999). *When Voices Clash. A Study in Literary Pragmatics*. Berlin: de Gruyter.

Palmer, Alan (2002). "The Construction of Fictional Minds." *Narrative* 10:1, 28–46.

Pascal, Roy (1977). *The Dual Voice. Free Indirect Speech and its Functioning in the Nineteenth Century European Novel*. Manchester: Manchester UP.

Quirk, Randolph & Greenbaum, Sidney (1977). *A University Grammar of English*. London: Longman.

Schmid, Wolf (2003). *Narratologiia*. Moscow: Iazyki slavianskoi kul'tury.

Short, Mick et al. (1996). "Using a Corpus for Stylistics Research: Speech and Thought Presentation." J. Thomas & M. Short (eds). *Using Corpora for Language Research*. London: Longman, 110–31.

Vološinov (Volochinov), Valentin (1973). *Marxism and the Philosophy of Language*. Tr. L. Matejka & I. R. Titunik. New York: Seminar Press.
Woolf, Virginia (1927). *To the Lighthouse*. London: Grafton Books, 1977.
– (2000). *Kum fara* [*To the Lighthouse*]. Tr. I. Vasileva. Pleven: EA.

TOMÁŠ KUBÍČEK
(Prague)

Focalization, the Subject and the Act of Shaping Perspective

A study of the history of the notion of focalization shows that the two distinct structural levels upon which it is considered[1] have, time and again, given rise to an endemic conflict, and that the ensuing disputes between two opposing camps of theorists have taken place not within the framework of either level, but across them. This is why they are constantly latent, and always ready to erupt. It would be possible to say that this occurs in this way because their subject (the subject of their investigation), in connection with the definition of focalization, is not the same. For Genette and his disciples this subject is the narrative (which itself is focal-

[1] Genette speaks about focalization at the narrative level, and for him this corresponds with "selection" of information (Genette uses the term "selection" even though he is aware of the danger this brings owing to an implied concept of mimesis). Focalization thus provides the basis for some kind of complex "view" of narration. Against this, Bal situates the entire theory of focalization on the level at which the characters of a narrative focalize the world of narrative events most simply: the story. She states: "In a story, elements of the fabula are presented in a certain way. We are confronted with a vision of the fabula" (Bal 1985: 100). The sentence, "Elizabeth saw him lie there, pale and lost in thought," is therefore for her an example of focalization, in which, for Bal, Elizabeth is the focalizer who does the focalizing, and she does not enquire whether there is also someone else, focalizing both "him" and "Elizabeth". Thus the "focus on narrative" (or, as Genette says, the narrator—or, beyond the convention that takes the fiction into account, the author) is a strategy that brings about this type of focalization. Moreover, Genette speaks also of focalization of the narrator, which, according to him, is logically implied in the case of first-person narration. Genette thus regards it as inapposite to personify focalization at the level of focalizers by whose mediation the elements of the story would be focalized: according to him only the narrative itself may be focalized, and as a complex entity. And Bal also says: "Focalization is the relationship between the 'vision', the agent that sees, and that which is seen. This relationship is a component of the *story part*, of the content of the narrative text: A says that B sees what C is doing" (Bal 1985: 104; italics added). Thus she provides a foundation for her theory of a mutually conditioned relationship between subject and object, in which she characterizes the seen as that which sees.

ized); for Mieke Bal and her disciples it is the story (which is focalized by means of the focalizers). The difference between their approaches is reflected also in Genette's reply to Bal in the book *Narrative Discourse Revisited*:

> The rest of the Balian theory of focalizations develops according to its own logic, based on her innovation (establishment of an instance of focalization composed of focalizer, a focalized, and even, page 251, "recipients of the focalizing"), like the idea of a focalization in the second degree. (Genette 1988: 76)

Bal thus establishes the instance (agent) of focalization, whereas for Genette it is rather the situation of focalization that is established. On the one hand, Gerard Genette refuses to connect focalization with any of the elements of narrative that we designate as the "narrator" or as "characters", considering it a higher category than these[2]; on the other, Mieke Bal claims it is possible to delimit the term "focalization" on the level of those elements, and in consequence to personify it, in the form of a focalizer. For Genette, focalization is connected with a limitation of the amount of information that the reader obtains through the text about the fictional world. In Bal, focalization is not connected with this phenomenon. It is a matter of an activity (of relationships) that produces information that has already been selected; this is why Bal does not speak of a zero-value focalization, and why she regards it as necessary to study both object and subject of the relationship, separately, in other words, what is focalized and what does the focalizing.

Therefore these two concepts can never be reconciled, despite the fact that they both use the common term focalization. Both consider the question that they answer with the term "focalization" quite legitimately—however, as mentioned above, each on its own structural level. One should be aware of these ambiguities in the term, and perceive them as a productive area to which the attention of narratology must be directed.

---

2 Genette defines focalization in terms of the character's "knowing more or less" than the narrator; however, in specific examples his "narrator" comes close to the concept of the author, and often overlaps with the concept of the implied author, which Genette refuses to admit to his theory. The peculiarity of the relationship between narrator and focalization is attested also by Genette's dictum: "For me, there is no focalizing or focalized character: *focalized* can be applied only to the narrative itself, and if focalizer applied to anyone, it could only be the person who *focalizes the narrative*—that is, the narrator, or, if one wanted to go outside the conventions of fiction, the *author* himself, who delegates (or does not delegate) to the narrator his power of focalizing or not focalizing" (Genette 1988: 73).

The attempt to reconcile these opposing views of focalization leads to paradoxical claims, also exemplified in Abbott's *Cambridge Introduction to Narrative* (2002). Here, focalization is a strategy at a higher level than either narrator or characters, but "it is important to keep in mind that focalizing is not necessarily achieved through a single consistent narrative consciousness. Focalization can change, sometimes frequently, during the course of narrative, and sometimes from sentence to sentence" (Abbott 2002: 190); Abbott consequently associates focalization with the narrative voice ("In this study I present focalization and voice as companion concepts", Abbott 2002: 190). While voice, for Genette, is the consequence of the strategy of focalization, for Abbott voice is focalization itself.

I would like here to adhere to the definition of Genette, for whom focalization is closely connected with the overall semantic construction of the narrative. It constitutes a sign of a strategy which distributes, and, from our point of view, generates, meaning in a literary text. I am interested in the moment at which, says Genette, only narration itself can be focalized, and the possibility of focalization is open only to that, who focalize the narration (or not focalize): this is the narrator, or—ignoring the convention that evaluates the fiction—the author himself, who delegates (or does not delegate) his task of focalization to the narrator (cf. Genette 1988: 73). To recapitulate: for Genette, focalization is connected with the level at which narration itself is focalized.

Before turning to my main topic, I would like to draw attention to another productive area which opens up when the concept of focalization is so defined, and which connects Genette's theories with those of the Prague structuralists, and of Jan Mukařovský. For Mukařovský, too, it was the question of intention that constituted the central question in connection with the generating of meaning: the text is the vehicle of the intention, and the intention at the same time refers to the situations of author, text and reader. For this reason, he introduced the notion of the subject in this context: it is an "abstract subject, contained in the structure of the work itself, which is merely a point from which the whole structure can be comprehended" (Mukařovský [1937] 2000: 258). Mukařovský then focused his attention on understand-ing the production, and the textual location, of the subject, at a time (the first half of the 1940s) when he was at the peak of his powers. And the essential content of the notions of "focalization" in Genette's writings, and "subject" in Mukařovský's, must prompt the question why the former did not need to use the term "implied author", and why the latter came so close to this concept.

In his *Poetics of Composition*, Boris Uspenskij distinguished a number of structural levels on which a narrative point of view is formed as a function, that he delimitated at a pragmatic level of the act of narration. The function of this point of view is to lead the narration to fulfil a certain purpose, and to understand this purpose it is necessary, according to Uspenskij, to investigate the principles of its constitution. Uspenskij convincingly demonstrated the way in which the processes through which the narrative point of view is manifested are closely connected with the formation of values in the fictional world. And his concept is in its own way confirmed by Schmid's model of the construction of perspective, which amplifies Uspenskij's four structural levels (ideological, phraseological, temporal-spatial and psychological) with a perceptual level that is hierarchically superior to them.

So if we perceive this point of view as a basic means of constructing value in the fictional world, then it is necessary to reformulate the question of the character and intention of a textual realization that produces the situation of focalization, or, more simply—of the character and intention of a textual instance of focalization. Therefore we are interested not only in the "range" and "depth", but also in the "quality" of a focalization of the fictional world. This quality cannot be connected merely with the "density" of the information that we acquire concerning the fictitious world, but also with its value. However, in the present context our questions concerning the principles through which meaning is generated in a text, and the principles through which the fictional world is constructed, come, by virtue of the strategy of focalization, very close to the questions of the intention of the narrative act, of the reading public, of the context, and of the principles through which the reader re-produces meaning in the form of a unique "sense". Our point of departure is the area of semantics, and we set out for the area of the pragmatics of a narrative act. Therefore the procedure is fully in the tradition of the Prague school, for whom the semantic gesture—the overall construction of meaning in a work—is a question of pragmatics.

1 The "Subject" According to the Prague School

The Prague structuralists connected the question of the subject closely with the concept of the semantic gesture, as the point of maximum meaning in the work where, according to Mukařovský, both author and recipient participate. The subject will then be the

> point from which the work's structure can be perceived in all its complexity and in its unity. It is therefore a bridge between poet and reader, who can project his own *ich* into the subject and thus identify his own situation in relation to the work with that of the poet. The subject may remain hidden in (but in no way absent from) the work, as for example in the "objective" epic, or, on the contrary, be realized more or less strongly (through first-person narration, the emotional cast of the work, the identification of the poet with one of the characters within the work, and so on). Therefore the subject cannot be identified with the poet *a priori*, even when the work seems to express the poet's feelings, his relation to the world and to reality in a direct way. (Mukařovský [1941] 2000: 264)

> And intentionality requires a subject, from which it proceeds and which is its source; thus it presupposes a human being. The subject is in no way located outside the work of art, but within it. It is a part of it. [...] The person who has worked out the words and their import is the subject; the person who is addressed by them is also the subject. And these are not in essence two subjects, but one. (Mukařovský [1944] 2000: 286)

> The subject is something other than a concrete individual [...]. As long as we remain within a work, the subject is a mere epistemological will-o'-the-wisp, an imaginary point. When it is made concrete, this point can be occupied by any individual at all, no matter whether this is the originator or the recipient. In any event, the individual is something that remains outside the scope of the work. (Mukařovský [1946] 2000: 307–08)

The extracts above are from various studies in which Mukařovský deals with the subject, cited here to provide a more focused idea of the form in which the subject is perceived by him, and the areas of discussion with which it is connected. But the basic features of the concept of the subject do not change: it is an entity (or point) realized by the work. At the same time, the work represents a boundary dividing the subject from its specific product or producer, author or reader—or rather a meeting-point between the intentions of reader and text. According to Mukařovský, the subject is a mental construct uncovering the intention of the construction of meaning and the unification of all its component parts. This point is fully realized within the work, but its recognition (the fulfilment or creation of meaning) depends on the activity of concretization, and therefore on the activity of the recipient. Its result is then the "subject", which is a product of the intention embedded in the work. Mukařovský speaks of a "point", which is the same term that he uses also in defining the semantic gesture. Therefore, but not only for this reason, his definition of subject and semantic gesture can be apprehended simultaneously. That is confirmed also by the similarity of their formulations and the identity of the terms used for their formation.

So if Mukařovský perceives the subject as a point, it is possible to understand it as a kind of understanding, closed in terms of process, or a subjectivization. On the other hand, however, Mukařovský regards this point as unattainable through any concretization whatsoever. So it is necessary to consider the nature of a semantic process where the task of delineating meaning lies constantly ahead of us. Here the subject is at one and the same time a unifying principle underlying the semantic structure (intention) as well as its realization in the form of a unique meaning, although it does not intersect with any potential unique sense. The temptation to perceive the subject univocally is caused by its delimitation as a "point", yielding a unique formation of meaning; a point from which it is possible to have a single bird's-eye view of the structure of the work. "It is a point at which the whole artistic structure of the work converges, and in relation to which it is assembled, but into which any personality may be projected, whether the perceiver or the author" (Mukařovský [1940/41] 2000: 15).

From the outset, Mukařovský's "subject" overlapped in part with the narrator of a literary work (as emerges from his opening quotation), but later its definition moved fully into the area in which the strategy of the overall construction of meaning is located—into an area which is used also by the narrator as an instrument of his intention. We are then able to perceive the "subject" in an analogous area where focalization (Genette) or an implicit, implied, abstract author is defined. The semantic gesture and the subject are then quantities of a pragmatic instantiation (situation), together constituted by all the components of the work, which it unifies, and which are related to it as their source.

The problem of the subject becomes central for Mukařovský in his later study, *Záměrnost a nezáměrnost v umění* ("Intentionality and lack of intentionality in art" [1943]). In it he reopens the problem of the identity of the literary work, which now becomes for him the problematic unity of sign and object, where the sign tends towards unity in meaning, and therefore towards concretization, and the object constantly resists concretization because, as a thing, it belongs to the world of natural facts which we cannot determine. In this productive tension Mukařovský is trying to redefine the identity of the work, and to establish the limits of the role and identity of the subject within this never-ending debate. He concludes accordingly that

> it is not only the poet and the structure he imposes on the work that are responsible for the semantic gesture that the recipient perceives in the work: a significant part is played also by the perceiver, and [...] the perceiver often substantially modifies the semantic gesture, in contradiction to the poet's original intention. (Mukařovský [1943] 2000: 373)

In this, the semantic gesture, as a principle of semantic unity, is recognized as both intentional and unintentional.

The concept of the subject as a construct dependent on the intention underlying the work and at the same time on a unique concretization (with which it, however, does not quite overlap) on the part of the individual recipient, is indicated by the mechanism of this production, which takes place in the area of intersubjectivity that we have recognized. Thus Mukařovský's concept of the subject has shifted from its original delimitation as the intention generating the work (the authorial intention) in favor of the intention that is fully realized in the work, and an increased focus on the act of concretization that recognizes and generates the subject. A similar shift also affects the semantic gesture, originally conceived by Mukařovský (in relation with the activity of the author) as "a significant process through which the work originates, and which is re-established in the reader by reading" (Mukařovský [1933] 2001: 451). The reader therefore becomes primarily a passive solver of puzzles—the addressee of a code. But the semantic gesture later shifts entirely into the framework of the work, defined in a broad sense, in favor of its own intention—the intention which is generated in the conflict between sign and object, and in which an essential role is now played also by the recipient.

Mukařovský's followers adopted this concept and virtually settled it in the form in which it was suggested in the essay "Intentionality and lack of intentionality in art". So to prevent the work dissolving in the multiplicity of its concretizations, Červenka (1992) sets up the authority of the work as their original stimulus. He then defines the work as an organization of linguistic signs, and at the same time as a structure of *stimuli* for further linguistic and extra-linguistic activities on the part of the perceiving subject (within the field of concretization). Červenka realizes that in the process of concretization the work enters a broad context that has an essential influence on the form of its unique concretization, and for this reason he also considers sociological problems, which are reflected in his concept of norms. (These norms help us understand the work, and are used by the work uses in order that it may be understood; they are a product of the work and themselves produce it.) For him, the norms are beyond man's reach but reflect human interests and values. So these norms are produced by history and develop in time. Červenka here develops Vodička's ideas (see his *Významová výstavba literárního díla* ["The Meaning Structure of a Literary Work" (1992)]), and his conception of the significance of context for the character of the work and for its semantic development.

Similarly, Milan Jankovič considers the relationship between a unique concretization and the intention of the work, and concludes that semantic motion in a work is not given and does not achieve closure. For this reason, the signified can never be definitively established in a work. This non-closure and non-givenness mean that the work constantly changes its meaning while still maintaining its identity—because possible meanings at the same time intersect in it. So for Jankovič the work is situated at the focal point of its interpretations (concretizations), behind which we identify its source, although this cannot be unambiguously designated, and it therefore becomes abstract, a mere procedural motion. Like Barthes, Jankovič in consequence inclines to dismissing a unique interpretation (concretization) as unimportant—he recognizes a specific message as irrelevant, even if it is the only possible one (see his *Dílo jako dění smyslu* ["The work as a semantic process"]).

From the above there emerge two important general questions: the social grounding of the work, and the connection between its semantic process and time, including its attachment to time.

2 How Narrative Models the Perspective

Our central question is the manner in which the perspective with which we attribute meanings to the work is modelled. If we define this perspective as an intersubjective space where the intention of the work meets a unique concretization, it will be necessary to observe two phenomena in succession: the activity of the text, and our reaction to this activity in this context[3]. Cognitive semantics can be invoked here.

---

[3] This unifying perspective, which we connect with the meaning of the notions of "subject" (as was specified by the Prague structuralists) or "focalization" (as understood by Genette), is the result of a pragmatic situation that is constructed by the text, but the reader creatively participates in it. However, it is necessary to distinguish this unifying

Let us now briefly refer to one specific type of narration from the Czech literature and let us examine the text written by Josef Čapek *Stín kapradiny* ("Shadow of a fern") (specifically the beginning of the novel) to discover the manner in which the perspective of reception is modelled through entering a fictional world.

> Rudolf Aksamit and Václav Kala, comrades through thick and thin, bent over the prey. You blue, black and green forest; you, forest brown and misty! Wild joy runs through their poachers' nerves; under their fingertips they had the carcase of an animal, that beautiful carcase of a roebuck. He was theirs.
>
> "Vašek – Vašek!" hissed Aksamit. "Rudy, oh Rudy!" breathed Václav Kala. They were trembling, spellbound, an ecstatic passion seething within them, a drunken giddiness coursing through their veins. Oh, my goodness, what luck we had today! There are no words to describe it.
>
> Vašek and Rudy were bending over the roebuck, under their fingers there was the carcase of the animal, yielding, still warm, still marvellously tense; and then a gamekeeper burst in from the thicket and roared: "Don"t move!" Those were old unsettled accounts, the gamekeeper's voice was choking with fury. You generous, wild forest! That roebuck carcase, still warm and tense. The joy of the poachers was cut short in an instant, and in a sudden eruption it boiled over in the red lava of anger. Rudy crouched behind the roebuck, an enraged beast raising its hackles within him; Vašek found himself being flung at the gamekeeper's throat. And now the fire of revenge has blazed up: a gun has gone off, and that is Rudy shooting the gamekeeper. "Bastards!" screams the enemy, and topples into the grass, head on one side. [...]
>
> You gave me one—the body gasps, but there is no stopping the boiling lava, it blazes volcanically and runs everywhere—beneath the fingernails, up to the hot earlobes, full to the height of the eyes.
>
> He's had enough, wail Rudolf Aksamit and Václav Kala, it's had enough, that corpse, still warm, still tense, that yielding corpse that will never be a gamekeeper again. He won't take away that roebuck from us again, he'll never strut about the woods again, he'll never go out to get his tobacco! (Čapek 1930: 5)[4]

The first view is presented from the perspective of an outside observer who at the same time confirms his knowledge of a wider context ("comrades through thick and thin"). Accordingly, we adopt an external perspective, at the center of which there appear two characters (identified by rigid designators). But we are quickly invited to amplify this view: the immediate surroundings of the scene are introduced, in the form of an expressive invocation ("you blue, black and green forest"). In the next sec-

---

perspective from those perspectives that mediate the story to us. Therefore, it is again the perspectivization of the narrative space (as its value anchoring) in relation to the narration (*récit*) on the one hand, and the story (*histoire*) on the other.

4 Tr. Tomáš Kubíček.

tion, we are encouraged by the text to alter our perspective or to unify it with the perspective of the poachers (see the evaluative term "beautiful," which is subsequently confirmed also by the tactile implications of "warm"). And in the section immediately following, the perspective moves through the space that is described (and represents it at the same time); it is amplified by the perspective of the gamekeeper, from which we perceive the scene once more (with identical motives—"roebuck, warm, tense carcase"), and as the internal perspective changes, its value criteria also change.

Clearly, thus, the space is modelled before us through a shifting perspective, which allows access to a great deal of information about the fictional world. Within an operation of consolidation, we can then create the complex perspective of the narrative scene. Conversely, we can then check the relevance of the expressive statement addressing the forest and judge it from the standpoint of any of the possible internal perspectives. Then we note that in this sentence, which represents a transition between the two internal perspectives, observed reality is strongly subjectivized, and we are invited to perceive it through the eyes of another, without being able definitively to refer the statement either to the poachers' perspective, or to an overall narrative perspective. The characterization of the two main characters (rigid designators), by means of the relationship between part and whole in the form of the expression "poachers' nerves," together with the unstable perspective, then suggests the form of the cognitive processes that we are to use for our operation of understanding. In this way, we are returned to the area of our own experience, with a similar type of literature and narrative style.

The unstable perspective that we encounter here guarantees that the mediation will involve a large number of elements, from which the fictional world is constructed, and at the same time the proximity of the point of view that we adopt in relation to this world (according to the demands of the text), giving the fictional world a strong "granularity". The perspective of the two poachers becomes the central axis of the narrative, and determines the selection of the elements of the action and the manner in which they are ordered. At the same time, however, it is continuously controlled by the authority of the superior narrator, one which therefore generates a perspective. The presence of this authority also confirms its interpretative activity in relation to the object of its observation, and therefore in relation to the perspective of the two poachers. It then uses linguistic means to establish the receptive perspective of the addressee.

The narrative world thus has located within itself a dialogue between both perspectives. It does not encompass merely a reciprocal confrontation of these two frameworks of knowledge and experience, even though, from the standpoint of the modelling of the reader's perspective as a cognitive action, it is precisely this confrontation that is its most important property. The framework that we identify as belonging to the two poachers conversely reveals the framework of the superior narrative authority as insufficient or incomplete, or breaches it (for example, it reveals the reluctance of the superior narrator to provide some information, or even reveals gaps in this superior framework). The reader then brings this dialogue up to date in the co-ordinates of the dialogue between the textual situation and his own, during this cognitive unifying operation he activates his experience with similar frameworks, and on the basis of them he creates the specific characteristics of the updated frameworks.

As for the modelling of the reader's perspective, the entry into the narrative space mentioned above also uncovers three further processes: (1) it shows that a high capacity to combine narrative elements will be necessary for the cognitive processes controlling the understanding and construction of the fictional world, in which (2) it will be necessary to refer to our cultural encyclopedia (to interpret the notions of poacher, gamekeeper, forest, roebuck and prey, as well as their mutual combinations), which also contains knowledge about social roles and possible relationships between individual elements within the narrative (for example, poacher and gamekeeper) and which shows us that the lexis that we use emerges from an environment of social interaction, in which is reflected not only the capacity to use it, but also more generally (3) its capacity for cognitive evaluation of our knowledge of the real world and our experience of it, as well as of the problem of the context to which the narrative refers. These three processes then control and determine the meaning which we assign to the narrative as its possible framework, and under the influence of which, during the course of the narrative, we decode both the partial and the more complex messages.

The perspective that is modelled in the narrative is totally dependent on the grammatical resources of language. With their aid, it determines its (and our) location in the narrative space, its distance from the object depicted, the manner in which it is represented (whether the perspective is stable or unstable) and at the same time, the logic of this representation (the subsequent move to a close perspective and a local space of observation[5]) and its direction in time (its concentration on the present temporal moment[6]). The intensity of the perspective is also established (not only through the expressive diction, but also in a number of the observed details) and the levels of the perspective are established hierarchically, together with the areas in which the fictional world is mapped (and their density) from the point of view of narrative strategy, and the manner in which this mapping is accomplished (the character of the information).

Within the framework of a cognitive operation of understanding, the conceptual connections are then made, which is a process in which a variety of otherwise disconnected conceptual material is brought together. This process draws on two basic overall forms of realization: connecting above the scene and connecting in time. In it, we determine which elements specify the structure of cognitive representation evoked by the given narrative. Leonard Talmy speaks in this case of a "scaffolding" or an "axis" around which linguistic material can be distributed or folded (cf. Talmy 2000: passim). But as it is a proposal (although we have established the manner in which the perspective is modelled by the narrative text), it is a subjective act, in which there occurs a preference for possible frameworks and in consequence a preference for the possible elements producing this meaning. The individual elements are then judged from the point of view of their capacity to be "inserted" in some meaningful way into this framework as a unifying complex. Without this operation, which is a parallel structuring of the fictional world, we would, in the case of the narrative, be dealing merely with an assemblage of individual juxtaposed elements and not with a universe that is being united as a meaningful complex of ideas.

To achieve this complex, it is necessary to supplement (concretize) it with certain actions or conceptual networks at the same time. The narrative challenges us to adopt this behaviour, whose consequence is an individual realization of the supplementation which is the basis of our interpretative activity. Within the framework of this operation of supplementation, we can distinguish between the elements (relationships and phenomena) that are obligatory, which must be supplemented, those which are optional, which it is possible to supplement, and those that are redundant. In the brief extract here quoted, trespassing can be seen as an obligatory element, the situating of the scene in the morning, for instance, can

5 The opposite would be a summary or synoptic perspective.
6 Alternatives would be retrospection and anticipation.

be seen as optional, and the question of animal rights is redundant. Whereas the former two operations of supplementation aid an understanding of the narrative or the scene of the narrative, and its possible meanings, the third leads us astray into misinterpretation. But supplementation is an operation that is evaluated during the course of time, and for this reason elements that have been considered obligatory can become less important during a subsequent reading, or vice versa—optional elements can become obligatory. It is also one of the ways through which unreliability is constructed. In such a case, the text challenges the reader to undertake a certain operation of supplementation in the framework of the obligatory area which will be recognized later as redundant, or vice versa. To make the unreliability a recognizable textual strategy and dominant within the semantic construction, it is of course necessary that this operation, intended by the text, be carried out.

But the reader does not undertake only this operation of supplementation, broadly conceived, when challenged to do so by such textual signals, but also a number of other operations, such as comparison (see above, a mutual comparison of perspectives formed in the text of narrators or reflectors), categorization (again determined in terms of the relationship between one perspective and another), abstraction or schematization, summarization, and so forth—in other words, operations that bear on the basic conditions of reading depend on the individual capacity of the recipient to carry out these operations, and on his widely based experience. Every lexical unit contains or evokes a series of cognitive domains (foundations of its meaning)—as an invitation to produce certain conceptualizations, which should lead to a certain level of understanding, and therefore to a certain form of the cognitive complex (but not, of course, its totality). In this process, the flexibility of lexical units, in the sense of their potential for incorporation in various complexes, is large, and the literary narrative of this capacity of theirs is often used also in dependence on the level of their literary or experimental qualities.

Interpretation is the basis of this operation, as is stressed for instance by Ronald W. Langacker, and is central to both semantic and grammatical structures[7]. Langacker further states that linguistic significance resides not only in the content of a lexical unit, but is a multidimensional phenomenon, whose individual aspects reflect some basic cognitive capa-

---

7 "Although long overlooked in traditional semantics, it is crucial to interpret (construct) for both semantic and grammatical structure." (Langacker 1999: 5)

cities, that can be summarized under five general headings: specificity, background, perspective, scope and prominence. In narrative, specificity refers to our capacity to denominate the narrative entity which evokes meaning on the basis of the information in the text, as well as our capacity to distinguish variant meanings of this entity. The background can be seen as the wide context (as well as the intertext) to which the given expression refers. We have already discussed the meaning and form of perspective, that bears closely on the value arrangement of the fictional world discussed above. The scope has a similar character, as well as the location of a narrative element within the scope or the distribution of the narrative scope, which then significantly models the hierarchy of values of the unit of meaning. So this might be constituted by a repetition of a certain expression at the beginning of the article, or its positioning in some key location in the text. For example, in Jan Čep's story *Do města* ("Journey to Town") we encounter three colours (gold, blue and red) that are individually varied in the text (for example, as corn, sky and poppies), but always in the same order and therefore constituting a hierarchy, so that these can be combined in the course of the text to construct an interpretation parallel to the three main characters of the story (father, mother and son), and also a parallel to a more complex cultural interpretation in which the colours are combined with the hierarchy of the family (God, Mary and Christ). The beginning and the end of the narrative are framed by the combination of father, mother and son (maintaining this order) and the colours (which acquire the character of symbols in relation to the above expressions) then appear in the same order in the center of the text. In this manner, the given terms emphasize their key semantic position. Prominence is a question of the denomination of the given element, for example on the basis of social experience or class structure (e.g. king, father, man, lad, human being). It is clear that the above categories refer immediately to the formation of value within the cognitive space of the statement (see below).Something substantial can now be said. The operations that we have mentioned enable us to understand narrative, indeed to read in the first place. But we should constantly be conscious of the general nature and indeed the production of these operations—only thus can we guarantee that during our reception of the narrative we will not be tempted by mimesis to replace the complex narrative structure with a unique ideological interpretation of our own. As we shall assert further below, but as we have already done in part in the introduction to this chapter, our interpretation must also be perceived as part of a productive dialogue between the potential capacities of the meaning and its realization in practice. This dialogue should lead to the communicative situation which the narrative makes possible, initiates and controls at the same time. Within the scope of the narrative, the causal (and temporally determined) perspective in this operation of connection is recognized and realized; it is not only questions of purpose but also questions of value that come into play here in relation to the meaning. Value, and evaluation, are relevant not only to the result of a narrativized process (poacher—prey—gamekeeper—carcase/corpse), but also to the perspectivization of this space, to each of its individual parts—and therefore also to the determination of the hierarchy of values through the allocation of perspective to it. In the opening quoted above, three perspectives are encountered (those of the poachers, of the gamekeeper and of the overall narrator), which impose a dialogue on this space and impart to it a three-fold set of values that the reader must unify. Boris Uspenskij earlier noted that value (the question of value as a structural and structuring element) is one of the basic properties or qualities of perspective (cf. Uspenskij 1975).

Although, as we have established, the narrative text plays a considerable role in achieving unification by issuing a challenge to undertake this cognitive operation, it is the recipient (the addressee) of the narrative text, who realizes it definitively, by selecting a specific framework—"scaffolding" or "axis", and the individual operation he carries out includes processes of combination and selection that happen in time and individually vary and combine the general scopes or frameworks. Here we are already in the area of the unique semiotic process, and the text holds controlling authority. This reciprocal activity points to the relevance to the process of intersubjectivity, and thus to an intersubjective construction of the fictional world. Hilary Putnam writes: "The elements of what we call 'language' or 'mind' penetrate so deeply into what we call 'reality', that the very project of presentation of ourselves 'mapping' something 'independent on the language' is fatally half-hearted" (Putnam 1990: 57). This observation, together with what has been said above, can be regarded as defining our position as the subject of reception.

References

Abbott, H. Porter (2002). *The Cambridge Introduction to Narrative*. Cambridge: Cambridge UP.

Abel, Günter (1999). *Sprache, Zeichen, Interpretation.* Frankfurt a. M.: Suhrkamp.

Bal, Mieke (1985). *Narratology: Introduction to the Theory of Narrative*. Toronto: U of Toronto P.
– (1991). *On Story-Telling: Essays in Narratology*. Sonoma, CA: Polebridge Press.
– (1988). *Framing the Sign: Criticism and its Institutions*. Oxford: Blackwell.
Čapek, Josef (1930). *Stín kapradiny*. Prague: Aventinum.
Červenka, Miroslav (1968). *Významová výstavba literárního díla*. Prague: Karolinum, 1992.
Chamberlain, Daniel Frank (1990). *Narrative Perspective in Fiction: A Phenomenological Mediation of Reader, Text, and World*. Toronto: U of Toronto P.
Chatman, Seymour (ed) (1971). *Literary Style. A Symposium*. London: Oxford UP.
– (1990). *Coming to Terms. The Rhetoric of Narrative in Fiction and Film*. Ithaca: Cornell UP.
Christensen, Carleton B. (1991). *Language and Intentionality*. Würzburg: Königshausen & Neumann.
Culler, Jonathan (1981). *The Pursuit of Signs: Semiotics, Literature, Deconstruction*. Ithaca: Cornell UP.
Doležel, Lubomír (1960). *O stylu moderní české prózy*. Prague: Československá akademie věd.
– (1973). *Narativní způsoby v české literatuře*. Praha: Československý spisovatel.
– (2003). *Heterocosmica*. Prague: Karolinum.
Genette, Gérard (1983). *Nouveau discours du récit*. Paris: Seuil.
– (1988). *Narrative Discourse Revisited*. Tr. J. E. Lewin. Ithaca: Cornell UP, 1998.
Herman, David (ed) (1999). *Narratologies: New Perspectives on Narrative Analysis*. Columbus: Ohio State UP.
– (1995). *Universal Grammar and Narrative Form*. Durham, NC: Duke UP.
Jakobson, Roman (1995). "Dva aspekty jazyka a dva typy afatických poruch." M. Červenka (ed). *Poetická funkce*. Prague: H&H.
Jankovič, Milan (1992). *Dílo jako dění smyslu*. Prague: Pražská imaginace.
Lamarque, Peter (1996). *Fictional Points of View*. Ithaca: Cornell UP.
Langacker, Ronald W. (1999). *Grammar and Conceptualization*. Berlin: de Gruyter.
Lanser, Susan S. (1981). *The Narrative Act: Point of View in Prose Fiction*. Princeton: Princeton UP.
Meggle, Georg (ed) (1979). *Handlung, Kommunikation, Bedeutung*. Frankfurt a. M.: Suhrkamp.
Mühl, Martin (1997). *Die Handlungsrelativität der Sinne*. Bodenheim: Philo.
Mukařovský, Jan (1933). „Významová výstavba a kompoziční osnova epiky Karla Čapka." *Studie II*. Brno: Host, 2001, 451–80.
– (1937). "Individuum v umění." *Studie I*. Brno: Host, 2000, 255–58.
– (1940/41). „Strukturalismus v estetice a ve vědě o literatuře." *Studie I*. Brno: Host, 2000, 9–25.
– (1941). „Básník." *Studie I*. Brno: Host, 2000, 259–74.
– (1943). „Záměrnost a nezáměrnost v umění." *Studie I*. Brno: Host, 2000, 353–88.
– (1944). „Osobnost v umění." *Studie I*. Brno: Host, 2000, 275–90.
– (1946). „Problém individua v umění.".*Studie I*. Brno: Host, 2000, 303–35.
– (1966). *Studie z estetiky*. Prague: Odeon.
– (1971). *Cestami poetiky a estetiky*. Prague: Československý spisovatel.

– (1982). *Studie z poetiky*. Prague: Odeon.
Palmer, Alan (2003). "The Mind Beyond the Skin." D. Herman (ed). *Narrative Theory and the Cognitive Sciences*. Stanford: CSLI, 322–48.
Prince, Gerald (1987). *A Dictionary of Narratology*. Lincoln: U of Nebraska P.
Phelan, James (1981). *Worlds from Worlds: A Theory of Language in Fiction*. Chicago: U of Chicago P.
– (1989). *Reading People, Reading Plots: Character, Progression, and the Interpretation of Narrative*. Chicago: U of Chicago P.
– (1996). *Narrative as Rhetoric: Technique, Audience, Ethics, Ideology*. Columbus: Ohio State UP.
Phelan, James & Rabinowitz, Peter J. (eds) (1994). *Understanding Narrative*. Columbus: Ohio State UP.
Putnam, Hilary (1990). *Realism with a Human Face*. Cambridge, MA: Harvard UP.
Rabinowitz, Peter J. (1987). *Before Reading: Narrative Conventions and the Politics of Interpretation*. Ithaca: Cornell UP.
Rescher, Nicholas (1973). "The Ontology of the Possible." M. K. Munitz (ed). *Logic and Ontology*. New York: New York UP.
Richardson, Brian (ed) (2002). *Narrative Dynamics. Essays on Time, Plot, Closure and Frames*. Columbus: Ohio State University.
Ronen, Ruth (2002): *Representing the Real*. Amsterdam: Rodopi.
Ryan, Marie-Laure (1991). *Possible Worlds, Artificial Intelligence, and Narrative Theory*. Bloomington: Indiana UP.
Ryle, Gilbert (1949). *The Concept of Mind*. London: Hutchinson's University Library.
Schmid, Wolf (2005). *Elemente der Narratologie*. Berlin: de Gruyter.
Shibatani, Masayoshi & Thompson, Sandra A. (eds) (1996). *Grammatical Constructions: Their Form and Meaning*. New York: Oxford UP.
Singer, Alan (1993). *The Subject as Action: Transformation and Totality in Narrative Aesthetics*. Ann Arbor: U of Michigan P.
Sternberg, Meir (1978). *Expositional Modes and Temporal Ordering in Fiction*. Baltimore: Johns Hopkins UP.
Talmy, Leonard (2000). *Toward a Cognitive Semantics*, Vol. 1. Cambridge, MA: MIT Press.
Uspenskij, Boris A. (1975). *Poetik der Komposition: Struktur des künstlerischen Textes und Typologie der Kompositionsform*. Tr. G. Mayer. Frankfurt a. M.: Suhrkamp.
Verhagen, Arie (2005). *Constructions of Intersubjectivity*. Oxford: Oxford UP.
Vodička, Felix (1948). *Počátky krásné prózy novočeské*. Prague: Melantrich.

CHRISTIAN HUCK
(London)

Coming to Our Senses: Narratology and the Visual

1 Introduction

Marco Polo is believed to have traveled about 14.000 miles during his lifetime; Ibn Battuta, the great Arab explorer of the middle ages, managed about 75.000. But both were dwarfed by the Englishman James Holman, a retired naval officer, who traveled roughly 250.000 miles in the first half of the 19th century—before the arrival of trains, steam boats and planes. He trekked deep into Siberia, sailed to Brazil, rode through southern Africa, explored unmapped parts of Australia and survived the bandit-infested Balkans. However, the most remarkable thing about all this is that Holman had been blind since the age of twenty-four—he made all his travels without seeing where he was going: he heard, smelled and felt his way cautiously through the world. "While vision gulps, tactility sips," his biographer notes, "an object yields up its qualities not all at once, at the speed of light, but successively over time, and in sequence of necessity." (Roberts 2006: 69) However, despite his obvious achievements, Holman was never taken seriously by his contemporaries, and was soon forgotten. His experiences were deemed invalid for the simple reason that he could not use his visual sense: "*His sightlessness makes genuine insight impossible*" (Roberts 2006: xii). The Enlightenment's epistemological paradigm of the eyewitness did not allow for other sense data to become the basis for new knowledge.

In this article, I want to compare two travelogues that mark the submission of the travel report to the paradigm of the eyewitness. The two texts in question are Daniel Defoe's *Tour through the Whole Island of Great Britain* (1724–26) and Edward Ward's account of his ramblings through London in *The London Spy*, originally published as a periodical between 1698 and 1699. While the two texts deal with roughly the same subject matter, London around the year 1700, they present two very different accounts of it. In line with the century's empiricist imperative to observe, both emphasize that they will only report those things they have personally witnessed. However, the resulting reports could not be more unlike. Defoe's calm, plain, and objective description of the streets and buildings of the city is contrasted by Ward's rushed, exuberant and excited account of its inhabitants. How can the two descriptions be so different, when the perceived object is basically the same?

A literary historian might credit this difference in description to different political aims: the Whig Defoe is trying to present an economically progressive Britain, while the Tory satirist Ward attempts to ridicule the human follies of his fellow citizens suffering the consequences of (early) modernity. Narratologically speaking, they consequently show very different points of view, they reveal a markedly different "perspective" on things, they "focalize" different aspects of the city. However, instead of explaining the differing accounts with reference to the ideological backgrounds of the authors and thus making "only" metaphorical use of the terminology, I want to analyze a difference manifested in the creation of two specific narrator-figures, the employment of their senses, and the relation between perception and reporting which these narrators reveal.

It becomes obvious, when analyzing the two texts more closely, that while perception in Defoe's text is restricted to the visual, the narrator in Ward's text employs all kinds of sensory perceptions. The attempt to describe and theorize the different narrators, then, leads to the question, whether there is an aural, olfactory or even a haptic equivalent to a point of *view*: a point of smell, maybe, or a point of taste? What would be the difference between these? And could a specific mode of perceiving (a story) influence the mode of reporting (in discourse)? As there are few predecessors which to build on, and as studies of the impact of perceptual regimes on modes of writing are still rare, all I will be able to offer here is a tentative investigation of what is at stake in the relation between "perspective" and the senses, and a few suggestions concerning how and why this relation could and should be further explored.

2 The Rise of the Visual

However persistent and/or ambivalent the classical "Greek privileging of vision" (Jay 1993: 33) and however "ocularphobic" (36) the Middle Ages might have been, the "ocularcentrism" of post-Renaissance culture would be difficult to deny: "vision, aided by new technologies, became the dominant sense in the modern world" (45). The importance of the visual soon became pervasive:

> From the curious, observant scientist to the exhibitionist, self-displaying courtier, from the private reader of printed books to the painter of perspectival landscapes, from the map-making colonizer of foreign lands to the quantifying businessman guided by instrumental rationality, modern men and women opened their eyes and beheld a world unveiled to their eager gazes. (69)

Although by no means a homogeneous field, the visual sense came to be dominated by the particularly influential scopic regime of linear perspective, embodied by the technical device of the *camera obscura* (cf. Crary 1990: 27–29). Lüdemann outlines how this scopic regime establishes a specific observer position: It gives

> the observer the illusion he could see without being involved, that he could see, without being seen, without changing the observed through observing and without himself being changed by the act of observing: The subject that sees by means of linear perspective installs itself behind the window of the "peep show" [...] in the position of a secret, for himself and others invisible voyeur. Consequently, he is an empirical subject only in a very limited sense. While he is *in* the world in the emphatic sense that the things of the world organize themselves according to his perspective [...], he is at the same time distanced from the world by this very act. Like the Cartesian *cogito* the observer is bereft of his body. (Lüdemann 1999: 66)[1]

As I want to argue in the following, it is such an observer position that a text like Defoe's ascribes to its narrator, a narrator curiously situated at the same time in and out of the world he describes. But it is also the observer position that forms the basis for the concept of the perceptive/reflective figure in (classical) narratology[2].

Throughout the nineteenth century, a new mode of observing evolved: the "mirror" was replaced by the "lamp" as the paradigm for (artistic) vision (cf. Abrams 1953). This new scopic regime was one of "subjective vision, a vision that had been taken out of the incorporal relations of the camera obscura and relocated in the human body" (Crary 1990: 16). Two aspects of this new development appear crucial. On the one hand, the replacement of the mirror by the lamp, or of the *camera obscura* by the *la-*

---

1 Here, as in the following, English translations of German texts are mine.

2 On perspective see also Jay (1993: 51–55). Crary emphasizes that linear perspective does not necessarily lead to the observer position embodied in the *camera obscura*, and that the two are similar but not identical (cf. Crary 1990: 34). The observer position described above is the effect of a scopic regime influenced by linear perspective and the *camera obscura*.

terna magica, is a replacement of one scopic regime for another; the dominance of the visual remains unaffected. On the other hand, the new scopic regime has to be interpreted in a specific way so that it can be integrated into the narratological framework. As Klepper (2004) has recently argued, the central shift from the old to the new scopic regime is based on the deconstruction of transparency: while older texts assumed the possibility of an impartial observer, later ones reveal the partiality of every (subjective) observation. It seems to me that narratological theory takes this later, adaptive, "Jamesian" stance as its starting point and reinterprets earlier narratives accordingly, i. e. that they, also, were biased. However, this theory inherits or adopts both the visual bias and the epistemological model of the older scopic regime, because it interprets a constructive mode of observation within the wider framework of perspectivism, of which the (Cartesian) linear perspective is understood to be only one particular instance. In the framework of narratology, the observer is, as I will argue, still watching from inside a *camera obscura*, albeit one which has a distorting prism in its hole.

3 Ut pictura poesis: Narratology and the Visual

Classical narratological theory, from Henry James to Franz Stanzel and Gérard Genette, was developed in response to the novel of the 18th and 19th centuries. Given that these centuries mark the heyday of the primacy of visual observation, it comes as no surprise that the classical texts of this era and subsequently the theories concerned with these should also show a strong visual bias (cf. Klepper 2004). The narrator—or character whose perceptions the narrator reports—is generally conceived as a subject that perceives its (fictional) world almost exclusively visually.

The question whether such visual bias poses a problem for narratology did not seem important to most theoreticians, who touch on it only slightly—if at all. Bal's definition of "focalization", for example, could not be more visual: "Whenever events are presented, they are always presented from within a certain 'vision'. A point of view is chosen, a certain way of seeing things, a certain angle". "Focalization is," she continues, "the relation between the vision and that which is 'seen', perceived" (Bal 1985: 100). Without further ado, she makes "seeing" stand in for all forms of perception. Bal seems to follow Genette, who thinks it enough to "take up [...] the slightly more abstract term *focalization*," to "avoid the too specifically visual connotations of the terms *vision*, *field*, and *point of view*"

(Genette 1980: 189). However, when revisiting his theory, Genette claims that his "only regret is that [he] used a purely visual, and hence overly narrow, formulation". Consequently, he wants to "replace *who sees?* with the broader question of *who perceives?*" (Genette 1988: 64). Similarly, in their chapter on "Focalization" Martinez and Scheffel appear to realize the reductive pairing of "who sees" and "who speaks", but think it enough to add in brackets: "('seeing' should be understood here in the more general sense of 'perceiving')" (Martinez & Scheffel 1999: 64). Finally, Rimmon-Kenan also hopes with Genette and Bal that the more abstract term of "focalization" can avoid "the specifically visual connotations of 'point of view'," but admits that even this new terminology "is not free of optical-photographic connotations" and proclaims that "its purely visual sense has to be broadened to include cognitive, emotive and ideological orientation" (Rimmon-Kenan 1983: 71). But although she declares her intention to transgress the limits of the "purely visual sense of 'focalization'" and acknowledges that perception also includes "hearing, smell, etc.," all her examples remain within the realm of the visual (77).

Quite obviously, this visual bias of narratological terminology and the failure to amend it have not gone unnoticed. In what might be called post-classical narratology, I found at least two possibilities to interpret these findings. The first follows the line set out already by Rimmon-Kenan and claims, in the words of Niederhoff, that "the metaphorical character of a scientific term does not diminish its suitability" (Niederhoff 2001: 4–5). The conceptual model, this suggests, remains unhampered by the terminology. Chatman, for example, claims: "Genette has always seemed to mean more by focalization than the mere power of sight. He obviously refers to the whole spectrum of perception: hearing, tasting, smelling, and so on" (Chatman 1986: 192). Prince takes the substitution of "seeing" for "perceiving" even further:

> Note [...] that the verb "perceive" is to be taken in a broad rather than narrow acceptation: to apprehend with the senses (to see, hear, touch, etc.) or with the mind, or with something like their equivalent. In other words, what is perceived may be abstract or concrete, tangible or intangible—sights, sounds, smells, or thoughts, feelings, dreams, and so on. (Prince 2001: 44)

According to this line of thinking, one can amend the terminology and leave the underlying model untouched. Consequently, Nelles, following Jost, distinguishes between "ocularization", the visual element of focalization, "auricularization", the "aural point of view" (cf. Jost 1983), gustativization, olfactivization, and tactivilization (cf. Nelles 1997: 95–96).

The problem I have with such supplementation lies in the subordination of different senses under a model that was quite obviously developed with the visual in mind. When Prince defines point of view as "yielding that which *might* be perceived from a certain perspective" (Prince 2005: 442), he is simply substituting the wider term perceiving for the old "seeing", but consequently must suggest that we smell or taste "from a certain perspective"—which, I think, already stretches the metaphor, and the model, a bit too far, as does the idea of an "aural point of view". I will return to the problem of "perspective" in regard to other senses later.

A second line of response to the visual bias of the terminology seems to accept that the terminology is not just arbitrary, but a metaphor we live by, not a surface problem, but one that conceptually frames our thinking. Consequently, Lanser affirms the visuality of the concept of "point of view" by conceding, with John Berger and others, the primacy of the visual over all other senses: "perception is always structured upon a relationship of perceiver and perceived—upon a *point of view*" (Lanser 1981: 4). In a similar way, Nünning and Nünning affirm the visual bias of their term "perspective": "The traditional correlation of visual-optic and cognitive aspects, which is already conditioned etymologically, is as much a constant of the term perspective as is the close relation to epistemological dualism." (Nünning & Nünning 2001: 8) Quite obviously, this is a perfect tool for analyzing works created within the 18th and 19th century framework of representational realism. For Nünning and Nünning, however, perspective is, systematically, "the prism through which all environmenttal stimuli are refracted" (12)—thereby turning a historically and culturally situated philosophical framework into a given premise for narratological reasoning. Neither can this model incorporate a sense like tactility, which defies a neat compartmentalization of object, idea and subject-observer, nor is it suitable for radical forms of subjective perception, where the creative act goes beyond the "refracting" of given stimuli. As I understand it, Nünning and Nünning's metaphor of the "prism" allows them to include a subjective/constructivist "perspective" into an otherwise Cartesian epistemology—by putting a prism into the hole of the *camera obscura*, and leaving it otherwise intact. As a consequence, the narratologically conceived observer sees the (fictional) world through a prism even if he is smelling or hearing.

Is "point of view", as much as focalization and perspective, then, just another example of the primacy of the visual in our culture and the hegemony of the scopic regime of perspective within this culture? Is narratology simply mirroring what a plethora of recent studies have identified as the dominance of the visual in modern culture? Is narratology, then, just another instance of what McLuhan understands as a central consequence of the rise of the Gutenberg Galaxy, that is, the "reduction of experience to a single sense, the visual, as a result of typography" (McLuhan 1962: 125)? Is there, as Uspenskij claimed in his article, a "Structural Isomorphism of Verbal and Visual Art" (1972)?

To a certain degree I would answer these questions positively. Consequently, a use of terms such as "point of view" or "perspective", which affirms its visual bias and consequently limits itself to analyses of visual perception within a certain cultural framework, is surely appropriate; also, such analyses should do justice to the bulk of mainstream 18th and 19th century novels. When it comes to dealing with other than visual sense perceptions, though, I would disagree with Nelles that we can successfully examine these within the given framework. In the following, I will attempt to exemplify the limits of the visual narratological terminology (and framework) in a comparative examination of the above mentioned texts by Defoe and Ward—and their differing perceptual and narrative modes. Here, McLuhan's claim of the relation between seeing and printing will also have to be re-examined.

4 A Terminological Re-Approximation

The fact that I am dealing with two factual texts seems to by-pass large parts of what is normally discussed under the terms perspective, focalization, or point-of-view, and what the title of this book reveals as the central function of these terms: mediation. As Nelles defines it: "Focalisation is a *relation* between the narrator's report and the character's thoughts" (Nelles 1997: 79). Or, as Jahn elaborates in more detail:

> Focalization denotes the perspectival restriction and orientation of narrative information relative to somebody's (usually a character's) perception, imagination, knowledge, or point-of-view. Hence, focalization theory covers the various means of regulating, selecting, and channeling narrative information, particularly of seeing events from somebody's point of view […]. (Jahn 2005: 173)

Stanzel's "Typenkreis", Genette's tripartition and Bal's refinement as much as Nünning's "Perspektivenstruktur", all deal, essentially, with the informational relation between a "character" and a "narrator". So what if there is no character-perspective from which to distinguish a narrator-perspective, and consequently no mediation between the two?

At first glance, there seems to be no immediate distinction between a subject of perception and a subject of narration in factual texts. Who perceives? Daniel Defoe. Who narrates? Daniel Defoe. Genette's famous incentive for dealing with focalization in the first place, the intention to distinguish between "who perceives" and "who speaks", seems to become rather irrelevant. But is that true? It is quite obvious that what Daniel Defoe perceives is not the same as what he narrates: the diegetic world, although not fictional, is still a "version" of the real world. It is as unlikely that Defoe never smelled anything in the whole of Britain[3] as it is that he never interacted with anyone on his travels—and of neither of which does he tell us. But that does not mean he is lying, he does not necessarily hold back information.

It is my conviction that both Defoe and Ward create a specific narrator-figure whose conception is responsible for the selection of perceptions. The relation that I want to focus on, then, is the relation between the "bias" of perception and the "bias" of narrating. As mentioned above, I am going to concentrate on sensory differences of perception, leaving ideological questions aside[4]. Also, I will leave aside the question what degree of "reality" the perceptual position of the narrator actually had for Defoe: was he so convinced of this perceptual position that he actually masked any smell, sound, etc., so that his conscious perception actually became purely visual? Or is it just a conceptual constriction of which he was well aware? Was his perception determined by the discursive cultural framework or did he simply write what he thought was expected from him?

Putting aside questions like these and despite the dangers of adding even more narratological terms to an already well stacked pile, I want to distinguish the two separate acts involved here as "slanted perception" on the one hand and "narrative focalization" on the other[5]. I think it important to uphold a distinction, terminologically and conceptually, between the act of perception and the act of reporting (cf. Schmid 2008: 129–

---

3 See further Cockayne's (2007) timely reminder of the sensual assaults the eighteenth century provided.

4 However, as might be deduced from the following, certain ideological positions seem to go hand in hand with certain perceptual positions.

5 Etymologically, the optical connotation of "focus" supplanted the older sense of "hearth". For me, then, "focalization" means concentrating on the heated center.

30)—even when dealing with factual accounts. My proposed distinction seems close to Jesch and Stein's contribution in this collection, although mine is not restricted to fictional texts, and neither does it deal with the perceptual act of characters as such: "The first element is the perception of the world invented by the author through narrators and other agents also invented by the author; the second element is the regulation of narrative information within the communication between author and reader" (59).

However, against Jesch and Stein I would argue that both entities are always present: never is there a perception without slant, and never is there a narration without focalization. While this, I assume, should be undisputed, as Schmid has successfully argued (cf. Schmid 2008: 120–21), the much more interesting question for me is whether there is a connection between the way perception is slanted and the way reporting is focalized. And more specifically: how does the way perception is conceptualized influence what one has to say about the world one travels? In my analysis of Defoe and Ward I will argue that there are culturally and historically specific models that suggest specific relations between the two acts, limiting the systematically available possibilities.

However, while the proposed terminology might be better adapted to diferent sense perceptions, it still remains within the realms of epistemological dualism. As long as the conceptual framework of diegetic world-making, of the distinction between narrator and story-world, forms the foundation of narratological theory (and it might turn out to be indispensable), "point of view" and related concepts remain central: "The novel and other narrative genres cannot escape the question at stake because they necessarily model a world and afford a specific viewpoint on this world" (Klepper 2004: 460). As will become clear, texts like Ward's reveal the limits of such frameworks; and all I can offer here is a pointer towards these limits from within this framework.

5 The Traveler's Senses

Daniel Defoe's *A Tour through the Whole Island of Great Britain* formed part of a new vogue in travel writing, dealing with Britain instead of faraway and exotic places on the one hand, and discarding scholastic accounts on the other. A predecessor to Defoe admits in his preface that "voluminous Treatises of this Nature" already seem to exist. But: "what so eminently distinguishes our Ingenious Author from most, if not all, is that he presents you here with nothing but his own Ocular Observations." Older authors, "confining themselves to their Studies," can only report what they "have taken upon the bare Credit of those, who were, perhaps, more slothful than themselves" (anon. 1694: n. pag.).

Defoe follows this new tradition. He also promises to report nothing "but what he has been an Eye-witness of himself" (Defoe 1724–26: I, 48), and he, too, praises his own work for not being "rais'd upon the burrow'd lights of other Observers" (48). When he relates a "long Fabulous Story" that some "Historians" (108) tell, he discards the fable with the following words: "I satisfy myself with transcribing the Matter of Fact, and then leave it as I find it" (108). However, this commitment is at the same time the source of a central problem in Defoe's book. Defoe's use of letters, which are supposed to be reports of several separate circuits, is to ensure his status as an eyewitness. In order to prove that his report is accurate, Defoe creates an easily discernible narrator figure who gives detailed descriptions of the traveled topography. In keeping with the empiricist doctrine of the age, the subjective point of view is to guarantee an objective account[6]. However, as we know today, the (empirical) author Daniel Defoe not only collected information on diverse travels that failed to match the reported circuits, he also used several secondary sources, and only much later brought the collected information into a coherent form. The narrative account, it appears, was created at another place, and another time, than the diverse perceptions.

What I want to argue now is that the temporal and spatial detachment of the act of perception and the act of reporting is mirrored in the perceptual position Defoe ascribes to his narrator. In whatever way the real author's perception was slanted, the narrator in the text has a peculiar and easily discernible slant of perception. In alliance with the 18th century's predominant concept of visual perception, Defoe seems to be traveling within a transportable walk-in *camera obscura*; he poses as a distanced observer to whom the world presents itself as if through an incorruptible machine. The following depiction of a *camera obscura* represents this conception perfectly.

6 See Jay (1993: 64): "Intersubjective visual witnessing was a fundamental source of legitimation for scientist like Robert Boyle." See further Crary (1990: 41).

Figure 1: Athanasii Kircheri, *Ars Magna Lucis et Umbrae*, 1671: 709 (extract).

The distance between Defoe's narrator, who poses as an experiencing figure, and the described objects correlates with the effects of the process of writing. The distance which the writer, sitting in his study, experiences in relation to the described objects finds its perfect embodiment in the idea of a transportable walk-in *camera obscura*. The *camera obscura*, as Crary has analyzed, "performs an operation of individuation; that is, it necessarily defines an observer as isolated, enclosed, and autonomous within its dark confines" (Crary 1990: 38–39). The observer is cast as "a free sovereign individual and a privatized subject confined in a quasi-domestic space, cut off from a public exterior world" (39). Incidentally, this is also a perfect description of the situation of writers and readers emerging in the eighteenth-century[7], sitting alone in their respective domestic, private closets (cf. Heyl 2004: 506–26): "The reader can open the door of a novel, enter, and quietly shut the door behind him" (Zimbardo 1978: 8). He or she is alone and not alone at the same time: "A thousand readers indeed stare, from their closets, into a single mirror of print, and each of them does it alone" (Hunter 1984: 285). The author, similarly writing on his or her own, by means of this device, can, as Fielding has it, "hold the

[7] The changes in question here are to be seen in relation to the older paradigm of the scribe—collectively writing in a monastery—and the paradigm of the audience—experiencing collectively in the theatre.

Glass to thousands in their Closets" (Fielding 1742: 6). Here, scientific-philosophical empiricism, the technique of the *camera obscura* and the new situation of the reader seem to converge: "The camera, or room, [or book; C. H.] is the site within which an orderly projection of the world, of extended substance, is made available for inspection by the mind" (Crary 1990: 46).

However, the concept of the *camera obscura* has consequences not only for the perceiving subject, but for the perceived object, too: a multi-faceted "thing" is turned into a purely visual semiotic sign—sound, smell, taste, touch; nothing of this can be reproduced within the box. Finally, objects can be looked at without having the chance of looking back; perception is bereft of any reciprocity. Correspondingly, in the act of reading, the object of observation is present only as mediated and physically absent: one can observe the object, without having to experience it in its full presence and without having to fear that it might stare back. (And if it does, as in some printed pictures, this feels uncanny.) Therefore, the sort of actual and symbolic distance involved when perceiving an object visually through the *camera obscura* makes possible the uninvolved stance of Defoe's account. Narratologically, this position is embodied nowhere better than in the heterodiegetic narrator of the classical realist novel, and although Defoe's narrator is strictly speaking homodiegetic, i. e. a part of the story of Britain, he nonetheless appears to remain external to this world. From this position, Defoe develops his calm and objective mode of writing, his now legendary "concise, clear prose," his "plain, easy, straightforward style" (Backscheider 1986: 46, 53). However, such narrative mode would seem quite at odds with an observer who claims to be "in the thick of it", interacting and turn-taking. Rather, this mode of narrating is only credible in relation to the peculiar narrator-observer position developed by Defoe, being there but not there at the same time—like the camera (and the audience) in a classical Hollywood production, protected by the "fourth wall".

The only time Defoe gets carried away is when describing the society at Tunbridge-Wells, a place full of "Fops, Fools, Beaus, and the like" (Defoe 1724–26: I, 165), where "you are surpriz'd to see the Walks covered with ladies compleatly dress'd and gay to profusion; where rich Cloths, Jewels, and Beauty [...] dazzles the Eyes" (164). Bedazzled by such spectacle Defoe rants about the dangers at such places, and the slander that increases such dangers, and finally has to cut himself short before becoming too agitated: "But this is a digression" (166). Apart from this perplexing encounter, Defoe appears to have avoided every contact with living human beings while on his travels. Although the subtitle of his book promises an account of the "Customs, Manners, Speech, as also the Exercises, Diversions, and Employment of the People," the inhabitants of Britain "receive little attention beyond the remark that the population is increasing" (Feldmann 1997: 37). When dealing with the capital, Defoe admits that "by *London* [...], I mean, all the Buildings, Places, Hamlets, and Villages contain'd in the line of Circumvallation" (Defoe 1724–26: II, 74)—an imaginary line Defoe has drawn in order to measure the city. The creation of this line seems to guarantee a vantage point, a perspective from which the "monstrous City" (74) that London is for Defoe can be tamed, that is, ordered, chartered. For him, London is nothing more than a "great Mass of Buildings" (74), and consequently he describes the appearance and function of every important building, market etc.—but never does he stoop to describe anything that cannot be contained within his "line of circumvallation" and would suggest a reciprocal, interactional approach: human beings, for example.

Ned Ward's *London Spy* develops a markedly different narrator-figure. In stark contrast to Defoe's distanced view of London's buildings, Ward constantly reports on not only seeing other people, but also hearing, smelling, and touching them. His slant of perception is noticeably different from Defoe's vision. Instead of looking down from above—Defoe variously describes ascents to specific vantage points in order to have a better (over-)view—, the Spy is at eye-level. Instead of being distanced, he is close. As a consequence, the Spy looks and is being looked at, he hears other people and is heard, he touches them and is touched. Unlike the linear perspective/*camera obscura* visual observer, Ward's narrator is all too aware of his own physical presence, aware of the effects his presence has on the observed objects and aware of the consequence such observations have on him. Finally, he interacts with people—and his report is full of people.

However, this experience of the social does not necessarily depend on which senses are used[8], but rather on how they are employed. The mode of observation, whether technically or discursively formed, determines whether co-presence, reciprocity and interaction, key elements of the social, are allowed for or not (cf. Bohn 2000). The perceptual stance of the

---

8 Kant thought the ear to be the privileged sense when it comes to the social, whereas Simmel opted for the eye; see Bohn (2000: 321–22).

narrator-observer predetermines, at least to a certain degree, the selection of as well as the relation to the objects described. And sometimes these "objects" even cease to be mere objects.

But Ward is no complete exemption from the 18th century's craze for all things visual. Rather, the Spy employs his visual sense without completely subjecting his environment to the demands of unilateral perspectival spectating. Because the Spy includes other than visual sensations, it seems his mode of visual observation is also different from Defoe's—he sees differently, because his relation to the objects of perception is formed by several senses. Most importantly, the Spy remains receptive on all channels. This, however, bears certain dangers. Again and again he seems overwhelmed by his sensory experiences: "nothing I could see but light, and nothing hear but noise" (Ward 1709: 29). He experiences the city with a very "acute, and sometimes over-powering awareness of [...] sensory experiences" (Hyland 1993: xv). His ears hear the "sundry passing-bells, the rattling of coaches, and the melancholy ditties of 'Hot Baked Wardens and Pippins!'" (Ward 1709: 29); he sees the "dazzling lights whose bright reflections so glittered in my eyes" (29); his nose smells the "narrow lane, as dark as a burying-vault, which stunk of stale sprats, piss and sir-reverence" (39).

In the realm of seeing there seems to be a strong preference for the observed object over the observer, especially under the scopic regime described in connection with Defoe. As described above, in the process of observation, the observed is turned into an independently existing object, while the observer is fashioned as a separately existing subject, uninvolved in the "creation" of the perceived object. On the other hand, most of the non-visual senses require a closer relation to the object of perception; hearing and tasting, for example, are often conceptualized as "taking in" the perceived object. The perceived object, finally, takes up such presence that a specific perspective, defining the individuality of the subject, is not necessarily easily to be made out—the distinction between observer and observed, subject and object threatens to collapse.

The completely opposite mode of writing—excited, emotional, exuberant—, with which Ward's perceptions are reported, seems to result from this closeness to the perceived objects and the way this closeness affects him. Instead of traveling in a confined, distancing and sensually diminishing *camera obscura*, Ward's experiencing figure walks among his fellow citizens. Being so close, he cannot help but experience other sensory experiences than purely visual ones. The writing style that results from this might be best described as "linguistically overstuffed" (Wall 1998: 137)—drawing attention to the utterance itself rather than the utterer. The attempt to render the vast amount of multi-sensorially experienced details into language leads to an exuberant style that constantly escapes into similes and analogies when a complete rendering of the multi-sensorial experience becomes impossible. As a consequence, the reader has great difficulty locating a similarly well-defined point of view to the one we find in Defoe. Only rarely can the reader follow where the narrator is, and whom he is speaking to. Often, the reader learns more about how the narrator is affected by his experiences than about the object that (apparently) emanates the stimuli. And only rarely is the localization of the experiencing figure possible: from where is an event heard, or smelled in the dark? A well-defined, easily locatable perceptual stance appears to be the privilege of the visual. Impressions, otherwise, do not seem to add up to a well-defined diegetic world. And although I think there is no doubt that Ward is narrating, it is not clear whether he is actually involved in world-making.

6 Consequences

The slant of perception of every experiencing figure is heavily influenced by the inclusion or exclusion of specific senses, by their emphasis or suppression. The perceptual position that results from such a slant, in turn, influences what a report can include, and how the report is fashioned; this, then, is what I termed "narrative focalization". No report, obviously, can render all sensory experiences. Therefore, every narration needs a specifically equipped and positioned experiencing figure, which filters what can be experienced and consequently determines, at least to a certain degree, what can be reported. In turn, every form of report needs an accompanying slant of perception. And while there is no strictly causal relation between a certain slant of perception and narrative focalization, there appear to be some culturally suggested default cases at least. Of course, there is no inherent superiority among different possible positions; Defoe is clearly able to see something that Ward can not, whereas Ward can render experiences that Defoe remains blind to. However, the specificity of these positions warrants close observation.

In the case of Ward and Defoe, attention to their perceptual stance helps understand their peculiar positions. Both pose as participant-observers, roaming the world they observe and subsequently describe.

Defoe's perceptual stance, however, reveals him as an observer rather than a participant, while Ward, on the other hand, is marked as a participant rather than a mere observer. The visual sense, and especially the scopic regime of the *camera obscura*, appears to appeal to those who try to be observers first, whereas a multi-sensorial approach seems to suggest participation. Closer attention to the perceptual situation and its technical and discursive determinations, then, might be able to distinguish historically and culturally specific embodiments of different narrative positions. Defoe's heterodiegetic narrator, who is at the same time close enough to see everything but distanced enough not to be seen, as well as Ward's specific homodiegetic narrator, can be more closely analyzed with regard to the use of their senses. And finally, looking at the cultural models or regimes of perception and reporting in factual accounts might also reveal what limitations and possibilities fictional narratives encounter.

References

Abrams, Meyer Howard (1953). *The Mirror and the Lamp: Romantic Theory and the Critical Tradition.* New York: Oxford UP.

Anon. (1694). *An Historical Account of Mr Roger's Three Year Travels over England and Wales. Giving a True and Exact Description of all the Chiefest Cities, Towns and Corporations*. London.

Backscheider, Paula R. (1986). *Daniel Defoe: Ambition and Innovation.* Lexington: UP of Kentucky.

Bal, Mieke (1985). *Narratology: Introduction to the Theory of Narrative*. Toronto: U of Toronto P.

Bohn, Cornelia (2000). "Sprache, Schrift, Bild." B. Heintz & J. Huber (eds). *Mit dem Auge denken: Strategien der Sichtbarmachung in wissenschaftlichen und virtuellen Welten.* Vienna: Springer, 321–45.

Chatman, Seymour (1986). "Characters and Narrators: Filter, Center, Slant and Interest-Focus." *Poetics Today* 7:2, 189–204.

Cockayne, Emily (2007). *Hubbub: Filth, Noise and Stench in England, 1600–1770.* Yale: Yale UP.

Crary, Jonathan (1990). *Techniques of the Observer. On Vision and Modernity in the Nineteenth Century.* Cambridge, MA: MIT Press.

Defoe, Daniel (1724–26). *A Tour through the Whole Island of Great Britain (1724–1726).* 3 vols. Ed. J. McVeagh. London: Pickering & Chatto, 2001.

Feldmann, Doris (1997). "Economic and / as Aesthetic Constructions of Britishness in Eighteenth-Century Domestic Travel Writing." *Journal for the Study of British Cultures* 4, 31–45.

Fielding, Henry (1742). *The History of the Adventures of Joseph Andrews*. London.

Genette, Gérard (1972). "Discours du récit." *Figures III.* Paris: Seuil, 65–278.

– (1980). *Narrative Discourse.* Tr. J. E. Lewin. Oxford: Blackwell.

– (1983). *Nouveau discours du récit.* Paris: Seuil.

– (1988). *Narrative Discourse Revisited.* Tr. J. E. Lewin. Ithaca: Cornell UP.

Heyl, Christoph (2004). *A Passion for Privacy: Untersuchungen zur Genese der bürgerlichen Privatsphäre in London, 1660–1800.* Munich: Oldenbourg.

Hunter, J. Paul (1984). "The World as Stage and Closet." S. S. Kenny (ed). *British Theatre and the Other Arts, 1660–1800.* Washington: Folger, 271–87.

Hyland, Paul (1993). "Introduction." E. Ward. *The London Spy.* East Lansing: Colleague P, xi– xxiii.

Jahn, Manfred (2005). "Focalization." D. Herman et al. (eds). *The Routledge Encyclopedia of Narrative Theory.* London: Routledge, 173–77.

Jay, Martin (1993). *Downcast Eyes: The Denigration of Vision in Twentieth-Century French Thought.* Berkeley: U of California P.

Jesch, Tatjana & Stein, Malte. "Perspectivization and Focalization: Two Concepts—One Meaning? An Attempt at a Conceptual Differentiation." In this collection, 59–77.

Jost, François (1983). "Narration(s): en decà et au-delà." *Communications* 38, 192–212.

Klepper, Martin (2004). *The Discovery of Point of View: Observation and Narration in the American Novel 1790-1910.* Unpublished *Habilitationsschrift*, University of Hamburg.

Lanser, Susan S. (1981). *The Narrative Act: Point of View in Prose Fiction.* Princeton: Princeton UP.

Lüdemann, Susanne (1999). "Beobachtungsverhältnisse. Zur (Kunst-)Geschichte der Beobachtung zweiter Ordnung." A. Koschorke & C. Vismann (eds). *Widerstände der Systemtheorie: Kulturtheoretische Analysen zum Werk von Niklas Luhmann.* Berlin: Akademie Verlag, 63–75.

Martínez, Matias & Scheffel, Michael (1999). *Einführung in die Erzähltheorie.* Munich: Beck.

McLuhan, Marshall (1962). *The Gutenberg Galaxy: The Making of Typographic Man.* London: Routledge & Kegan Paul.

Nelles, William (1997). *Frameworks: Narrative Levels and Embedded Narrative.* Frankfurt a. M.: Peter Lang.

Niederhoff, Burkhard (2001). "Fokalisation und Perspektive. Ein Plädoyer für eine friedliche Koexistenz." *Poetica* 33:1–2, 1–21.

Nünning, Ansgar & Vera Nünning (2001). "Von 'der' Erzählperspektive zur Perspektivenstruktur narrativer Texte: Überlegungen zu Definition, Konzeptualisierung und Untersuchbarkeit von Multiperspektivität." A. Nünning & V. Nünning (eds). *Multiperspektivisches Erzählen: Zur Theorie und Geschichte der Perspektivenstruktur im Englischen Roman des 18. bis 20. Jahrhunderts.* Trier: WVT, 3–38.

Prince, Gerald (2001). "A Point of View on Point of View or Refocusing Focalization." W. van Peer & S. Chatman (eds). *New Perspectives on Narrative Perspective.* Albany: SUNY Press, 43–50.

– (2005). "Point of View (Literary)." D. Herman et al. (eds). *The Routledge Encyclopedia of Narrative Theory.* London: Routledge, 442–43.

Rimmon-Kenan, Shlomith (1983). *Narrative Fiction: Contemporary Poetics.* London: Methuen.

Roberts, Jason (2006). *A Sense of the World. How a Blind Man Became History's Greatest Traveller.* London: Simon & Schuster.

Schmid, Wolf ([2]2008). *Elemente der Narratologie*. Berlin: de Gruyter.

Uspenskij, Boris (1972). "Structural Isomorphism of Verbal and Visual Art." *Poetics* 5, 5–39.

Wall, Cynthia (1998). *The Literary and Cultural Spaces of Restoration London.* Cambridge: Cambridge UP.

Ward, Edward [Ned] ([4]1709). *The London Spy*. Ed. P. Hyland. East Lansing: Colleague Press, 1993.

Zimbardo, Rose A. (1978). "Imitation to Emulation: 'Imitation of Nature' from the Restoration to the Eighteenth Century." *Restoration: Studies in English Literary Culture, 1660–1700* 2:2, 2–9.

Part III: Transliterary Aspects of Mediation

ROLAND WEIDLE
(Hamburg)

Organizing the Perspectives: Focalization and the Superordinate Narrative System in Drama and Theater

1 Introduction

Epic elements in drama and theater have been the subject of wide interest in the last decades and especially in the last few years. Particular attention has been paid to so-called narrator figures who present the audience with embedded narratives. These teller-figures have been compared to intra-, hypo-, meta-, homo-, hetero- or even "privileged intradiegetic" (Korthals 2003: 310) narrators in narrative fiction. Approaches like these have opened up a new branch of academic interest "toward a narratology of drama" (Sommer 2005: 123). Research has led to valuable insights into the various dramatic functions and effects of such embedded narrators and narratives (such as addressing the audience, distancing, alienation, irony), the underlying assumption behind these approaches being "that narrative storytelling is not only to be found in narrative literature but in all literary genres, and thus also in poetry and drama" (Nünning & Sommer 2002: 108)[1]. This statement requires no further explanation and is amply illustrated by the publication of whole monographs and anthologies devoted to the analysis of embedded narratives with a transgeneric and even transmedial perspective[2]. In the following, however, I would like to pursue a somewhat different line of inquiry which so far has only attracted the interest of a limited number of critics[3]. These scholars promote the investigation of "extradiegetic" narration of drama (as opposed to the focus on intradiegetic narration in drama). Given the wide interest that has been bestowed upon extradiegetic narration in other genres and

---

1 Here, as in the following, English translations of German texts are mine.

2 See Nünning & Nünning (2002); Herman (1999; 2003; 2004); Ryan (2004).

3 Such as Brian Richardson, Manfred Jahn, Richard Aczel and Holger Korthals, and, to some extent, Rolf Fieguth, Patricia Suchy and Horst Spittler.

media, such as film and poetry, "narratology's neglect of the narrating voice in performance is actually quite surprising" (Richardson 2001: 682). It is my contention that narratological concepts such as extradiegetic narration and focalization can be fruitfully applied to, or at least tested in, the analysis of drama in order to show that drama, like narrative literature and poetry, is also narrated, if only in a broader meaning of the term. However, I do not wish to focus on locating the extradiegetic narrator in the communicative system of drama and clarifying his ontological status. It is far more rewarding to concentrate on the question how and to what effects drama is narrated than to concern oneself with the question as to who narrates, that is, whether the extradiegetic narrator in drama is synonymous with the author, the implied author or yet another agency.

When applying transgeneric narratological terms to drama one has to be aware of several methodological pitfalls. Before setting out on the course just laid out, it is therefore necessary to tackle briefly some of the essential problems associated with such an approach.

2 Story, Narration, and Narrating

At the end of their helpful explication of the various layers of fictional narration, Martinez and Scheffel come up with a table of six main planes: event (*Ereignis* [*Motiv*]), story (*Geschehen*), plot (*Geschichte*), plot-scheme (*Handlungsschema*), narration (*Erzählung*) and narrating (*Erzählen*)[4]. Whereas the first four levels belong to the realm of *Handlung* (action, understood as the sum of all the elements that constitute what is being told), the latter two belong to the category *Darstellung* (presentation), meaning: they deal with the how of telling[5]. For the purpose of this analysis I would like to argue that *Geschehen* (story), as understood by Martinez and Scheffel, constitutes the most relevant layer in the realm

4 Martinez and Scheffel understand *Erzählung* as the narrated events in the order of their representation in the text and *Erzählen* as the actual presentation of the plot in a manner particular to a specific language, code or media (cf. Martinez & Scheffel 1999: 25). For my choice of using the English "narrating" for the German *Erzählen* (instead of "discourse", as one might also suggest) and its significance for my intermedial approach see below.

5 See Martinez & Scheffel (1999: 25). In the subsequent chapters the authors refer to the aspect of representation (*Darstellung*) as the "How" (*Wie*) and to the aspect of the represented (*Handlung*) as the "What" (*Was*).

of the represented, whereas on the side of presentation the two categories "narration" and "narrating" are of equal importance for our perspective. Martinez and Scheffel understand story in a similar vein as Edward Morgan Forster, as a chain of chronologically ordered events without causal relationships. Such a broad conception of story may not be necessary when discussing plays of Shakespeare, Dryden, Lillo or Shaw. Here the objects of presentation are never interconnected without causality. But what about the drama of Beckett, Pinter, and Stoppard? Is causality a useful concept when trying to analyze the actions of Stanley, Goldberg, and McCann in *The Birthday Party*? Where is the causality between Vladimir and Estragon's final decision to leave and their subsequent not moving in *Waiting for Godot*?

> VLADIMIR: Well? Shall we go?
> ESTRAGON: Yes, let's go.
> [*They do not move.*] (Beckett 1990: 88)

With regard to the narrative contents of the plays of Beckett and Stoppard it becomes evident that Genette's "relations of linking, opposition, repetition" (Genette 1983: 25) are just as valid in constituting stories as is causality for pre-modernist drama[6].

I am aware that a strict separation of narrative content and narrative presentation is problematic. After all, even our minimal definition of story as events linked by repetition, chronology, similarity or any other relationship presupposes an agent that does the linking, a consciousness that generates and/or identifies these links[7]. As mentioned earlier, Martinez and Scheffel define two aspects of presentation in their theoretical overview: narration and narrating. The former is more or less synonymous with Genette's "récit" and Rimmon-Kenan's "text", designating "the narrated events in the order of their representation in the text" (Martinez & Scheffel 1999: 25), differing from the story above all in the ways the

---

6 Whereas the contrast between Vladimir and Estragon's words and their subsequent action, or rather: non-action, at the end of *Waiting for Godot* constitutes an oppositional relation, the beginning of Stoppard's *Rosencrantz and Guildenstern are Dead* may serve as an example of a repetitional relationship between events. The first scene of the play shows the two protagonists flipping coins with Rosencrantz always winning (cf. Stoppard 1966: 11–12). The coin-flipping-business, which continues well into the first act, is of course only one of the many instances that contribute to the repetitional character of the play (cf. also the verbal and gestural repetitions in the play).

7 Jonathan Hart argues with reference to Ross Chambers and Seymour Chatman that it "is difficult to separate stories from their telling" (Hart 1991: 140).

events are temporally restructured and regrouped[8]. The latter category (narrating), refers to the actual process and form of narrating, including the different possible forms of presentation as regards language, code or media (cf. Martinez & Scheffel 1999: 25). Martinez and Scheffel's inclusion of the aspect of narrating seems to be a very useful approach in applying narratological concepts to the analysis of drama. It draws attention to the fact that narrations are always linked to actual narrating processes that can occur in different semiotic systems, codes, languages, genres, and media, and not only in narrative literature. Bearing in mind the dramatic focus of this article, this inevitably leads us to reconsider our notions of the text containing the narrated events, and even more so to reconsider our ideas of the conditions that are constitutive of the narrating process. I will first deal with the conditions defining the dramatic narrating situation and then comment on the textual character of dramatic narration.

In the *Routledge Encyclopedia of Narrative Theory* Marie-Laure Ryan posits six dilemmas in trying to define narrative. Apart from discussing the problematic notion of narrative universals and other issues, she also mentions the aspect of mediation:

> Does narrative presuppose a verbal act of narration by an anthropomorphic creature called a narrator, or can a story be told without the mediation of a narratorial consciousness? […] Some scholars have attempted to reconcile the narrator-based definition with the possibility of non-verbal narration by analysing drama and movie as presupposing the utterance of a narratorial figure, even when the film or the play does not make use of voice-over narration […]. (Ryan 2005: 346)

In her summary of approaches—narratives are either verbally mediated, told without mediation, or non-verbally mediated—only the last definition seems to offer a viable approach when applied to drama and its enactment on stage. The scripts for Beckett's mimes *Act Without Words I* and *Act Without Words II*, which consist solely of secondary text, are neither verbally mediated on stage, nor is dramatic representation in general devoid of mediation[9]. Both as playtext and as performed drama the story always depends upon mediation, either via the arrangement of written

---

[8] For Genette's definition of "récit" see Genette (1983: 27 and passim). For Rimmon-Kenan's definition of "text" see Rimmon-Kenan (1999: 3 and passim).

[9] Stefan Schenk-Haupt drew my attention to the fact that mimes do not consist of secondary text, but contain solely "directive" information as to how to play the mime. Yet, as is the case with secondary text proper, the "directive" text is not verbally mediated on stage but itself mediates—via other semiotic channels—the story of the mime.

words on the page (primary and secondary text in the script), or through various linguistic and non-linguistic sign-systems on stage. Thus dramatic stories are selected, arranged, mediated, and, in a wider meaning of the term, narrated to us. Ryan's third option, which allows for an "utterance of a narratorial figure" behind stories, points in a more helpful direction, although—as so often in recent discussions—with an undue focus on the narratorial agent. I would therefore like to postulate—in slight modification of Jahn's concept of a "superordinate narrative agent" (Jahn 2001: 672)—the existence and working of a "superordinate narrative system" in drama with "an anonymous and impersonal narrative function controlling the selection, arrangement, and focalization" (674) of the story-data. Before illustrating some of the levels on which this superordinate narrative system operates, I would like to discuss the "textual" character of dramatic narration and the problems associated with an unduly narrow focus on the dramatic playtext.

Playscript Mode

Holger Korthals' German monograph *Zwischen Drama und Erzählung: Ein Beitrag zur Theorie geschehensdarstellender Literatur* (*Drama and Narration: A Contribution to the Theory of Story-representative Literature*), published in 2003, is, to date the only monograph on the subject of superordinate narrative structures in drama, or rather "poetic drama", because Korthals makes it very clear that he is solely interested in the dramatic playtext. "By displacing the literary text of drama from the theatrical performance we arrive not only at a seeming but at a genuine comparability to other story-representative genres such as the novel or novella" (Korthals 2003: 60). According to Korthals, such a concentration on the written text endows the reader of drama with privileges formerly ascribed only to readers of narrative literature, such as the suspension of the "irreversible linearity" (Pfister 1977: 63) of dramatic performance. As practical as such a comparison of dramatic and narrative texts may be, it neglects the essential and defining feature of drama: namely, that it is written to be performed. Although Korthals later concedes that there is "a link between the literary dramatic text and its performance" (Korthals 2003: 74) and that the play-text always has to be seen with a view to its performance, he ascribes a greater presentational force to the written secondary text than to its enactment on stage[10] and concludes that the presented story can in principle be deduced from reading the dramatic playtext without having any notion about the norm of theater (cf. 58–59).

The question as to whether drama should be approached mainly as a dramatic text or a theatrical performance has been widely (and controversially) discussed. For the present purpose I will refer to Manfred Jahn's short and useful summary of the main views on this subject. He differentiates between three interpretive approaches. Whereas the "school of Poetic Drama roundly prioritizes the dramatic text," whose "main interpretive strategy is a close reading which aims at bringing out the dramatic work's full aesthetic quality and richness," the "school of Theater Studies, by contrast, privileges the performance over the text" (Jahn 2001: 661). The main strategies of this approach include, according to Jahn,

> considering a performance as the product of historical and cultural theatrical conditions, describing the sociology of drama, analyzing stage codes and semiotics, stage histories, and the dynamics of collaborative authorship. (661)

This approach attacks the school of Poetic Drama for its academic isolation, and it considers the performed play as "really the only relevant and worthwhile form of the genre" (661). The third school of "Reading Drama," however, is an approach that Jahn favors and that I also would like to take as a basis for my understanding of drama. It combines the approaches of Poetic Drama and Theater Studies:

> Reading Drama is a school that envisages an ideal recipient who is both a reader and theatergoer—a reader who appreciates the text with a view to possible or actual performance, and theatergoer who (re)appreciates a performance through his or her knowledge (and rereading) of the text. Its interpretive strategies include performance-oriented textual analysis, paying particular attention to the "secondary text" of the stage directions, and comparing the reading of plays to the reading of novels. (662)

Such an approach requires careful reading and analysis of the play text, but it also challenges us in our imaginative efforts to visualize what we read: "if we are to make sense of the play, we must read with especially active visual imagination" (Campbell 1978: 187). Not only do we have to pay "particular attention" to the secondary text of the stage directions, we

---

10 See for example his disputable comment on the final lines of *Waiting for Godot*, already referred to above: "Thus the note in the secondary text makes the contradiction between talking and acting far more visible for the reader than for the spectator who can only be made aware of the importance of this contradictory behaviour through the players' demonstrative and conspicuous performance" (Korthals 2003: 67).

also have to pay particular attention to the "performative" messages encoded in the primary text (the implied stage directions) that tell us something about how the story is to be enacted on stage. It is, however, important to draw a line here between drama and performance analysis. I am not suggesting the inclusion of every possible way of visualizing and enacting the play-text on stage, nor do I propose to engage in an analysis of individual performances by "production collective[s]" (Pfister 1977: 11) with a specific aesthetic and/or ideological motivation. Instead, the play-text has to be understood as the playwright's instruction of how to present or envision things on the stage. The written text, be it secondary or primary text, does not only narrate (as Holger Korthals argues) but it also has a clear referential and sometimes even imperative function in providing the recipient of the dramatic text (reader or production collective) with the minimum information necessary to visualize or to enact the textual data[11]. The imperative function can be aptly illustrated with the opening passage from Beckett's *Krapp's Last Tape*:

> *A late evening in the future.*
> KRAPP'S *den.*
> *Front centre a small table, the two drawers of which open towards the audience.*
> *Sitting at the table, facing front, i.e. across from the drawers, a wearish old man:* KRAPP.
> *Rusty black narrow trousers too short for him. Rusty black sleeveless waistcoat, four capacious pockets. Heavy silver watch and chain. Grimy white shirt open at neck, no collar. Surprising pair of dirty white boots, size ten at least, very narrow and pointed.*
> [...]
> KRAPP *remains a moment motionless, heaves a great sigh, looks a this watch, fumbles in his pockets, takes out an envelope, puts it back, fumbles, takes out a small bunch of keys, raises it to his eyes, chooses a key, gets up and moves to front of table. He stoops, unlocks first drawer, peers into it, feels about inside it, takes out a reel of tape, peers at it, puts it back, locks drawer* [...]. (Beckett 1990: 215)

Whereas the first line "A late evening in the future" does not provide concrete information as to its enactment on stage, the description of the room, of Krapp's appearance, and his movements are very specific and tell us exactly how Beckett wanted the play's beginning to be staged[12]. It is of course a far more difficult matter to talk about an author's intention if—as for example in Shakespeare's case—we do not have an original

---

11 For a discussion of the illocutionary force of stage directions see Jahn (2001: 663–69).

12 The importance of the detailed stage-directions becomes evident in the course of the play, as the desk, its position on the stage, and the drawers play an integral role in the play's story.

text, licensed by the author. As this is not the moment to engage in a postmodern debate about the valid or invalid concept of the author, let it suffice to say that even dramatic texts, where it is difficult to arrive at the author's intentions, provide the reader with signals as to their scenic enactment. Thus, reading and analyzing plays in this "*playscript mode*" (Jahn 2001: 673) entails "performance-oriented textual analysis" (662). It avoids treating the play-text as a purely textual phenomenon without taking into account its theatrical orientation.

3 Superordinate Narrative System

Repudiating the idea of narratorless narratives, which holds "that certain sentences of fiction do not occur in the spoken language and cannot be said to be enunciated by a narrator" (Banfield 2005: 396), Richard Aczel prefers to see

> the "narrator" as an umbrella term for a cluster of possible functions, of which some are necessary (the selection, organization, and presentation of narrative elements) and others optional (such as self-personification as teller, comment, and direct reader/narratee address). (Aczel 1998: 492)

Such a view goes back to Chatman's differentiation between diegetic and mimetic narration[13], which in turn derives from a broader interpretation of Aristotle's concept of mimesis not only as the imitation of words but also as the production of "larger structures—in particular, structures of plot" (Chatman 1990: 110). According to Aristotle (*Poetics* 9.1451b) the poet is a "*maker* of plots [...] and his mimesis is of actions" (Aristotle 1995: 61; emphasis added), which holds true for both the epic genre and tragedy. Aczel's differentiation between necessary and optional functions of the narrator is interesting and to some, like Genette, inacceptable because it renders actual telling as a possible but not necessary requirement for the act of narration. Shakespeare's *Pericles* presents an interesting case in point for both the necessary and optional functions of a narrator. Before the play proper begins, an actor impersonating John Gower, the 14th-century poet and author of the *Confessio Amantis*, one of the sources of Shakespeare's play, appears and speaks the following lines:

---

13 See Chatman (1990: 109–23). "To 'show' a narrative, I maintain, no less than to 'tell' it, is to 'present it narratively' or to 'narrate' it" (113).

To sing a song that old was sung
From ashes ancient Gower is come,
Assuming man's infirmities
To glad your ear and please your eyes.
It hath been sung at festivals,
On ember-eves and holy-ales,
And lords and ladies in their lives
Have read it for restoratives.
[...]
This' Antioch, then; Antiochus the Great
Built up this city for his chiefest seat,
The fairest in all Syria.
I tell you what mine authors say.
This king unto him took a fere
Who died, and left a female heir [...] (I.1–8, 17–22)[14]

The prologue introduces himself as the resurrected poet ("Assuming man's infirmities") and author of the story of Pericles that the audience is about to witness. Does this fulfil Aczel's optional criterion of the "self-personification" of the teller? Do we really have with Gower the superordinate narrative agent of Shakespeare's play *Pericles* personified on stage? Does the fact that Gower reappears throughout the play "as a perceptive moderator who introduces each of the remaining acts" make him, as Jahn states, the "behind-the-scene show-er agency in control of selection, arrangement, and presentation" (Jahn 2001: 671)[15]? I agree with Jahn when he concludes (although with caution) that "Gower's discourse acquires the status of an *inset*" (672), that is, in narratological terms, Gower has to be understood as an intradiegetic narrator, who is part of the diegetic level[16]. The prologue appears at regular intervals in the play, announcing, summarizing, and commenting on the hypodiegetic story enacted by the actors who play the roles of Pericles, Marina, and the rest. The interplay between the different diegetic levels of the prologue on the one side and the playworld of the other figures on the other side is an integral part of the play's composition and bespeaks a "behind-the-scene show-er

14 Quotations from Shakespeare's plays are from the Norton-Edition (1997), unless otherwise indicated.

15 Jahn also uses the terms "narrating instance" (660), "dramatic narrator" (669), "superordinate narrative agent" (672), and "impersonal narrative function" (674).

16 I disagree, however, with Jahn's statement that Gower's diegesis is a "first-degree narrative" (672) which is shadowed by the superordinate narrative agent's first-degree narrative. Gower's narrative is secondary to the extradiegetic narrative of the superordinate system.

agency" that stands also behind or rather above[17] Gower. Gower's referring to his own sources in the quoted passage ("I tell you what mine authors say") aptly illustrates his embedded position and dependence on other authorities.

3.1 Overt vs. Covert

Can one therefore argue that the narrative superordinate agent in drama, unlike its extradiegetic counterpart in narrative literature, is always covert and never visible in the play-text or the enacted play? The production *Isabella's Room* (2004) of the Belgian theater group *Needcompany* provides an interesting case in this respect. The protagonist Isabella, aged 94, sits in her room in Paris, which is filled with archaeological objects. These objects assist her in reflecting on her past life. At the beginning of every performance the author of the play, Jan Lauwers, who is also the founder and artistic director of *Needcompany*, appears on stage and makes an announcement:

> Good evening ladies and gentlemen,
> Welcome,
>
> We will perform for you tonight "Isabella's room". But before we start with the performance, I would like to tell you a bit more about the text I have written. You see, my father died a few years ago. He left me a huge collection of more than 4000 archaeological and ethnographical objects. Some of them are presented here on stage.
> [...]
> And so, I wrote the story of Isabella Morandi, performed by Viviane De Muynck.
> [...]
> Next to Isabella, on my left, we have her dream: the desert prince, [...] played by Julien Faure and born out of a lie. [...] The music is written by Hans Petter and Maarten Seghers. Maarten also plays the grandson of Isabella, Franky. Can you still follow?
> [...]
> And in the corner, Misha Downey, the narrator, who—and this is unique in the history of theatre—will play Isabella's erogenous zone for you.
> [...]
> Sound: Dré Schneider, Light: Jeroen Wuyts.
>
> Oh, I will play the man in the white suit. Now we can start. Misha, it's all yours. (Lauwers 2006b)

[17] Or "below" in Genette's taxonomy.

Lauwers then remains on stage for the whole performance, sitting at the upper side stage, dressed in white, observing his play, and from time to time handing props to the actors[18]. At the end he takes part in the performance of a song. The matter becomes even more complicated as we also have a narrator on stage, "Misha", who fulfils the traditional functions of epic commentary, interaction with the audience, and standing in for other characters. One has seen similar metalepses where a narrator-figure interacts with the audience and the other actors. The stage manager in Thornton Wilder's *Our Town* or Scullery in Jim Cartwright's *Road* are a case in point. However, the situation here is different. Lauwers is the author and superordinate narrative agent of *Isabella's Room* and he is present on stage in every performance of the play. But he is also, as prologue and observer, part of the presented story-world and visible throughout the performance, although his function is restricted primarily to "behind-the-scene" tasks as handing props. In the prologue, Lauwers conflates the levels of author and character. Whereas the introduction of the actors and the production ensemble and the teasing of the audience ("Can you still follow?") fulfil more or less conventional functions of the prologue, Lauwers' references to his biographical background (his father's death, the collection of objects) and the comments on his motivation to write the play bring together the worlds of the extra-textual and the diegetic. In other words: the superordinate narrative agent assumes an overt presence in the play, or at least almost, because in the end Lauwers' prologue is part of the written play-text, performed in the same way—with minor alterations—in every performance, and thus acquires the status of an inset. His interfering with other characters of the play-world, his visible presence, and the ensuing tension between the different narrative levels are an integral part of the play and contribute to its intricate design in which "times and places dissolve into another" (Lévesque 2005). Yet again, there is one aspect which supports the view that it is Lauwers as superordinate narrative agent, and not as intradiegetic narrator figure, who is overtly present in the performed play. In the published version of the

[18] For a detailed account of the performance I am very grateful to Felix Sprang, an ardent supporter and follower of *Needcompany* and their productions. This paper benefited greatly from his knowledge and viewing experience. Felix Sprang also was so kind as to provide me with the manuscript of his article on "Turns on the Narrative Turn. Showing and Telling in Needcompany's Early Shakespeare Productions and *Isabella's Room*" (cf. Sprang 2007).

play[19] Lauwers does not appear; except for a short introductory note he remains absent from the play. In the play-text the author and "behind-the-scene show-er" remains hidden. Only through Lauwers' self-personification on stage are we made aware of the actual presence of the superordinate narrative agent. That it is in fact in this function that Lauwers appears on stage, and not as author, is confirmed by Lauwers himself:

> It may seem paradoxical, but it is precisely for this reason that I take part in the performance myself this time. [...] You might say that the simple fact that I am there on-stage without taking part in the action makes sure that it is no longer about me.[20]

Taking *Isabella's Room* then as an exception to the rule that the superordinate narrative system is generally covert, the question remains, how does this system manifest itself, or rather, how does it operate and how can it be described?

3.2 Analepsis, Prolepsis, and Syllepsis

Korthals sees three possible planes on which dramatic texts reveal their narrativity: (1) figural speech—what I prefer to call intradiegetic narration—, which so far has been the major focus of narratological analysis; (2) secondary text, which explains the temporal and causal relationships between individual scenes; (3) "narrative-analogous structures" constituted by the interplay between figural and authorial speech, primary and secondary text (Korthals 2003: 186). In the following, I would like to focus on the latter, "narrative-analogous structures", and more specifically on dramatic examples of narrative order and narrative mood.

Most of the discussions of temporal relations between story and narration tend to focus on intradiegetic manifestations of analepsis and prolepsis, such as messengers' reports, flashbacks of epic narrators or prophecies. To name only a few: Salieri's retrospective showing, telling, and reenactment of his life in Mozart's Vienna in Shaffer's *Amadeus*, Enobarbus' account of Cleopatra's arrival at Tarsus in *Antony and Cleopatra* (II.ii,196 and passim), and the witches' prophecies in *Macbeth*. Drawing

---

19 A French edition of *Isabella's Room* was published along with Lauwers' *The Lobster Shop* in May 2006 (cf. Lauwers 2006a).

20 Lauwers in an interview with Pieter T'Jonk in the *De Tijd* ("Because Women are Tremendously Important" ["Omdat vrouwen ontzettend belangrijk zijn"], 21.9.2004), quoted in the English translation from *Needcompany's* website <www.needcompany.org>.

on Bernhardt Asmuth's classification of four possible types of dramatic prolepsis (authorial, plot-engendered, mantic, and presentational)[21], Korthals privileges authorial prolepsis as constitutive of extradiegetic narration and sees its main realization in the secondary text and prologues (cf. Korthals 2003: 215)[22]. Because of my doubts mentioned above regarding the extradiegetic qualities of written secondary text and prologues I would like to focus on Asmuth's fourth type of prolepsis, neglected by Korthals: the presentational prolepsis. Presentational prolepsis functions on two levels, plot-externally and plot-internally, by drawing our attention to particular props, characters, words or moments, and thus endowing them with specific (proleptic) meaning. On a level external to the plot this can be done by virtue of specific lighting techniques, sound, music, and other theatrical means. As this type of external prolepsis is most often employed by the production collective and not the author, it is of minor relevance for this analysis. The plot-internal prolepsis, however, is part of the plot and depends to a large extent on "the conventional expectations of the audience concerning the genre, story, motives, props, characters and manners of speech" (Asmuth 1997: 121). Thus, for example, the repeated appearance, hiding and finding of parts of clothing in Orton's farce *What the Butler Saw* anticipate the great finale of un- and cross-dressing in the second act[23]. Or to take an example on a more microscopic level: Faustus' last hour in Marlowe's play, in which he awaits the arrival of the devils. The striking of the clock at eleven, eleven-thirty, and midnight at shortening intervals mirrors (and heightens) Faustus' and our own anticipation of his death. Another manifestation of the temporal relationship between story and narrative is defined by what Genette calls "syllepsis," the "ana-

---

21 Asmuth (1997: 114–22) differentiates between authorial (*auktoriale Vorausdeutung*) and plot-internal prolepsis (*handlungsinterne Vorausdeutung*) subsuming under the latter the certain (*zukunftsgewisse*) and the uncertain (*zukunftsungewisse*) variants of plot-engendered (*handlungslogische Vorausdeutung*) and mantic prolepsis (*mantische Vorausdeutung*). As a last type he defines presentational prolepsis (*darstellende Vorausdeutung*).

22 Korthals implies that authorial prolepsis and analepsis can also be achieved by means of an "interplay of secondary text signals, story-constitutive speech and narrative figural mediating speech" (218). In his subsequent discussion of an obscure play, however, he falls short of illustrating this point convincingly (cf. 218–20).

23 See also the ominous "small cardboard box" (act I; Orton 1976: 7) carried by Geraldine at the beginning of the play. It is repeatedly referred to (and handled), and the disclosure of its contents ends the play.

chronic groupings governed by one or another kinship (spatial, temporal, or other)" (Genette 1983: 85).

Shakespeare's *A Midsummer Night's Dream* (ed. 1993) illustrates variants both of spatial and thematic syllepses. Variants, because—apart from a minor anachronistic slip at the beginning of the play[24]—the play adheres to a strictly chronological sequence. As Pfister has shown, the four plot lines of the Theseus-Hippolyta wedding, the four lovers, the fairy world, and the mechanicals are grouped and thus "narrated" along the spatial axis court-city-wood (cf. Pfister 1977: 259). However, these plot lines are also arranged around a central motif, the moon. Not only is the moon referred to in almost every scene, it also plays a prominent part as an appointed date for the royal wedding (I.i,1–3), as the appointment time for Lysander and Hermia (I.i,209–13), as a source providing the necessary "moonlight" (cf. I.ii,83) for the mechanicals' rehearsal of *Pyramus and Thisbe*, and in setting the atmosphere in Oberon and Titania's first meeting (cf. II.i,60)[25]. Finally, the moon even appears on stage, albeit not personified very successfully by Starveling. The moon suffuses the plot lines of the play with its polyvalent, ambiguous, and often contradictory meanings, consequently establishing a sylleptic, superordinate narrative web[26].

A similar narrative and structuring function is fulfilled by the tape in Beckett's *Krapp's Last Tape*. The three time-levels of Krapp at the age of 69, 39 and 29 are all arranged thematically around the actual process of listening to and narrating on tape[27]. The important "narrative" role of the tape is also supported by the prominent position of the tape recorder on the table situated "*front centre*"[28] and by the title of the play. Especially with this type of thematic syllepsis, as Korthals poignantly states, "it is not the memories of a participating character but the *arrangement* of the

---

24 Theseus announces at the beginning of the play that his wedding will take place in four days, at full moon (cf. I.i,1–3). The subsequent events until the wedding, however, take up only three days.

25 According to Harold F. Brooks, the "moon in her many aspects is regent of the *Dream*" (Shakespeare 1993: cxxviii).

26 In his *Dictionary of Symbols and Imagery* Ad De Vries lists a variety of different meanings with which the moon in western culture has been associated. One of the striking features of the meanings—besides their richness—is their often contradictory character. Thus, the moon "stands for opposing values: female and male, fluid and volatile, constancy and inconstancy, etc." (De Vries 1976: 326).

27 For a helpful visualization of the time structure of the play see Jahn (2003: D 7.3).

28 Stage direction at the beginning of the play (Beckett 1990: 215).

narrative discourse" (Korthals 2003: 193) that performs the functions of the narrative agency.

4 Focalization

Genette separates the notions of voice and mood and argues that we have to differentiate between the agent who narrates and the agent who perceives[29], or, as he reformulates in his *Narrative Discourse Revisited*, between the question who narrates and the question "*where is the focus of perception*?" (Genette 1988: 64) I will briefly repeat the three well-known types of focalization (1): zero focalization: the narrator knows and says more than any of the characters knows; vision from behind; (2) internal focalization: the narrator says only what a given character knows; vision from within; (3) external focalization: the narrator says less than the character knows; vision from without.

For Korthals external focalization constitutes the default mode of drama. Characters, actions, and events are shown to us on stage and we perceive them from the outside without a narrator giving us additional information (cf. Korthals 2003: 273–74). Zero focalization on the other hand occurs, according to Korthals, through explanatory secondary texts—what Issacharoff calls "autonomous stage directions" (Issacharoff 1989: 20)—, providing the reader with additional information that helps him or her to transcend the perceptive horizon of the characters (and eventually of the audience sitting in the theater). The following stage direction from Stoppard's *Travesties* (act I) may serve as an example:

> *A note on the above: the scene (and most of the play) is under the erratic control of Old Carr's memory, which is not notably reliable, and also of his various prejudices and delusions. One result is that the story (like a toy train perhaps) occasionally jumps the rails and has to be restarted at the point where it goes wild.* (Stoppard 1974: 11)

---

[29] It is interesting to note that there is still no general agreement on the difference between the narratological notions of focalization, point of view, and perspective—see Prince (1988: 31, 73); Niederhoff (2001); Surkamp (2005: 424); Prince (2005: 442–43). Genette explains the introduction of the term "focalization" on two grounds: (1) "to avoid the too specifically visual connotations of the terms *vision*, *field*, and *point of view*" (Genette 1983: 189), and (2) to distance himself from earlier "confusions [...] between *mood* and *voice*" (Genette 1988: 64) connected to the term "point of view".

The problem with autonomous stage directions of this kind is that they do not reach the audience, only the reader of the play-text. Thus they cannot contribute to the narrative set-up of "reading drama" as sketched out above. Korthals' second manifestation of zero focalization, prologues, and epilogues, similarly falls short of proving the existence of zero focalization in drama, because they are not, contrary to Korthals argument, external to the presented story and they do not deliver "quasi secondary text made audible on stage" (Korthals 2003: 278). Does this inevitably lead to the conclusion that zero focalization is not possible in drama? The following scene from Patrick Marber's *Closer* (1997) proves otherwise. The play is about four characters—two men, Larry and Dan, two women, Anna and Alice—who attempt to find intimacy, but after various attempts and partner changes in a "pass-the-lover"-fashion fail to get any "closer" to each other. The following passage is from a scene (scene 8) which begins at a restaurant in the evening. Anna tells Dan about the encounter she has had with her freshly divorced husband Larry, which had taken place only hours before at the same restaurant:

> DAN So has he signed?
> ANNA *Yes*
> DAN Congratulations. You are now a divorcée—double divorcée. Sorry. (*Dan takes her hand.*) How do you feel?
> ANNA Tired. (*Dan kisses her hand, Anna kisses his.*)
> DAN I love you. *And...* I need a piss. (*Dan exits. Anna reaches into her bag and pulls out the divorce papers. Larry enters.*)
> LARRY (*Sitting.*) Afternoon.
> ANNA Hi. (*Larry looks around.*)
> LARRY I hate this place.
> ANNA At least it's central. [...] (Marber 1999: 57).

With Dan leaving the table, Anna pulling out the divorce papers, and Larry joining Anna at her table Marber goes back in time half a day to Anna's meeting with her soon-to-be ex-husband ("Afternoon"). In the following dialogue Larry offers to sign the divorce papers under the condition that Anna sleeps with him for one last time: "Be my whore and in return I will pay you with your liberty" (58). Before Anna can respond, Larry goes to the bar (he exits) and Dan appears again and resumes the previous dialogue "he is going to have" with Anna that evening. She tells him that she in fact did sleep with Larry, a piece of information which upsets Dan and occupies most of the ensuing dialogue. The scene ends with a fusion of both time levels and all three characters present on stage:

DAN [...] I think you enjoyed it; he wheedles you into bed, the old jokes, the strange familiarity, I think you had "a whale of a time" and the truth is, I'll never know unless I ask *him*.
ANNA Well why don't you? (*Larry returns to the table with two drinks. Vodka tonic for Anna, Scotch and dry for himself.*)
LARRY Vodka tonic for the lady.
ANNA (*To Larry*) Drink your drink and then we'll go. (*Larry looks at her. To Larry.*) I'm doing this because I feel guilty and because I pity you. You know that, don't you?
LARRY Yes.
ANNA (*To Larry.*) Feel good about yourself?
LARRY No. (*Larry drinks.*)
DAN (*To Anna.*) I'm sorry ...
ANNA (*To Dan.*) I didn't do it to hurt you. It's not all about *you*.
DAN (*To Anna.*) I know.
Let's go home ... (*Dan and Anna kiss.*) [...] (61)

By leaving Dan on stage during the analepsis the audience is able to assume a perspective superior to the characters Larry and (especially) Dan, because we—unlike Dan—do not have to rely on Anna's account and her internal focalization of her meeting with Larry. We can "witness" the encounter at the same time from a superior perspective. Or, in other words: when viewing this scene the audience is able to share in the superior knowledge that results from being able to compare simultaneously Anna's version with "reality", something that cannot be done in narrative fiction. Another example of zero focalization occurs in the third scene of the same play, in which Dan and Larry chat on the internet. It is a split-scene showing Dan sitting at his computer in his flat and at the same time Larry at his computer at work. They type the words as they speak and their dialogue "appears on a large screen simultaneous to their typing it" (22). The audience obtains a bird's-eye view sharing the superordinate narrative instance's vision but also each of the characters' internal focalization of the screen with the words appearing as they are typed (and spoken). The contrast between the limited perspectives of the figures on the one hand and the superior perspective is even heightened by the fact that Dan pretends to be Anna, which of course Larry cannot see. These are extreme examples of zero focalization in drama and one could in fact argue that the physical nature of the performance and the fact that we—unlike readers of narrative fiction—are always able to see and compare perspectives for ourselves, move drama in general closer to zero than to external focalization[30].

This still leaves Genette's third type unaccounted for, internal focalization, of which Korthals says that it can appear either on the plane of the figures' speech such as in soliloquies, asides, and in narrative mediations like reports and teichoscopies, or in the form of "theatrical stagings of mental events" (Korthals 2003: 282)[31], such as apparitions, dreams, memories, and the like (cf. 282–95). It is almost self-evident that, for example, Katherine's dream in Shakespeare's *Henry VIII* (cf. IV.ii,80–84), which is being performed while she is shown sleeping on stage, presents an instance of internal focalization. However, one may ask whether the fact that we can see the focalizing agent on stage, the sleeping Katherine, would not also allow for zero and external focalization. In this respect, it is worth noting that the simultaneous presence of focalizing subject and focalized object on stage seems to be the standard case in drama. Due to the corporeal nature of scenic presentation and the immediacy of visual perception the focalizing subjects on stage are always at the same time focalized objects[32].

Hamlet's vision of his father's ghost in the closet-scene is another example, although more complex because of the fact that the ghost was in fact seen by Horatio, Barnardo, and Marcellus in the first act, but is not visible to Gertrude in this scene. If Hamlet were not the main character of the play, one could actually view this scene as an illustration of Gertrude's, and not of Hamlet's internal focalization (cf. Korthals 2003: 283). The matter becomes even more complicated once we turn to modern and postmodern drama. In Stoppard's *Travesties* the old Carr remembers, or thinks he remembers, the events that occurred in the years 1917/18 in Zurich when he was in his twenties, employed at the consulate and when he met James Joyce during his involvement in an amateur production of Oscar Wilde's *The Importance of Being Earnest*. His faulty memory twists the facts and conjures up fictional encounters not only with Joyce, but also with the Dadaist Tzara and Lenin. In a stage direction (act I) Stoppard says that during the first encounter between Joyce, Tzara, and

---

[30] For a brief discussion of the differences between Pfister's concept of perspective structure, Spittler's presentational perspectives, and Genette's types of focalizations see Korthals (2003: 274–76).

[31] Korthals borrows this phrase from Richardson (1988: 204).

[32] For a differentiation between focalizing subject and focalized object, and between focalization from within and without see Rimmon-Kenan (1999: 75–76).

Lenin it "*is possible that* CARR *has been immobile on stage from the beginning, an old man remembering*" (Stoppard 1974: 5). If that suggestion is taken up by the director and old Carr is on stage while we see his faulty recollections, we have a similar case to Katherine in *Henry VIII*, who is presented sleeping on stage while the audience sees her dream enacted, namely: a case of "impure" internal focalization. Both focalizing agent and the focalized are visible on stage. If, however, Carr is absent from the stage or is part of the recollected memories as young Carr—and this is the case several times in the play—, the presented memories clearly seem to be a case of internal focalization. But that leaves us with another problem and lays open the unreliability of Carr's memories. One may ask how Carr can focalize anything which he was not a part of[33]? Another scene (act II) from the same play shows young Carr denying having fantasies about the librarian Cecily, followed by an enactment of exactly these fantasies from "Carr's-mind view":

> [CECILY: …] don't talk to me about superior morality, you patronizing Kant-struck prig, all the time you're talking about the classes you're trying to imagine how I'd look stripped off to my knickers—
> CARR: That's a lie!
> (*But apparently it isn't. As CECILY continues to speak we get a partial Carr's-mind view of her. Coloured lights begin to play over her body, and most of the other light goes except for a bright spot on Carr.*) (*Faintly from 1974, comes the sound of a big band playing "The Stripper". CARR is in a trance. The music builds. CECILY might perhaps climb on to her desk. The desk may have cabaret lights built into it for use at this point.*) […] (Stoppard 1974: 52)

Not only do we have here Young Carr's "impure" internal focalization (both the focalizer and his fantasies are focalized), but this scene also represents Old Carr's—probably faulty—internal focalization of Young Carr's internal focalization of his fantasies about Cecily.

5 Conclusion

The narratological concept of focalization as a filter through which the act of narrating takes place is problematic when applied to the analysis of drama. Because of drama's physical and visual nature and the material presence of the actors, focalization in drama, or to be more precise: in

[33] Young Carr leaves the stage for the first time well into the first act on p. 34 and returns as Old Carr on p. 42, shortly before the end of the first act. Thus, the intermediate scenes are focalized by someone who actually was not in the position to focalize them.

"reading drama", appears to be less dependent on the mediating process. Of course, even in drama, focalization does not take place without narration (by means of a superordinate narrative system), but the relation between narration and focalizing seems to be less prescriptive and more flexible than in narrative fiction. Mieke Bal's formula for fiction "x relates that y sees what z does" (Bal 1985: 45) turns into "x relates *while* y sees what z does," and here the "y" refers both to characters on stage and to the audience. As for the extradiegetic narrative voice of drama, the superordinate narrative system, I hope to have shown that a transgeneric and transmedial application of a broader conception of narration lays open the narrative planes and channels of drama and directs more attention to the how of dramatic mediation than to the question, who narrates drama.

References

Aczel, Richard (1998). "Hearing Voices in Narrative Texts." *New Literary History* 29:3, 467–500.

Aristotle (1995). *Poetics*. Ed. & tr. S. Halliwell. / Longinus. *On the Sublime*. Tr. W. H. Fyfe. / Demetrius. *On Style*. Ed. & tr. D. C. Innes. Cambridge, MA: Harvard UP.

Asmuth, Bernhardt (1997). *Einführung in die Dramenanalyse*. Stuttgart: Metzler.

Bal, Mieke (1985). *Narratology: Introduction to the Theory of Narrative*. Toronto: U of Toronto P, 1997.

Banfield, Ann (2005). "No-Narrator Theory." D. Herman et al. (eds). *Routledge Encyclopedia of Narrative Theory*. London: Routledge, 396–97.

Beckett, Samuel (1990). *The Complete Dramatic Works*. London: Faber and Faber.

Campbell, Sue Ellen (1978). "*Krapp's Last Tape* and Critical Theory." *Comparative Drama* 12, 187–99.

Chatman, Seymour (1990). *Coming To Terms: The Rhetoric of Narrative Fiction and Film*. Ithaca: Cornell UP.

De Vries, Ad (^{2}1976). *Dictionary of Symbols and Imagery*. Amsterdam: North-Holland Publishing Company.

Fieguth, Rolf (1973). "Zur Rezeptionslenkung bei narrativen und dramatischen Werken." *Sprache im technischen Zeitalter* 47, 186–201.

Genette, Gérard (1972). "Discours du récit." *Figures III*. Paris: Seuil, 65–278.

– (1980). *Narrative Discourse*. Tr. J. E. Lewin. Oxford: Blackwell.

– (1983). *Nouveau discours du récit*. Paris: Seuil.

– (1988). *Narrative Discourse Revisited*. Tr. J. E. Lewin. Ithaca: Cornell UP.

Hart, Jonathan (1991). "Narrative, Narrative Theory, Drama: The Renaissance." *Canadian Review of Comparative Literature* 18:2–3, 117–65.

Herman, David (ed) (2003). *Narrative Theory and the Cognitive Sciences*. Stanford: Center for the Study of Language and Information.

– (ed) (1999). *Narratologies: New Perspectives on Narrative Analysis*. Columbus, Ohio: Ohio State UP.

– (2004). "Toward a Transmedial Narratology." M.-L. Ryan (ed). *Narrative Across Media: The Languages of Storytelling*. Lincoln, NE: U of Nebraska P, 47–75.

Herman, David et al. (eds) (2005). *Routledge Encyclopedia of Narrative Theory*. London: Routledge.

Issacharoff, Michael (1989). *Discourse as Performance*. Stanford: Stanford UP.

Jahn, Manfred (2001). "Narrative Voice and Agency in Drama." *New Literary History* 32:3, 659–80.

– (2003). *Poems, Plays, and Prose: A Guide to the Theory of Literary Genres*. <http://www.uni-koeln.de/~ame02/ppp.htm> (6.10.2006).

Korthals, Holger (2003). *Zwischen Drama und Erzählung: Ein Beitrag zur Theorie geschehensdarstellender Literatur*. Berlin: Schmidt.

Lauwers, Jan (2006a). *La Chambre d'Isabella / Le Bazar du Homard*. Arles: Actes Sud.

– (2006b). *Isabella's Room*. Script (Work Version), 33 pp. Supplied by Needcompany on 21.9.2006.

Lévesque, Solange (2005). "An Ode to Life, Disguised as Kaddish." *Le Devoir*, Montreal (3.6.2005), quoted on Needcompany.org (s. below).

Marber, Patrick (1999). *Closer*. New York: Dramatists Play Service, 2000.

Martinez, Matías & Michael Scheffel (1999). *Einführung in die Erzähltheorie*. Munich: Beck.

Needcompany.org. <www.needcompany.org> (9.10.2006).

Niederhoff, Burkhard (2001). "Fokalisation und Perspektive. Ein Plädoyer für eine friedliche Koexistenz." *Poetica* 33:1, 1–21.

Nünning, Ansgar & Sommer, Roy (2002). "Drama und Narratologie: Die Entwicklung erzähltheoretischer Modelle und Kategorien für die Dramenanalyse." V. Nünning & A. Nünning (eds). *Erzähltheorie transgenerisch, intermedial, interdisziplinär*. Trier: Wissenschaftlicher Verlag Trier, 105–28.

Nünning, Vera & Nünning, Ansgar (eds) (2002). *Erzähltheorie transgenerisch, intermedial, interdisziplinär*. Trier: Wissenschaftlicher Verlag Trier.

Orton, Joe (1976). *The Complete Plays*. New York: Grove.

Pfister, Manfred (1977). *Das Drama: Theorie und Analyse*. Munich: Fink, 1997.

– (1993) *The Theory and Analysis of Drama*. Tr. J. Halliday. Cambridge: Cambridge UP.

Prince, Gerald (1988). *A Dictionary of Narratology*. Aldershot: Scolar Pr.

– (2005). "Point of View (Literary)." D. Herman et al. (eds). *Routledge Encyclopedia of Narrative Theory*. London: Routledge, 442–43.

Richardson, Brian (1988). "Point of View in Drama: Diegetic Monologue, Unreliable Narrators, and the Author's Voice on Stage." *Comparative Drama* 22:3, 193–214.

– (2001). "Voice and Narration in Postmodern Drama." *New Literary History* 32:3, 681–94.

Rimmon-Kenan, Shlomith (1999). *Narrative Fiction: Contemporary Poetics*. London: Routledge.

Ryan, Marie-Laure (2005). "Narrative." D. Herman et al. (eds). *Routledge Encyclopedia of Narrative Theory*. London: Routledge, 344–48.

Shakespeare, William (ed. 1993). *A Midsummer Night's Dream*. Ed. H. F. Brooks. London: Routledge.

– *The Norton Shakespeare* (1997). Eds. S. J. Greenblatt et al. New York: Norton.

Sommer, Roy (2005): "Drama and Narrative." D. Herman et al. (eds). *Routledge Encyclopedia of Narrative Theory*. London: Routledge, 119–24.

Spittler, Horst (1979). *Darstellungsperspektiven im Drama*. Frankfurt a. M.: Peter Lang.

Sprang, Felix (2007). "Turns on the Narrative Turn: Showing and Telling in Needcompany's Early Shakespeare Productions and *Isabella's Room*." C. Stalpaert et al. (eds). *No Beauty For Me There Where Human Life Is Rare. On Jan Lauwers' Theatre Work With Needcompany*. Gent: Academia Press and International Theatre & Film Books, 132–48.

Stoppard, Tom (1966). *Rosencrantz and Guildenstern Are Dead*. New York: Grove, 1967.

– (1974). *Travesties*. New York: Grove, 1975.

Suchy, Patricia A. (1991). "When Words Collide: The Stage Direction As Utterance." *Journal of Dramatic Theory and Criticism* 6:1, 69–82.

Surkamp, Carola (2005): "Perspective." D. Herman et al. (eds). *Routledge Encyclopedia of Narrative Theory*. London: Routledge, 423–25.

SABINE SCHLICKERS
(Bremen)

Focalization, Ocularization and Auricularization in Film and Literature

In the following, I will limit my discussion of focalization to fictional films although it cannot really be limited to these only. But fictional films are more complex than factual ones or documentaries, because, like literary narrative texts, they are based on a double communication situation: the implied director or author is not identical with the narrative entity of the film, which I term "camera"[1]. Therefore, we have to differentiate between the implied director and viewer on the one hand and the "camera" as intermediator of visual and acoustic information as well as the narratees of this information on the other.

In her study of point of view in three Spanish films adapted from literary texts, Susan Rubio Gribble (cf. 1992: 25–26) argues that the "camera" cannot be equated with the narrator of a literary text. What is at stake, however, is not what we call this narrating agent in the film, but the fact that, in film too, the act of narrative mediation is located on the extradiegetic level. This is why we have to speak of the filmic narrator instead of the author as does Rubio Gribble, who is conscious of introducing a polyvalent and therefore problematic term: "author" means (a) the actual author or director, (b) the implied author (whom she fails to mention), (c) that agent which Michel Foucault terms author and which, when we inspect it more closely, turns out to be a mixture of implied author[2] and narrator[3] and, finally, the "auteur" of New Wave Cinema. In

1 In this article, I will use quotation marks ("camera") in order to differentiate this narrative agent from the technical instrument. For more details on the following modeling see my book *Verfilmtes Erzählen* (Schlickers 1997).

2 "Everyone knows that, in a novel narrated in the first person, neither the first-person pronoun nor the present indicative refers exactly either to the writer or to the moment in which he writes, but rather to an alter ego whose distance from the author varies, often changing in the course of the work. It would be just as wrong to equate the

my argumentation, however, I will not focus on the entity of the author, but rather on perspectivation. In film, as I will show, perspectivation is mediated in the form of focalization—by the help of the "camera" as a filmic narrator—and its interplay with "seeing" (ocularization) and "hearing" (auricularization) as well as through editing and montage. On the level of the intended meaning, perspectivation has to be connected with the agent of the implied author or the implied director.

As in literary narrative texts, the "camera" as narrator can be located on the extradiegetic, intradiegetic, hypodiegetic, etc. levels. Nevertheless, in the vast majority of cases, the "camera" is located on the extradiegetic level, as illustrated in the figure below. We can locate it on the lower levels only when the "camera" is visible as a camera on these lower levels of the shown world serving a diegetic function, for example, when a film is being shot within the film.

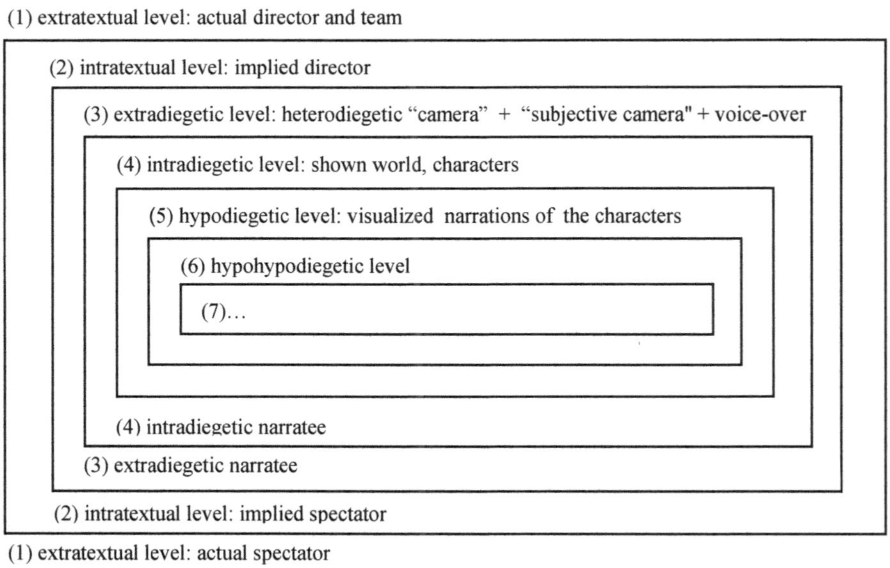

Table 1: Model of Narrative Levels in Fiction Film

author with the real writer as to equate him with the fictitious speaker; the author function is carried out and operates in the scission itself, in this division and this distance." (Foucault 1984: 112)

3 "The text always contains a certain number of signs referring to the author. These signs [...] are personal pronouns, adverbs of time and place, and verb conjugation." (Foucault 1984: 112)

What is more complex is the case of the so-called “subjective camera” or “point-of-view shot”. Here, the takes are recorded (virtually) from the point of view of one character—the “subjective camera”, as an agent of enunciation, is located on the extradiegetic level. As a consequence, what it is showing, i.e. the enounced or rather the view of the character, must be located on the intradiegetic level[4]. This interplay of enunciation and enounced can be compared to the way speech is rendered in narrative literary texts: what the characters say is located on the intradiegetic level, yet it is the extradiegetic narrator who quotes, selects, and condenses these items of speech.

As a narrative agent, the “camera” can track sound as well as images, which means it is not limited to “showing” only. What is more, film as a plurimedial semiotic system is capable of simultaneously transporting visual and acoustic information about the fictional world. Decoding this fundamental double perspectivation is not an easy task, particularly because the perspective and the flow of information keep changing incessantly and hardly ever remain constant over a longer period of time. Moreover, pieces of visual and acoustic information can be concordant or discordant and likewise, discrepancies regarding information can be created among the various characters. And there is yet another factor: only the selection and composition of the individual shots and takes or rather the *mise en scène* create the meaning of the filmic narration[5].

Before I go on to illustrate these possibilities with examples of films, I would like to present a typology of filmic perspectivation which is based mainly on François Jost’s critique of Gérard Genette’s typology devel-

---

4 At this point, I wish to correct the thesis I put forward in 1997 in *Verfilmtes Erzählen* (*Filmed narration)* according to which the “subjective camera” is homo- and intradiegetic, because this would mean that there are two “cameras” in every fictional film, an extra- and an intradiegetic one, which keep taking turns.

5 In earlier publications (cf. Schlickers 1997), I located the artistic-compositional organizing principle of the montage on the level of the implied director, who, analogous to the implied author, governs the entire dimension of image and sound but possesses no semiotic signs of his or her own to articulate him- or herself and therefore has to utilize the “camera” as a narrative agent. Contrary to this earlier description, I would like to agree with Markus Kuhn’s conception (see his contribution in the current volume) and locate the montage also on the extradiegetic level. After all, filmic narration only comes into existence through the combination of the different takes and shots, and filmic perspectivation is the result of this composition, in which the sequence of the individual takes determines the type of focalization.

oped for literary perspectivations. I developed this typology of literary and filmic perspectivation in *Verfilmtes Erzählen (Filmed narration,* 1997). In this contribution, I will simplify and abridge it as well as, regarding certain points (see above), correct and supplement it.

Genette's distinction of focalization and voice was intended to contribute to the analysis of the fundamental option of double perspectivation in terms of "knowing" versus "showing/telling" which we always have in narrative literary texts too.

> However, to my mind most of the theoretical works on this subject [perspective] (which are mainly classifications) suffer from a regrettable confusion between what I call here *mood* and *voice*, a confusion between the question *who is the character whose point of view orients the narrative perspective?* and the very different question *who is the narrator?*—or, more simply, the question *who sees?* and the question *who speaks?* (Genette 1980: 186)

Reducing the question "who is the character whose point of view orients the narrative perspective?" to the formulation of "who sees?" limits focalization to the visual aspect, which is what Genette aims to avoid. Reducing focalization to "seeing" precludes analyzing those passages in which the narrator is not viewing through the eyes of a character but nevertheless is able to penetrate into his or her interior, for instance: "As she was crossing the bridge, she was thinking of her ailing mother." At a later point in his works, Genette expanded the category of focalization in order to include the knowledge of the narrator—and thus merged what he had originally set out to distinguish "the regrettable confusion between [...] *mood* and *voice*" (Genette 1988: 64). I therefore aim to distinguish once more between "seeing" and "knowledge". After all, especially when we consider film, it becomes clear that this is a medium which employs double perspectivations even more so than does literature—which, moreover, are usually being mediated simultaneously.

François Jost defines focalization as the knowledge of the narrator in relation to the characters (cf. Jost 1989: 71). Unlike Genette's characterization of focalization, in his definition, "seeing" and "hearing" are replaced by the categories of ocularization and auricularization respecttively. Admittedly, these are awkward categories, but after years of consideration, I have not been able to come up with a better idea, so that I will carry on using these categories[6]. Jost adopts the forms of focalization which Genette introduced drawing on Jean Pouillon and Tzvetan Todorov. In spite of the fact that the term zero focalization has been rightfully criticized in narratological discussion for implying that there is an absence of perspectivation, I would like to continue employing this term, because it is well-established internationally. Therefore I will continue to distinguish:

zero focalization: narrator > character ($n > c$)
internal focalization: narrator = character ($n = c$)
external focalization: narrator < character ($n < c$)

Table 2

Even without a narrator, various forms of focalization can be used. This is why it seems necessary to expand this well-known typology in order to include focalization on the level of the characters (i.e. the intradiegetic and lower levels). Thus we render more dynamic the interplay of knowledge, lack of knowledge, and the conscious withholding of information of the various characters from each other as well as in their relationship to the extradiegetic narratee and the implied reader/viewer. On the intradiegetic level, the narrator should be replaced by "c_n" for *character$_{narrator}$*, the former character becomes *character$_2$ (c_2)*.The formulas are thus:

$c_n < c_2$
$c_n = c_2$
$c_n > c_2$

Table 3

The second expansion is implied in table 3 because it refers to an entity which Jost and other narratologists and scholars of film leave out: the extradiegetic narratee (n_{ee}, table 4) or the intradiegetic narratee (c_{ee}, table 5), who also plays a significant role in the reconstruction of focalization:

6 Lintvelt (1981) coined the term "plan psychique", which could be equated with the term of focalization employed here, his "plan perceptif" to ocularization and auricularization.

$n + n_{ee} > c$
$n + n_{ee} = c$
$n + n_{ee} < c$

Table 4: Focalization of Narrator and Narratee on the Extradiegetic Level

$c_n + c_{ee} > c_2$
$c_n + c_{ee} = c_2$
$c_n + c_{ee} < c_2$

Table 5: Focalization of *character$_{narrator}$* and intradiegetic narratee

Alfred Hitchcock's *Notorious* (1946) serves as a particularly intricate example: character c_1, played by Ingrid Bergman, is a secret agent. Her mother in law (c_2) and her husband (c_3) have found out about this. C_2 is planning to kill slowly her son's wife and therefore puts every day some poison in the young woman's coffee. The extradiegetic narratee (n_{ee}) is aware of the fact that c_2 wants to "see to that problem", yet knows nothing about her concrete plans. The extradiegetic narratee then experiences how c_1 is getting a little sicker every day ($c_1 + n_{ee} < c_2 + c_3$: external focalization). The very moment, however, that c_1 realizes that she is being poisoned, her cup of coffee is frozen in an extreme close-up that lasts several seconds, to the effect that, at this short and slowed down moment, the narratee goes through the same terror that c_1 is experiencing. We can thus detect, from the side of the "camera" and its extradiegetic narratee, internal focalization regarding c_1 ($n + n_{ee} = c_1$). At the same time, however, we can detect zero focalization regarding the other characters of the world shown ($c_1 + n + n_{ee} > c_2 + c_3$), because those that have been administering the poison have no idea that they have been found out.

Jost postulates three forms of ocularization, which, for practical reasons, I have chosen to reduce to two:

zero ocularization = "nobody's shots", hetero- and extradiegetic "camera"
internal ocularization = "subjective camera" and mindscreen

Table 6

The most common case is that of zero ocularization, or "nobody's shots," as Nick Browne (1976: 5) terms them: the "camera" is showing the character from the outside and does not count as a diegetic agent within the fictional world. It is thus marked as hetero- and extradiegetic and does not usually mark its enunciation. Unlike Jost (1989) I also count the marking of enunciation by the help of peculiar camera movements or changes in color as zero ocularization if this makes the "camera" self-referential or rather foregrounds its *hic et nunc*. In this case, the narrative mode of the "camera" can be regarded as authorial. The use of an unsteady hand-held camera may be involuntary as a result of the lack of better equipment, for instance in the production of cheap documentaries. It may also be a result of aesthetic and intentional principles, as is the case in the "Dogma Films", whose directors have subscribed to a "vow of chastity"[7].

Unlike zero ocularization, internal ocularization refers to subjective images which can be ascribed to a diegetic agent. Here we can often find the use of the "subjective camera" mentioned above, in which recording takes place almost completely from the point of view of one character. However, subjective images can also be created by the use of montage, lap dissolves, fade-over, color fade, slow-motion, distortion of sound, music and other devices. Although ocularization can always be defined in purely technical terms, when looking at the specific semiotic-narrative context we can only classify it in its interplay with focalization. Thus a segment of what a character remembers is not tied to internal ocularization. Instead, conventional flashback-structure first shows the character in zero ocularization and only then slides into this character's visualized flashback which itself is mediated in zero ocularization

This conventional structure is dissolved in Francesco Rosi's adaptation of Gabriel García Marquez's short novel *Chronicle of a Death Foretold* when at first somebody's dream is shown and we see how the dreamer wakes up only after that. In film, dreams and memories are thus visualized from the characters' interior perspective while the characters see themselves as acting characters from the outside. We cannot describe ocularization as internal in this context (since then the character of the dream would not be visible). Nevertheless, this flashback-structure has become conventionalized as a subjective form of remembering or dreaming and must therefore be described as internal focalization.

---

7 See < http://www.martweiss.com/film/dogma95-thevow.shtml>.

Analogous to ocularization, Jost distinguished three forms of auditory "point of view", that is, auricularization, which I have also chosen to reduce to two:

zero auricularization: the sound cannot be ascribed to a shown agent
internal auricularization: auditory subjectivity

Table 7

Zero auricularization refers to those cases in which the sound cannot be located and is indeterminate and extradiegetic. This is quite obvious when we have off-screen sound and voices which are mediated by the help of the "camera", but in most cases zero auricularization is a sound whose source is on-screen. Conversely, internal auricularization constitutes auditory subjectivity—the sound track mediates what the character is hearing in the shown world. It must therefore be located on the intradiegetic levels or those below, just like the enounced of the "subjective camera". An unambiguous ascription can be undertaken when a character is eavesdropping at a door: in this case, the sound can be ascribed to this character's auditory perception. Alejandro Amenábar's film *Tesis* (1996) manages to mediate internal auricularization in a more unique way. Both protagonists are sitting in the university cafeteria, a few meters from each other, and are listening to their walkmans. She is listening to classical music, he is listening to loud rock. Whenever she is looking at him, we can hear classical music (internal ocularization + auricularization), conversely, we can hear strident rock when he is looking at her (internal ocularization + auricularization). At one point, the "camera" shows him jumping up angrily and running over to her (internal ocularization → zero ocularization; his internal auricularization). Only as he comes to a stop at her table, does he take out his headphones, she takes out hers simultaneously—and the viewer sighs with relief because the noise has finally stopped.

Cases of change of both forms of auricularization are very rare. In *El Sur*, a fictional film of Spanish filmmaker Víctor Érice, which I will discuss in more depth below, we can nevertheless find an example: Estrella, a young girl, is hiding under the bed and hears intimidating, repeated pounding from the room above (internal auricularization). The next shot shows where the sound originates from (zero auricularization): her father is sitting in an armchair in his chamber in the attic, gazes into space, and, with a stick, beats the wooden floor at regular intervals. The noise grows louder as it is carried on and resonates through the whole house. The next cut leads us back to Estrella, who is lying under the bed crying. Her mother enters the room, stops, and hears the intimidating pounding (internal auricularization).

Establishing those sounds of which we do not know for sure to which part of the shown world they belong is more difficult. In this case, their point of origin can be either mental (as in an acoustic hallucination) or be located outside the diegesis. Thus the visual sphere gains significance in determining auricularization, particularly because our sense of hearing is less evolved than our eye sight. On the other hand, the sound quality of a human voice is very distinctive and unambiguous, and can therefore be more easily ascribed to a character in a film than a particular way of looking could be.

Making use of a voice coming from off-screen is a popular device of auricularization. Often, a homo- or autodiegetic narrator-character is introduced at the beginning of the frame story. This narrator then leads the viewer through the film, just like in Francesco Rosi's *Chronicle of a Death Foretold.* Sometimes it only returns towards the end of the film, just like the (fictitious) writer Marguerite Duras in the filmic adaptation of her novel *L'Amant* (which has the same title as the novel). I would now like to put forward the thesis that it is irrelevant for determining auricularization whether the extradiegetic voice from off-screen is part of the shown world[8]: although speakers of the voice from off-screen are often homo- or autodiegetic, i.e. they are usually characters of the world shown, they might just as well be heterodiegetic. In this case, the speaker of the off-screen voice takes on the function of the classical heterodiegetic literary narrator—for instance in *Y tu mamá también*, where the elaborated speech of the off-screen narrator forms a sharp contrast with the colloquial Mexican Spanish of the on-screen characters.

Luchino Visconti's *L'Étranger* (1967), based on Albert Camus's 1942 novel of the same name, demonstrates the option of combining zero auricularization with zero ocularization, which has nevertheless to be described as internal focalization: after Meursault killed an Arab and was arrested, he is now sitting in his prison cell brooding. While the camera closes up on Meursault's silent face (zero ocularization), Meursault's autodiegetic voice is rendered in zero auricularization. In the original

[8] This thesis is contrary to my earlier descriptions in *Verfilmtes Erzählen* (*Filmed Narration,* 1997).

Italian version, it is actually actor Marcello Mastroianni's voice coming from off-screen. Although the acoustic and visual perspectivation chosen is not internal, this interior monologue of Meursault must be established as internal focalization. The main difference from the autodiegetic narrative mode of the novel consists in the use of such "objective" forms of auricularization and ocularization which paradoxically effect subjective perspectivation. Visconti's film does not only use auricularization and ocularization in interior monologues in order to effect subjectivization. In fact this strange way of rendering the outside world through the protagonist's internal perspective thus objectivized is characteristic of the entire film—which, therefore, adapts the similarly strange focalization of the novel adequately[9].

In the context of this article, I cannot elaborate further on the characteristics of the three types of focalization and their interplay with the two types of ocularization and auricularization which we find in filmic and literary texts (cf. Schlickers 1997: 153–67). Instead, I would like to examine more closely another film adaptation in order to exemplify further options of perspectivation in film and to investigate more profoundly the above mentioned determination of focalization in terms of the extra-, intra-, and hypodiegetic narratees and the implied viewer.

Victor Erice's film *El Sur* (1983) is based on Adelaida García Morales short novel of the same name (written in 1981, published in 1985). Fifteen-year-old Estrella is the autodiegetic narrator-character of the film. Following the opening scene, the film is presented as an extended flashback which sets in as Estrella is eight years old and which continues till the fictional present time of the narrative situation, thus covering seven years of narrated time. In the novel, the protagonist—whose name there is Adriana—addresses her second person narrative to her father, trying to shed light on their (platonic) incestuous relationship[10]. Nonetheless, what

---

9 Genette reconstructs the perspectivation in Camus's novel at first as "internal focalization with an almost total paralipsis of thoughts" (Genette 1988: 124). Yet then he moves away from this formula because it implies that Meursault was actually thinking—something we cannot see in the text. Genette thus comes to the conclusion that in *L'Etranger* we have "a homodiegetic narrating that is 'neutral', or in external focalization" (124; cf. Schlickers 1997: 165–66).

10 See Rubio Gribble (1992) and Nimmo (1995) as well as the scene of initiation with the pendulum in the novel which reads like a sexual act: "When I had it in my hands, [...] its stillness discouraged me. I was scared that it would never move in my hands. 'Now' you were telling me in a whisper [...]. When you turned off the lights, without ceasing the soft murmur which was more and more occupying my mind, I felt my heart beat

is covered up by the constant presence of the intradiegetic narratee is the factual absence of the father: we learn soon that he committed suicide and that Adriana is directing herself at a dead person. Neither of the media tells us how much time has passed since the father's suicide and the protagonist's return to the house of her father.

In the film, however, the role of the narratee Estrella addresses as narrator remains unspecific. While working through her memories, Estrella/Adriana is continuously growing aware of the fact that her father (Rafael in the novel, Agustín in the film) was not only the magician who used to swing his pendulum, who was from the "other" Spain, that of the south, and who withdrew to the rough north because of his longing for solitude and for political reasons. Rather, he was a lonesome person, a coward, who betrayed the love of his life for reasons of bourgeois conventions, and slowly perished because of it. After reading this gloomy epistolary narrative for the first time, one is led to think that the challenge of a film adaptation would mainly be the lack of dialog and the brevity of the text. In fact, the last 12 pages of this 47 page long novel, that is one quarter of the text, which cover Adriana's journey to the south, constantly evoked in its mythical quality, do not even form part of the film—they were left out in order to keep costs low. The film was very successful at the 1983 Cannes Film Festival, although the originally planned sequence was never made and the film thus remains uncompleted.

The perspective in the novel is limited to the perception and knowledge of auto(intra)diegetic narrator Adriana. In the film, too, the protagonist is the character that is directing the narratee's attention: as the one who is remembering (in the extradiegetic voice-over) and the one who is being remembered and who is acting in the world shown (intradiegetic). In terms of its aesthetics, the film follows a structural principle which is not very common today: each intradiegetic memory sequence is framed by a black screen: the world shown is being opened by the help of a slow fade-in to one of the images that constitute it; the sequence ends with a slow fade-out to black-screen. We must, however, be wary of the world shown. After all, some of the images that we see derive from Estrella's imagination and bear no relation to the fictional reality. For instance, right at the beginning of the film, the "camera" shows 15-year-old Estrella, who is holding her dead father's pendulum. She closes her eyes, a tear

with violence, my breath going faster and that I was beginning to tremble [...]." (Garcia Morales 1985: 11–12; tr. S. Sch.)

runs slowly down her face (zero ocularization). This is followed by black screen, a slow fade-in shows the father, sitting beside his pregnant wife and using his pendulum in order to determine the baby's sex. On-screen he tenderly speaks to his wife: "Her name will be Estrella."[11] A slow fade-out leads back to a black screen that finishes this memory sequence. Meanwhile, the narratee can hear Estrella's voice from off-screen (zero auricularization): "They told me that my father had predicted that I would be a girl. That's the first memory that comes to my mind—a very intensive image which, in fact, I invented." The fictitious character of this pendulum-scene is thus established by the autodiegetic narrator's voice-over only—a scene that works beautifully in order to illustrate the power of the word or to oppose the theory of the primacy of the image. At the same time, this scene demonstrates that Estrella as narrator is capable to control the images of the "camera" and, therefore, that she is the one carrying out the central narrative function in this film.

Another scene, however, illustrates the narrative power of images and contains a congenial time lapse: the narratee sees eight year-old Estrella as she leaves her parents' house by bicycle and rides down the long avenue, her little dog, almost a puppy, trotting behind her. The "camera" remains in the same position and shows the empty avenue. An unnoticeable lap dissolve takes us to the next scene: the "camera", still in the same position, shows Estrella as she is returning on her bicycle. She is still accompanied by her dog, now fully grown, and has herself become a fifteen year-old teenage girl.

In a key scene of the film, eight year-old Estrella discovers that the mysterious Irene Ríos, her father's former lover, does in fact exist. The narratee shares the experience of this process of recognition purely through the images shown: one late afternoon, Estrella sees her father's moped parked in front of the Arcadia cinema. She looks at the poster of the movie which they are showing (zero ocularization). Over the following two minutes, the "camera" keeps changing, through shot-reverse-shots, between Estrella's looking at the poster (internal ocularization) and backward-moves to show her face (zero ocularization), continuously enlarging the position of the internal ocularization. At first, we can see the movie poster in its full size, as though looking at it with Estrella's eyes. The movie is titled "Flor en la Sombra" ("Flower in the Shade"), and the poster shows the drawing of a woman who, from a very short distance, is

[11] Here, as in the following, English translations of Spanish texts are mine.

looking at a man yearningly. Another woman can be made out in the background; she is essentially overseeing the entire scene. In the right hand lower corner, the names of the main actors are shown, the first one on the list being Irene Ríos. The "camera" rolls back to Estrella's incredulous face; closes up more on the letters of the actress's name, and then rolls back again to Estrella. She enters the lobby of the movie theater where she can see more movie posters. She eyes these black-and-white publicity stills critically, the "camera" pans to follow her gaze from the right to the left till it gets stuck on a picture of Irene Ríos. In two reverse-shots, the "camera" zooms in till, in an extreme close-up, it fills the entire screen. Estrella walks over to the box office and asks the cashier there whether the blond actress is Irene Ríos but the woman cannot help her. Estrella leaves the movie theater and observes its entrance from the other side of the street. Another internal ocularization transports her gaze over to the movie theater; a travel shot slowly glides up the façade and comes to a rest on a brightly illuminated round glass arch. A humming noise can be heard from off-screen, without any mediation, a cut leads to a scene of the hypodiegetic film within the film: Irene Ríos is humming a song and looks straight into the camera while she is brushing her hair. A cut shows Estrella's father from his side in a close-up, as his gaze is glued to the screen—he is thus the intradiegetic narratee or the viewer of the film within the film. Another cut jumps back to Irene Ríos, whose direct look into the "camera" seems to be addressed directly to Estrella's father.

Since Estrella is waiting outside while this happens, these and the following passages, which uncover the film within the film, cannot be ascribed to her as a narrator. If at all, then they must be ascribed to her imagination as Martín-Márquez suggests (cf. 1994: 134)—an explanation that is not very convincing when we consider her young age. Rubio Gribble (1992: 185), on the other hand, recognizes that "the narration has shifted to another narrative level (another focalization)". Instead of reconstructing, thus, the depicted scene as Estrella's internal focalization, we have to attribute the narrative function in this sequence to the extradiegetic "camera", which consequently leads us to replace the internal focalization hitherto dominant by zero focalization ($n + n_{ee} > c$).

When we refer to the implied viewer, we can attest internal focalization also in this scene, because he or she decodes the character of *mise-en-abyme* of this melodramatic sequence of a film within a film with which Estrella's father identifies: when, in the melodramatic *film noir*, Irene Ríos is shot dead by her jealous lover, the "camera" pans to show

Agustín's very sad face from the front. The extradiegetic narratee's knowledge regarding Estrella, however, corresponds to zero focalization, because, unlike her (whose focalization with respect to her father is external), the extradiegetic narratee sees the passages of the film within the film and, just a moment later, hears her father's voice coming from off-screen, as he sits in a café, writing a love letter to the actress after he has left the theater. Agustín's voice-over can be heard by the extradiegetic narratee only, yet it can't be perceived by intradiegetic Estrella, who is curiously peeking at the writing paper through the window as her father is coming out of the café towards her. Significantly, the extradiegetic narratee's knowledge is more substantial even than that of Estrella's extradiegetic voice when she formulates ideas about the content of what seems to be a letter.

In the scene following the next, Agustín sits in another café and reads the letter which his former lover sent to him as a reply. This time, the extradiegetic narratee hears the actress's voice from off-screen. Agustín is shown as he is reading the letter (zero ocularization) and is imagining the voice of the woman who wrote it. In spite of this internal process, the auricularization in this scene, analogous to the example given above, that is Visconti's *L'Étranger*, must be described as zero. With regard to Agustín, the narratee's and implied viewer's focalization is therefore internal; with regard to Estrella, however, focalization must be considered external also in this scene, because Estrella does not know the letter of the former lover. It is therefore the "camera" that takes on the narrator's function in this sequence and eliminates Estrella as a narrator: the narratee learns at the same time as Agustín why Estrella never heard of Irene Ríos again—she gave up acting when Agustín left her. Now she can't understand why Agustín is contacting her again, after so many years, she wants to let bygones be bygones and does not want to hear from him again. The scene foreshadows Agustín's own end as in reaction to the actress's refusal to take up again the love story of the past, he will commit suicide.

In the novel, the second person narrative, directed at an extradiegetic narratee, which Adriana uses to address the intradiegetic You of her late father, works to exclude him or rather to push him into the role of a voyeur (cf. Rubio Gribble 1992: 174–75). In the film, however, these newly added scenes do not only bestow on him a certain presence but also give him superior knowledge. At the same time, these scenes illustrate the perfect interplay of image ("camera"/ocularization) and sound (Estrella's voice-over/auricularization), yet also the competition between the two modes of expression. In each sequence, we can detect anew the dynamic and often changing focalization in terms of the extra- and intradiegetic agents. Nevertheless, this does not only hold true for *El Sur* but for every intellectually and artistically demanding fictional film and literary text.

Translated from German by Katharina Kracht.

Films cited

Amenábar, Alejandro (1996). *Tesis*. Video.
Annaud, Jean-Jacques (1992). *L'Amant*. Video.
Cuarón, Alfonso (2002). *Y tu mamá también*. Video
Érice, Victor (1983). *El Sur*. DVD.
Hitchcock, Alfred (1946). *Notorious*. Video.
Rosi, Francesco (1985). *Chronicle of a Death Foretold*. Video.
Visconti, Luchino (1967). *L'Étranger*. Video.

References

Browne, Nick (1976). *The Rhetoric of Filmic Narration*. Ann Arbor: UMI Research Press.
Camus, Albert (1942). *L'Étranger*. Paris: Gallimard, 1957.
Foucault, Michel (1984). "What Is an Author?" P. Rabinow (ed). *The Foucault Reader*. New York: Pantheon Books, 101–20.
García Morales, Adelaida (1985). *El Sur*. Barcelona: Anagrama.
Genette, Gérard (1972). "Discours du récit." *Figures III*. Paris: Seuil, 65–278.
– (1980). *Narrative Discourse*. Tr. J. E. Lewin. Oxford: Blackwell.
– (1983). *Nouveau discours du récit*. Paris: Seuil.
– (1988). *Narrative Discourse Revisited*. Tr. J. E. Lewin. Ithaca: Cornell UP.
Jost, François (1983). "Narration(s): en deçà et au-delà." *Communications* 38, 192–212.
– (1984). "Le regard romanesque. Ocularisation et focalisation." *Hors Cadre* 2, 67–84.
– (1987). *L'Œil - Caméra. Entre film et roman*. Lyon: Presses Universitaires, 1989.
Lintvelt, Jaap (1981). *Essai de typologie narrative. »Le point de vue«*. Paris: Corti.
Martín-Márquez, Susan L. (1994). "Desire and Narrative Agency in *El Sur*." G. Cabello-Castellet et al. (eds). *Cine-Lit II. Essays on hispanic film and fiction*. Oregon: Oregon State U, 130–36.
Nimmo, Clare (1995). "García Morales's and Erice's *El Sur*: Viewpoint and Closure." *Romance studies* 26/26, 41–49.
Rubio Gribble, Susana (1992). *Del texto literario al texto fílmico: Representación del punto de vista en tres adaptaciones del cine español de los ochenta*. Dissertation, New York State University.

Schlickers, Sabine (1997). *Verfilmtes Erzählen: Narratologisch-komparative Untersuchung zu «El beso de la mujer araña» (Manuel Puig/Héctor Babenco) und «Crónica de una muerte anunciada» (Gabriel García Márquez/Francesco Rosi)*. Frankfurt a. M.: Vervuert.

MARKUS KUHN
(Hamburg)

Film Narratology: Who Tells? Who Shows? Who Focalizes? Narrative Mediation in Self-Reflexive Fiction Films

1 Introduction: Narrative and Narrative Mediation

With the exception of focalization, there is hardly a field in the area of film narratology that has been discussed as controversially as the question of narrative mediation. Does employing the construct of a "film narrator" make sense? David Bordwell and his followers reject a "narrator" and emphasize the part of reception[1]. Other scholars defend the concept of a "narrative agent" and locate it within a multi-layered communication model. Thus terms such as "grand imagier" (cf. Metz 1971), "image-maker" (cf. Kozloff 1988), "fundamental narrator" (cf. Gaudreault 1988) or "cinematic narrator" (cf. Chatman 1990) were coined, without, however, gaining general acceptance[2].

Naming and locating a presumed narrative agent in the film communication model is one of the areas which should be investigated further. Another area is that which we encounter in the context of an intermedial narratology extending beyond narrative literature and film to include further visual, auditory, and audiovisual media—such as drama, cartoons, video games, comic strips, animations, radio plays, paintings, music etc. How can we define narrativity in such a way that the definition does not only apply to verbal narratives? "Narrow" definitions of narrativity, like those in classical German narrative theory, postulate the existence of an instance of narrative mediation; "broad" definitions refer to the level of the represented and define narrativity in terms of events or changes of state[3].

---

1 See Bordwell (1985: 62); Branigan (1992: 108–10); Fleishman (1992: 13), et al.

2 Griem & Voigts-Virchow (2002: 161–63) list different positions, although with too great an emphasis on the aspect of anthropomorphization of the film narrator.

3 See Chatman (1990); Jahn (1995); Schmid (2005), et al. The discussion revolving around a universal term of narrativity is extended by combinatory, functional, and

It is quite obvious that a broad definition serves as a better foundation for the application of narratology to all kinds of media. However, we have to ask: how do such a definition of narrativity and the models derived from it benefit the narrative theory of the media in question and facilitate the analysis of works of art in such media? Doesn't too broad a definition run the risk of overlooking the basic narrative patterns of the medium in question? From the point of view of film study, for example, it is surprising that broad intermedial narratological approaches often ignore the film apparatus that mediates the events, thus regarding film as a mimetic narrative medium or as a medium without a mediating agent[4].

If we decide to apply narratological concepts to film analysis, we need to develop an awareness of the strategies of narrative mediation in film to explain the basic structures of a certain work, genre or epoch. Narrative mediation, if not bound to the concept of an anthropomorphic narrator, is a *tertium comparationis* between narrative fiction and fiction film. Comparing the devices of narrative mediation in literature and film can offer new impulses for the study of literary screen adaptations and prevent that studies of crossmedial influences—which are encompassed in such terms as *filmische Schreibweise* (filmic style of writing)—remain stuck in vague aesthetic categories[5].

---

gradual definitions (cf. Fludernik [1996]; Wolf [2002]; Herman [2002]; Ryan [2005], et al.). See Prince (2003: 1–2): "As we know, nothing like a consensus has been reached on that subject. Some theorists and researchers believe that everything is a narrative; others maintain that everything can be; and still others contend that, in a sense, nothing is (because narrativity is culture-dependent and context-bound). Some define narrative as a verbal recounting of one or more events and others as any kind of event representation (including non-verbal ones) [...]."

4 In his otherwise very convincing essay on intermedial theory of narration, Werner Wolf (2002) omits the aspect of narrative mediation and credits drama with a higher narrative potential than film. Although Seymour Chatman subsumes film under the "mimetic narratives" (Chatman 1990: 115), he discusses the problem of narrative mediation in film very thoroughly when he describes his concept of the "cinematic narrator" (Chatman 1990: 124-38)—unlike many scholars who quote the schemes he has developed (Jahn [1995]; Bach [1999], et al.).

5 This does not give preferentiality to a narrow definition of narrativity within the framework of intermedial narratology. However, in the area of film narratology, which is not as sophisticated as language-based narratologies, a systematic description of the various forms of narrative mediation has yet to be developed.

2 The Model of Narrative Levels in Fiction Film

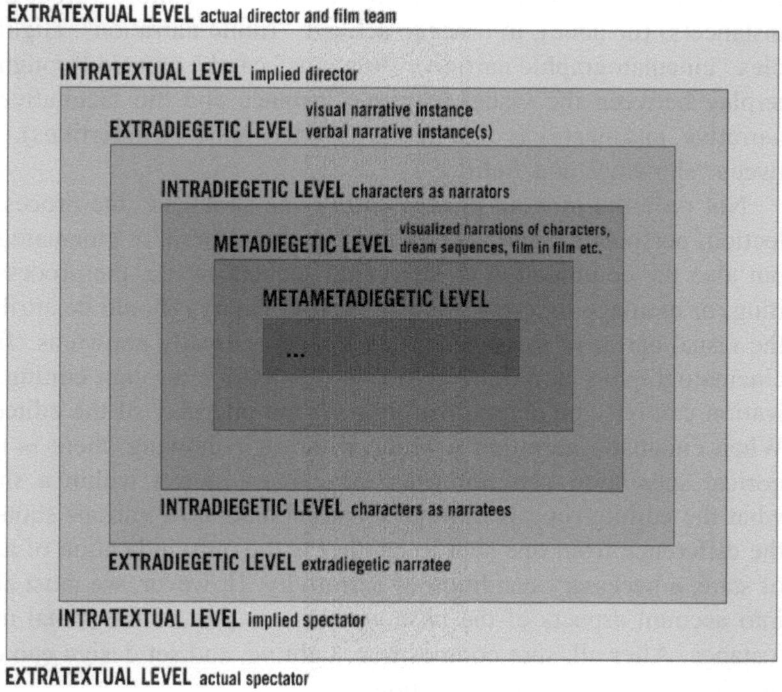

Figure 1: Model of Narrative Levels in Fiction Film

The model I propose is an adaptation of the communication model of narrative theory in literary studies, such as can be found in Fieguth (cf. 1973: 186) or Schmid (cf. 2005: 47–48), to the film medium. It is largely analogous to that proposed by Sabine Schlickers and in many aspects resembles Seymour Chatman's notion of levels[6], but differs from them insofar as I divide the category of the "filmic narrative agent" (i.e. Schlickers's "heterodiegetic camera" or Chatman's "cinematic narrator") into an "audiovisual narrative instance", which I term "visual narrative instance"/ "visual NI", and one or more facultative "verbal narrative instance(s)"/

[6] See Chatman (1990); Schlickers (1997) and Schlickers' article in this publication, pages 243–58.

"verbal NI(s)"[7]. Thus the "implied director", who does not have any semiotic sign systems "at his disposal", employs, on the extradiegetic level, the visual narrative instance as well as one or more verbal narrative instance(s) (or none), in order to achieve "filmic narration". Highly complex "cinematographic narrative situations" can be created through the interplay between the visual narrative instance and the facultative verbal narrative instance(s) (voice-overs, inserted texts or intertitles), i.e. between "showing" and "telling".

Not only the moving picture within one shot[8] (i.e. the process of selection, perspective, and accentuation by the camera, or cinematography), but also the combination of shots into sequences (i.e. the process of editing, or montage in terms of classical film theory) should be attributed to the visual narrative instance. That which is generally known as "filmic or cinematographic narration" comes into existence through editing. Focalization can only be determined through the interplay of the edited shots. When cinematic narration is realized through showing, there is no categorical separation between what the camera shows within a shot, and what the editing reveals through the combination of various shots. Often the difference from one shot to another is the only indication of a change of state, a necessary condition of narrativity. However, we must also take into account aspects of the *mise en scène* as part of the visual narrative instance. After all, shot composition, lighting, and set design can contribute significantly to visual narration.

The implied director can be found on this level, on which the aspects of all narrative instances in film come together. The implied director serves as an explanation for the complex interplay of visual and verbal narrative instances and for the analysis of certain forms of unreliability[9].

---

7 The "point of view shot" does not represent a transition to the intradiegetic level because the camera does not become an element of the diegetic world. In the instance of the point of view shot the extradiegetic visual narrative instance approximately shows what a character is seeing (internal ocularization).

8 A "shot" can be defined as the time in which the camera runs without interruption or as a continuous strip of motion picture film.

9 As is the case with all instances that can be derived from the structure of the work in question, the "visual narrative instance", the "verbal narrative instances", and the "implied author/director" are instances assumed theoretically and not existing entities (and much less anthropomorphous figures). If we use analysis only in order to prove these assumed instances or if we abuse these instances as advocates of a certain interpretation, we run the risk of ending up in a tautological short-circuit. However, particularly in the area of film analysis, narratological categories can ward off the temptation

3 Focalization

A basic idea of my proposed concept of focalization is understanding it, as Sabine Schlickers and François Jost do, in terms of knowledge, i.e. the relation of knowledge between the narrative instance and the character, and separating it from questions regarding perception in the narrow sense. In the context of the visual aspects of perception (seeing) I will use the term "ocularization", and the term "auricularization" for the auditory aspects (hearing)[10].

This classification of focalization categorizes the relation of knowledge between the narrative instance and the character(s) into (a) zero, (b) internal, and (c) external focalization, that is when the visual/verbal narrative instance shows/tells the narratee (a) more than, (b) as much as, and (c) less than the character(s) know. It has proven to be a valuable tool in the comparative analysis of literature and film. I will thus maintain the term "zero focalization", despite its sometimes inopportune implications, and use it only to refer to the relation of knowledge between narrative instance and character and not to the limited or unlimited knowledge of the narrative instance per se, which would require a complex model of perspective. Focalization thus defined can usually only be classified in the succession of shots. However, it is impossible to identify distinctly each sequence in its focalization. It is therefore necessary to highlight clearly ambivalences and uncertainties in focalization.

4 The Visual Narrative Instance in its Interplay with Facultative Verbal Narrative Instances

The proposed method of distinguishing between the narrative instances shows its value in the analysis of films such as R. W. Fassbinder's epilogue of *Berlin Alexanderplatz* (West Germany 1980). Next to the

of an approach too grounded in the aesthetics of the process. Far too often, we encounter film analyses which focus heavily on the production. The question whether we can omit the history of the term "implied author/director" and its contended theoretical implications arises quite naturally (cf. Booth 1961; Chatman 1978 and 1990; Nünning 1993; Kindt & Müller 1999 and 2006; Schmid 2005). In the context of this article, I will use this term only referring to provable intratextual aspects.

10 See Jost (1987); Schlickers (1997) and Schlickers's contribution in this collection in which she discusses the relationship of focalization, ocularization, and auricularization in detail.

visual narrative instance, various verbal narrative instances are employed on the extradiegetic level (in the form of various voice-overs, intertitles, and text captions). Every extradiegetic verbal narrative instance can be both heterodiegetic or homodiegetic in its relation to the diegetic world. They can each focalize differently and be in opposition to the visual narrative instance, which in turn can also focalize independently[11]. Whether a visual narrative instance can actually also be homodiegetic (i.e. whether some form of "first person narrative situation" [*sensu* Stanzel] can be accomplished on the visual level) must be discussed with the help of borderline cases (part 7).

Contrary to what has been widely declared, there is no primary relationship of dominance between visual and verbal narrative instances in film, in effect there is no primacy of the image (i.e. the narrative instances cannot be located on two levels that stand in a hierarchic relationship). The verbal narrative instance is not automatically located in a position above the visual narrative instance or vice versa. The reliable extradiegetic visual narrative instance can uncover the unreliable extradiegetic verbal narrative instances (*All about Eve*, Joseph Mankiewicz, USA 1950). However, the visual narrative instance can also be unreliable (*Stage Fright*, Alfred Hitchcock, USA 1950; *Fight Club*, David Fincher, USA 1999), or its reliability can be called into question with the help of verbal narrative instances (*Rashômon*, Akira Kurosawa, Japan 1950). An extradiegetic verbal narrative instance can dominate the visual narrative instance and reduce it to an illustrating function (opening of *Magnolia*, Paul T. Anderson, USA 1999). However, it can also serve to structure that which the visual narrative instance shows, order it in time and space or summarize past history (expository voice-overs, intertitles indicating the action's setting in silent movies). This relation can be as alternating and ironical as in François Truffaut's *Jules et Jim* (France 1962) or as ambivalent as in Alain Resnais's *L'année dernière à Marienbad* (France/Italy 1961). In silent movies this interplay is also encapsulated in a complex way because of different methods of speech representation, such as reports by a narrator or quoted direct speech in intertitles.

---

[11] Just as Jost (1987) and others proposed, I assume that narrative instances are able to focalize and therefore do without the instance of a "focalizer".

5 The Relationship of Narrative Instances

In order to illustrate the interplay of verbal narration and visual images in film, Sarah Kozloff (1988: 103) suggests "a continuous graph" comprising three areas: "disparate," "complementary," and "overlapping." Kozloff does not attempt to introduce either binary or clearly delimited categories. Instead, she speaks of the "degree of correspondence between narration and images"—which is sensible because no clearly defined dividing lines can be drawn. To use Kozloff's scheme as a framework to describe the dynamic relationship between visual narrative instance and verbal narrative instance, we have to complement her three categories. If both instances are in a disparate relationship, we have to detect whether both instances stand in evident contradiction to each other, or just tell disparately about different facts. In a complementary relationship, we are confronted with the question as to whether both instances mesh to tell the main story or whether they illuminate different facts or storylines which each complement the other. In an overlapping relationship, each instance can equally paraphrase the other, or the visual narrative instance can merely illustrate that which the dominating verbal narrative instance reports and vice versa. Between the overlapping and the complementary relationships, we find a polarizing relationship which we refer to when one narrative instance embeds the other, each resolving the other's ambivalences or uncertainties. The resulting categories are: contradictory, disparately, complementary, meshing, polarizing, illustrating, paraphrasing.

In practice, of course, these overlapping categories have no clear limits. There could be a relation of dominance for each of these relationships, but it is impossible to point out general guidelines for the specification of these relationships and the resulting relations of dominance which might arise. There are films in which this relationship can be detected quite obviously; others, however, show no clearly distinguishable relations. The relationship between visual and verbal narrative instance within one film is hardly ever static. In more complex cases (for instance, when questions of unreliable narration arise or in films with various verbal narrative instances) we have to analyze how the interplay of the instances throughout the film has been organized by the implied director.

Even when we analyze conventional forms of transition between different diegetic (or narrative) levels, the heuristic value of the analytical distinction between visual and verbal narrative instances becomes obvious. This applies all the more when analyzing complex forms of narrative mediation in films which use voice-over and have a multi-layered structure (part 6), or the special cases of "film within the film". We will stress this highly self-reflexive phenomenon in two cases: the shooting of a film shown in a film (part 6) and film-making as a central theme having influence on both form and plot (part 7).

6 Narrative Mediation in Self-Reflexive Multilayered Film: Pedro Almodóvar's *La mala educación*

The opening film of the 2004 Cannes Festival, Pedro Almodóvar's *La mala educación* (*Bad Education*), narrates the story on three encapsulated diegetic levels, which the following short summary will highlight. After the credits are shown, the diegesis is located with a caption: "Madrid 1980." Successful director Enrique Goded (Fele Martínez) is looking for inspiration for his next movie. Ignacio, a childhood friend of Enrique who is now an actor under the stage name Ángel (Gael García Bernal), coincidentally shows up with a short story he has written. Entitled "La visita" ("The Visit"), the story is based on their childhood. Parts of this story are shown as a metadiegesis: Ignacio, as a transvestite, returns to the town where he went to a Catholic elementary school. He intends to blackmail his former teacher, Father Manolo, with a story about his childhood. On the level of metametadiegesis, this fictitious childhood is also shown: Enrique and Ignacio discover the first blossoming of their tender homosexual love. Their friendship is nipped in the bud by Father Manolo, who is in love with Ignacio and uses his position of power as school principal to abuse Ignacio. Whether, on the level of the metadiegesis, Ignacio is successful in his attempt at blackmail, is not shown in the film. However, later on the happy ending of the short story is mentioned.

On the level of diegesis, director Enrique decides to make "La visita" into a movie. His researches lead him to the house of Ignacio's parents, where he discovers that Ignacio died three years ago. Ignacio's younger brother Juan, taking the name Ángel, falsely presented himself as Enrique's friend Ignacio. Ignacio however, is the real author of "La visita". Ignacio's mother shows Enrique a letter he never received. In this letter Ignacio explains his attempt at blackmailing Father Manolo.

For the screen adaptation of "La visita", Enrique adds a tragic ending to the story: Father Manolo kills the transvestite Ignacio, because he is scared he will continue to blackmail him indefinitely. Towards the end of the film shoot, which is shown in part (the second metadiegesis), a stranger appears: Señor Berenguer. He later unveils himself to Enrique as Father Manolo and tells him how Ignacio really died. This is shown in a third metadiegesis: Ignacio, as a drug-addicted transvestite, tries to blackmail Señor Berenguer/Manolo. Berenguer makes the acquaintance of Ignacio's younger brother Juan/Ángel as he tries to delay Ignacio's blackmail attempts and becomes romantically involved with him. Together they kill Ignacio with an overdose of narcotics.

Firstly we can observe that however complex the structure of levels might be, all levels are indicated unequivocally. They can be located within the hierarchy, and all meta- and metametadiegeses are embedded in a narrative situation, on the next highest diegetic level[12]. Telling and adapting stories is a central topic of *La mala educación*. We see Enrique as a director collecting clippings of bizarre stories and discussing whether they have the necessary qualities to be turned into a film. The *discours* presents us with various embedded literary stories, a number of letters, and a "film within a film". Functionally the different embedded fictitious narratives have consequences for the plot on the diegetic levels above them. The topic of storytelling and narration is complemented by the film's reflexive way of dealing with the relationship between factual and fictional narration. Ignacio and Enrique's childhood and the decisive act of abuse committed by Father Manolo are, for instance, only presented through "narrated narrated narration". Nevertheless, this fictitious narrative of a childhood experience is considered to be truthful enough to serve as the basis for blackmail.

The crucial question is how the narratives within the film are being mediated. The diegesis, i.e. the plot level that revolves around director Enrique Goded, is mostly shown through an extradiegetic visual narrative instance (visual NI). In the second third of the film, an extradiegetic, homodiegetic verbal narrative instance (realized through a voice-over of Enrique) interferes for a short while. This verbal NI meshes with the visual NI. The verbal NI summarizes the impressions during the film shoot (internal focalization on the "Experiencing-I" of Enrique). This internal focalization corresponds to the focalization of the visual NI on Enrique (which, however, is often interrupted by zero focalization).

---

[12] This is in contrast, for instance, to some of David Lynch's films, in which we cannot reconstruct the level structure unequivocally, see *Lost Highway* (USA 1997), *Mulholland Drive* (USA/France 2001), *Inland Empire* (USA/Poland/France 2006).

The most conventional change of levels in the film is the last one: Señor Berenguer is sitting in Enrique's office as he prepares to tell Enrique how Ignacio died. In this scene, Berenguer starts telling as intradiegetic, homodiegetic verbal NI: "About three years ago, someone put a copy of 'The Visit' on my desk [...]." While the last words of his reply ("Ignacio Rodríguez") are spoken, the visual NI changes to the metadiegesis: Berenguer as an editor in a publishing company receives a phone call by Ignacio Rodríguez, threatening to blackmail him. The following scenes alternate the diegetic and metadiegetic levels. Because the voice-over of Berenguer reappears several times during this metadiegesis and the "situation of conversation" on the diegetic level is frequently intercut with the metadiegesis (altogether five times), this prolonged visual metadiegesis is linked unequivocally to the "situation of conversation". In some transitions, Berenguer's voice is used in a classical overlap: it starts in the scene on the diegetic level, is continued as voice-over (while the visual NI changes to the metadiegetic level) and stops when the metadiegesis is (re)established visually.

The first change of levels in the film is equally conventional. The extradiegetic visual NI shows Enrique reading the title "The Visit" out loud. His lip movements are synchronized with his voice. His reading of the story, however, is then rendered through a voice-over. His lips have stopped moving—the classical form of the "filmic interior monologue" used to represent thoughts and inner voices[13]. The visual NI slowly fades over to the first shot of the metadiegesis and the voice-over soon ends. The metadiegesis is unequivocally linked to Enrique who is reading, which becomes even clearer when, throughout this sequence, the visual NI jumps back to this reading situation several times. We should take note that it is the voice of Enrique as reader that we hear in this voice-over and not that of the author of the text. This constellation is reversed in another part of the film, when Enrique is reading Ignacio's letter and we hear Ignacio in the voice-over (although, on the level of plot, he is already dead). When analyzing transitions to the level below, it is generally advisable to observe in which situation of conversation or narration the

[13] Strictly spoken, his voice is not an element of the diegetic world. "Filmic interior monologues" can usually be described as extradiegetic, homodiegetic verbal NIs with internal focalization on the "Experiencing-I".

lower level is embedded, part of whose narrative the lower level forms, and whose voice is heard in the voice-over[14].

The first transition from the metadiegesis to the metametadiegesis is somewhat more conspicuous. Within the metadiegesis shown, Ignacio is visiting Father Manolo with his childhood story threatening to blackmail the priest. The visual NI shows how Ignacio indicates a text passage to Father Manolo. A child's voice (as homodiegetic voice-over) begins reading the text (the exact part of the text which can be seen in frame). There is a cut, and the visual NI shows the face of Manolo reading (still in the metadiegesis) while the child's voice continues reading aloud and without interruption. Another cut takes us to the level of the metametadiegesis and we see children playing. This meshing of verbal and visual NI represents a rather conventional transition of levels. However, the voice we are listening to now is not the inner voice of Manolo reading, but the conspicuously high-pitched child's voice of the homodiegetic author of the text—after all, the text which the "metadiegetic Ignacio" threatens to use for blackmail was already written by Ignacio as a young boy. That means that the "Narrating-I" of the metametadiegesis is the voice of young Ignacio who wrote it down after the experience (indicated by the use of past tense). The "Experiencing-I" of the metametadiegesis is the young Ignacio who is shown in the scene. The visual metametadiegesis is thus linked to the narrating child's voice of Ignacio, which

[14] When embedding and attributing visual metadiegeses, we can also find forms that are far more complex and ambiguous. The mere opposition of contradictory attributions through visual and verbal markings, missing markings, narrational forms of attribution and contradictory denouements of metadiegeses when returning to the diegesis, result in manifold forms. Kozloff (cf. 1988: 49–53) elaborates on the various possibilities of anchoring voice-over narration in the diegesis, however, she does not take into consideration visual and complex forms of attribution. The first metadiegesis in *La mala educación* is additionally marked by a frame on the left and right of the film picture. A black bar moves from the left and right into the picture when changing into the metadiegesis, and back out of the picture when changing back to the diegesis. With the second and third metadiegesis of the film there is no such framing (also the transition from the metadiegesis to the metametadiegesis is not marked by additional framing). The ambiguous framing of the first metadiegesis can be interpreted, in respect to the relationship of factual and fictional narration, as an indicator that the visual representation of the novel is fictional.

keeps reappearing as voice-over, as well as to Manolo reading, to whom the visual NI changes repeatedly[15].

I have thus given an idea of how the transitions between the levels are constructed in the film and how the respective meta- and metametadiegeses can be attributed to a reading, writing, or narrating intra- or metadiegetic character. The question to be answered is who actually "narrates" the meta- and metametadiegeses. Although the meta- and metametadiegeses can be attributed to a certain telling or reading situation, and they are usually introduced by a verbal NI, the larger part is shown by a visual NI. Consequently, the narration relies predominantly on visual showing (and the showing of dialogues) rather than on verbal telling (through the short voice-overs). Logically following the proposed construction of levels, the visual NI should be classified as (a) intradiegetic or (b) metadiegetic if it shows (a) the metadiegesis or (b) the metametadiegesis. Firstly, however, the visual NI that shows the metadiegesis is not an element of the diegetic world that frames it, i.e. it is not a "shown showing instance" (comparable to what we know in literature as "narrated narrating instances"). And secondly, neither in the way and style of showing, nor in focalization and perspectivation, nor in the pace of editing and *mise en scène,* does the intradiegetic visual NI differ from the extradiegetic visual NI (the same holds true for the level below).

This is where we can detect an inherent contradiction which can be found not only in this film. On one hand, levels can be unequivocally identified in terms of their diegetic rank. On the other, they are shown through a visual NI which does not seem to be linked to one particular inner rank of levels. This is related to the fact that a film narrative embedded within a film is usually supposed to simulate a narrative in another medium. The filmic metadiegesis within the filmic diegesis is supposed to represent a written text, a novel, a letter read aloud, a stream of consciousness, an oral account, a recorded tape, etc. It is only very rarely used as what it really is, as a subordinate film sequence within a film. The rarer case of the unequivocal visual change of levels, i.e. actually "shown visually-showing narration", can be found in two forms in *La mala educación*: firstly, the shooting of the "film within the film" and secondly, protagonists watching a film. The second form can be found more

[15] Another form of transition between levels in *La mala educación* works entirely without voice-over: at first, the visual NI shows a page of text being read and then fades over to the next-lowest diegetic level.

frequently in fictional film: the extradiegetic visual NI shows the intradiegetic narratee who is watching a film, which in turn is being shown by an intradiegetic visual NI. Film production within a film, however, is an exception.

In the case of an ascription of a filmic metadiegesis to a verbal narrative situation of the diegesis, there is usually no unequivocal visual change of levels. The visual NI of the diegesis cannot be distinguished systematically from the visual NI of the meta- or metametadiegesis. While I can only treat it as an example in this context, I will term this phenomenon a "visual short-circuit of levels". This short-circuit arises from the fact that a visual NI—which is not an element of the diegetic world and must therefore be located on the extradiegetic level—narrates stories through showing which, with the help of specific markings, are attributed to intra- and metadiegetic characters (although they are not told by them, or, if so, only in part)[16].

This visual short-circuit of levels can be irrelevant in the context of certain films. In *La mala educación*, however, it leads to a clear dominance of the visual. Most of the episodes told on the various diegetic levels are being shown by an extradiegetic visual NI in the same characteristic style. They are thus focalized and assessed. This is how the metametadiegesis of Ignacio's and Enrique's childhood is endowed with a greater sense of reality than it would have in terms of the logic of levels—which in turn is significant if we want to assess the relationship of fictional and factual narration.

One of several prominent sequences demonstrating the potency of the visual NI, situated beyond the diegetic levels, is a sequence in which a

---

[16] This phenomenon, which I subsume as a "visual short-circuit of levels", has not been extensively discussed yet. It is evident in many fictional films with multiple levels or with embedded voice-over narration. Things are somewhat different when the whole metadiegesis is marked visually (for example throught the use of black and white footage within a color film, special lenses and filters, etc.). When applying the model of diegetic levels in literature to the film medium, special mention has to be made of the problem of the "visual short-circuit of levels". How this applies specifically to film depends on our understanding of diegetic levels. There are substantial reasons to maintain the term of levels (alternatively one could speak of "pseudometadiegesis", etc.) and to investigate which function or effect a "visual short-circuit of levels" can serve in a film. Kozloff (cf. 1988: 43–49) circumvents this question when she refers to the viewer (whom, however, she does not define as a category) who attributes everything that is shown to a character, even though she maintains that a "more powerful narrating agent, the image maker" (49) is positioned above any homodiegetic voice-over.

transition from the metametadiegesis to the diegesis occurs, skipping the metadiegesis. In a shot-reverse-shot beginning on the level of metametadiegesis, showing Ignacio and Enrique as young boys looking at each other, the visual NI shows a time-lapse of young Ignacio's face maturing to his presumed age on the level of diegesis (yet not showing an adult Ignacio, but Ángel's face). Subsequently, the visual NI shows young Enrique's face changing into the face of an adult Enrique, on the level of the diegesis. The film continues with the transformed characters on the diegesis. This transition from the metametadiegesis to the diegesis, created by a technical device, is not irrelevant for the assessment of the figuration. After all, the visual NI indicates that Ángel is Ignacio—which proves wrong in the course of the plot. The narratee of the extradiegetic visual NI is being deceived, just like Enrique by Ángel.

The dominance of the extradiegetic visual NI becomes even more apparent in the only sequence in which a real intradiegetic visual NI is present in form of the camera shooting the film within the film. The sequence begins with the take being shot by this intradiegetic camera: Ignacio threatening to blackmail Father Manolo. The clapperboard onscreen and several off-screen voices ("quiet," "roll camera") are clear markings of the film shoot. The sequence then cuts away to a shot of the film team and camera on set. After two alternations between the filmed situation (metadiegesis) and the filming situation (diegesis), a longer episode of the metadiegesis follows. In order to be consistent, this metadiegetic sequence should be shown as a single shot from a single camera position. However, we are confronted with evident use of editing: Ignacio, Manolo and his associate are shown in a shot-reverse-shot, which would require three camera positions in the diegesis. Following the return to the diegesis, we are left in no doubt that there is only a single camera on set. Thus we cannot attribute the metadiegetic sequence to this one intradiegetic camera. What we are confronted with at this point is a latent "visual short-circuit of levels": the extradiegetic visual NI has taken over the film within the film without breaking the illusion of the metadiegesis, or showing the intradiegetic camera again. The extradiegetic visual NI shows the metadiegesis of the film Enrique is directing in the same stylistic manner as the first visual metadiegesis, namely Enrique reading the short story. We could interpret the film adaptation as a continuation of the short story. Alternatively Enrique's reading of the story could be interpreted as his "inner film", the director's vision of the completed film. Further indicators support both these interpretations, making *La mala educación* an increasingly reflexive film about visual storytelling. This ambivalence can only be resolved through interpretation, and not by systematic analysis. If, in this context, we decided to cross the boundaries of the work itself, we could even go a step further and suppose an autobiographic connection between director Almodóvar and his fictitious character, director Enrique Goded. At the very least *La mala educación* is equally a result and an account of all its reflections about the issues of adapting literary narratives for the screen.

The layering of diegetic levels in *La mala educación* functions as an important device in the creation of suspense. Playing the possibilities of its various subplots, the film mainly builds suspense on the level of "discourse". *La mala educación* can thus be viewed as part of a tendency in contemporary cinema: films that self-reflexively put the possibilities of cinematic narrative to use in order to build immensely dense movies and to create suspense through their narrative realization.

7 Film Production within the Film and the Question of "First-Person Film": Lars Kraume's *Keine Lieder über Liebe*

Lars Kraume's film *Keine Lieder über Liebe* (Germany 2005), literally "No Songs Of Love", presents us with an unusual example of self-reflexivity without transition between diegetic levels. The film blurs the borders between documentary and fiction film in several points. It's a fictional documentary about the Hansen Band, a band of real actors and musicians cast for the film, touring Germany. This "real" tour serves as the set-up for a fictitious *ménage à trois* revolving around the film's three main characters: Tobias, his brother Markus, and Tobias's girlfriend Ellen.

Aspiring filmmaker Tobias Hansen (Florian Lukas) is making a documentary about his brother Markus (Jürgen Vogel), who is the lead singer of the Hansen Band. Tobias takes his girlfriend Ellen (Heike Makatsch) along on the tour, and soon discovers she cheated on him with Markus a year earlier. The film *Keine Lieder über die Liebe* purports to be Tobias's documentary film. The development of the *ménage à trois* increasingly pushes Tobias into the focus of "his" film, turning the project into a filmic self-portrait.

On the extradiegetic level we have a visual NI which is flexible in terms of focalization, ocularization, and auricularization and which makes use of various visual stylistic elements in order to suggest either a high degree of immediacy or its presence within the diegesis. Moreover,

Tobias Hansens's voice-over must be considered a homodiegetic verbal NI on the extradiegetic level. Depending on the point of the story that is being told, it fluctuates between internal focalization on the Experiencing-I and zero focalization when the Narrating-I tells more than the Experiencing-I knows. In many of the voice-over replies, these two "I's" can easily be distinguished from one another (e.g.: "I swear that at the time *I* had no idea this would become a film about the three of us"[17]).

When the visual NI is showing Tobias, the shown character corresponds to the Experiencing-I of the verbal narrative situation. This "Shown-I" of the diegesis is aware of the fact that it wants to turn all the material it is collecting into a film. This is why it sometimes announces specific information about time and setting in front of the camera or once whispers an account which is supposed to be seen and heard only by the camera (and not by his girlfriend who is in the adjacent room). The scenic Shown-I that talks to the camera upfront wants to make a documentary which is—and this is where we find the first (self-)reflexive feedback—already completed at the moment it is being shown by the visual NI and being seen by the extradiegetic narratee. The second feedback is created when Tobias Hansen, as the fictitious filmmaker who edits all the material afterwards, ostensibly takes on the position of the implied director who organizes the interplay of verbal and visual NI.

This constellation brings the act of narration to attention in a self-reflexive way, and is comparable to constellations in literature where the narrative takes the form of a text written by an extradiegetic homodiegetic narrator. This type of literary narrative situation is usually adapted to the film medium with the help of voice-overs and/or framing narratives. The film is then meant to be a novel written by a (intra)diegetic character[18]. However, the constellation found in *Keine Lieder über Liebe* is much rarer: the film is meant to be a documentary film made by one of the film's characters.

Do we then have a homodiegetic cinematic narrator in the narrow sense, i.e. a human character who narrates in a cinematic format? In sections of the film that use voice-over, we can detect a homodiegetic verbal NI (and thus a first-person narrative situation in the narrow sense). This is

---

[17] Here, as in the following, English translations are mine.

[18] This attribution in a different medium is in part comparable to the attribution of a filmic metadiegesis to a verbal narrative situation in the diegesis found in *La mala educación*.

particularly true for the exposition in which the homodiegetic verbal NI dominates the visual NI. On the visual level, there are only rare instances of a homodiegetic NI. However, the structural position of the implied director is in part filled by Tobias, a diegetic character. But there are two things to take into account: firstly, the intratextual implied director must be distinguished from the extratextual actual director of the film, Lars Kraume (there is no autofictitious short-circuit). Secondly, there is a difference between the character designated as implied director and the instance of the implied director that actually structures the film itself. The difference is hardly noticeable at times, at others it can be clearly detected, particularly if we look at the structures that establish Tobias as director within the film. The character of Tobias is not the implied director (which is why we should rather speak of a fictitious director). Nevertheless, the processes that structure the film, which are usually attributed to the implied director, can be attributed to Tobias, or he can be seen as the image of the director conveyed by the film. However, the question of whether Tobias has carried out certain filmic structures consciously or unconsciously can only be answered through interpretation. Just as in every self-portrait, we cannot draw clear lines between conscious, unconscious and coincidental. Additionally Tobias is just a character created by a film purporting to be his work—*Keine Lieder über Liebe* is thus in a way a cinematic counterpart of M.C. Escher's *Drawing Hands*.

The film alternates various narrative constellations. There are montage sequences to the band's songs in which the heterodiegetic visual and the homodiegetic verbal NI mesh to summarize longer developments in the relationships (summary; both instances: zero focalization). The absence of a verbal NI and the visual NI's stepping back through the use of inconspicuous cuts, with close shots and close-ups bringing the characters' emotions into focus, create a strong sense of immediacy during conflict scenes. In other scenes the presence of the camera is mentioned by the characters without a visual cue ("Shall we take the camera with us to bed?"). They interact consciously with the camera, making signs to it, speaking to it directly, or they block the camera's view, not wanting to be filmed any longer. In some of these sequences we can detect a rare form of the homodiegetic visual NI without use of voice-over, a sort of purely visual first-person narrative situation[19]. In these scenes the visual NI can-

[19] For the question of "first-person film" see Kawin (1978); Hurst (1996); Brinckmann (1988); Bach (1999), et al.

not be attributed to Tobias, but rather to an anonymous cameraman, or the camera itself. The camera, which is not seen on-screen, is only part of the scene because the characters interact with it. When the film shows what the camera is recording at the current point in time, the camera is a part of the diegetic world (it is therefore homodiegetic) but it also creates the diegetic world (and is therefore extradiegetic)[20]. These few sequences in which we can speak of a homodiegetic visual NI are unedited. The end of these scenes is a natural result of the action, for example when Tobias puts down the camera he has been speaking to when his girlfriend enters the room. We can partly detect an "anthropomorphization" of the "homodiegetic camera"—for example when it is being carried around like a video camera (idea of someone who is live on scene). In other scenes the camera is used as a purely technical instrument which, for instance, is being put on a tripod.

These scenes in which a camera is used as a homodiegetic visual NI are short and in most cases, editing indicates an interference with the immediacy of the scene. Thus a conspicuous temporal difference is created: the "homodiegetic camera" is located on the temporal level of the diegesis, editing on the temporal level of the narration afterwards. This time gap corresponds to the temporal difference between the Narrating-I and the Experiencing-I: the simultaneousness of the camera's recording corresponds to the simultaneousness of the Experiencing-I; the temporal delay of the editing corresponds to the temporal delay of the Narrating-I. However, this special case of the "homodiegetic camera" can only be attributed to Tobias Hansen's Experiencing-I in short passages of the exposition. In all other cases, it remains a homodiegetic technical instrument or, in the case of anthropomorphization, it is attributed to an anonymous character: the camera as an anonymous "homodiegetic Observer-I" or as a "first-person observer".

A scene in which Markus and Ellen flirt in Tobias's absence illustrates the interplay of instances. Both are aware they are being filmed, the camera as Observer-I is present, and Markus takes off his coat to give it to Ellen—just like in "one of those old movies"—he looks directly into the camera and says: "Let him see this. If he doesn't like it because he is

[20] The visual NI/camera is not intradiegetic because it is never seen on screen, even if the characters interact with it (not a case of a "shown showing camera"). Instead, it shows what the camera is "seeing" at the same moment (internal ocularization)—that what the camera is "seeing" in these sequences is simultaneously the diegetic world which only exists because it is shown.

jealous *he* can cut it out." "He" is Tobias, who will edit the video material afterwards. The fact that Tobias, the editor, leaves this passage in the film, in spite of or even because of the risky flirt going on, draws our attention to the fact that he is the organizing presence after the shooting. He saw the scene and decided not to cut it out. The conscious nature of this decision is emphasized by a noticeable cut immediately after Markus's reply. Tobias's "I", the "Editing-I", is present, without the presence of the scenic Shown-I of Tobias. The Observer-I, the anonymous cameraman, is not Tobias, but he is not independent of Tobias because of Tobias's influence as the filmmaker either.

This constellation, characterized by two exceptions, the character as a fictional director and the camera as a homodiegetic observing instance, is extremely rare in film. *Keine Lieder über die Liebe* complements this with highly specific narrative situations. Such constellations featuring a diegetic character filling a position endowed with multiple functions, metaleptic short-circuits, and a complex interplay of instances in unusual narrative forms are also known in classical narratology. Because of their similarities and differences to comparable literary constellations, some of the narrative situations which we have analyzed in both films might hopefully inspire the imagination of transmedial narratology.

References

Bach, Michaela (1999). "Dead Men—Dead Narrators: Überlegungen zu Erzählern und Subjektivität im Film." W. Grünzweig et al. (eds). *Grenzüberschreitungen. Narratologie im Kontext.* Tübingen: Narr, 231–46.

Booth, Wayne C. (1961). *The Rhetoric of Fiction.* Chicago: U of Chicago P.

Bordwell, David (1985). *Narration in the Fiction Film.* Madison: U of Wisconsin P/Methuen.

Branigan, Edward (1992). *Narrative Comprehension and Film.* London: Routledge.

Brinckmann, Christine N. (1988). "Ichfilm und Ichroman." A. Weber & B. Friedl (eds). *Film und Literatur in Amerika.* Darmstadt: Wissenschaftliche Buchgesellschaft, 65–96.

Chatman, Seymour (1978). *Story and Discourse. Narrative Structure in Fiction and Film.* Ithaca: Cornell UP.

– (1990). *Coming to Terms. The Rhetoric of Narrative in Fiction and Film.* Ithaca: Cornell UP.

Fieguth, Rolf (1973). "Zur Rezeptionslenkung bei narrativen und dramatischen Werken." *Sprache im Technischen Zeitalter* 43, 186–201.

Fleishman, Avrom (1992). *Narrated Films. Storytelling Situations in Cinema History.* Baltimore: Johns Hopkins UP.

Fludernik, Monika (1996). *Towards a 'Natural' Narratology.* London: Routledge.

Gaudreault, André (1988). *Du littéraire au filmique. Système du récit.* Paris: Klincksieck.

Griem, Julika & Voigts-Virchow, Eckart (2002). "Filmnarratologie: Grundlagen, Tendenzen und Beispielanalysen." A. Nünning & V. Nünning (eds). *Erzähltheorie transgenerisch, intermedial, interdisziplinär.* Trier: WVT, 155–83.

Herman, David (2002). *Story Logic. Problems and Possibilities of Narrative.* Lincoln: U of Nebraska P.

Hurst, Matthias (1996). *Erzählsituationen in Literatur und Film. Ein Modell zur vergleichenden Analyse von literarischen Texten und filmischen Adaptionen.* Tübingen: Niemeyer.

Jahn, Manfred (1995). "Narratologie: Methoden und Modelle der Erzähltheorie." A. Nünning (ed). *Literaturwissenschaftliche Theorien, Modelle und Methoden. Eine Einführung.* Trier: WVT, 29–50.

Jost, François (1987). *L'Oeil—Caméra. Entre film et roman.* Lyon: PU de Lyon.

Kawin, Bruce F. (1978). *Mindscreen. Bergman, Godard, and First-Person Film.* Princeton: Princeton UP.

Kindt, Tom & Müller, Hans-Harald (1999). "Der implizite Autor: Zur Explikation und Verwendung eines umstrittenen Begriffs." F. Jannidis et al. (eds). *Rückkehr des Autors. Zur Erneuerung eines umstrittenen Begriffs.* Tübingen: Niemeyer, 273–87.

Kindt, Tom & Hans-Harald Müller (2006). *The Implied Author. Concept and Controversy.* Berlin: de Gruyter.

Kozloff, Sarah (1988). *Invisible Storytellers. Voice-over Narration in American Fiction Film.* Berkeley: U of California P.

Metz, Christian (1971). *Langage et cinema.* Paris: Larousse.

Nünning, Ansgar (1993). "Renaissance eines anthropomorphisierten Passepartouts oder Nachruf auf ein literaturkritisches Phantom? Überlegungen und Alternativen zum Konzept des *implied author.*" *Deutsche Vierteljahresschrift für Literaturwissenschaft und Geistesgeschichte* 67, 1–25.

Prince, Gerald (2003). "Surveying Narratology." T. Kindt & H.-H. Müller (eds). *What is Narratology? Questions and Answers Regarding the Status of a Theory.* Berlin: de Gruyter, 1-16.

Ryan, Marie Laure (2005). "On the Theoretical Foundations of Transmedial Narratology." J. C. Meister (ed). *Narratology beyond Literary Criticism. Mediality, Disciplinarity.* Berlin: de Gruyter, 1–23.

Schlickers, Sabine (1997). *Verfilmtes Erzählen. Narratologisch-komparative Untersuchung zu «El beso de la mujer araña» (Manuel Puig/Héctor Babenco) und «Crónica de una muerte anunciada» (Gabriel García Márquez/Francesco Rosi).* Frankfurt a. M.: Vervuert.

Schmid, Wolf (2005). *Elemente der Narratologie.* Berlin: de Gruyter.

Wolf, Werner (2002). "Das Problem der Narrativität in Literatur, bildender Kunst und Musik: Ein Beitrag zu einer intermedialen Erzähltheorie." A. Nünning & V. Nünning (eds). *Erzähltheorie transgenerisch, intermedial, interdisziplinär.* Trier: WVT, 23–104.

JAN-NOËL THON
(Hamburg)

Perspective in Contemporary Computer Games[1]

1 Toward a Model of Perspective in Contemporary Computer Games

While the relatively new medium of the computer game has elicited an increasing amount of academic attention from a variety of disciplines in the last few years, research on perspective and point of view in computer games generally focuses on questions regarding the presentation of space, i.e. on perspective as being determined by a point of view in the purely spatial sense[2]. Within narratology, on the other hand, it is quite common to conceptualize point of view and perspective as multidimensional phenomena, both with regard to literary texts[3] and, albeit to a lesser extent, narrative films[4]. It therefore seems as if our understanding of perspective in computer games could benefit from the complex models of perspective that narratology has developed. Computer games, however, are neither literary narratives nor narrative films, and although the results of narratological research on perspective are doubtlessly inspiring, most of the models developed for the description of literary texts (or narrative films, for that matter) cannot be directly applied to computer games without missing some of their most central characteristics. Hence, the present paper proposes a multidimensional model of perspective in computer games that takes into account their specific medial properties.

For this purpose, we distinguish between three dimensions of perspective. The first dimension is that of spatial perspective, which is determined by the point of view, i.e. the spatial position from which the game

---

1 A longer version of this paper was published online in 2006 as "Toward a Model of Perspective in Contemporary Computer Games." <http://www.icn.uni-hamburg.de/images/download/beitrag_thon_bfs.pdf> (15.9.2008).

2 See Poole (2004); Rumbke (2005); Wolf (2001).

3 See Chatman (1978); Schmid (2005); Uspenskij (1973).

4 See Branigan (1984); Mitry (1998); Smith (1995).

space is presented audiovisually (this includes the presentation of sound which is often presented from the same position that the game space is presented from). Since the presentation of space in computer games is audiovisual instead of verbal and therefore closer to the movies than to literary narrative texts, we will mainly draw on film theory and works on perspective from computer game studies, rather than try to adopt models developed in literary narrative theory. The second dimension is that of actional perspective, which is determined by the point of action, i.e. the position from which the player can interact with the game space. Here, we will mainly refer to Neitzel's work on the point of action in computer games (cf. Neitzel 2002). The third and most complex dimension is that of the ideological perspective structure, which is determined by the various positions from which the events in the game are evaluated. Although we will focus mainly on the question of how characters in computer games evaluate events and situations, this dimension also refers to other positions within a game, namely that of the player and the implied game designer. With reference to the spatial perspective determined by the point of view and the actional perspective determined by the point of action, we will here speak of an ideological perspective that is determined by the point of evaluation.

Before we discuss these types of perspective in more detail, it has to be stressed that the three dimensions of perspective distinguished here are not all that could be considered. Although the spatial, actional and ideological dimensions of perspective seem to be most central, the analysis of particular games might well make it necessary to examine dimensions of perspective not treated in this paper[5]. Especially the analysis of the ideological perspective structure of a game may make it necessary to describe other forms of perspective that may be used in the presentation of fictional worlds in contemporary computer games. Our main aim, however, lies in the introduction of the idea that perspective in computer games consists of more than just spatial perspective, and the distinction of three dimensions of perspective seems to be enough for this purpose.

---

[5] With regard to additional dimensions that could be considered in the analysis of computer games, one can examine the narratological models of perspective already mentioned. Schmid (2005), for example, distinguishes between five dimensions of perspective in literary narrative texts, namely spatial, ideological, temporal, linguistic and perceptual perspective. Both the linguistic and temporal perspective may occasionally be worth analysing, especially with regard to the narrative elements of computer games.

2 Point of View and Spatial Perspective

There is a wide variety of ways in which computer games can construct the space in which they take place, from "all text-based" (Wolf 2001: 53) via various forms of two-dimensional spaces (cf. 55–65) to "[i]nteractive three-dimensional environments" (65). However, since many if not most contemporary computer games present a three-dimensional space on a two-dimensional screen, it is this form of computer game space that the present paper is mainly interested in. Before we can examine more closely the various forms of spatial perspective that can be found in such games, it has to be made clear to which parts of these games we refer. Since many computer games are set in complex fictional worlds, one has to distinguish between the space of the fictional world as a whole and the spaces that the player can interact with through the interface. Jesper Juul draws a similar distinction between "world space" and "game space" (cf. Juul 2005: 164–67). Since most of the events in computer games take place in the game space, it seems to be mainly this part of the space of the fictional world that is of interest with regard to the question of spatial perspective in computer games.

Such game spaces often are three-dimensional environments in which the player can more or less freely move certain objects such as his or her avatar (i.e. representative in the game space) as well as the point from which the space is presented and which, in games using an avatar, is often in some way connected to the position of the latter (thereby moving automatically when the avatar is moved). When referring to the point of view in computer games, one of the more commonly used terms is that of camera position (cf. Rumbke 2005: 244–45). This is not too surprising since, according to Wolf, many contemporary computer games "follow, to some degree, the precedent set by the space represented in classical Hollywood film" (Wolf 2001: 66) and accordingly the presentation of the game space in computer games may at first glance seem similar to the presentation of space in film. But while terminology originating from film theory is doubtlessly useful for describing spatial perspective in audiovisual media, it has to be emphasized that all talk of a camera or a camera position is metaphoric when referring to computer games since game spaces are generally not created by actual film cameras. Hence, it seems more precise to speak of a point of view as the spatial position from which the game space is presented aurally as well as visually and which determines the spatial perspective of a computer game.

One of the most common distinctions between different types of spatial perspective in computer games is that of first-person perspective, where the game space is presented from the spatial (and sometimes even perceptual) position of the player's avatar, and that of third-person perspective, where it is not. Aside from the fact that the category of "third-person perspective" is very broad (cf. Rumbke 2005: 246–48), this distinction is also inappropriate in its reference to grammatical categories that cannot be applied to audiovisual presentations of space in such a straightforward manner. A more appropriate and differentiated categoryization of audiovisual point of view in computer games has been proposed by Neitzel (2002). Referring to Mitry's *The Aesthetics and Psychology of the Cinema* (1998), she distinguishes between subjective, semi-subjective and objective points of view. Although this distinction is relatively broad as well, it provides a good starting point for a description of the spatial perspective(s) used in actual games.

3 Subjective, Semi-Subjective and Objective Points of View

Computer games using a subjective point of view have the position from which the game space is presented coincide with the position of the player's avatar. This perspective is, most prominently, used in so-called first-person shooter games such as *Doom* (1993), *Halo* (2001), or *SWAT 4* (2005). One can, in fact, observe an increasing sophistication in the way first-person shooter games realize their respective subjective points of view. While early games such as *Doom* use nothing more than a hand holding a weapon protruding into the presented space to indicate the existence of the player's avatar, more recent games such as *Halo* show its avatar on various occasions. Nevertheless, the hand holding a weapon is still seen most of the time (figure 1). There is, however, a tendency towards an implementation not only of the spatial but also the perceptual perspective (cf. Schmid 2005: 131–32) of the player's avatar that has led to games such as *SWAT 4*, where grenades, pepper spray and flash packs not only affect the avatar, but also have an effect on the audiovisual presentation of the game space. Another instance of a game that simulates the perceptual perspective of its avatar is *World of Warcraft* (2004), where the avatar's drunkenness affects the presentation of the game space.

Figure 1: Subjective point of view in *Halo* (2001)

According to Neitzel, one can speak of a semi-subjective point of view when the "point of view is connected to the movements of the avatar; it is not a substitute for the viewpoint as in case of the subjective POV, but rather a *viewing-with*" (Neitzel 2002: n. p.) the player's avatar. The camera follows the avatar at some distance, allowing for a better sense of its precise position in the game space than is the case in games with a subjective point of view. This form of spatial perspective is typically used in action adventures from *Tomb Raider* (1996) to *Grand Theft Auto: San Andreas* (2005) as well as in more recent role-playing games such as *Fable* (2004), *Jade Empire* (2005) or *World of Warcraft*. A closer examination of these games reveals that although the category of semi-subjective point of view allows for some variation as to the distance between the position of the camera and the avatar or the angle from which the avatar is shown, many games using a semi-subjective point of view use it in quite a similar manner. Most of the time, the camera floats slightly above and some way behind the avatar, showing it in relation to its surroundings (figure 2).

Although the spatial position of the avatar is not the same as that of the camera, the camera's position is always linked to the avatar.

Figure 2: Semi-subjective point of view in *World of Warcraft* (2004)

When the game space is presented from a position that is not connected to an avatar, one can speak of an objective point of view. This "oldest and most diversified" (Neitzel 2002: n. p.) perspective is used in a wide variety of games, but most obviously in strategy games such as *Z* (1996), *Warcraft III* (2002) or *Warhammer 40.000: Dawn of War* (2004). The main aim of these games is to build large armies and take control of the game space, which normally consists of a more or less extensive landscape. Hence, the objective point of view in these strategy games offers the possibility to observe a large game space without being constrained by the spatial perspective of an avatar or comparable entity. The objective point of view shows a game space from a position that is not part of this game space (as is the case with a subjective point of view) and is not connected to an entity in the game space (as is the case with a semi-subjective point of view). However, most strategy games do not show the whole game space at once, but present only a small part of it at a time, allowing the player to determine which part is shown (figure 3).

Figure 3: Objective point of view in *Warhammer 40.000: Dawn of War* (2004)

4 Point of View and the Player

Although one could further distinguish between various forms of objecttive point of view (especially when attempting to describe not only computer games presenting a three-dimensional space on a two-dimensional screen but also games presenting two-dimensional game spaces), Neitzel's "general distinctions that can be mixed and altered in the games" (Neitzel 2002: n. p.) seem to be appropriate for a categorization of spatial perspective in computer games. Nevertheless, it should be emphasized that many contemporary games not only combine various forms of spatial perspective but also allow their players to control camera movements (which is an essential part of the gameplay in most strategy games) and switch between different perspectives themselves. While such a player-controlled change in perspective is naturally rare in first-person shooter games that derive their name from a constant use of the subjective point of view (although *Halo* switches to a semi-subjective point of view when the avatar is controlling vehicles), it has become common in games using a semi-subjective point of view to allow the player some degree of control over the camera position. There are even games such as *World of Warcraft* that allow their players to switch from a semi-subjective to a subjective point of view if they so desire.

In *Tomb Raider*, which founded the action-adventure genre, the player cannot change the semi-subjective point of view the game uses to present its game space. It is, however, possible to influence the position from which the game space is presented by way of making Lara Croft, the avatar of the game, look in various directions. Without switching to a subjective point of view, the camera will then change its position, allowing the player to see what Lara sees—or would see if she was not an avatar in a computer game but a real person capable of seeing (figure 4).

Figure 4: Lara Croft in *Tomb Raider* (1995), looking to her upper-left hand side

Obviously, the ways in which the player can influence the camera position have evolved since 1996, the year in which *Tomb Raider* was published. Hence, *World of Warcraft* allows its players not only to change the camera position in order to look at the avatar from virtually all angles but also to change the distance between the camera and the avatar, which can be adjusted on a scale of 15 steps. While the largest distance allows the player to see the most of the surroundings of his or her avatar, the smallest distance makes the position of the camera coincide with the spatial position of the avatar, thereby allowing the player to switch from the semi-subjective point of view (which is the standard mode of the game in version 2.0) to a subjective point of view.

It can be concluded that many contemporary computer games allow their players an ever greater amount of control over the spatial perspective(s) used in the presentation of the game space. While this is particularly the case with action-adventure and role-playing games, it is also true for most other games with the previously mentioned exception of first-person shooters. Since strategy games do not present the player with a single avatar, the occurrence of a genuine semi-subjective or even subjective point of view seems unlikely here. Nevertheless, most of the more recent strategy games, e.g. *Warcraft III* and *Warhammer 40.000: Dawn of War*, allow the player not only to change the part of the game space that is presented on the screen, but also to change the camera angle from which it is presented. Finally, it may be noted that while players generally like the opportunity to take control of the camera, they rarely use the possibility to change the default point of view. This has to do with the fact that the default point of view is often best suited to the interaction with the game space required by the game. And although the appreciation of beautyfully designed game spaces is surely a part of the pleasure in playing a computer game, the interaction with the game space will, of course, be more important to most players than the game space itself.

5 Point of Action and Actional Perspective

Unlike the spaces that are presented in Hollywood film, computer game spaces allow players to interact with them through the interface. The importance of this interactive nature of computer games leads us to the question of how the interaction between player and game can be described in terms of perspective. For this purpose, we will build on Neitzel's notion of a point of action, by which she refers to "the position from which action can be taken, and the way it will be taken in" (Neitzel 2002: n. p.), determining the actional perspective of the computer game. So what exactly is meant by "actional perspective" with regard to computer games? Neitzel describes the relationship between the seeing and acting of the computer game player as follows: "The computer takes the effects of the actions out of the spatial-material reality of the player and distributes them in the space of the monitor. This space, including the effects of the actions, is observed and interpreted [by the player, J.-N.T], which then influences the subsequent actions" (Neitzel 2002: n. p.). It is not, however, the case that a player can choose freely what he or she sees or does when playing a computer game. As we have seen, computer games present their game spaces using different points of view that result in different spatial perspectives and thereby determine to a great extent which part of the game space can be seen by the player and how he or she sees it.

In much the same way, computer games use different points of action that result in different actional perspectives and thereby determine what the player can do in the game and how he or she can do it. Neitzel argues that the point of action in computer games can be described using three basic distinctions. Firstly, the point of action "can reside either within or outside the diegesis, so that one can speak of an intradiegetic and an extradiegetic point of action" (Neitzel 2002: n. p.). Secondly, Neitzel distinguishes between a concentric and an ex-centric and, thirdly, between a direct and an indirect point of action. Since an intradiegetic point of action means that the actions of the player result in actions that can be ascribed to some character or object within the game world, every game that uses an avatar automatically uses an intradiegetic point of action. An extradiegetic point of action means that the actions of the player result in actions that cannot be ascribed to some character or object within the game world. This is typically the case in strategy games that do not cast the player in the role of some "ruler character, who then guides the fortunes of his subjects" (Neitzel 2002: n. p.).

The distinction between intradiegetic and extradiegetic points of action is often not very clear-cut, since games such as *Warcraft III* or *Warhammer 40.000: Dawn of War* do not in any explicit way construct a ruler character to whom the results of the player actions could be ascribed, but still have the player-controlled troops react to the players' commands with expressions of obedience such as "Yes Sir!", thereby implying that the result of the player's actions can actually be ascribed to some entity within the game world (the same entity that is addressed as "Sir" in the above example). Although there seem to be considerable differences between the ways in which the points of action in these strategy games and those in games such as *Grand Theft Auto: San Andreas* that have the player control the same avatar through the whole game are related to the entities in the fictional worlds of these games, one would have to describe both points of actions as intradiegetic. Hence, the usefulness of that first distinction may be doubted.

Neitzel's second distinction is much clearer. She proposes to distinguish between a concentric point of action, meaning that the player's actions are executed at only one location in the game space and an excentric point of action, meaning that the player's actions can be executed at multiple locations in the game space. Hence, games such as *Grand Theft Auto: San Andreas* which have the player control a single avatar to which the result of the player's actions can be ascribed would be categorized as using a concentric point of action while games such as *Warhammer 40.000: Dawn of War*, where the player uses the keyboard and mouse to control huge armies, taking control of individual troops or buildings as he or she pleases would be categorized as using an ex-centric point of action. While this distinction helps to describe which objects in the game space are controlled by the player, it does not answer the question of how they are controlled, i.e. how the actions of the player influence objects in the game space.

It is this question to which Neitzel's third distinction refers. Many games using an avatar allow the player to control the avatar directly. This means that every press of a button or movement of the mouse results in an instant action of the avatar. Among many other games, first-person shooters generally use such a direct point of action. On the other hand, there are many games where the relation between player actions and avatar actions is not as direct. Strategy games such as *Command and Conquer*, *Warcraft III*, or *Warhammer 40.000: Dawn of War* often allow the player to take control of many different objects in the game world. In these games, a click with the mouse is enough to make a large number of troops move over a large distance, and another click will make them attack the enemy. It is not necessary (or even possible) for the player to control directly every movement of his or her troops. This also means that there is no constant association of the pressing of a certain button with a resultant movement of the avatar. Hence, one can say that these games use an indirect point of action. Neitzel also notes that some games combine a direct and indirect point of action. This is the case, for example, in

World of Warcraft, where the player controls the basic movements of the avatar directly, but also has to employ the mouse to make the avatar use its abilities or interact with other characters by clicking on a variety of icons or on the character he or she wants to interact with.

6 Subjective, Semi-Subjective and Objective Points of Action

Although especially the latter two of Neitzel's distinctions seem quite useful, it is questionable if a typology as complex as the one proposed by Neitzel is necessary. Alternatively, we propose to distinguish between only three different kinds of point of action, applying the distinction between the subjective, semi-subjective and objective point of view to the point of action. In games that use a subjective point of action, the action position of the player coincides with that of the player's avatar. Here, the player has direct control over the movements of his or her avatar, "every press of a button instantly results in an action" (Neitzel 2002: n. p.). This also means that the player can control his or her avatar and nothing else. The player cannot interact directly with the game space.

In games that use the semi-subjective point of action, the interaction with the game world is connected to an avatar, but the player also has to interact with the game space directly. Interaction does not exclusively happen through the avatar, as is the case in games using a subjective point of action. In games such as *World of Warcraft*, the player controls the basic movements of the avatar in the same way as in games using a subjective point of action. He or she does, however, also have to employ the mouse to make the avatar use some of its various abilities or interact with other characters. In games using an objective point of action, the interaction with the game world is not connected to a single avatar. This is, for example, the case in strategy games such as *Warhammer 40.000: Dawn of War* where the player uses the keyboard and mouse to control huge armies, taking control of troops or buildings as he or she pleases.

Although there may be a certain tendency for the three types of point of action to converge with the respective forms of point of view, this is by no means generally true. *Tomb Raider* combines a semi-subjective point of view with a subjective point of action, *Baldurs Gate* (1999) combines a semi-subjective point of view with an objective point of action and *Myst* (1993) combines a subjective point of view with an objective point of action. Furthermore, although of central importance for the gaming experience, the spatial perspective as determined by the point of view and the actional perspective as determined by the point of action are not the only ways in which the presentation of events in a computer game is perspectivated.

7 Point of Evaluation and Ideological Perspective

While Chatman does not go into too much detail in his treatment of different dimensions of point of view, he rightly emphasizes that the term "point of view" can refer not only to the position from which events are perceived (which he calls the perceptual point of view), but also to the position, from which events are evaluated (which he calls the conceptual point of view). The idea that a character's "world view (ideology, conceptual system, *Weltanschauung*, etc.)" (Chatman 1978: 151) should be conceptualized as a dimension of point of view can also be found in Uspenskij's seminal work *A Poetics of Composition*. Uspenskij claims that one of the most basic aspects of point of view is "manifested on the level we may designate as ideological or evaluative (understanding by 'evaluation' a general system of viewing the world conceptually)" (Uspenskij 1973: 8). While this paper cannot hope to discuss exhaustively the question of how the events and situations in a computer game are evaluated by the avatar and the other characters in the game (or even the game as a system of rules), these questions are nevertheless of central importance for the analysis of perspective in computer games. In order to distinguish these evaluative positions from the notions of point of view and point of action already discussed, we will refer to them as points of evaluation. However, ideological perspective as determined by a point of evaluation is not as easily identified in the analysis of computer games as is the case with the dimensions of perspective in computer games already discussed.

According to Ryan, the observation that events in fictional worlds are connected to certain goals, plans and psychological motivations, which can be ascribed to the characters populating such worlds also applies to computer games (cf. Ryan 2001). The fact that the player can ascribe a specific "world view" to the characters in a computer game does not necessarily lead to a more compelling story, but does function as a means of orientation for the player. The different points of evaluation and ideologyical perspectives of the characters in a computer game result in a certain system of norms and values in which the player has to position him- or herself. Smith notes that, for an understanding of films, it is important "to consider, first, how such 'systems of value' are constructed; secondly, the range of possible types of moral structure; and thirdly, the different ways in which a narration may unfurl these moral structures over time" (Smith 1995: 189). This is also true for computer games. However, due to the limited scope of this paper and the fact that most systems of norms and values in computer games tend to be rather simple, we will mainly discuss the first question, which is how these systems are constructed with regard to the points of evaluation that can be ascribed to the various characters.

Ansgar Nünning has treated the notion of perspective within the framework of possible worlds theory, emphasizing that it is applicable "not only to the rhetorical structure of narrative transmission," but also to "the world-models of the fictional individuals that populate the represented universe projected in narrative texts" (Nünning 2001: 207). Hence, we can describe the point of evaluation of a character in a computer game as being determined by the character's model of the fictional world. But how can a player ascribe a certain "world view" to the characters in a game? Nünning emphasizes that in narrative texts "each verbal utterance and each physical or mental act of a character provides insights into his or her perspective" (Nünning 2001: 210). Once again this is true for computer games. A computer game's fictional world and its characters are conveyed not only through the presentation of the actual game spaces (to which the previously discussed dimensions of perspective in computer games mainly refer), but also through a variety of narrative techniques. While most of the information about mental acts of characters in a computer game will be conveyed through cut-scenes and other forms of narrative techniques, the main part of physical acts will be presented in the form of ludic instead of narrative events[6]. Therefore, in order to determine the point of evaluation of a computer game character, one has to examine the narrative as well as the ludic elements of the game.

For the purpose of the present paper, however, the actual form of these narrative elements is less important than the function that they have for the rest of the game, i.e. the game space and the ludic events. Narrative events in computer games not only constitute a story and contribute to the construction of the fictional world, but they also convey information about the ludic structure of the game. Rune Klevjer even claims that "giv-

[6] In computer games, one can distinguish between narrative events that are already determined before the game is played and ludic events that are determined at the moment of playing. Due to spatial limitations, the present paper cannot discuss this distinction in any detail. See Thon (2006 and 2007) for a more detailed discussion of these different kinds of events and the narrative techniques used in their presentation.

ing meaning and sensation to the actions when they are performed by the computer and the player" (Klevjer 2001: n. p.) is the main function of narrative elements in computer games. He distinguishes between three levels on which this "signification" of ludic events takes place. Firstly, on the most important level, narrative (as well as ludic) events introduce a certain evaluation of possible actions. In every shooter-themed game, be it *Tomb Raider* or *Halo*, "it is important for me [the player, J.-N.T] that the objects I [the player's avatar, J.-N.T] 'shoot' are 'bad guys' with 'guns' who 'fight' back, and who can be 'killed'" (Klevjer 2001: n. p.). This is not a question of ethics, but of effective action. The player of *Halo* has to be able to distinguish between his opponents (the "bad guys") and his allies. In order to be successful he should refrain from letting his or her avatar shoot the latter. Secondly, most games will use narrative techniques to give the player "some kind of motivation for performing the specific actions that the game requires" (Klevjer 2001: n. p.). In *Halo*, the avatar is a (super) soldier named Master Chief who, together with his human allies, tries to save the universe from various aliens. Here, we have a more specific level of meaning than is constituted by the mere distinction between opponents and allies. Thirdly, many games use a chronologically and causally ordered chain of predetermined narrative events (which is, of course, continuously interrupted by ludic events) to present a (possibly non-linear but nevertheless consistent) story. This is, of course, relevant with regard to Smith's question of how "a narration may unfurl these moral structures over time" (Smith 1995: 189). One example of a story that forces us to change our initial conception of the ideological perspective structure is *Halo 2* (2004), where it becomes clear during the course of the story that certain aliens are actually allies instead of opponents in that they help the Master Chief to save the universe.

8 Ideological Perspective Structure and the Player

Unlike the point of view and the point of action, which can both generally be determined without too much of a problem, one has to consider the various points of evaluation of the different characters to arrive at an appropriate description of this most complex level of perspective in computer games. According to Nünning, "the term perspective structure can be defined as the general system formed by all the character-perspectives and narrator-perspectives as well as by the patterns of relationships between them" (Nünning 2001: 214). While the present paper can only sketchily show how a computer game's ideological perspective structure with its various points of evaluation is constructed and can be analyzed, this structure does indeed play a central part in the presentation of ludic as well as narrative events in most contemporary computer games. As we have seen, the first step in the analysis of the ideological perspective structure of a game aims to reconstruct the points of evaluation of the characters in the fictional world of the game. Furthermore, the characters are generally connected to each other, either in a relation of opposition or similarity of the respective points of evaluation. But as the above quotation from Nünning suggests it is not enough to analyze the constellation of the various characters in a computer game. Although one would have difficulties finding a narrator perspective in most games[7], it is nevertheless the case that an analysis of the ideological perspective structure of a game should also consider the choices that the player is allowed to make with regard to his or her actions and the norms and values that are implied by the game itself.

There is obviously a certain relationship between how the avatar evaluates the various events and situations in a game and how the player evaluates them. However, this does not mean that the player uncritically assumes the avatar's position towards these situations and events. Rather, the player will use the ideological perspective structure of a game to orient him- or herself within its ludic (as well as narrative) structure. This also explains why the player of *Halo* will normally act according to the avatar's point of evaluation, and not try to befriend the aliens (which is, as was previously mentioned, different in *Halo 2*). The player acts according to the avatar's point of evaluation since such action is in compliance with the aims of the game. The game itself does not allow the player to choose his allies freely or to decide that shooting aliens is not an action to be evaluated positively. While the player may decide not to make his or her avatar shoot aliens, this will most likely result in the death of the said avatar and the player losing the game. However, we have already mentioned that events and situations in computer games are not only evaluated on the level of character. In many contemporary computer games, one can distinguish between the points of evaluation of the various characters in the game, the point of evaluation that the game constructs for the

---

7 There are certain games that use character narrators for their (at least partially linguistic) narration. Here, the notion of "narrator's perspective" may be useful. It has, however, to be emphasized that neither the player nor the avatar are narrators.

player and the point of evaluation that can be inferred from the overall design of the game.

The relevance of a character's point of evaluation for the whole game becomes most obvious in games with a single avatar. The avatar's model of the fictional world determines to a great extent the ways in which the player can interact with the game world. Lara Croft, the avatar in *Tomb Raider*, seems to have no doubt about the appropriateness of shooting the various animals, humans and demons that act as her opponents throughout the game. The game would be entirely different if Lara was a female Hamlet, considering and re-considering the commands given by the player before finally deciding to act. It is clear that the player of *Tomb Raider* is not entirely free in his or her decisions. Lara cannot be made to join the bad guys (the main bad guy being a woman in *Tomb Raider*) in their attempt at world domination. Another example previously mentioned would be the avatar in the science-fiction-themed first-person shooter *Halo*, who is presented as a soldier loyal to the human army. Here, the player is not free to choose the alien alliance as an ally. It is true for most contemporary computer games that many of the norms and values attributable to the avatar are not decided upon by the player. Although the player has not much choice but to follow the avatar's evaluation as far as his (inter-)actions are concerned (since these evaluations generally define the goals of the game), this does not necessarily mean that the player is embracing these evaluation in any other way than with regard to the ludic structure. The fact that a player of *Tomb Raider* makes the avatar of the game shoot wolves does not imply that this player generally believes shooting wolves to be a good thing. Indeed, it does not even necessarily imply that the player believes that the fact that Lara Croft is shooting wolves in the fictional world of *Tomb Raider* is a good thing. It is simply a part of the game rules that Lara has to shoot wolves in order to survive.

While most computer games operate with clear-cut polarities of good and evil, this does not mean that the player never has a choice between the two. In games such as *Fable* or *Jade Empire*, the player can choose which course of action to evaluate as the "right" one. Even in these games, the possibilities for choice are strictly limited by the program, but the player at least partly decides on the avatar's norms and values. Another example where the player can influence the avatar's point of evaluation is *World of Warcraft*. Here, the player gets to choose whether his avatar is a member of the Alliance or the Horde. The player's choice will strongly influence the point of evaluation of his or her avatar, since the two parties are constantly at war with one another. In these cases, the point of evaluation of the player influences how the avatar evaluates the events in the game and what course of actions it then holds to be the "right" one. However, it has again to be emphasized that what we propose to call the point of evaluation of the player does not refer to the player's model of the actual world. Instead, it refers to the player's model of the fictional game world and his or her evaluation of the events and situations that occur in it[8]. While some games allow their players to influence the point of evaluation of his or her avatar, one should also keep in mind that the choices a player can make in these games are generally choices between narrowly defined alternatives.

We have seen that the player of a game using an avatar usually assumes that avatar's point of evaluation in order to orient him- or herself within the ludic structure of the game. This process of orientation, which is necessary to play a game successfully, is also influenced by those norms and values that are not directly connected to characters (be it the player's avatar or other characters) but can be attributed to the game designer(s). For the purpose of this paper, it is not relevant whether the game designers really subscribed to these norms and values or had any intention to have them ascribed to them. If, for example, no children appear in most parts of the game world in *Fable*, this is a conscious design decision that was intended to prevent the players' from letting their avatars kill children without obviously restricting their possibilities for interacttion with the game world. But, whether there was a conscious design decision behind it or not, the fact that no children can be killed may be read as part of a system of norms and values that includes the norm that it is not acceptable to have children killed, even in the fictional world of a computer game. Another example is that Lara Croft can carry a variety of weapons and kill an impressive number of various beasts in *Tomb Raider* without getting problems with the authorities (or animal rights organizations). The point to be made here is that a particular ideological perspective manifests itself in the overall design and presentation of a game

---

[8] See also Smith's discussion of allegiance. Smith assumes that "something like a suspension of values must occur, if we are to explain the spectator aroused by a gangster film, against her 'better' (i.e. everyday) judgement" (Smith 1995: 189). Although such a suspension of values in computer games will most likely focus on the necessity to act in compliance with the ludic structure of the game, it nevertheless occurs. See also Schirra & Carl-McGrath (2002) on how the process of identification with characters in computer games differs from the process of identification with characters in film.

world as well as in the rules and goals of the game. Here, one can speak of the point of evaluation of an implied game designer.

A reconstruction of the system of norms and values inherent in computer games might also contribute to one of the most controversial questions concerning this relatively new form of entertainment, namely how their often violent and politically incorrect[9] content should be evaluated from an ethical point of view. Buchanan and Ess claim that

> this debate threatens to become paralyzed on the one hand by simple-minded [...] characterizations of e-games and their impacts, and, on the other hand, by overly simple ethical analyses that would force us to choose between Manichean polarities of absolute evil vs. absolute good. (Buchanan & Ess 2005: 3)

Without intending to further discuss this question here, it seems likely that an (ethical) evaluation of the events and situations in a computer game would benefit from considering how these events are evaluated within the game itself. Sicart claims "that players act as moral beings, that they reflect upon those values that are contained in the system of the game, and that they evaluate them keeping in perspective the values of the game world" (Sicart 2005: 17), but before discussing these questions, one should probably examine exactly how "values [...] are contained in the system of the game" (17).

9 Conclusion

This paper has proposed a model of perspective in contemporary computer games consisting of three dimensions. It has become clear that the presentation of the game space in computer games differs from the presentation of space in narrative films and literary narrative texts. While the perspective of the audiovisual presentation of the game space in a computer game is generally determined by a relatively constant point of view, most games allow the player to control the spatial perspective at least to a certain degree. In fact, the most obvious difference between computer games and narrative films or literary narrative texts is the possibility to interact with the presented space, which makes it necessary to include in a model of perspective in computer games the notion of an actional perspective as determined by the point of action in addition to the spatial perspective as determined by the point of view.

---

9 See Jahn-Sudmann & Stockmann (2008).

Although we could only sketch the last dimension of our model of perspective in computer games, it has become clear that the ideological perspective structure that is determined by various points of evaluation and conveyed through narrative as well as ludic elements plays an important role in the perspectivation of events and situations in contemporary computer games. There is still some conceptual and terminological work left to do especially with regard to the ideological perspective structure. Nevertheless, we believe that the three dimensions of perspective described in this paper allow an analysis of the most central ways in which the events in computer games are perspectivated.

In conclusion, it can be stated that models of perspective developed for literary texts and narrative films cannot be directly applied to computer games. It has, however, also become clear that the concepts and terminology developed in literary and film narratology possess considerable heuristic value for the analysis of different media, such as computer games. When attempting to transfer theoretical concepts such as "perspective" to new domains, awareness of the specific characteristics of the respective medium is of central importance. Nevertheless, differences between media do not necessarily prevent such a transfer from being successful.

Games Cited

Doom. ID, 1993. (PC)
Fable. Lionhead / Microsoft, 2004. (Xbox)
Grand Theft Auto: San Andreas. Rockstar, 2005. (PC)
Halo. Bungie / Microsoft, 2001. (Xbox)
Halo 2. Bungie / Microsoft, 2004. (Xbox)
Jade Empire. Bioware / Microsoft, 2005. (Xbox)
Myst. Cyan Worlds / Brøderbund, 1993. (PC)
SWAT 4. Irrational / Sierra, 2005. (PC)
Tomb Raider. Core / Eidos, 1996. (PC)
Warcraft III. Blizzard, 2002. (PC)
Warhammer 40.000: Dawn of War. Relic / THQ, 2004. (PC)
World of Warcraft. Blizzard, 2004. (PC)
Z. Bitmap Brothers / Renegade, 1996. (PC)

References

Branigan, Edward (1984). *Point of View in the Cinema. A Theory of Narration and Subjectivity in Classical Film*. Berlin: Mouton.

Buchanan, Elisabeth A. & Ess, Charles (2005). "Introduction: The Ethics of E-Games." *International Review of Information Ethics* 4, 2–7. <http://www.i-r-i-e.net/inhalt/004/004_full.pdf> (31.3.2007).

Chatman, Seymour (1978). *Story and Discourse. Narrative Structure in Fiction and Film*. Ithaca: Cornell UP.

Jahn-Sudmann, Andreas & Stockmann, Ralf (2008). "Anti-PC-Games. Exploring Articulations of the 'Politically Incorrect' in *GTA San Andreas*." A. Jahn-Sudmann & R. Stockmann (eds). *Computer Games as a Sociocultural Phenomenon. Games without Frontiers—War without Tears*. Houndmills: Palgrave, 150–61.

Juul, Jesper (2005). *Half-Real: Video Games Between Real Rules and Fictional Worlds*. Cambridge, MA: MIT Press.

Klevjer, Rune (2001). "Computer Game Aesthetics and Media Studies." Paper presented at the 15th Nordic Conference on Media and Communication Research, Reykjavik, Aug. 2001. <http://uib.no/people/smkrk/docs/klevjerpaper_2001.htm> (31.3.2007).

Mitry, Jean (1998). *The Aesthetics and Psychology of the Cinema*. London: Athlone Press.

Neitzel, Britta (2002). "Point of View and Point of Action. A Perspective on Perspective in Computer Games." Paper presented at the The Challenge of Computer Games Conference, Lodz, Oct. 2002. Manuscript kindly forwarded by the author.

Nünning, Ansgar (2001). "On the Perspective Structure of Narrative Texts. Steps toward a Constructivist Narratology." W. van Peer & S. Chatman (eds). *New Perspectives on Narrative Perspective*. Albany: SUNY Press, 207–24.

Poole, Steven (2004). *Trigger Happy*. New York: Arcade Publishing.

Rumbke, Leif (2005) *Pixel³. Raumrepräsentation im klassischen Computerspiel* (Hausarbeit Kunsthochschule für Medien, Cologne). <http://www.rumbke.de/data/text/pixel3%20-%20leif%20rumbke%202005.pdf> (31.3.2007).

Ryan, Marie-Laure (2001). "Narrative Beyond Myth and Metaphor." *Game Studies* 1:1, n.p. <http://www.gamestudies.org/0101/ryan/> (31.3.2007).

Schirra, Jörg R. J. & Carl-McGrath, Stefan (2002). "Identifikationsformen in Computerspiel und Spielfilm." M. Strübel (ed). *Film und Krieg. Die Inszenierung von Politik zwischen Apologetik und Apokalypse*. Opladen: Leske+Budrich, 149–63.

Schmid, Wolf (2005). *Elemente der Narratologie*. Berlin: de Gruyter.

Sicart, Miguel (2005). "Game, Player, Ethics: A Virtue Ethics Approach to Computer Games". *International Review of Information Ethics* 4, 13–18. <http://www.i-r-i-e.net/inhalt/004/004_full.pdf> (31.3.2007).

Smith, Murray (1995). *Engaging Characters*. Oxford: Oxford UP.

Thon, Jan-Noël (2007). "Schauplätze und Ereignisse. Über Erzähltechniken im Computerspiel des 21. Jahrhunderts." C. Müller & I. Scheidgen (eds). *Mediale Ordnungen. Erzählen, Archivieren, Beschreiben*. Marburg: Schüren, 40–55.

Uspenskij, Boris (1973). *A Poetics of Composition. The Structure of the Poetic Text and Typology of a Compositional Form*. Berkeley: U of California P.

Wolf, Mark J. P. (2001). "Space in the Video Game." M. J. P. Wolf (ed). *The Medium of the Video Game*. Austin: U of Texas P, 51–76.

Authors

DAVID HERMAN, who co-founded the Project Narrative initiative at Ohio State University (http://projectnarrative.osu.edu) and served as its inaugural director, teaches in OSU's English Department. He has authored, edited, or co-edited eight books on aspects of narrative and narrative theory, and he also serves as editor of the *Frontiers of Narrative* book series and of the new journal *Storyworlds*, both published by the University of Nebraska Press. He was recently awarded a research fellowship from the American Council of Learned Societies for his 2009 project on "Storytelling and the Sciences of Mind".

CHRISTIAN HUCK is principal investigator of the research project "Travelling Goods // Travelling Moods: A Transcultural Study of the Acculturation of Consumer Goods, 1918–1939". He took his PhD at Tübingen University and received his *Habilitation* at the University of Erlangen-Nuremberg. The topics of his publications range from Irish poetry and 18th-century travel literature to rockumentaries and music videos. He is currently preparing a monograph on *Fashioning Society, or, The Mode of Modernity: Observations of Clothing in Eighteenth-Century Britain.*

PETER HÜHN is a professor of English Literature, Hamburg University (retired since 2005) and member of the *Interdisciplinary Center for Narratology*. He has published books and articles on theory of poetry and history of British poetry, narratology, application of narratology to poetry analysis, and detective and crime fiction. He is author of *Geschichte der englischen Lyrik* (1995), co-author of *Der Entwicklungsroman in Europa und Übersee* (2001), *Die europäische Lyrik seit der Antike* (2005), *The Narratological Analysis of Lyric Poetry* (2005), *Lyrik und Narratologie* (2007) and co-editor of the *Living Handbook of Narratology* (to appear in 2009).

TATJANA JESCH is working on a postdoctoral thesis about theory and empirical experience in the field of narratology and didactics at Jena University. She is the author of *Das Subjekt in Märchenraum und Märchenzeit* (1998), co-author of *Texte lesen* (2008), and editor of *Märchen in der Geschichte und Gegenwart des Deutschunterrichts* (2003). In addition, she has published several theoretical and empirical articles on (psycho)-narratology and on understanding and teaching literature.

TOMÁŠ KUBÍČEK, PhD, is a researcher in the Department of the History of Literature at the Institute for Czech Literature, Czech Academy of Sciences. Until 2008 he was a researcher in the Section Narratology, which he directed from 2002 to 2007. He also lectures on literary theory, narratology and literary history in the Department of Czech and Comparative Literature and Literary Theory at Charles University, Prague. He has published studies on narratology, literary theory, Czech literary structuralism, and Czech prose. He is the author of the books: *Intersubjectivity in Literary Narrative* (2007); *Vypravěč. Kategorie narativní analýzy* (2007); *Vyprávět příběh. Naratologické kapitoly k románům Milana Kundery* (2002). He was editor in chief of the book series *Theoretica* and is co-editor of *Library of the Possible Worlds*.

MARKUS KUHN, M.A., is a visiting lecturer at the Institute of Media and Communication (IMK) at the University of Hamburg and has just finished his PhD thesis on film-narratology. He studied German language and literature, media and communication studies, history of arts and journalism in Göttingen and Hamburg. He works as a freelance journalist for print and online media. His M.A. thesis on "Narrative Situations in Literature and Film" was awarded the "Karl H. Ditze-Preis" for outstanding Master's theses.

URI MARGOLIN is a professor emeritus of Comparative Literature at the University of Alberta, Edmonton, Canada. He has been working for many years in the fields of narratology and general literary theory, and has published close to 70 articles in collective volumes and professional journals in Europe and North America.

GUNTHER MARTENS is a postdoctoral fellow of the Flemish Research Council (FWO), affiliated with the German Department at the University of Ghent and Visiting Professor of Literary Theory at the Free University of Brussels. Publications on literary modernism, literature and ethics, and the relation between rhetoric and narratology. Activities: in 2005, research stay at the *Narratology Research Group* Hamburg; in 2007 (jointly with the *Interdisciplinary Center for Narratology* Hamburg) and 2008, co-organizer of the International Narratology Workshops at Ghent University; in 2008, co-organizer of the Inaugural Conference of the European Network for Avant-Garde and Modernism Studies (EAM). Most recent publications: E. D'hoker & G. Martens (eds): *Narrative Unreliability in the Twentieth-Century First-Person Novel* (2008); G. Martens & B. Biebuyck: "On the narrative function of metonymy in Heine's *Ideen. Das Buch Le Grand* (Chapter XIV)." *Style* 41:3 (2007).

JAN CHRISTOPH MEISTER has taught at the University of the Witwatersrand, Johannesburg, and at the University of Munich. He is currently professor of German Literature, Literary Theory and Literary Computing at the University of Hamburg. His publications include *Computing Action. A Narratological Approach* (2003). Among his major research topics is the computational modelling of narrative structures and narrative competence in Story Generator Algorithms.

ALAIN RABATEL is a professor of Language Sciences at the University of Lyon 1 (University Institute for Teacher Training). He specializes in discourse analysis, particularly in literary, media, religious and political text and discourse. He is the author of several books including *Une histoire du point de vue* (1997), *La construction textuelle du point de vue* (1998), and *Homo narrans* (2008) as well as of some one hundred articles setting out an enunciative-interactional narratological approach, working within a dialogical and polyphonic framework.

BRIAN RICHARDSON is a professor in the English Department of the University of Maryland. He is the author of *Unlikely Stories: Causality and the Nature of Modern Narrative* (1997) and *Unnatural Voices: Extreme Narration on Modern and Contemporary Fiction* (2006), winner of the Perkins Prize for the year's best book on narrative studies. He has written numerous articles on different aspects of narrative theory, including plot, time, cause, closure, character, narration, reader response, reflexivity, and the narratives of literary history. He is the editor of two books, *Narrative Dynamics: Essays on Time, Plot, Closure, and Frames* (2002) and *Narrative Beginnings: Theories and Practices* (2008). He is currently completing a book on modernism, misreading, and the theory of the reader.

SABINE SCHLICKERS is a professor of Spanish and Latin American Literature at Bremen University, Germany. She is the author of *Verfilmtes Erzählen: Narratologisch-komparative Untersuchung zu «El beso de la mujer araña» (Manuel Puig/Héctor Babenco) und «Crónica de una muerte anunciada» (Gabriel García Márquez/Francesco Rosi)* (1997), *El lado oscuro de la modernización: Estudios sobre la novela naturalista hispanoamericana* (2003) and, most recently, of *»Que yo también soy pueta«. La literatura gauchesca rioplatense y brasileña (siglos XIX-XX)* (2007) as well as of numerous articles on narratology, literature and film.

WOLF SCHMID is a professor of Slavic Literatures at the University of Hamburg. He founded the Hamburg *Narratology Research Group* (www.narrport.uni-hamburg.de) and is currently director of the *Interdisciplinary Center for Narratology* (www.icn.uni-hamburg.de) and executive editor of the series *Narratologia*. With his Hamburg colleagues, he founded the *European Narratology Network* (www.narratology.net). He has authored *Elemente der Narratologie* (Russian 2003, 2008; German 2005, 2008) and edited two collections on Slavic narratology.

JÖRG SCHÖNERT is a retired professor of Modern German Literature, Hamburg University, and member of the *Interdisciplinary Center for Narratology*. He has published on the theory and practice of the social history of literature (with an emphasis on structural and functional text-theoretical models), on the history of the humanities and on problems of literary theory and methodology. Co-author of *Lyrik und Narratologie* (2007) and co-editor of the *Living Handbook of Narratology* (to appear in 2009).

VIOLETA SOTIROVA is a lecturer in stylistics at the University of Nottingham. She has published articles on narrative point of view in the journal of the Poetics and Linguistics Association, *Language and Literature* ("Connectives in free indirect style: continuity or shift?", 2004, for which she was awarded the PALA prize for best first publication), in *Style* ("Repetition in free indirect style: a dialogue of minds," 2006) and in *Poetics* ("Reader responses to narrative point of view," 2006). Her publications also include articles in *English Studies* (2006), *Études Lawrenciennes* (2007; 2008) and a chapter in *Contemporary Stylistics* (2007). She is currently working on a monograph on consciousness presentation in modernist fiction.

MALTE STEIN, former member of the *Narratology Research Group*, Hamburg University, is a teacher at the Hansa-Kolleg in Hamburg, Germany. He wrote his dissertation on family violence in the novellas of Theodor Storm (2006), is co-author of *Lyrik und Narratologie* (2007) and has published several articles on the intersection of literature, narratology and psychoanalysis.

JAN-NOËL THON is a PhD student at Hamburg University, working on a project in the field of transmedial narratology. He has authored several conference papers, articles, and book chapters on the theory and aesthetics of contemporary computer games, focusing mainly on space, interaction, simulation, narration, communication and immersion.

ROLAND WEIDLE presently holds a position as substitute professor for English Literature at the University of Hamburg. He has published on Shakespeare, drama and theatre from the early modern age to the present, contemporary fiction and transmedial and transgeneric narratology. Most recently, he co-edited a volume on contemporary British literature (*Cool Britannia*, 2006) and was the focus editor of the issue "Transmedial and Transgeneric Narration" for the journal *Anglistik. International Journal of English Studies* (2007).

Bei Fragen zur Produktsicherheit wenden Sie sich bitte an:
If you have any questions regarding product safety,
please contact:

Walter de Gruyter GmbH
Genthiner Straße 13
10785 Berlin
productsafety@degruyterbrill.com